Monochromatic Heart

Monochromatic Heart: On Grief and Love and Still Being Here

ISBN 13: 979-8-218-60606-0
Library of Congress Control Number: 2025901893
Edited by Bruce Latshaw, Jessica McCann, and Stefanie Seamster
Layout and Cover by Helen Ounjian

This work depicts actual events of the author, recalled and recorded as truthfully as permitted to remain consistent with the recollection. Dialogue may be embellished but within the nature of the character depicted. Some names of characters have been changed to respect their privacy.

JessicaLatshaw.com

For inquiries, email monochromaticheartbook@gmail.com

Jessica Latshaw

MONOCHROMATIC HEART
on grief and love and still being here

To TJ, my forever Boaz

Luca, my light

Charlee, Willa, and Noa–
my mirror, my teacher, my muse

Acknowledgments

I'd like to acknowledge my pop, an English teacher and pastor, who went through my manuscript with a fine tooth comb. The hours we spent together over this book will be some of my most cherished with you. Sorry for constantly getting us off-topic. Thanks for your patience, expertise, and love. Considering how much we belly laughed together while editing this—a book about my grief over the death of my son—is a testament to our relationship. Thank you. (P.S. If people don't like this book, I will blame it on your edits.)

I also must joyously acknowledge my friend Stefanie, who is a surgeon when it comes to editing. She poured her precious heart and brilliant mind all over these pages and made them better. You remind me how collaboration—both with God and each other—is our highest calling.

And how do I acknowledge my TJ, always the hero of my story? Without you, I'd probably live in a cave with no internet. I am sort of joking. Your encouragement is hard to believe. (But I believed it enough to write a book.) You know what I need; you are what I need. I love you, I love you, I love you.

Contents

"For love is strong as death..."
Song of Songs 8:6 KJV

"But, that's not my order."

Chapter 1

Discharge
(three months after)

Never in my life have I been more aware of what the inside of my underwear looks like. Apparently, it's the egg white-ish stuff I want. This is the first book I've published, and those are my first two sentences. They surprise me too.

My friend recently burnt our lunch.

"This isn't what I expected," she said, scraping off the black parts of the grilled cheese sandwich over the sink.

"That could be my life motto, actually," I told her.

Hi, nice to meet you. Welcome to my world. God, I want a baby (if you haven't already guessed).

My poor pop is reading this book and wondering why I can't write about growing up in the green rolling hills of Pennsylvania, the years I spent touring with Broadway shows, or even my first marriage and its disastrous end—really, anything other than my current preoccupation with discharge. Not that this book is about that (sorry to disappoint)—but what this book *is* about has me hyper focused on it.

(At least I'm not writing 'vaginal discharge.' But then again, I think you guessed it from the underwear reference. So, whatever—let's dive right in.)

Actually, I've googled 'vaginal discharge' more times than I can count, and every time the results are the same: When it looks like someone cracked an egg, withheld the yolk, and dumped what's left into your underwear, it's time to make a baby. I've carried two healthy babies—had no problem getting pregnant with either of them—and I never knew this before now.

Why do I know this now? Because my second baby—my firstborn son—died at 35 weeks, a cord accident. He died inside me. A stillbirth. It is a death unlike any other. Some call it the invisible loss, leaving an inexplicable pain, the death which we are least prepared for.

We are never truly prepared for tragedy (I recently read that 85% of the things we worry about never come to pass. So when you start to worry, just assume it's part of the 85% and let it go. There, now you've got some encouraging news right off the bat—in a book about somebody's baby dying, no less). But in most cases, we are not busily preparing for someone's arrival—having filled empty drawers with baby clothes, filled your own body with a baby, filled your own heart with the flood of a mother's love—only to have that person suddenly gone. It is an extraordinary grief that follows the extraordinary love you hold for your baby who doesn't come home.

My son died, and I want another baby so desperately that I can barely say it out loud. But I can quietly stare at my discharge all day long and try to glean from it some kind of deeply personal sign that another baby is not only coming, but also coming home. I stare at it like it's one of those Rorschach ink blots, willing myself to see a baby, a future, something—anything—better than this grief.

Writing a book is like taking a microscope to your insides and publishing your findings. If you want it to be honest and interesting, you need to dive in and tell the truth. Take a picture and show it. Maybe use a filter, but that's it. Best-selling author and humorist David Sedaris makes this wonderful comparison to how writing should be much more like peeling off your skin than like a Hallmark card. But the thing is, a Hallmark card is generally accepted in society and very easily digestible for mass consumption. My parents would be comfortable with the world reading any number of Hallmark cards written by their daughter. (*Sam from the Post Office, here you go! Sally who works at church, you can read every single one of Jess's Hallmark cards!*) But in an effort to peel off my skin, I am letting the world know about me in the bathroom, staring at the discharge in my underwear, grasping at hope while grieving my son's death. The stuff I wash off my underwear is base, raw, gross, yes; and also deeply vulnerable—and dare I say—hopeful. I watch it intently the way you'd read tea leaves, drawing purpose from some inanimate part of nature. Willing it to tell a better future than what anxiety predicts.

With apologies to my parents' and all their friends, there is no Hallmark card for this.

Chapter 2

When Even the Jokes Stop
(eight weeks after)

When I first text my family the autopsy report, eight weeks after losing my son, I write that it was a "chord accident." Like death by G minor when you forget the B flat or something. My family is comprised of people who will go for every single joke that comes our way. And when one doesn't come our way, we will make one anyway. We are Italian and Cornish—both tribes full of storytellers. We are loud, we gesticulate wildly with our hands, and (just about) nothing is sacred. When my mom's mom died, she wanted to watch Chris Farley comedies and eat candy, so that's what we did. Her grief looked like laughter and togetherness and nostalgia over movies we all knew and loved, which seems nonsensical, but I've learned that our emotions have a way of informing us of what we need. I've learned to listen to them. Anyway, my family will pick the low-hanging fruit, then climb the tree and balance precariously to grab the highest fruit that most mortals would never bother with—all this just to laugh. We love jokes, typos included.

I don't realize my misnomer until later—when I also realize that not a single person in my family made fun of it. I not only write this to assure you that my family actually has some tact, but to let you know how serious and devastating my son's death continues to be. Of course, I will make a dark joke from time to time. Like when my birthday arrives two weeks after Luca's death. Birthdays show up regardless, even during times of grief; if you're alive, they come for you, whether you feel like celebrating or not. Life parades on as normal, whether you feel like getting up in the morning or not. It can be awful.

What do you get for the girl whose baby just died? It's the million dollar question this year. My mom decided the answer is a self-sustaining ecosystem. I stare at the small glass orb that has what looks like tiny, shrimpy crayfish swimming blithely around in it. Like lice, if they lived in water. They need nothing; no food, no freshly changed water, not one thing. They are the anti-pet pet. I can see my mom is trying to give me something easy, something happy.

"How long are these little guys supposed to live, Mom?" I ask, watching them swim around and around. My mom starts to say something, but I cut her off. "Let me guess—they are perfectly healthy for 35 weeks and then die unexpectedly," I say dryly. "Jess," my mom says, in the hushed tone we use to let people know they are inappropriate. "Hahahahahahaha. Come on, Mom. It's funny."

Those little creatures did not, however, live forever. Turns out they do need something. Turns out they need to have their glass home *not* accidentally dropped and smashed by my husband TJ, their little strange suddenly still bodies littered all over the floor while he apologizes profusely for killing my birthday present. He starts to vacuum while I think but do not say that it makes a kind of terrible poetic sense. I numbly watch him clean up the ecosystem. I really don't care that they didn't make it; I don't have room inside me to care right now.

Chapter 3

When You Can't Choose the Details
(four months after)

Even as I write this story down—over three months since Luca died—I can hardly believe it's my story. That my husband had to bury his firstborn son. That my daughter doesn't know her little brother. That my parents are missing their eleventh grandchild. I hate this story, but it's mine, so I make room for it. Right now, it feels like fire. Nobody is ambiguous about a flame. You can't be, because it's consuming; it changes the atmosphere. You can't stay the same amid it. A fire can devastate, level everything. And a fire lights up the dark and purifies certain metals. Someday the thought might comfort me, but not today. I am not metal. Surely metal doesn't cry itself to sleep or stop talking to friends who have babies.

I leave home and find a little bit of comfort among strangers who do not know what's happened. They smile at me on the train. Here, I'm not grieving, and nobody knows I was so recently pregnant.

But I have to get off the train. I walk into the spin studio where I taught classes for years. I taught throughout my pregnancy, right up until the day they induced me to deliver Luca. Now I slip in quietly, say hello to a few familiar faces, and jump on a bike in a blessedly dark room. One woman yells over the pop music pumping through the speakers while I'm putting on my shoes.

"Did you have baby number two, then?!"

I pause. This narrative. This damn narrative must be explained over and over again. I take a deep breath.

"I did. He died."

If you ever want to stop a conversation short, just say someone died. If you want it to end even faster, say it was your baby. People stammer their "I'm sorrys," and there is nothing more to say. I used to excuse myself to the restroom to get out of tedious conversations, but now no need. I just mention the truth; silence ensues and I'm on my way.

I walk into class and the repetitive motion of pedaling on a bike that goes nowhere gives my mind room to wander. Too much room, maybe. I brush tears away and keep going. I do this a lot, lately—on the bike or not. It's a theme. Brush tears away and keep going. Or stop, cry really hard, then keep going. It's an appropriate response to the tremendous loss. It is as appropriate as others telling me they're sorry it happened. It is recognizing both what should be and what isn't—and just how terrible the gap between them is. The goal here isn't necessarily focusing on death or even on all the life that is still here; it is simply to keep going. To see the space left when What Should Be vanished. To sit down, look around, hate it, and realize there's a little dirt here. One day run your fingers through the dirt. And maybe one day after that—it doesn't have to be soon—realize dirt is the only place where seeds grow.

Chapter 4

My Grief Asks Questions
(five months after)

The loss is so pervasive because the love was so pervasive—and a love like that stays. When I scroll through social media and see a newborn baby boy staring up at me, I have a physical reaction, a heart-dropping sensation. Someone else's baby reminds me of the question that haunts me: *Why do so many women get to keep their babies, hold their babies, but I didn't? Why do so many babies get to stay, when Luca didn't?*

I am not sure there's a satisfying answer.

There are plenty of people who try to provide one. In my experience, canned answers only make me feel worse. Their explanation is a band-aid for a bullet hole, woefully inadequate for the loss of my son I got to hold for five hours total.

"God needed one more angel."

Really?

God created the universe; creating a few more angels can't be that hard. He can't get by without recruiting angel trainees from earth and breaking hearts while he does it? Also, people are not angels. We are made of different stuff.

"Everything has a reason."

You will never tell me a reason good enough to kill my baby. Please, try. No really—I'll wait. I've been to plenty of theater auditions in New York. I'm not sure if I got any better at acting, but I sure got GREAT at waiting.

"God only gives the hardest trials to the strongest people."

This is a compliment, then? *Congratulations! I am SO STRONG that God killed my baby! Instead of a funeral, let's throw a party!* If that's the case, thanks for the compliment, but I'd rather be weak and see my baby grow up. It's a strange sort of priorities we mothers have, I guess. I may not understand everything about God, but I don't believe for a second that he would kill a baby to teach me some sort of lesson.

Let's change the narrative. When something terrible happens—when grief replaces the blood in our veins, the air in our lungs, the ideas in our head. When it is lightning fast to come, but its work is as slow as forever, let's help each other and refrain from saying, "God needed another angel."

I don't think God needs anything. He's God. But if he does need anything, I do not think he'd kill a baby to get it. Perhaps I could take it as a compliment that "God gives the hardest battles to the strongest soldiers." But I'm not a soldier. I used to be a little girl who mostly read stories. Then I tried to tell stories in every way I could—with words, songs, dances, pictures. I'm still that girl, but I got taller and fell in love and got hurt to the point that I eventually discovered myself the way I once discovered the bones of a bird while dissecting an owl pellet: in a million little pieces spread over the kitchen table (all the gross, indigestible parts of the animals the owl eats and then spits up are called owl pellets and given to elementary students to examine. The owls don't even charge us for these). *Oh, this should only take forever to put back together*, I thought, and promptly stopped trying. Until God came in—it's always this way!—and, together, over time, we built something remarkable that I get exhausted by every single day. It's my family, and I love this story that is told through the intersection of our lives.

But I don't feel particularly strong. I feel very well acquainted with how tiring, exhilarating, and at times profoundly disappointing it is to be here. We are skin that moves over bones, telling stories with our scars. We are longings — both met and still felt deep within us. We are wonderful, resilient, adaptable, vulnerable, in dire need of protection. I feel like God loves my ragged edges and the weakness that keeps me asking for mercy—for grace for me and the people over there that aren't like me at all. I feel like rocks are strong, but I am not a rock; I have become liquid, ebbing and flowing with the seasons.

So, what do we say to the grieving among us?

"I'm sorry."

"I'm so incredibly sorry the person you love has died."

"I don't understand it, either."

"I think God is here; He is close to the brokenhearted."

"Church makes me cry, too."

"I'm dropping off food."

★ ★ ★

If someone you love is grieving, do variations of this over and over again. Tell the truth: that life is difficult and painful, and you don't understand it. Don't rush their grief. Sit with it, with them, and allow them to feel it. One day, they will (most likely) tell you they are better, but that day is theirs to choose. (Telling you about it, I mean—but, man, would I love to be able to *choose* the day I feel better, too.)

I know how it feels to hear the opposite—the explanations, the justifications. The (well-intentioned but misguided) attempts to make things okay. They hurt, and make you feel like your grief is an overreaction to something that can be explained so well; an overreaction to something that is captured in a meme your Aunt Cathy sends.

The best explanation I've heard so far is simply: Sometimes bad stuff happens. It happens to everyone. Not the exact same kind of bad stuff—not even to the same degree, which is good news for some—but still, nobody's life remains unscathed. And without reducing grief by putting a positive spin on it or oversimplifying it, you can offer small reminders of hope. You can light a very small and non-judgmental match in the darkness, if only to remind them that you're there, too. Or you can simply tell them that you have a match, but if it's too bright today, you can come back with it tomorrow. It's in your pocket; you're not getting rid of it and just say the word, should you ever feel the need for the extra light.

When I feel sadness or jealousy over the healthy babies I see on my social media feed or on television or in the lives of my community, my husband TJ gently tells me it's a good thing so many people have healthy babies. It's good for everyone—including us.

"It means a higher probability that we'll have another healthy baby, too, Jess," he tells me—reminding me, for the twentieth time that day, to hope.

Chapter 5

I Don't Want to Have to Be Brave
(three months after)

I'm checking my underwear, aware of what my body is doing now, more than ever before—because I want another baby. I wish I had Luca. The word *wish* is not strong enough. I wish my husband and I were talking about potentially having a third child to raise right now, not a second. But as Sheryl Sandberg writes in her book *Option B*, "Option A is not available. So let's kick the sh*t out of Option B."

What does that mean? My friend Mercy gave birth to her daughter Pearl last year; she was stillborn. She also gave birth to her son Jude this year, a little early but entirely healthy. He is her rainbow baby, the term we use for the baby that comes after miscarriage, stillbirth, or infant loss. It implies the return of light, hope, and brilliant color to our skies after the storm. It doesn't negate or replace the storm; it is the beauty that comes after the storm. It is even the beauty that comes because of the storm. Mercy and I have had many discussions about pregnancy after such a tremendous loss. What does it mean to have a rainbow pregnancy, to deal with all the emotions and hope and anxiety while also deeply grieving the child who isn't here? "It means being brave," she tells me. "Again and again, it means choosing bravery over fear, despite the terrifying risk of losing another child."

In *A Grief Observed*, CS Lewis writes, "Nobody ever told me that grief was so like fear." Contemplating another pregnancy, I'm afraid. I'm afraid that I will always feel that the death of my son made the bottom fall out of my life. That nothing is now sure, that I can no longer count on any of the things I thought were guaranteed in life. I am not sure why I suddenly feel this; I've known for quite a while that people die. I guess it is simply our nature to hope that we are specially blessed, that these terrible things could never actually happen to us. In theory, death makes sense, but in the context of our own precious lives, it becomes utterly senseless.

I will never forget, at age seven, I was struck by the realization that someday my parents would die. As one of five siblings, privacy was a rare and precious commodity in our house and I had to duck into random closets to sob alone for the deaths that I knew would someday happen. This was my first preview of grief, the first time I felt the relentless weight of my own fragility. For one full day this terrified me, and I could not regulate my emotions. Then, in the absence of any resolution, I just kept going. To school, to dinner, to ballet class, to church, to the bathroom, to bed. The busyness of everyday life saved me, making me forget my epiphany that this life would eventually give me grief. It's a lot for one young heart to hold, for any heart to hold. So I didn't hold it for long.

In the weeks after Luca dies so unexpectedly, I darkly wonder who will be next. My brain jumps weirdly from the mundane to the morbid countless times a day. I wonder what I should make for dinner, then the phone rings, startling me into panic—who's died now? If my husband TJ doesn't text me back right away, my heart starts racing, my body re-reacting to what happened once before, overreacting to what is happening now. I wake up this morning terrified that my mom has died until I reach her on the phone. I feel embarrassed at my panic, I don't mention it, willing my conversation to sound casual as my heart rate finally starts to slow back down. This afternoon, when TJ comes home a bit later than usual, I am absolutely sure he has died.

But here's the good news: Since 4:30 PM today, I have not thought that one person has died. Maybe tomorrow I will practice that brave truth even earlier. Like, by noon or something crazy like that. (FYI: Nobody that I know died today. I love it when my fears are proven untrue. Almost every day now this happens.)

Chapter 6

Coming Home
(two days after)

As we leave Massachusetts General Hospital, everything feels wrong. Boston feels like Vegas in the thick 90-something degree heat, I think, as I sit empty-handed in a wheelchair before climbing slowly into the car. It's strangely hot for May.

But my son died; everything is strange.

When we arrive home, I walk slowly through my building, saying hello to our neighbors as quickly as possible so as not to invite conversation. I don't want to talk. Especially not to the curious passerby who remembers how pregnant I was and naturally thinks that after such a round belly, there must be a baby to bring home.

I get it; I thought that, too.

I avoid eye contact. My neighbor blessedly looks the other way.

I walk into our apartment and notice the fridge looks like it's for sale. It's been wiped clean of anything personal—of all three rolls of Luca's ultrasound photos. I don't say anything. We are loved. Someone has been here, cleaning, wanting to protect us from the grief that comes anyway.

I wake up this morning to the sound of my two-year-old daughter, Charlee, crying from her crib and forget for a moment. I think I feel Luca move, then I remember. I hear my mom go to Charlee and feel TJ pull me in close.

I forget to thank God in that moment, but I am thanking Him now. For Charlee's beautiful cries and for a husband who loves me like I've never been loved before. For all my brothers and sisters who've come to Boston from Los Angeles, Maryland, Pennsylvania—making me laugh, reminding me of better days, and sitting with me while I cry. When life is so very dark, the light sure does stand out, I notice.

★ ★ ★

It's Tuesday but it doesn't matter. Every day feels the same. I'm sitting in a dark room with my dog Luna sleeping beside me. She is a blessing, I think. God, I don't have to look far for my blessings.

TJ. I love everything about him. He holds my hand, and I marvel at the dark hair on his arms. How the bones of his fingers curl around mine in perfect symmetry. I don't think I've ever needed another human as much as I need him. I want to protect him; I am so deeply sad that he lost his son, too. Too. I wonder how both of us can be so low and end up okay. I try to trust God with TJ's heart. I try to believe there is something deeper at work than the pain.

Charlee. She walks around asking everyone within earshot what their "favorite color in the most whole world" is. We try to quietly pay for parking as we drive out of the Boston Public Market garage, but she insists on knowing the name of the man in the booth. We ask him sheepishly, telling him our daughter would like to know, hesitant to break the barrier that exists between strangers. But she's right: Orlando's name is important. He smiles when he sees us now. Charlee does that, you know.

She leaves a trace of smiles and warmth and strewn-about toys wherever she goes. She's a force of grace in my life, and I love even the broken branches the tornado of her presence leaves behind.

I think about Luca's clothes, washed and folded, and how he'll never wear them. I had so much fun picking them out. I was skeptical that dressing a boy could be even close to as much fun as dressing my Charlee. But the bow ties, suspenders, and alligator- and dinosaur-print onesies proved me wrong.

It turns out that dressing my child—any sex—is a gift.

I ask God to tell Luca about his family and how much we love him. I don't think he needs anything at all, but I know Jesus is in the habit of giving all of us more than we need. So, I appreciate the fact that He meets my boy's needs, but I also remind him that Luca is not just anybody. He's our son. I run my hand over my dog Luna's fur, willing myself to feel her closeness in addition to the tears that run down my face.

Chapter 7

When Everyone Sends You Books on Grief
(six weeks after)

I am reading a book called *Pregnancy After Loss*. It is summer, six weeks after Luca's death, and my family is vacationing at Bethany Beach in Delaware, something we've done forever. My mom gave me the book when we arrived.

"This may be too soon, Jess. But I wanted you to have it, for if and when you're ready," she says. I dutifully take it down to the beach and open it right away, reading it in the mornings when we laze around the pool.

I would be pregnant right now if I could. I have already asked the doctor when we can start trying again. I want a sibling for Charlee on earth. I want another child for me and TJ. I want Luca's little brother or sister here with us, even if I can't have Luca.

At first glance, the book I'm reading is written by a legit, just-the-facts-ma'am journalist. I am a big fan of stories, but statistics don't move me quite as much. The author lost a baby very late in her pregnancy too. I open the book hoping for the comfort that comes when someone else's story makes you feel less alone.

Except everyone is different. Whereas statistics help calm and comfort this author (she notes this up front), reading about the many ways a baby can die before it takes its first breath makes *me* feel even more depressed. For her, it helps to know that many things are out of our hands; for me, it makes me wonder how any baby ever makes it to 40 weeks. I don't finish the book. I am okay with only knowing the first hundred ways a baby can die in gestation and missing out on the next fifty.

My brothers, sister, sisters-in-law, nieces, nephews, parents, TJ, myself, and Charlee are all gathered around the pool on this particularly hot July day. The original plan was that TJ and I would stay home with newly born Luca while Charlee went down to the beach with my family. Instead, TJ and I are here, and Luca is not. This feels as bitter as it sounds.

I try to make the best of it. Is there anything as pitiful as a newly made loss-mama trying to "make the best of it"? It's mostly just hard. There's too much to make the best of. This is not a hook for any of you who are grieving. This is me saying you are off the hook. It's okay to not make the best of it. It's okay to not smile or engage happily with your family. It's okay to look out at the light reflecting off the ocean and find the beauty overwhelmingly painful because the person you love has died. Because they aren't seeing it too.

But I try. I try to just be, to feel, to love those around me and listen to them be themselves, because it's comforting to find that my life is still here in the sounds of my family around me. I try to connect with the people who are here, even as my thoughts are never far from the one person who is not. I try to make the best of it, I guess, because it helps. And God, I need help.

That book about pregnancy after loss is lying on the table, face down and open to the page where I stopped reading, the title in full display. My brother Josh glances at the open book and asks, "That book any good?"

My oldest brother Josh is wonderful for many reasons, but his attention to detail is not one of them. One time years ago, another brother, Jonathan, and I spent all of our homeschooled day (Yes, we were homeschooled. Yes, my parents knew about public and private school. I know, I find it amazing that they did this for us, too. They weren't even forced into it by a pandemic; they freely chose it.) discussing the best way to use our newest toy: a perfectly coiled fake turd. After much deliberation, we planted it on the edge of the toilet in Josh's bathroom for him to discover when he returned home from high school. Game on.

It felt like forever until Josh finally got home. Turns out that thing about a watched pot never boiling can also be applied to a watched plastic turd you put on the toilet to prank your brother never paying off. Josh finally got back, and we followed at a discreet distance as he made his way to his bathroom. We put our ears to the door, stifling our laughter and anticipating the reaction that would surely come. He would groan in disgust or scream in outrage—man, this would be good.

But then…nothing. The toilet flushed, the sink ran for a bit, and Josh emerged from the bathroom. "Hey, guys," he said casually.

We peered around Josh at the toilet, wondering where our fake poop went. We looked at each other in disbelief.

"Uh. Did you notice anything different in there?" Jonathan asked.

"No."

"Nothing?" Jonathan demanded.

"Nothing."

"DID YOU NOTICE A POOP ON THE TOILET, THOUGH?" I finally asked, my voice high with desperation.

Josh thought for a moment. "Oh! Yeah, I figured I just missed the toilet bowl this morning, so I knocked it back in and flushed it."

"YOU FLUSHED IT?" we chorused, crestfallen.

"Yeah … why?"

"That wasn't your poop! How could you think that was real poop? It was fake poop mom bought us. We put it there to gross you out!" Jonathan explained, talking fast.

"Oh, sorry about that," Josh shrugged, and walked away. And that was that.

This is Josh—not exactly a noticer of details. (And apparently, in high school, he missed his toilet enough times to not think anything of it on this particular afternoon.)

Now he's sprawled beside the pool, looking at me over his sunglasses, asking me if my book on pregnancy loss is any good.

"It's…um…yeah, I guess. I mean, it's about your baby dying and getting pregnant again, so I guess it's good. Not exactly what you'd call a summer read, though."

"Oh," he says, "But it's a pretty good read?"

"Yeah, I guess you could say…it's a pretty good read."

That night in our room, I fill TJ in on the exchange, and we both laugh. Most people would not say anything aloud about the fact that I am reading a book on one of the most painful subjects possible. Most people would try to change the subject, to ignore the fact that my life has made this kind of reading necessary. But not Josh. Instead, he acts like it's the most normal thing in the world for me to be reading this book, and the conversation surrounding it is no different than if I were reading a Nicholas Sparks book on this hot July day by the pool. I love him for that.

Also, you might not find it shocking that, years after he flushed away our fake turd, we were all at the Pennsylvania

Renaissance Faire, in line to get lunch, when Josh saw what he assumed were free samples. Without hesitation, he grabbed one, and while bringing the food to his mouth, the guy behind the cash register said in a panicky tone, "Sir! SIR! This isn't real food! It's only a display—IT'S NOT TO EAT!" But it was too late. After taking a very short-lived bite, Josh sheepishly put the plastic food back on the counter while we all tried and failed to stifle our laughter.

Chapter 8

Parenting Now
(one week after)

It's 5 AM, a week after we lost Luca, and Charlee has been waking up repeatedly since 2:45. Since giving birth, I'm not supposed to lift anything heavier than 7 lbs, so TJ insists I lay down as he gets up with her repeatedly. We're exhausted, but we can't be upset, because she's here. She's crying. She's our child, and she's alive.

All our former complaints about parenting have been silenced. Usually, Charlee sleeps through the night and wakes at 6 AM; usually, we would be irritable at this point. But lately I'm already awake at night, just listening for her. She cries, and I breathe a sigh of relief. She's still here. We get to be her parents on earth. I thank God, and I don't care so much that I'm tired.

Our white sheets are dotted with purple. I've been stuffing red cabbage leaves down my bra at night, trying to get my body to realize there's no newborn to feed; they are supposed to dry up the milk and reduce the swelling. After I gave birth to Luca, I assumed my care team would give me something for the milk I wouldn't need. Maybe a shot, a pill. I don't know, I didn't care, but I'd take it. I was shocked when there was nothing they could do.

"So just let the milk come in and try to figure out how to make my body stop producing it?" I asked quietly. The nurse nodded compassionately and mentioned the cabbage leaves, so here I am. Luca's milk came in this past weekend, and it's as cruel a reminder of his absence as you'd think. The first night, I was so engorged and in so much pain that TJ stayed up with me as I sat and cried in the shower. I expressed my rock-hard breasts and let the hot water, Luca's milk, and my own tears blend before draining away.

But here's the grace: Charlee hasn't yet stopped nursing, so I'm giving her small amounts. I walk a fine line; if I give her too much, my body will make too much, and I'll be walking around with a whole newborn's amount of milk inside of me, minus the newborn who needs it. But I like to think of Luca's milk nourishing his sister.

"It tastes like cookies, Mama," she tells me, and I'm grateful this is not a bitter thing for everyone.

★ ★ ★

I still use my maternity pillow. I curl myself around it, pressing my shrinking belly into it, and I cry. TJ is asleep while I cry, until he's not. Until the warmth from his hand rubbing my back changes things again.

Pain, comfort, pain, comfort … lots of pain.

I'm a pendulum swinging back and forth between the two. It's all my brain can think, all my heart can feel. Pain, comfort, pain.

"Will we ever not be so sad?" I ask him in the darkness.

"But I'm happy even now with you," he tells me quietly.

And he's right. Even in the consuming pain, *we* are not consumed forever. At least never longer than until the next time we're together.

A stranger contacts me on social media. She has been following me online, reading my personal account of grieving Luca, and she tells me her story. She, too, has faced tremendous loss. She understands that the clichés don't help. She understands that statistics don't reach the part that is so raw and broken inside. Not when you're crying yourself to sleep again, your whole body aching for the baby who filled your belly, the baby who should fill your arms, the baby who still fills your heart. And not when you're taking your two-year-old toddler to the public pool, trying not to stare at the woman sitting beside you with her toddler daughter and healthy newborn son.

This kind stranger shares a poem that has helped her. I read it and marvel, because the tone is just right. I'd never heard of Nessa Rapoport and her poem, 'Suffering' (*A Woman's Book of Grieving*), but as I read it, something happens. I feel less alone. I understand that I am not the only one who has lost too much. It is comforting to read the powerful, resonant words another woman writes about her grief.

This is why author and humorist David Sedaris compares writing to peeling off our skin. We dare to look inside without the filters that make it palatable and describe what we find. And then, a revelation. It *helps* us to describe our pain, to somehow circle the details of our grief with words, organize them like a game of Tetris. Our nervous system gets a break as our brain works in a different way to solve this problem of exactly *which* words to use to reveal what we look like under our skin. We find that, while our grief feels both impossible and impassable, the problem of fitting words together is solvable. Blessedly solvable. We can put together syntax and create sentences that make sense, when nothing else does. And to those who are also grieving, our stories not only describe our grief, they also carry a powerful message: Me Too.

Grief goes from isolation to a common bond. And just like that, the grieving person is no longer alone. Our stories are not just ways to tell each other about what broke us. Our stories are bridges, giving passage to others who are also grieving. Our stories are permission for the world to allow grief, to count it sacred. Our stories are flashlights, revealing a way forward in the dark. We scrape meaning from the stories we share, the stories we hear from friends, family, books, and narratives online. And when we walk through suffering, we find that meaning is still there, under our fingernails, hanging on, present and palpable, a lifeline.

Jewish tradition is good at emphasizing the importance of grief. Two thousand years before psychologists talked about "grief work," Judaism held space, with specific stages, rituals, and boundaries for the grieving. My therapist, who is Jewish, mentions this to me, and I realize this kind of map is a godsend. With directives like exemptions from focusing on anything other than the funeral immediately after the loss, then, for seven days, simply sitting at home—not working—while your community visits and, together with you, honors the memory of your loved one in conversation punctuated by tears and laughter—it's a gift to simply know how to go about the act of grieving. What it looks and sounds like (sitting, talking about your loved one, praying the *Mourner's Kaddish*, avoiding entertainment and celebrations for a set time).

"Every stage of mourning in the Jewish tradition involves community," my therapist tells me. "We're not necessarily trying to make someone in grief feel better—certainly not right away—but rather, the goal is to make sure that person stays connected to others," she explains.

When grief has made it impossible to make decisions, or even ask someone to come sit with you, tradition lightens the burden with a directive: this is when you sit, talk, listen, cry, laugh, eat the food we prepare for you, say the prayer of mourning, and stay within the circle we've constructed around you, ensuring you know you're loved and seen, carried by a collective.

I listen to her and nod—for the first time, the need for these beautiful, social and religious traditions makes profound sense to me.

Chapter 9

Willing My Body to Work
(five weeks after)

In the weeks after I birth Luca, I anxiously await my period. I find myself dodging the illogical, overwhelming thought that it will just never come again, that Luca was the last baby I have. One Friday night, I diligently seek wisdom on the matter by hunching over my phone and googling: HOW TO MAKE YOUR PERIOD COME BACK AFTER HAVING A STILLBIRTH.

I hope none of you ever have to google this, but in case you do, let me save you a google. There's no way to force your period. It's kind of like a toddler: It's messy, and it does whatever it wants.

You're better off just googling the regular stuff. You know:

What day of the week is Christmas this year?

How old is Jennifer Lopez?

You're kidding about Jennifer Lopez's age, right? (She looks great!)

That Friday night, as I sit on the toilet googling, I realize something. (I mean, I could tell you I'm sitting on our very classy chaise lounge, but I'm trying to be honest here—plus, we don't own a chaise lounge.) I realize, once again, that I am not in control. Not of my body, and not of my babies. I ask God for help. I ask Him to give me back my period, to give me some sort of encouragement. The next morning, my period comes. I've never been so happy to see blood. *Thank you, Jesus,* I pray. This Name isn't mentioned in the Bible, per se, but *Giver of Periods* has a ring to it. This is way better than what Google ever does for me. And for the first time since Luca died, I feel like maybe there is life for me, still. I feel encouraged. I feel a little better.

And better is amazing.

I text my mom, and she is even more excited about this period than she was for my first, when she finally stopped me from using wads of toilet paper stuffed in the crotch of my underwear. (Alright, I can't leave you hanging on "toilet paper stuffed in the crotch of my underwear"—not figuratively—and definitely not literally, either (gross). You deserve more, as we all do.)

When I was newly thirteen, before I got up the nerve to tell my mom what happened and ask for something a little more discreet—not to mention effective—than an entire roll of toilet paper, I had to go to a church-wide Labor Day picnic. Two of my older brothers drove me, and I made sure to grab my newly acquired tote bag for the sole purpose of keeping toilet paper with me.

Considering it was Pennsylvania in the late summer, it was a hot day, but last minute, I stuffed a jacket into the bag, too. This way, if a brother questioned why I'm suddenly going everywhere with this huge bag over my shoulder, I can show him the jacket in the bag and mention how it could get chilly. A sort of alibi, if you will. I mean, if there was a complete break from normal weather patterns, sure, it COULD get cold, but I figured that would at least get me out of explaining why there was a single roll of toilet paper in a bag that I wouldn't put down. Also, worth mentioning is that I'm not sure why I thought the bathrooms at this picnic wouldn't have toilet paper. Our church picnic wasn't located in the rain forest or on a safari or along the many miles of the New Jersey Turnpike between rest stops—places that warrant bringing your own TP, I imagine. I guess I just wanted to take a little control over a destiny that had completely shocked me by suddenly soaking my underwear in blood, and really, can you blame me?

That night, my brother Jonathan came into my room to talk before we went to bed. He brought up the bag and I started sweating.

"I know what that bag means," he announced. *Oh my gosh, mention the jacket. The fool proof jacket alibi will throw him off,* I thought (I hoped).

"I used it to carry my jacket," I stated casually, the way any innocent person would.

"It's *hot* out," he countered.

"I didn't know how late we'd stay out—it could get cool," I said, not missing a beat.

"Jess. That bag can only mean one thing. Women who get their periods carry bags because they need tampons. You got your *period*, didn't you?"

I saw a thin crack in the prosecution. Finally, a way out, so I charged forward, proudly armed with the truth. "I didn't have ONE SINGLE TAMPON in that bag," I stated, imagining the jury hanging on my every overly annunciated syllable. "I've never USED a tampon; you're totally wrong about that." I said this with the confidence of one who is stating facts. Before God! I have never used a tampon! I don't even have one! (*Now please don't ask me if I need one. The toilet paper is not a great system.*)

It was awkward and weird, which is exactly how I felt about puberty, so perhaps it was just right. I was comforted by the thought that Jonathan went to bed thinking I was still the same old Jess I'd always been. No periods here, changing everything and driving a massive wedge between me and the brothers to whom I'd always felt so similar. Anyway, when I told my mom, she immediately introduced me to pads, and I ditched the old toilet-paper-in-a-tote-bag-but-also-include-a-jacket-to-cover-up-the-toilet-paper (she swallowed a spider to catch the fly!) trick.

A few months before I got my first period ever (and, coincidentally, my first tote ever), I had a vivid dream that I was being chased by a blob called *Obulation* (Freud would have a hay day with this!). The blob got one letter wrong—or maybe I just remembered it wrong, considering I had no idea about ovulation, had never even heard the word. I recounted the odd dream to my older brother Jase and his girlfriend at the time, thinking they'd be like, "Weird, Jessica." Instead, they exchanged the kind of glances grownups give each other when they know something the kids in the group do not. It's that super parental look. I didn't love it.

"Do you know what ovulation is, Jessica?" my brother asks, finally. I shake my head no.

"It has something to do with your period and having babies," he explains, which is more than enough information for me. If I'd known that, I certainly would not have shared this dream in the first place. I blush heavily, my attempts to make conversation with him and his super-cool girlfriend having gone terribly awry. That blob, of course, caught up with me later that summer.

And now it's the other way around. I've been chasing it, and I am so grateful it's back. I feel the way I do when I see buds on magnolia branches in April. It's the first sign of spring. I hope so, anyway.

Chapter 10

Grieving While Hoping
(six weeks after)

My baby—my firstborn son—died, and I'm walking through a hell that only baby-lost mamas know.

And I want another baby.

There are no words for this kind of loss. No words for being in Labor and Delivery among all the joyous parents, their happy sounds mingling with the cries of newborn life. There you are, in a silent room, laboring to bring forth your child whom you will not bring home, will not raise, will not get to know beyond the kicks you felt, the perfect face that showed up on the ultrasound, and his beautiful, still form in your arms.

There are no words for this kind of loss, but I'm using lots anyway as I navigate through it. These words help me frame my story as nuanced and dappled, and yet still beautiful, as I write about the "bad stuff" that has happened to me.

Highlight reel: My first husband made lots of terrible choices. Having an affair with a family member tops the list, but also lying to me throughout our entire relationship, stealing from me, and being emotionally abusive were pretty bad, too. And of course, some years later, my baby dies. (There are clearly some things I need to work through.)

These words I am finding, perfect or not, help me describe what I have seen, what I continue to see, and remind me that the story does not end with just the loss. They help me see that God is not doing the bad stuff, but man; He is here close to me through it all. Sometimes He feels closer in the worse times. It's a terrible price to pay for it, but the closeness and the beauty that show up in the grief and pain is real. Just as real as these circumstances and longer lasting. I tell myself this repeatedly in the darkness. It's a lifeline.

I am afraid that pain is a better teacher than comfort. I am afraid of this because I hate pain. But still, I seem to grow when I suffer and I stay put when I'm comfortable. As a kid, when things wouldn't go my way—and I am talking middle-class, first-world "not going my way," like I didn't get the role I wanted in the Nutcracker Ballet, and I'd cry with my mom—it was (and is) hard for me to accept that a loving and powerful God doesn't make sure I'm always happy.

"I know He could have given me the role I wanted—so why didn't He?" I'd ask my mom sitting at our dining room table.

"God cares more about our hearts than our happiness," my mom told me, "And He always brings happiness eventually."

I didn't get it then, but maybe I am starting to. Maybe God allows hard things so that, eventually, our hearts become mature, and we are freed from the pain and the meaninglessness of a self-absorbed life. So that we become the lucky ones who see well, who don't waste time and energy on what does not matter. Maybe if we were only ever happy, we'd have nothing to say to the grieving mother, the addicted father, the people living in poverty, abuse, etc., because we simply cannot relate. We wouldn't speak the language of grief because we've never been there, never been forced to use it ourselves.

One of my dearest friends had, in more than one way, a tough childhood. Honestly, I didn't. She'd come over to my house and see two parents who love each other and nobody wondering how the bills would be paid this month. When my first husband left,

I experienced more pain than I'd known a person could survive. And Ireland was there, telling me about her own pain, letting me see her scars, and also showing me that people can not only survive trauma, but even thrive. I'd take away the suffering she endured in a heartbeat, but that's not my choice—it's not even hers. And I am also grateful that her ability to grow, heal, deepen her faith and widen her heart *through* the trauma was a beacon of hope for me when it was my turn for deep pain.

I am learning that happiness alone cannot be the goal. That goal gets moved by hands that aren't our own, becoming inaccessible. Our person leaves or dies and, through no failing of ours, we are no longer happy. But let's say that to love others and be loved is our purpose—well, that's great news. Because whether or not we feel happy in any given season, that goal remains. Pain and suffering are horrible (full stop), and they can also allow our hearts to stay soft and our need for help to remain so great that it is either reach out and let people in or don't make it at all. Instead of a life that is simply about ourselves, our own happiness, it becomes richer, deeper, greater as we see others and let them see us. What if it is love, our connection to others—that brings us the deepest happiness and joy available? And again, love, respect, dignity, joy, hope, honor—the things we hold within that nobody can take from us—are always available.

World famous psychiatrist, Auschwitz survivor, and creator of *logotherapy*, Dr. Viktor Frankl, writes in his incredible book, *Man's Search for Meaning,* about discovering our purpose in every season. While Dr. Freud had offered that the purpose of mankind is pleasure, and Dr. Adler had stated that, no, actually, the purpose of mankind is power—Frankl negated both of these theories with his own: the purpose of mankind is *deriving meaning throughout all of life.* As a prisoner in a horrific Nazi death camp, where neither pleasure or power were accessible to him, and in which, he notes, he had a 1 in 28 chance of even surviving at all—he discovered firsthand that meaning was still within his grasp. Frankl takes my breath away as he writes about the potential in every man to live well, with dignity, honor, and even faith, despite the basest of circumstances. He describes his generation as realists. After all, he explains, they'd seen that man had invented the gas chambers of Auschwitz. And yet, he goes on (boldly declaring that there is more to this story than the horror of the gas chambers alone), it is also man who entered those gas chambers with head held high, the Lord's prayer and *Shema Yisrael* on their lips. Perhaps, like Dr. Frankl says, there is more to life than what happens to us. Perhaps we get a say as to how and what life is.

After my divorce, I became close to a friend. A male, single, kind, handsome friend (oops). I pointed my whole broken heart towards him and finally exhaled. *Things are going to be okay,* I'd think, my face buried in his chest in a parking lot while we took hours saying good-bye, only to see each other the very next day. But then, they weren't—at least not with him, at least not in that way.

The blow was crushing.

I felt like the sun had abandoned the sky.

Eating was exhausting and uninteresting.

Even the work of breath—my lungs laboring over the seemingly impossible task of moving the heavy bones of my ribcage—felt hard as I lay in my bed, the morning no longer promising and the evening something to dread. I was profoundly sad. This, on the heels of having already been profoundly sad. It was not the straw that broke the camel's back—it was the *boulder* that broke its back, and everyone said: *Well, yeah! I mean, it was a boulder! And the camel wasn't exactly strong to begin with! And what did the camel THINK was going to happen, hanging out with a single, male, kind, handsome friend while recovering from a divorce like that?* (Thank you, everyone; you've said quite enough!)

This was my state when my mom found me sitting in the dark one evening. "Jess," she said, "I need to tell you something. I've been married to your pop since I was 19. We've raised five babies and built a church together. He is my person. And yet, if he died, I wouldn't lose my purpose. How could I, when my kids and their kids are here, too? When my faith drives me on, reminding me I have life to live and people to encourage? I know you are heartbroken, and with all my heart, I wish I could change that—but please know your life hasn't ended. You have so much to offer, still."

Please don't confuse the feeling of happiness alone with purpose. For, though it is very hard to grieve and feel happy, we can grieve and have purpose. And as we continue to walk in our purpose, our grief sharply highlights the grace we find. The people who drop off meals, who write heartfelt notes, encouragement laced through the syntax. The books we devour containing stories of suffering and creativity, mourning and joy—how these correlations offer us hope, keep us here. We find grace is greater than whatever else it is we don't have enough of—whether it's money or husbands who stay or babies who come home or self-confidence or healthy family dynamics or whatever.

Everything runs out, yet grace remains. It shows up even brighter when the noise fades and the only sound left to compete with is our own tired tears traveling a well-worn path on our faces. Grace is God telling us that we are loved, therefore lovely. That His plan for us is kind and detailed. That joy is involved. When we know this, when we learn how vast grace is, we become liberal with it. For when we lean on grace, we tend to give it to others, too. It becomes the currency we're familiar with, the thing we give and get, give and get, give and get.

When we remember well, we wake up and realize that none of us have ever done this before. This season, this project, this problem, this grief, this joy—heck, none of us have ever even done this day before. So we don't walk with the casual shuffle of those who have been here many times over. We walk with our eyes wide, noticing. We walk in awe of how little we know. On very good days, doing our best might feel like enough, but eventually, a day will teach us it wasn't/isn't/won't be enough. Our best falls short. Our happiness runs out.

Which brings me back full circle—back to grace. Generous, expansive, I-live-here-now grace. It takes our hand and gently walks us through change. Often the door is labeled Grief or Pain or Suffering. Sometimes it's not, and I do love when that happens. But Grace is a gentle leader, always reminding us we are loved and therefore lovely. That life is still ours. We still get to enter in. And joy is still here, present and holding its breath, waiting for us to round the corner and see it—know it intimately—again. If not this corner, then next—I will say this forever, because I've seen it. At the intersection of grief and grace, I have seen it.

* * *

Now I'm back home from the hospital, and I am afraid of everyone in our building. The drive home from Massachusetts General is quiet and empty, my husband navigating the streets we know so well. There isn't much to say; there's so much to cry about. We park and, for the first time, I hate that we live in an apartment building with neighbors everywhere. For the first time, running into friendly faces feels intrusive; I am not ready.

On the long walk from our parking spot to our apartment, I am acutely aware of how much smaller my belly is, afraid of the questions this will invite. *Surely you had your baby?* everyone's prying eyes seem to ask. I keep my own eyes down, a clear message to leave me alone. My grief is too sacred, too private, too intense for the lobby of our building, too intimate for conversations among neighbors who can't know there is nothing left inside—not my baby boy—not even the courage to say hello anymore.

My family is home with Charlee—sweet, wonderfully innocent, two-year-old Charlee, who is only happy to see us. She doesn't know to be sad, doesn't understand that death has just robbed her of her brother. I'm grateful for this; I want to protect her from all of it, forever. I know I can't, but I will try anyway.

I think about God and his love for humanity. It's the first love, the greatest love, the love that brought us all here. But it doesn't necessarily mean that He always shields us from heartbreak. There is a line in C.S. Lewis' famous children's book, *The Lion, The Witch, and The Wardrobe* that stays with me. This is right after Aslan, who all the animals of Narnia look to rescue them from the White Witch's reign of terror, has been killed by the White Witch, but shockingly comes back to life—bigger, brighter, stronger, more alive than ever before. Lucy and Susan, two of the heroines of the story, love him dearly, and are beyond relieved to see him alive once again. They ask him if he's a ghost, because they saw the White Witch kill him.

Aslan tells the girls that, though the Witch knows the Deep Magic, there is a Deeper Magic still that she doesn't know. I think about all the terrible things that can happen to us during our journey through life. How there are the Big Things—things I find overwhelming, because I don't know what I can do to fix the holes in the ozone layer or reverse global warming. (Okay, I know there are a few things I can do. I am not proposing we do nothing. We should absolutely do lots of whatever we can. Thankfully, there are people much more knowledgeable than me on this subject, and they have written books, and you should definitely read those books because this is not one of them). And there are all the terrifying things that can happen to make us lose the ones we love. I think many of us know the first kind, the "Deep Magic" Aslan means—that a heart breaks and is never the same. That darkness descends on a soul, and it isn't just that we can no longer see, but that we no longer even care to try. We think we know what's in front of us, and we think it's always this darkness, discouraging and bitter, forever.

I wonder how many of us know the Deeper Magic that Aslan refers to, the magic that God knows: that brokenness leads to healing and that those who go through the pain of healing and come out the other side as some of the most grateful and loving and compassionate people on earth. That joy killed can lead to joy reborn. That in pain, our hearts expand and grow in a way that they simply cannot do in happiness alone. And maybe it is because God sees this Deeper Magic that He allows us to experience suffering.

Have you heard about trees and the role of wind in their life? I need to tell you, I need to tell myself over and over again. Scientists trying to study trees in a controlled environment created their own biosphere. They found, however, that the trees kept collapsing under their own weight before ever reaching maturity. This, despite the trees seemingly having everything they need. These scientists soon realized there was no wind in this biosphere. And they learned that the wind in a tree's life keeps it moving and fighting as it grows to position itself for the best light. The resistance the wind provides causes a tree to create something called *reaction wood*. And it is this reaction wood that causes the tree to be strong enough to reach full maturity and thrive. Imagine! The very thing that is considered the hardest burden in a tree's life ("Can't I just have *one day* where I'm not fighting to remain upright?!" Bob the Tree complains to a very sympathetic squirrel) is what actually allows the tree to make it. Maybe the horrible things in life create some sort of *reaction wood* of the soul.

I am not saying anything as annoying as, *So it's all worth it! Or next time you're grieving, just think of the reaction wood coming your way.* Life is really, unbearably hard sometimes. In a moment, sometimes that's all it is. And yet, reaction wood. Resilience. The beauty of brokenness. The softness of our hearts after. The trees and wind. It's got to all mean something. It's got to line up in our own hearts as some kind of map that shows us which way is up. It's got to be like Orion in the winter, his bright clear belt high above a cold dark world, letting me know there's a guardian here. That I'm not alone. That I am small, but as long as the One looking out for me is big, it's okay.

There is the time Jesus restores the woman who the Bible describes as having "lived a sinful life."

"She loves much, because she has been forgiven much. But whoever has been forgiven little, loves little." (Luke 7:47)

There's something about brokenness, that, once healed, ushers in love.

The Deeper Magic is the one that sounds like a fairy tale, I realize, but I don't care. It gives me hope, and hope is the thing I need more than anything else. There is heaven. There is much

more than we can see. There is a place where Luca is right now—
and he is not sad there.

Chapter 11

Telling People

(three days after)

After I come home from the hospital without Luca, I go back and forth between the isolation of my bedroom, where I can cry freely, and the living room crowded with the people I've known forever. I like the normalcy of my siblings talking about whatever, just like we've always done. I like the way Charlee makes them all laugh, how even though they don't get to know my second child, they are busy knowing my first. It's also shocking that people can talk and laugh and live. I can't seem to do any of it. The cognitive dissonance of trying to reconcile Luca's death with everyday things and small talk is at times too much. So I go back to my room, fall into my bed, and sob until there are no tears left. For now, anyway.

One of these times when I've fallen back into bed, I grab my phone: It's time. I write out the birth and death announcement for Luca. It's the first time I've written about him, and something surprises me. I don't feel worse while doing it. There is a kind of puzzle to arranging the perfect words to tell the world what has happened to my boy, what has happened to us, that they will never get to meet him here on earth. That I didn't either—at least not earth-side. The visceral, raw parts of me get a break—strangely, the pain somewhat subsides—as a different part of my brain takes over and I simply tell my story in words that I choose. It's still terrible, but I'm no longer just a victim of that terrible thing. Now I'm a writer, describing something terrible. There is a difference that makes me feel, for the first time since, powerful.

I finish writing and ask TJ to read it.

"Is it okay?" I ask. "Should we let everyone know now?"

"If you're ready, Jess, I'm ready," he says. "And what you've written is beautiful; it's perfect."

There are no perfect words for this, but for the first time, I realize there are many words to choose from to tell my story. And there is so much grace, so much empowerment in the choosing.

★ ★ ★

Luca Thomas Taormina
May 17, 2017

The nurses keep asking my pain scale from 0-10. They are so kind, so caring. They don't ask about my heart, though; there is no number for how it feels.

I don't know how to do this.

Another whole mountain to climb.

It's grief and loss, and I suppose I start here and keep putting one foot in front of the other.

Today we left the hospital without our baby boy. I couldn't do it; I had to do it. We are alone in our grief. We are also surrounded by family who flew here, who drove here, who came as soon as they heard the news.

God, every part of my body aches for him. And at the same time, I'm smiling for my precious Charlee because she's asking me, "Mama, where did your smile go?"

Our Luca is doing well; he is with God. We are not doing as well, but we trust that we will be okay. This is what God does: He is close to the broken hearted; He heals us.

We miss our son with everything that makes up us. It is not natural to bury your baby. It is not okay to say good-bye at the very same moment you get to say hello. It's part of our story, though, and our son makes our story even more precious. He was perfect, with ten fingers and toes, and a little round nose like his sister. I had 35+ sacred weeks with him—weeks that I would never trade, not even to escape this present pain.

Luca Thomas Taormina, your mama loves you. That is the beginning of this story, and that is the end.

Love.

I'm just so profoundly sad that we don't get to spend more time together here on earth. It's not the same without you.

Chapter 12

They Keep Asking for Details
(two weeks after)

I reach out to a therapist because I prefer not to become mentally unstable. At least not permanently. I email her, ask about insurance, location, and if she has room for one more.

Though it feels ridiculous, like I'm shouting, "I'M BLEEDING OUT! Before you, um, help me, do you take Blue Cross?"

Speaking of the inane details we must address while bleeding out: Right after discovering our son Luca is dead at 35 weeks, my doctors discuss whether I can deliver him vaginally because now he's breech.

"Maybe we'll do a C-section," another suggests.

No wait, here's another doctor who's better at figuring these ultrasound-ey things out. She's saying that yes, he's breech, but since he's my second, and since he's already dead, he essentially cannot be further harmed. Doing a vaginal birth should be fine.

Small victories, am I right?

But right after that whirlwind of a good time, a doctor stands in front of us with many papers and even more questions.

"I'm so sorry I have to ask you these questions now, but it's just how it is."

I've learned that a lot of terrible things are just how they are and there is no comfort in this.

And then TJ and I are telling her about the respective genders with which we identify, the race by which we identify.

And then she asks, "Your level of education?"

I can feel the terrible stillness in my huge belly. My mind is wrapping around what is, trying to ready myself to deliver my son's dead body—as I explain that I have a BFA in dance performance and graduated with high honors. I don't think she cares about the high honors, but none of this is relevant, so I throw it in there anyway.

We are stunned and quietly recounting details about our lives that pale so ferociously to the here and now, that it is like asking a starving human being if they prefer sourdough over seven-grain bread before finally feeding them.

God, these things don't matter—doesn't anybody else in the world see the enormity of how much nothing matters compared to THIS?

But TJ and I try to be polite. We even thank the doctor for the questionnaire, like two gracious little frogs slowly being boiled alive. Thank you so much for this very warm bath (it's actually getting a little too hot, but God forbid I say anything). Politeness before all else.

Some of the most horrible things in life are accompanied by papers. I remember walking into the courthouse and seeing the word DIVORCE on a list of items to buy. It had a price next to it. Like a dollar menu. Could I buy a burger and fries along with the dissolution of my marriage and heart, or do I need to stop at McDonald's on the way home?

But there are good papers, too.

Just today, I finally have the energy to organize our bedroom and sort through the many piles that these last two weeks have accumulated. I come across Charlee's dedication certificate—a reminder of the day we gave her to God in front of a bunch of people who celebrated with us. The day we told Jesus she belongs to Him.

Just like we'd have done with Luca. He ended up in the same place we'd imagined—just so much sooner than we ever expected.

Chapter 13

Holding Him
(five weeks after)

It's been five weeks and one day since I held Luca.

Life has happened in the meantime. We've celebrated birthdays. I baked cakes and swam in the pool and had a million deep and shallow conversations. It's all been punctuated by tears—sometimes quietly falling, and sometimes shaking my whole body with the sound the universe recognizes as a mother grieving.

There's no sound like it.

Having written songs for as long as I can remember, I feel this great expectation to write powerful songs about this experience. But I sit at the piano and nothing comes. I play the chord progressions that flow easily, but they are tired and feel hollow. I cannot write lyrics about this. There is no rhyme to be found.

What I can do is think about what has happened. I do this a lot. From the outside, I look like any other mom—buying groceries or holding my daughter's hand tightly to avoid her falling when she trips over Boston's uneven (albeit charming) sidewalks.

But inside, I am remembering.

Always remembering.

I have read about mothers who lose a child and wash and fold every garment their child wore. They do it as a ritual, to mother the child who is no longer here. They put the clothes away lovingly, perfectly. But, I imagine, not before holding each piece to their face and sobbing into the cotton that will no longer cover the body they'd give anything they have—or find anything they don't have, if that is what's required—to simply hold again.

I do that, too, but with my thoughts, with my memories. (Come on, there's no way I am folding unnecessary laundry. Not even now.) I sit down and create space in my mind for all the thoughts about Luca that are available today. They hurt, but I need them. Taking care of these thoughts is the way I can mother my boy now. I grab the memories and lay them out, one by one. I fold them again and again inside my mind; I wonder if there are new details I will discover this time. I open the drawers inside me—the ones you don't know about, the ones the world can only guess at—and I put my thoughts away. They are not gone. They are here and safe and waiting until the next moment when I can pull them out and bury my face in them, breathing deep all the evidence of the boy I carried, my forever baby. I recently read a line by Viktor Frankl in *Man's Search For Meaning* and, though I took it out of context, the words basically carried Luca into the forefront of my thoughts: "Having been is also a kind of being and perhaps the surest kind."

Perhaps the surest kind—yes.

* * *

Now I am laying on the hospital bed, having just pushed my baby out of my body. I am afraid, at first, to hold him, because (this is obvious, but I will write it down anyway) he's dead.

"You don't have to hold him, Jess," TJ tells me, trying, like always, to shield me from as much pain as possible. The thought of holding a dead baby is not exactly something you wake up to and want to do.

"Yes, I do," I say simply.

Because I do. We both do. We are his parents, and although we don't stand up in front of a crowd of witnesses with a formal set of vows we take, there is still a binding contract between parents and their children that I will not break. Not even in death.

I am Charlee's mama, and I get all the good parts that come with it. I am the first person she wants to hug in a crowded room. I am the one she calls for when she wakes up in the morning. When she's tired—because the day has filled her to capacity and then some, and it's the witching hour—her clinginess finds me first. She's been walking for well over a year, but every part of her needs to be held, because it's not about her ability to move herself around the room anymore. It's about needing to be close, to be safe, to be held by someone who loves her.

And it's no different now.

I know Luca has flown already. I know he is in heaven and I'm not sure how it works there. Maybe he can see us. Maybe he will see us holding him with reverence for the body that housed him during the thirty-five weeks he was on earth, growing inside me. Maybe he will see his mama touch his tiny nose the same way I've touched Charlee's nose in wonder a thousand times.

And he will know that he is loved.

He will know that he was brought into this world by parents who want him and couldn't wait to show him that Mondays could be wonderful, too. That there are a lot of great things to make, but jokes are some of the best. That you can never go wrong with love, and you will learn that truth, here and now with us, your family. Then you take that idea into the world, and we'll all feel so proud as we watch our world get brighter because of it, because of our boy Luca. I know that my final physical acts on earth with Luca—as his mother—are first delivering him and then holding him. Of course I would do it. Just like of course I hold Charlee every single day.

I had never touched a dead body before, but I think that no amount of experience with handling the dead could prepare you for holding your own dead son. I reach for him, not knowing quite what to expect. I thought I would hesitate, but I am his mama: There is no hesitation when it comes to putting him where he belongs. He is wrapped in a hospital baby blanket with the same kind of hat Charlee wore right after birth, only he has no bow, because he is a boy. Our boy. God, I was so excited to have a son, too. *Am* excited? No, *was* excited—past tense, I guess.

I let out the breath I didn't even know I was holding as I study his little face. He is perfect, with even features and beautiful red bow lips. He reminds me of Charlee, except he's the kind of still I've never seen in my daughter. His skin is marked by little bloody patches that surprise me.

"Why is he bleeding?" I ask the nurse.

"It doesn't take long for their bodies to break down once they're gone," she answers quietly. "Babies have very delicate skin, so it goes first, Hon," she tells me, with nothing to soften the hard truth except the hushed tone of compassion I hear in her voice.

Chapter 14

Hope, That Old Tough Bird Who Keeps Showing Up
(two hours after)

TJ and I are alone with Luca for a while. I'm holding him, his body settled into the crook of my arm the way a mama who has done this before can do. Finally, my mom and sister arrive. They are crying, but then they see him, and they start *oohing* and *aahing* over his beauty the way you do over any brand-new baby.

For a moment, it is almost normal.

My mom reaches to hold him, and I'm so sorry I can't give her a living grandson right now. He is her eleventh. Before he was born, I joked with my mom that she didn't have to pretend to be excited anymore. Like, we'd all understand if she was a little bit ho-hum about another grandkid to join the already full ranks.

"Are you kidding me, Jess?" my mom said with real consternation in her voice. "I cannot wait to meet him! We get to have another baby in the family! Christmas will be amazing with a three-year-old and a six-month-old this year!" Every sentence deserves an exclamation point; that's how excited she was.

And I agreed. What a lot of joy for one family, for one season, for one mama.

The thing is, no matter how many grandbabies are presented to my mom, she thrills over each like it is her first. And it is no different now. She's thrilling over him, too.

I watch her move his little hat so she can peak at what's underneath. And how kind of a nurse to put him in a hat. It's not that he needs to stay warm, but still, they give my Luca a hat, anyway.

"So much hair!" my mom exclaims quietly. "He's got a full head of it!"

I'm glad my mom thought to move his hat. Being so afraid to disturb his fragile skin, I hadn't thought to see what's underneath. Now I know that my son has hair and considering how little I get to know of him on this earth, this is a gift. He's like TJ, I think to myself. I was born bald and stayed that way a while. What an honor it is to have had a little boy with hair like TJ's.

Then something strange happens. Two of my brothers arrive, having driven up from Pennsylvania and Maryland, and they each hold Luca, too. They *ooh* and *aah* like my mom and sister did, and we settle into a rhythm of conversation as we pass Luca from one to another. It's not as depressing as you might think, either. It's not the scene you would imagine for a dead baby and his family. It was somehow special. Not that sad moments aren't special; they can be sacred, holy. But this is different— weaving in and out between profound sadness and everyday conversation and laughter. It's strange, I know. I'm learning that I have no idea what to anticipate.

As long as I can remember, my family has talked. When I visit other families at dinnertime, I am still shocked by the sound of silverware clinking on dishes throughout the meal. Like eating is the main event or something. I generally leave dinners with my family with an even fuller heart than belly. And we never ever hear the silverware.

The first time I brought TJ home to visit, my nieces and nephews, parents, brothers, and sisters-in-law sat around my parents' large dinner table, firing questions off rapidly. I left TJ with no shield, standing on his own two feet in this firestorm, knowing that all his years on the radio had more than prepared him to give answers now.

We laughed as the questions got more and more ridiculous. "Have you ever gone number two in public, TJ?" my brother demanded. (Turns out, he has, for those of you who are curious.)

"What do you think of Aunt Jessica?" my niece asked.

"I think she's beautiful," TJ answered simply, halting my family's riotous laughter and questions all at once with this perfect, lovely answer.

After dinner, we moved to the living room; it was my mom's birthday, so we launched into one of our favorite traditions. One by one, from the very young to not-so-young, we each told my mom one thing we love about her. I remember TJ's face, how he couldn't stop smiling at all the words pouring out in the moment—words to build up and connect, the best kind of talking.

"Okay," someone said, as always, "Now let's say what we DON'T like about Mom!" Everyone laughed and no one said anything, just like always. The truth is, there is very little that any of us dislike about her.

And even now, while my boy Luca is being held reverently by my family, we still haven't run out of words. I can't remember what we talk about, specifically, but I remember how we laugh and cry, depending upon the moment. I remember how grief is present, but so is love. There is a sense of togetherness and family; a suspicion that we might still get to be us. Not that it is okay that my baby is dead, but that, by the kind of saving grace that is impossible to describe (in the same way a miracle is not easily broken down into three simple steps)—there are moments when I think we might end up okay.

I feel that my very bones are heavier with the weight of my loss. But I wonder about the miracles of which I've heard. Wonder if something that's both a part of grief and also deeper than grief is at work, battling for our lives. I hope for something that is hard to explain, because a true miracle cannot be found in the pages of a self-help book or easily understood by someone whose life isn't the one brought back by it.

As I hold Luca, I know he will not come back. I am not hoping for this anymore. I am hoping for wholeness again someday. I am hoping that grief will do its healing work and will someday be replaced by something else. Something that doesn't leave my family with an emotional limp as we continue walking this journey, this life, this beautiful life, dammit. Does that sound insane? Yes. It makes no sense, but we do not hope because it makes sense. We hope because we have felt the desperation that comes without it, and we want something more. We need something more. One of the great poets of the 19th century, Emily Dickinson, wrote:

Hope is the thing with feathers —
That perches in the soul —
And sings the tune without the words —
And never stops — at all.

Never stops at all.

I'd always imagined the "thing with feathers" to be a dainty, flittering bird, the kind that hangs around Disney princesses, never doing anything more than singing sweet notes in blue skies. But, in this moment, what I'm wishing for is that I'm wrong. Because I need hope to be the toughest and oldest bird in existence—the kind that isn't known as much for its beauty as it is for its ridiculous persistence. For its ability to keep showing up. This bird has seen the ugliest things—stuff that would send the dainty hummingbird flying to the furthest ends of the sky—but she remains unafraid. She knows her place, and she will not leave. There is a viral video of a seagull eating a rat off the street here in Boston. The bird just eats it whole—pointy nose to the end of its tail—and it is shocking to watch. (Google it if you're curious. Even if you know what to expect, it still catches you off guard.) This is the kind of bird I'm talking about. Unafraid like that. She's been around long enough to see a rat and knows just what to do with it.

Hope is the thing with feathers that stays with those of us living through ugly things, whose lives are not dainty or perfect. While others might not need this tough old bird to shade them with her wings, to surprise them with the fact that hope remains even in the darkest, ugliest places—I do. I need her here, especially, in the places that should never be. Like death when everyone told you there'd be birth. Like what should have been a double stroller, a birth announcement, and the good wishes and shared joy of a thousand friendly faces but is grief instead.

But maybe there's something more here, too. Maybe hope, the thing with feathers—the tough-as-nails, old, unafraid, most-showing-up bird there is—never leaves at all. Maybe she crouches there in the shadows, waiting for when we need her, for when our grief is so big we cannot see beyond it. Maybe grief and this bird know each other well, having sat like sentries through the dark night of the soul. Maybe they sit side by side, shepherding our hearts through it.

Let it be.

I think about Luca's twenty-week ultrasound. TJ has to work, so I go alone. There is no reason to be afraid or feel like I need someone else with me. And sure enough, everything is perfect.

"The dark days of pregnancy are over," the doctor tells me after thoroughly assessing Luca's brain, heart, growth, limbs, fingers, toes—everything. "We expect to see a healthy baby boy in another 20 weeks or so," he says, turning off the machine and handing me paper towels to wipe the goop from my belly. I leave feeling grateful and happy, fumbling for my phone to call TJ and give him the good news. I bring home a new scroll of photos of our baby and show my sister. She immediately tapes them to our refrigerator door.

Everyone I see remarks how lucky we are to be having a boy to add to the girl we already have. Our neighbors tell me that our family will be perfect: "You're done after this, if you want to be!" they say, smiling. And I smile back, though I'm not quite sure we are done. I'm not ready to say that Luca is our last baby.

The dark days of pregnancy are over. I think about that phrase, spoken to me by a doctor, and I am still shocked by how wrong it proved to be. I realize that, statistically, it is a mostly true statement to tell pregnant women with a healthy 20-week-old fetus. I get it. But I never would have predicted that the very darkest days of my life were looming just fifteen weeks away. And maybe Hope, the thing with feathers, was there at the ultrasound, saw the darkness coming, and steeled herself to stay perched in my soul anyway.

Chapter 15

Therapy

(two weeks after)

I'm seeing a therapist tomorrow. Her name is Nancy. This is a good sign, because the Nancy I grew up with was Nancy Drew. You know, the girl from the books who always solves the mystery in 150 pages. I bet this Nancy will, too. She'll take out a magnifying glass and, together, we will study the shape of my heart.

"Here it is," she'll say, matter of fact, because she sees this stuff all the time.

"Here's where it's broken. But look! There's something else you should see."

She'll take off her glasses. (All the best professionals wear glasses, so they can take them off for added emphasis when need be.) She'll make sure I'm following where her fingers are pointing.

"Here is a scar. Every scar tells a story. Do you know what this one tells me?" she'll ask.

"Would you like my last therapist to email you the notes?" I'll joke.

She'll smile at my snark and continue, "This scar indicates that your heart has a great capacity to heal. To knit back together. To grow even stronger where the break once was. This is good news."

Good news.

Oh God, please.

I'll take that good news in the way the dry Pennsylvania fields of my girlhood—bleached from the summer droughts—softened when the rain finally came. The clouds rolled in, bearing relief from the endless hot sun, convincing the dry cracked earth to open back up. To trust that there is good here, that maybe it never even left, because look. The rain comes. It always comes again.

"I never bought a double stroller," I tell Nancy, "Or a rocking chair—which is something I told TJ was a must for this baby. I didn't have one when Charlee was tiny, and I always wished I did during those long nights when your baby needs rocking and your body needs help. So I kept telling TJ that we needed a double stroller and a rocking chair. But there I was, 35 weeks along, and we still hadn't bought either. Do you think deep down I somehow knew? Do you think there was a subconscious part of me that just felt like he wasn't actually going to live with us?"

I'm not sure why I am saying this. I know nobody can answer this question, not even myself.

"Other parents who've lost their babies at or near full term have told me the same thing. Did you know? Or is it just because it's the second baby and you're so much busier this time around so things got pushed off? Who can really say?" she replies. "But I can tell you that you're not the only one dealing with loss who wonders this."

"I never worried once about Charlee not making it," I continue. "But I worried about Luca. I was afraid he wasn't moving enough—a little more than a week before he died, I went into Mass General Hospital because I felt like he wasn't moving as much as he should. They did an ultrasound and he scored an eight out of eight. Like, he couldn't have done better. But then the following week, he wasn't moving again, and I was worried all over again. And that time it was for good reason, obviously. I never felt that way with Charlee. Maybe she moved a lot more because she was healthier. Or maybe it's because a good friend of mine had a stillbirth just last year and we sometimes texted about it..."

I trail off into silence, knowing again that nobody has sufficient answers for me. But this doesn't stop me from voicing the questions anyway.

"I just wonder," I keep going—in the doorway now, as my session ended five minutes ago, "I wonder…if I get to be pregnant again—how I will feel. Will I be anxious over the baby every single day? And there are so many days when you have to grow the baby, unable to do anything but wait and trust that your baby is okay. Two hundred and eighty days of this. That's a lot of days to try not to worry. How am I going to do that?"

Nancy nods and trains her eyes on my face. "It is a lot of days to try not to worry, Jess. I can tell you that your next pregnancy will be different from Charlee's, but also different from Luca's. Your next baby's story is just that: unique to him or her. It will not be Charlee's story, but it will also not be Luca's story. Of course, you will be very aware of your loss, which is understandable. There will be scary moments. But there will also be many other moments, wonderful moments, that will make the scary ones worth it."

I agree. Then I quietly walk away from Suite 307, where I come once a week and describe to Nancy how it feels to be me now that Luca has left.

Chapter 16

We're Still Us

(three weeks after)

TJ and I are in bed when I turn to him and say, "Can I tell you something that's been bothering me? Something I feel guilty about?"

TJ is looking at me now, his book closed, his face an invitation to tell him anything, just like always.

"His tiny feet, TJ. I didn't look at Luca's tiny feet. I can remember the weight of him in my arms, but I can't picture his feet, and I'm sorry I can't. What kind of mom can't picture their baby's feet?"

I'm crying now. TJ is just listening, silently, so I continue.

"I didn't know how to do it. I didn't know how to say goodbye in the perfect way. I was afraid to disturb his little body. Afraid to make his fragile skin bleed even more if I moved him too much. So I didn't. I just held him in his blanket and stared at his face and felt his weight against me and tried to love him the best that I could. Tried to love him a lifetime's worth in the few hours we had with him. But I forgot to look at his feet. I'm so sorry about that."

"Jess, there is nothing to feel guilty about," TJ says, now pressing my body close. Shoulder to shoulder and knee to knee, eliminating the space, willing the hurt away with his proximity.

"There was never going to be a perfect way to say goodbye to our baby. Luca knows we love him. He also knows that by the time we held him, he was no longer here. We know that, too. It's okay that you haven't seen his feet yet; you'll see them someday. There is no one way to do this, but it's hard enough without letting guilt add to it. Please, don't listen to it. You said goodbye in the best way you knew how. I'm so sorry you had to."

I still regret not looking at his feet. I didn't think about it at the time. I also apparently had full conversations—agreeing to things that, afterward, I had no recollection of—while I was saying goodbye to my son. It was, to put it lightly, a hard time. I don't think I even knew how hard it was while I was in it, really. None of it had set in yet; I was reeling from shock, blindly feeling my way through. So when I think about this, I have to let it go. It's not a measure of my love for him.

How do you say goodbye to your baby? You cannot. You do it. Both are true, somehow.

★ ★ ★

I think TJ is doing better than I am. I think everyone is doing better than I am. At least today. It's raining and cold and it's my birthday soon. For the first time ever, I really feel sad about my birthday. (I feel like writing it's my "f***ing birthday," but that would make my pastor mom so sad. So, I add the asterisks and hope she can get past it. Once, when I was rehearsing for the Broadway tour of *A Chorus Line* in Manhattan, they did a press release with photos of the cast. My mom, silently pouring over the photos, taking in the fact that her daughter was playing in the big leagues, so to speak, finally said only, "Why do you always have to be the one showing your belly?" It's true, I was often showing my belly. I was a dancer and had this tiny little belly and got hot when I danced, and so these factors coalesced into me often dancing in a sports bra. And I know my wonderful pastor mom had to really ask for grace about all the midriff showing which was quite a contrast to my growing up years, that's for sure).

Anyway, it especially hurts that it must be my birthday—now, of all times.

All year, I've anticipated this birthday with such joy because Luca was coming right after. And if he came early, maybe he'd come on my birthday. Even better. TJ joked about him coming on his birthday, six days after mine. "He'll come on mine, and I can kiss my birthday good-bye after that," he'd joke.

At which point I'd remind him of how much I celebrate him and how that's not changing. "I've already planned your birthday, actually," I told him. "I've had it planned for a year, and you'll love it. We just need to pray Luca doesn't come that day!"

And he didn't. Oh God. He didn't.

"What do you want for your birthday?" my mom asks me, as she does every year.

"Nothing, Mom."

I am dreading the upbeat, stupid birthday wishes from people this year. And I am also dreading people saying nothing at all, like I fully *did* disappear into my grief, the way I suspect I have.

But on my birthday, I will breathe and write and my heart will keep beating, I am guessing. I will eat cake for Charlee, who enjoys birthdays quite a lot. Thank God for Charlee.

And maybe I will get the gift of editing something of TJ's again. Grammar makes sense to me in a time when not much does. TJ asked me to edit something of his last night, and I am like little Oliver Twist—starving Oliver Twist, who has the temerity to ask for more gruel—hungrily rearranging words, trading out an ellipsis for a dash. Putting sentences in the kind of order I can't quite make of my heart, my feelings, my life.

I keep writing because I don't know what else to do. I keep writing because it helps to choose the words of this narrative, at least, if I can't choose the narrative itself. I'm struck by both the pain and the love that keep coming back. The love from TJ and Charlee and my family and friends and perfect strangers, and yes, God too.

But the pain never leaves; it just mingles with the love, creating something else entirely. Like when I first learned about primary colors and what they can do when you blend them. I'm here watching red and blue—pain and love—continue to intersect. I follow the traces of a bold new purple down my arms, my legs, over my shoulders, and down my chest.

Purple. It's not what I want. It's not what I asked for. But maybe it's beautiful, too.

Chapter 17

Other People and My Grief
(three months after)

I text my friend. She lost her baby just under a year ago, so she's farther down this path than me.

"When did you start hanging out with people again?" I ask.

I still have no desire to do that—people ask, but I politely decline. Unless it's for Charlee—then I smile and hang so that she gets to play with a friend.

"I'll let you know," my friend texts back. "I still don't do it."

Grief is isolating. It feels suddenly impossible to relate to a non-grieving world of people who still think things like vacations and weekend plans matter. And at the same time, there is still a vulnerable spot inside that reminds you of your humanity, that you are built for community. And that spot also hurts when the feeling of being part of that community vanishes just as suddenly as your loved one.

A few months after Luca's death, I scroll through social media and see a photo of all my former co-workers at a bridal shower. I'd been left off the invite list. I feel an immediate sting, but I understand. Would I want to go at this point? Probably not. Do I want other people to want me there, though? I do. Proof of life keeps showing up like that. These smalls inklings of wanting something, reminding me that I'm here, that I am entering into whatever it is that's in front of me, despite the forever ambivalence that grief has promised me.

I'm surprised that I have not developed a thicker skin while going through this. I feel like the person who has survived a major accident yet obsesses over a tiny scratch on my arm. I text the same friend who lost her baby last year, asking her if she found she was even more sensitive while grieving.

"You don't develop a thicker skin, Jess," she says. "You develop no skin. It's all been ripped off. You're incredibly sensitive to everything and easily hurt by everyone."

Oh.

I work out a plan. If I am hurt and it is something that will affect a relationship I want to keep, I will address it (Fun! Who doesn't want to be the grieving woman who confronts her normal, happy friends?). Otherwise, I will forgive, assume the best about whoever unknowingly hurt me, and let it go. Do I do this perfectly? Nope, nope, nope. But the goal helps guide me forward, step by step, through the minefield of my emotions.

At three months after Luca's death, I am wondering why most people in my immediate family have stopped reaching out. The more I wonder, the more hurt I feel. I see their happy posts on social media, and it makes me feel even worse. One night I cannot sleep, so I compose this email:

Dear Family —

I appreciate and love you all very much. More than I can say, I appreciate when you showed up to be with me and TJ and Charlee after Luca died — how you showed up to be at his funeral, too. This means so much, will always mean so much. You showed love and support right away — which, again, I can't adequately say how much I appreciate that for the lifeline it was.

I met someone who lost her twin boys the day before I lost Luca. We connected on Instagram and we've been writing to each other a lot, forging a friendship through our parallel grief. She told me this advice a rabbi shared with her: Many people will want to help but won't know how. Her rabbi explained that she and her husband will have to teach others how to support them in their grief.

That sounds exhausting, honestly. When you are grieving, you want as little responsibility as possible. And being promoted to everyone's guide on "how to handle me in grief" sounds like lots of responsibility. But I have found this to be true. Direct and honest communication makes a big difference. Especially when I'm grieving and need others' care and understanding more than ever before.

So here goes. My son died three months ago. I'm still grieving. Sometimes it's really hard. I would very much appreciate hearing from you. I miss you guys. I don't know if this is how little we communicated before Luca died or not (it's hard to remember, honestly), but I'd love you to tell me that you think of us, that you think of Luca, that you're with me.

Lately, I've felt isolated and lonely. I miss my life, but I can't get that back, necessarily. I also miss my family, though—and that's one thing I don't have to miss, because you guys are all still here. You are all awesome and kind. Maybe you think I'm fine now, because, through social media, you see me re-entering into life. But I am not fine, and I need you.

Not hearing from people who are close to me makes me wonder, erroneously or not, if they think my baby's death is not a big deal. It can leave space for me to make wrong assumptions and withdraw further into myself. Obviously, that's my choice, and I can choose not to do this. But I can't really know how people feel if they don't tell me. It goes without saying that you never have to reach out if you don't want to—but I suspect that you want to. It's not like I need to hear from you every day by 5 o'clock Eastern Standard Time or anything. There's no rule, but it helps when you reach out.

I love you, and I'm proud of each one of you. Please don't feel defensive; I'm not sitting here mad. I just thought it might be a good idea to help teach you how to be there for me now. Even just a text every so often is awesome.

Love, Jess

* * *

The responses pour in.

One brother says, "I know this sounds dumb, but I didn't want to make you sadder by bringing it up."

That doesn't sound dumb, because I understand the instinct. But there is nothing anyone could say now that would make me sadder than how sad Luca's death has already made me. Instead, you can let me know that you care in specific and direct ways. If you don't mention it, don't reach out, and just assume others are reaching out, I start to wonder if you care at all. Meanwhile, others are probably doing the exact same thing—so perhaps nobody is reaching out with words that break the silence and let me know I am not alone; that I am cared for.

Another family member writes, "I am so sorry that I haven't been better at reaching out. I've been busy. I know that's a terrible excuse. Please forgive me."

I do—I forgive you. I also think being busy is a pretty good excuse. I'm busy and often don't do things because of it.

A sister-in-law tells me, "I am so glad you told us this. Thank you. It was brave and vulnerable, and now I know what to do."

You're welcome. And I can't really nurse my offense if I don't at least give you the chance to correct it. If you still don't correct it, then I will make sure to feed and nurture this baby offense every day so it can grow up to be a huge offense that takes over my life and calls the shots until I am no longer here, just the offense. So remember that when you ask to hang out in about a year. And for the rest of our lives, I will distance my heart, so you might miss the benefit of a deep and true connection with yours truly. So choose wisely.

(Just kidding. Hahahahaha. Grudge jokes that make people wonder if you're really joking are so good.)

No matter how people react when you are grieving, no matter how wronged you might feel, these people you love are probably trying their best. Try not to nurse the offense. Forgiveness is always the better choice. Forgiveness leads to freedom from being held down by a debt that someone else may or may not ever repay. And in many cases, they cannot ever repay it. How does one repay you for sleeping with your husband? How does one repay you for taking the life of a loved one? They can't; they don't. Therefore, if your forgiveness of their offense hinges upon their ability (or lack thereof) to repay you, then you are once again a victim, because you have no say over whether or not you will forgive them. It strips you of your power, of your agency.

The truth is: You are powerful. You call the shots of your wonderful, painful—whatever, it's yours, and it's probably both—life. You can forgive an offense and enjoy the freedom that follows, no matter what anybody else—especially the one who hurt you—does or doesn't do. We can forgive the debt another owes us, whether or not they have the ability or initiative to pay it back. We can walk around without being owed. In the end, it's our choice. And though you didn't have a choice in the matter of getting hurt, you do have a choice now. Note: Forgiving someone is not saying, "What you did to me is okay."

It is not saying, "What you did to me is not a big deal."

It is not even saying, "When I think about what you did to me, I no longer have feelings about it.

We can think an act against us is a big deal, not okay, *and* have feelings about it. And we can forgive the person responsible for the act. Forgiveness is letting them off the hook for the debt they owe you. It is taking back the key and walking out of the prison they landed you in when they hurt you. It is no longer putting your own life on hold while waiting for them to "pay you back" from what they stole from you. It is the decision to extend them grace and not act in vengeance.

It is saying, "You are free and so am I."

Forgiveness also does not mean you have to enter into a close relationship—or any relationship at all—with the person who hurt you. I have no relationship with my ex-husband. There is simply no room in my life for it. I have forgiven him and sincerely hope he is well. And we have zero communication. He owes me nothing, and so I am free. Forgiveness is one of the best gifts we give to each other; but first and foremost, we give this gift to ourselves. Choosing to hold onto bitterness is like drinking poison, thinking it will kill someone else. Forgiveness is an act of bold and radical faith.

It is saying, "Instead of waiting around for this person who stole from me to give it back, I am going to release them of their debt and trust that God will give me exactly what I need to be okay."

Wild, right? It reminds me of the line in Song of Songs: "Who is this coming up from the wilderness, leaning on her Beloved?" (Song of Songs 8:5 NIV)

When we forgive someone, first of all, it's a recognition of how we are: hurt. We find ourselves in the wilderness where we're not safe and life no longer looks familiar. But then we get to come up out of the wilderness by leaning on our Beloved. By trusting that God can do for us what no person can. By telling the person who hurt us they don't have to help us find our way out of this terrible wilderness, we know a guy.

(Jessica, stay in your lane! Last I checked, this was not a book about forgiveness.

Dear Reader: You're right. But when we grieve, chances are we're going to have the option to forgive some people who get it wrong in how they handle our broken hearts. I'm simply saying that in my experience, forgiveness is not only an option, but also the best way forward. And since you're the one who is taking your precious time to read my book, then it's you that I care about. PS even though you told me to stay in my lane, thank you very much for reading my book!)

Chapter 18

Out and About with Grief
(one week after)

"Oh! Did you have the baby, then?" our concierge asks.

"We lost the baby, actually."

"Ooooh," he says, scrunching up his face, "I'm so sorry."

"Thank you. It's hard."

Silence.

"You know," he tells me, "I could see it in your face. I took one look at your face when you walked in, and I knew something happened."

"Yeah. I guess so."

And then while the concierge is busy staring hard at his computer screen, my dog Luna and I wait for what feels like five years or so for TJ to meet us in the lobby so we can finally leave.

Do you know how when you hurt your toe, suddenly everybody and their cat is stepping on it and you also cannot remember ever being this clumsy and banging it against this many inanimate objects before? Really, you were probably always this clumsy, and people and their rude cats stepped on this particular toe just as much, but the fact that it's hurting makes you aware of it.

It's the same now with me and pregnant women. They're everywhere. No, I'm not using hyperbole. Boston might as well add a baby bump to its shape on a map, because the streets are rampant with them.

And not just the streets, either. For the first time in the history of walking Luna in the park behind our building, there is a round happy pregnant woman doing her maternity shoot. She is literally getting photographed on the hill where Luna likes to crap. As this woman glows in her billowing white Etsy-inspired dress that shows off her bump beautifully, Luna is nearby, wondering just where, exactly, she should take a dump.

My thoughts exactly, Luna.

The hill isn't even that nice. And there's construction right behind it, so the view isn't anything to write home about. And the photographer is shooting with her *iPhone*, for goodness' sake. There are so many reasons this maternity shoot is unlikely, but here it is, right in front of us. My baby died, so of course this is necessary on an otherwise peaceful walk. Dumb cats and people stepping on my broken toe, I guess.

(Dear Jessica, I must say, what have you got against cats. You have now called them both rude and dumb in the space of three paragraphs and it's beginning to feel like pure libel.

Dear Reader, are you a cat? If so, I do apologize, because you are clearly very smart — you're reading a book! My book! And for this, I thank you. I will no longer write ill of cats in this book. In fact, I will no longer even write about cats in this book at all. This will be difficult, considering how integral they are to this narrative, but I will restrain.)

I've become so good at spotting a pregnant woman. I'll see someone with just the beginning of a round little baby belly, and I'll think, *Aha! She's still hiding it, but I know she's pregnant.*

(Yes, it's a little crazy being me right now.)

Yesterday, as TJ and I walk to the North End with Charlee in her stroller, I glimpse a form walking through the distant foliage. Spotting a little round belly, my Spidey senses tingle: *We've got a live one here, folks!* But when the person emerges into plain view, I see a completely harmless middle-aged man with a potbelly. It's wonderful how *not* pregnant he is. My Spidey senses quickly change their tune: *Abort mission! No pregnant lady in vicinity, and therefore no need to hurt extra right now. Regular levels of hurt will suffice.*

Thank God for middle-aged men who like their everything bagels and cream cheese. That was a close one.

We go to church this morning, and I mostly sit and cry. I feel out of sync with all the smiling people, like I am lying if I smile too. So I don't. But I agree with what I hear. I touch the place where my heart is buried in my chest and ask God how long it will hurt this much. I don't hear an answer, but at some point I put my hand down and TJ grabs it. I wonder if there is an answer after all.

Tonight we are listening to Chance the Rapper in the car. It's like church again, but without all the smiles and happy greetings, so I feel better. The song goes: "Are you ready for your blessing, are you ready for your miracle?" And this time I sing along. This time I find the breath and the courage to do so, and then I think about how blessings don't always look like blessings.

I think about fields, of all things. Maybe it's because my grandfather was a man who bred horses and had land, but I think about farmers ploughing fields, and how this is a fancy way of saying they tear them to shreds. But they plough to make the soil soft, to expose deeper, richer layers of earth. And then they plant things—beautiful things. Necessary things like food. And it all starts with tearing the field up. To the field, this beginning probably feels like death. But the death doesn't end in death; remarkably, life comes afterward. And God, more than anything I just want my baby. But that's not my choice. So I lean my head against the car window and think about the torn fields, how their story will unfold with life and growth and better things than just tearing for tearing's sake, and I find some comfort in that.

Chapter 19

The Grace Here
(one week after)

The whole story is important, and right now I can't see it. The present, glaring season feels all-encompassing, but the truth is that it's not the whole story. More of the story is this: A girl is born in Pennsylvania to two parents who love her.

Grace.

There are three older brothers who teach her loyalty and humor and resilience, then a younger sister who fits into these same lessons seamlessly with a laugh that could wake the dead—or at least make them smile. It's not nearly perfect, but a lot of it is good.

There is a marriage and a betrayal that leaves her gasping for air, but even that can't erase the older story. The story that was here first, as her therapist explains, "You've been hurt badly by a man who promised to love you. But your heart remains open and trusting and intact simply because your family has taught you the lesson of trust from the beginning. And this lesson remains, even if your marriage does not."

Again: Grace.

And then there is TJ. Meeting him in one of the tallest buildings she's ever stepped foot in, falling in love under the shadow of a crooked skyline. Becoming each other's world in the center of the universe. She's never heard him on the radio, but just about everyone else has. Suddenly the terrible tearing that led her here makes some sense. Because here is worth anything.

Every single tear that stole her sleep, her pride, her blind belief in her former love, was a path through the dark leading to this clear bright joy. Some kind of wonderful life. There is a move, a marriage, a Labrador—then the incredible gift of a baby named Charlee Jane.

And now this! Everything that led to here, all the parts before now still exist. It's still just as present as the loss is now. Not to mention all the stages all over the world this girl from Pennsylvania has danced on, sang on; not to mention the friends who have changed her heart for the better.

I dare to say this is a good story. Our beautiful firstborn son is part of it. I miss him the way no mother should have to miss her baby—with tears that come while reading Charlee all the books I don't get to read Luca. But there is comfort in the fact that I know where he is. That he's lacking for nothing. That our baby boy is well, even if not here with us. That grace keeps rising, creating a narrative that I cannot and would not escape. The darkness comes, but it cannot stay. And what I am always so shocked to see, no matter how many times I do, is how the darkness sets the kind of stage for the light that I simply cannot miss. And this story, my story, is a constant, present reminder that it's-not-okay and I'm-going-to-be-okay are two realities that can exist side by side.

It still doesn't feel real.

Sometimes TJ and I look at each other and quietly say, "I can't believe this is our story." But the construction outside our building is steadily progressing towards its finish. We're walking Luna, putting Charlee to bed every night, and flossing our teeth. We keep up with all the mundane things that mark the relentless passage of time, and now I'm fitting into my jackets again, my body finding its shape without Luca. I am thinner and infinitely sadder, like when I was going through a divorce. I look at photos from that season and see I was a waif. A ghost. If you reached out to touch me, perhaps your hand would go right through.

No wonder my pop made me sandwiches and, armed with my lunch one day, found me in the dark, curled up and crying on the bed. He wanted me to eat; I tried to explain that taking in grief every day was enough for my soul and my mind and even my belly. That there was no room for anything else—not even food. He put the sandwich down and held me and let me cry. He stopped trying to convince me to eat and told me I would be okay. My body was diminishing and my grief was spilling out, covering the area around me like liquid on a smooth, flat surface. At one point, there was more grief to me than flesh, I am sure.

Side note: When telling TJ this story, his first question was, "Was it awkward as a grown woman to have your dad hold you?"

"Well, it wasn't, like, normal."

Pause.

"So it was awkward?" he asked again.

I thought about it for a second. "I was out of my mind with sadness, TJ," I explained. "I was sobbing so hard; I could barely breathe. So yeah, it wasn't normal, because it's not like we had this ritual where my pop would hold me in bed every night— with a sandwich in one hand—but, again, I was out of my mind."

I stopped, grasping for the right way to tell him how it was, before adding, "It's kind of like asking someone who survived getting shot in the chest if they were embarrassed when the paramedics ripped open their shirt to stop the bleeding."

By now TJ was laughing and nodding. "Gotcha," he said, "Okay, yeah, that makes sense."

When I got surgery last summer for a lipoma—a benign lump (and if that's not sexy enough, it was a lump in my armpit)—my doctor told me the space left after removing it would be filled. "Empty space just doesn't stay empty forever," he explained.

I'm thinking about that this morning, considering it a promise. Because I have a lot of empty space right now. TJ asks me a question, but instead of answering, I just stare.

"What are you seeing? What are you thinking?" TJ says.

And the truth is, it can be hard to describe my interior landscape. I'm dwarfed by its vast endlessness. Friends mention fun and interesting things to me and I try to respond appropriately. But mostly I just don't care.

I see empty space instead of a full summer spent at home with a brand-new baby that we're learning as he's learning us. But empty space just doesn't stay empty forever. We will fill it; we are filling it. With trips to Target and the sounds of Charlee ecstatically laughing over the bubbles we make with wands in our living room. With long talks after Charlee goes to sleep, because now it's just the two of us—and always That Great Sadness that sits with us on the couch, weighty enough that I swear it leaves an imprint, too, once we all get up and go to bed.

I read the words of St. Augustine: "God gives where he finds empty hands." I mostly spend my energy believing this: That we have all the time in the world for God to out-give the emptiness we hold.

Chapter 20

My Small Intestine on Grief and Trauma
(one week after)

It's been a week since Luca died. Yesterday I showered, put on lipstick, and went out with TJ. (Hold for applause.) No mascara yet; I'm still crying too much. That's why texting goes better with grief than talking. I can respond to people while crying and the words still come out. Here's to grieving in the 21st century. But lipstick, I feel, is a great step forward.

Today I feel a different kind of pain. You know there's a lot of pain when you start developing a finer palette for it. Like one of those people who take a sip of wine and can tell you the year, the province, the everything that I don't care about. The ones who can differentiate between the stuff that costs $8 and the stuff you give your boss and hope she googles the price.

Speaking about pain, I'm texting a friend that the terror group ISIS has done terrible things to people—so look! I have a lot to be grateful for. "I know. But when you have to compare your life to people attacked by ISIS to feel better, you know you are hurting," he writes back.

"LOL," I reply.

Because all I want is my baby, but life is still funny—and yes, so terrible, too—but thank God for friends who get it and motivate an LOL even now.

TJ and I are doing what the social worker told us to do—normal, simple stuff we're used to enjoying. Brunch on Sunday after church and pretending to care about the small talk the waitress makes with us. But then my abdomen is ablaze with an unbearable pain, and I can barely walk. We call my amazing angel of a midwife who trusts us with her cell phone number. She says to go back to Labor and Delivery, and we find ourselves amidst all the happy glowing pregnant ladies of Boston again. Yay.

I am laying on a cot in one of those backless hospital gowns holding TJ's hand again—and this time, afraid the week will be topped off with me dying or something.

"We're not worried that it's serious," the doctor tells me.

"Well—it's been a pretty bad week, so it wouldn't surprise me."

She agrees about the week. (Everyone agrees about the week.) She says I am dehydrated and constipated. Very sexy—but then again, my right eye is just about swollen shut from crying, so I'm not about to win any Sexiest Woman Alive contests. Maybe Sexiest Grieving Woman Alive, but honestly, probably not—I'm also postpartum and just not feeling it. Might as well be constipated too.

All I can think of is Charlee and TJ and how wonderful it is to want to be alive—and not just alive, but well, so that I can have a full life with them. So I'm drinking my water. I'm paying more attention to self-care. And I don't mean pedicures or those weird face masks that make you look like Jason from *Friday the 13th*. I mean just the basics: hydration and sleep. The basics are hard enough right now, but it's worth it. I've got a couple of people who need me healthy.

Oh wait, there's more. My small intestine fell asleep. There's a medical term for it, but I can't remember the word. It can happen in trauma, apparently. I don't blame the thing at all—if

I could sleep for a few days and Charlee wouldn't be any worse for it, I would. So now I take meds for my brain to sleep at night and meds to wake up my belly. I'm also on a diet—Jessica Can't Eat Any Comfort Food at All. Come on. That's funny. Like rain on your wedding day, funny. For the first time in my life—now of ALL weeks—I can't have gluten (I love gluten). Or dairy. Not even an avocado to ease the pain. And so much food is showing up at our place right now. An entire box of pastries just arrived from my friend. But it's okay, my appetite isn't exactly raging. And now I know that gluten-free bread isn't that bad when toasted (who am I kidding, it's still pretty bad). And at least I'm not dying, which was my original self-diagnosis.

My brother texts that of course I'm not dying. Of course God is keeping me around.

"I know," I say. "Who would God give the sh*t sandwiches to if I weren't here?! He'd notice I'm not on earth, and there'd be a pile up of tragedies on hand because WHERE DO THESE GO NOW?"

My brother and I text Bible verses to each other, too. Ancient biblical texts. Sh*t sandwich jokes. You know, balance.

I'm quiet as I walk through our building. I don't say hi much because it just feels too normal, and nothing is normal. But there's one neighbor who, when TJ says hello and I say nothing, loudly says, HI JESSICA! She says it so brightly, as if trying to force a response. She hangs out in the lobby and when she sees us, jumps up and gets in the same elevator. She stares at me and asks how I'm doing, winks and says she's thinking of me.

"I'm fine," I finally say, eyes down.

Please don't talk to me, I want to say. This pain is too raw to show you—too sacred to spill into an elevator. Let me choose the time and the place to tell my story. I did not choose all the details, but I can now choose the words with which I frame it. There's some power in that, at least.

* * *

We walk into the hospital to check on my sleeping small intestine, back to where, before last Tuesday, we'd gotten good reports about Luca. Where he'd scored an 8/8 on his ultrasound. I left with the kind of 3D photos that pepper Facebook, Instagram, refrigerators; we'd kept them to ourselves, planning to show his perfect little face to the world in a few weeks.

I pass the ultrasound tech who first showed me Luca. She doesn't remember me. Maybe I look different in my sadness. She'd told me how perfect my baby was; she even told me he was a boy. "I shouldn't say anything about sex this early, but no girl has *that*," she said, pointing between his little legs.

A son. I just figured we'd have another girl. It never dawned on me that I could make a boy, too. When I got home, I wrote down names. I wanted something with meaning, something that goes perfectly with Charlee. I couldn't believe how blessed I was.

A lifetime ago—but just some years, really—I moved back home to my parents' basement while going through my divorce. I lived with their three Alaskan Malamutes that took huge dumps outside my door. It was almost poetic, matching my life. I'd gingerly step over it and think, *of course*. All the days left before me, a 20-something in deep emotional pain, felt like a life sentence. But now. Oh God, now! The contrast between where I was and where I am takes my breath away.

I thought, *Somebody should tell that girl what's ahead. Let her know that it's not just going to be okay—that her heart will be fuller than she can imagine. Tell her to keep walking, because the scenery changes. Winter is swallowed up in the kind of spring that reminds us our story doesn't end until redemption shows up.*

And I would still tell her this, still. Over and over again, I'd tell that sad girl with her hair bleached platinum in an attempt for change she could actually control, that it'll be okay. I'd say it so much that the walls themselves would start saying it, too; so that when her heart breaks again, she can still hear an echo that tells the truth.

It'll be okay. Life is a changeling, *and* it is beautiful. It hurts like hell, *and* it is worth it. This present unbearable pain burns you up from the inside, but it can't take what matters. The people who are here, our Luca who is not but is somewhere far better. These people live within, they help create us. The love between us is a bridge that takes me to a better place and that bridge stays buried in my heart still.

Ancient mystic and anchorite (one who withdraws from secular society to lead a simple life centered on prayer) of the Middle Ages, Julian of Norwich, survived the Black Plague. As everyone did who stayed alive then, she saw a lot of people die. You either died or witnessed others do so. Maybe you even did both. She is the first woman to ever have published a book in the English language (*Revelations of Divine Love*), and is credited for writing, "All shall be well, all shall be well, and all manner of things shall be well." Centuries later, I imagine her in prayer, in grief, in peace, still, with those words forming in her spirit, an anchor that ties her to hope, despite what she sees and feels and mourns.

All shall be well, all shall be well, and all manner of things shall be well.

Chapter 21

The Day We Found Out
(when it happened)

Let me tell you about grace and what's fair and how none of it makes any sense at all. Like how the same storm that ends the drought will sweep away something precious in the swells of rain. It's not fair, and it's also grace. Like how this regular Tuesday morning begins with the mundane task of getting a haircut—a haircut that makes me just plain mad because I tell the stylist I want bangs, thank you. That I need a change.

"We don't cut bangs between May and September," he tells me.

"What? Not even for money?"

"You don't want bangs," he maintains. "It's too hot. Plus, you're pregnant, so no big changes for you."

I leave feeling frustrated and basic, with a slightly trimmed version of the same boring hairstyle I had when I walked in.

That is right before there is no heartbeat. That is a long time ago, I think. It's in the chair at the salon when I realize I haven't felt Luca move yet this morning. Suddenly, the stylist is taking way too long. I get super antsy and a little anxious as he finishes. I finally pay and leave and go home to try to make my baby move. Surely once I'm on the couch with a bag of frozen peas on my belly, he'll move.

I try all the tricks—drinking orange juice and putting all the frozen things on my belly. I poke and prod him, trying to wake him up. It's now been thirty minutes of trying, so I call the hospital, and they tell me to come in. It's just me and Charlee at home, so I plop her in the stroller and we walk to the hospital. When we arrive, they have us wait. We wait for a long time. It feels interminable, but it was maybe an hour, though it's hard to remember. I'm busy entertaining my two-year-old with the few stray stickers I manage to find in my bag, while also telling myself Luca is fine and trying not to walk up to the front desk and demand they just get me back to someone who can tell me my baby is alive, please.

He's not moving.

I'm trying to be calm and I'm laughing at Charlee's toddler antics while my insides have turned to water because the baby inside me hasn't moved all day.

Finally, they call me back. Charlee, my best sidekick, is right next to me when they pull that wand over my large belly. I will never forget how Charlee looked the day I found out her brother died. She is wearing a pink dress from my favorite children's boutique store. The skirt is a full tutu, and the bodice is a soft velvety fabric with the depiction of a little girl holding a lamb. Charlee's dirty blond curls are in her typical completely unkempt all-over-the-place style as she sits next to me. Her big brown eyes and lashes that are so thick they actually look fake are always a wonder. She is the cutest thing I have ever seen.

"Will I get a shot, mama?" Charlee asks in the exam room. She takes one look at the nurse preparing to listen to my baby and says, "I don't want her to touch me." I laugh; that's grace. Genuine laughter on that day is only grace.

There are muffled sounds as the tech keeps moving the wand back and forth over my huge belly. But beyond that, it is silent. I don't say anything because I know what this means. She goes to get someone else, someone who is better at this than her, she tells me. She is trying to give me some hope. It is a Hail Mary pass and I take it. The next tech asks me questions as she searches for a heartbeat.

"Have you felt nauseous at all?

I haven't.

"Did you notice any difference in movement before now?"

I hadn't.

She explains that the next step is an ultrasound, and I am quietly listening and nodding and wondering when I will get to step back into my own life. As we walk from the failed non-stress test room to the ultrasound room, Charlee leans in and kisses me repeatedly. I am hoping desperately for a better outcome this time. I am numb. Charlee's over-and-over-again kisses are grace. I notice them.

There is a picture on the screen in the dark room. It is entirely still. The wand is cold on my belly and Charlee is clinging to me so close; these sensations are pulling at me to stay present while I hear, "There's no heartbeat."

I swallow. I blink. I lay there and feel Charlee shift a thousand times because toddler bodies keep moving until sleep finally makes them stop. I say something.

"So what does this mean?" I ask quietly, meaning what do I do with my baby inside me when he's also in heaven.

"It means your baby is dead," the doctor says, matter of fact. She says it so plainly. It is horrible and startlingly obvious—like I'm the only idiot in the world who thinks anyone at all can be alive without a heartbeat. She says it like I ordered chicken salad and they're out of chicken salad, sorry.

"I understand that. I—I—just meant...what do I do now?"

And that's the question I ask every single day. Maybe ten times a day. In grief. In faith. In how the two intersect and somehow create a path forward.

It is painfully unfair that Luca left so soon. But it is also unfair that we get to have our Charlee; not everyone gets a perfect little girl to kiss them over and over while they hear unthinkable news. That is more than I deserve, and I remain grateful. I am also grieving. That is grace. I will keep looking for it, and I will keep finding it.

Sometimes I sneak onto TJ's phone to look at the photos he's taken. I like to see our life from his point of view. I pause, looking at one I've never seen before, remembering the perfect May morning he captured here. It is cool and sunny and, more than anything, I remember how I feel. Like I could barely contain my heart, it was so full. Luca is alive inside of me, with Charlee beside me and Luna between us and TJ across from me. And I'm just there, in that moment, unable to figure out what I'd done to deserve to be connected to so many wonderful creatures.

But I also remember an earlier time. An earlier marriage, an earlier moment when I couldn't figure out what I'd done to deserve so much pain.

Sometimes the only thing we can do is sit in the enormity of the moment. Acknowledge that we don't fully understand it and embrace the good that will eventually come of it. Because I'm convinced that neither pain nor joy is an isolated thing. There is always good that comes, too, because there is always

God who brings it. It comes eventually. It comes despite the convictions, the fears, and the days we have that say otherwise. And sometimes we recognize this great good suddenly. It is unexpectedly captured in the flash of a camera—just another one of the many photos we take throughout the day—but this one leaves our eyes lit up with wonder at what our life has become.

Chapter 22

Breathe

(two months after)

It's a summer unlike any other. I just keep breathing in and out. I do it over and over again until it's a whole day's worth of breaths that I've taken. But it's also a whole day's worth of breaths further away from the night we said good-bye to our boy. So you can see my problem with time.

Luca.
Born at 4:15 PM on May 17.
5/17/2017.

And now whenever I see a date—any random date, really—my brain immediately calculates its relationship to this past May 17. Tonight I see a photo someone posted on May 19. They look happy. They are doing touristy things. For a second, I can't understand how they can be so happy. It had only been two days.

I know this is ridiculous thinking. Of course people are touring the national monument. They do this every single day of the year. But my visceral reaction is not always logical. This is why I don't answer the phone. This is why I don't go to parties. My grief is a lion on a leash, and every time I look down, I see the other end of the leash is tied tight to my wrist. I can't go anywhere alone. I have with me a constant and unpredictable beast who could show up at any moment and ruin it. I am not in control. Grief takes every waking moment. It rises with the day hungry, devours all my hours.

Luca weighed five pounds and was 17.5 inches long. He had dark hair on his head, and the nurse said he looks like me. *Looks,* present tense—because he still looks like me, just not here. He has delicate, even features on his face. I wish I could've seen his eyes open.

We kept him with us for five hours before we said good-bye to our forever baby.

Five hours.

We've had not quite two and a half years with our Charlee Jane, and it's nowhere near enough. Five hours with our firstborn son is a hard part of life to reconcile. I watched TJ carry Luca back to his crib, lay him down and kiss his perfect head one last time. The nurse knew how sacred this time was and didn't try to cheapen it with words as she took him from our room. God bless her. There is a memory box that I will look through eventually, but not today, and probably not tomorrow, either.

* * *

"I'M A WET BABY!" Charlee yells between squeals of laughter while running in and out of the city fountains, and TJ and I laugh, too. Summer in Boston is the absolute best. It's the carrot dangling at the end of the long, long stick called winter.

And Charlee is a wonderful kind of contagious. I can't help but laugh with her. There is so much joy in these moments, and I'm a grateful mama. As we're walking home from the T (Boston's public transit, affectionately called the "T"), we run into one of our midwives.

"How are you guys?" she says, asking the obvious question.

"I started therapy today," I blurt out, needing her to know that I'm not okay but I'm working on being okay.

She nods, and we talk about how hard it is but there's Charlee, so we have to be present and that's both a good thing and a hard thing at once. I tell her that sometimes I cry in front of Charlee, and we talk about being sad and how sadness is an okay thing to feel. Then, we segue into how close we live to each other, and how we never knew it. Because there's no list of what to talk about in these situations; there's nothing normal about this. And just like it's okay to feel sad, it's okay to talk about grieving your child and then come up for air with a lighter topic—like, "Look how close we live!"—all in the same breath.

I mean, you just can't stay in the deep waters forever. You dive as much as you need to, but eventually you must come back to where you can stand. Treading water is exhausting. We all need a break.

Tomorrow is my birthday, and I'm deciding now with you, Dear Reader, as my witness, to be brave. Because Charlee is very excited and has already told me she has gotten me a toy monkey, a Peppa Pig robe, and brand-new Play-Doh (all which sound suspiciously like her own wish list, but whatever). She's also been singing "HAPPY BIRTHDAY TO MAMA!" for about 24 hours now, so the least I can do is smile and act happy about it. TJ, too, loves me and wants to celebrate, and who am I to deny him celebrating the girl he loves? How am I so lucky?

I don't think I will answer the phone tomorrow—phone calls are taxing even on good days, and absolutely overwhelming now—but I will thank God for this gift of life and all these relationships that have changed the shape of my heart for the better. Soon, I hope, this will be easier. Until then, I just breathe. In and out.

Chapter 23

Grief Shared
(six weeks after)

My friends and co-workers surprise me with a gift—a hair appointment. "For whenever you're ready," they say. "Does the stylist…know about me?" I ask, so I know what to expect. I would rather know if a stranger is going to greet me with "I'm sorry" or not.

"Just that we love you."

I arrive at the salon and am struck by the warm light, the plush chairs, the sunlight filtering through leafy green plants. I watch my new stylist, Jason, hug his client, saying good-bye like old friends. I realize a lot more than hair gets taken care of in this place.

He has the kind of amazing long beard that our hippie dads could only dream of, and I like him immediately. I settle in a chair, and he runs his fingers through my hair.

"Is it dumb if I want bangs?" I ask. "My last stylist wouldn't do it—he said it was too hot. But nobody has ever died of heat exhaustion because of bangs." I don't say the last stylist also said I was too pregnant for big changes. Big changes. Like I was trying to move to Vegas or wielding a Bic razor and threatening to shave my head. (At least that wouldn't be too hot in the summer, I guess.)

Jason says he will be right back and nonchalantly hands me a brush. He doesn't say anything about the tangles in my hair that I'd been unaware of until now. He makes no comparison to stray dogs. I like him even more now. He returns with scissors and mischievously catches my eye in the mirror.

"I think bangs are a great idea," he says. With one quick movement, he grabs the hair in front of my eyes, pulls it up straight, and cuts it right off. "Here," he tells me, "Before you can change your mind."

I am delighted. I like the way he not only agrees with me, but makes it happen, too. TJ does that at home all the time. It's a good way to take care of someone. I wasn't planning on telling Jason much, but then he begins to tell me about his divorce. I realize, *Oh, he gets it. He's grieved, too.* So we swap details. Now there are foils in my hair and empathy in our words. It's one thing to share scars, but another thing entirely to reveal an open wound. I feel safe here, though, so I tell him about Luca.

He takes a deep breath. "When?"

"They couldn't find his heartbeat six weeks ago today."

It's easy to tell him everything, and by the time we're admiring his finished work, I realize the walls I'd walked in with are on the floor with my hair. He walks me downstairs and I thank him. As he hugs me hard, he says quietly in my ear, "Life is dog sh*t."

I laugh because sometimes it is.

I tell him I'll be back soon for a trim.

This morning, I open Instagram and find a direct message from a stranger. My husband TJ hosts a radio show and some of his listeners have found me on the internet. Messages like these never cease to encourage me:

Dear Jessica,

Every morning I wake up and check your IG to see how you're managing. Most mornings, before I pray for you and your family, I cry for you. I've wanted to message you and let you know you have people praying for you, but it just felt weird. Then I went to get my hair cut on Tuesday. As Jason was hugging me goodbye, I saw you out of the corner of my eye. You smiled, and I was so happy you were able to even manage that. I wanted to tell you I knew you and hug you, but that would've been weird. So I went to the bathroom, sat on — yes — a public toilet, and cried. God bless you. May you find at least one smile a day until you can find more. Thinking of you and praying for you.

I stare at the words and am stunned by their content. This kind stranger bears no responsibility for carrying anything for me, least of all grief. I immediately screenshot the message and send it to TJ.

"Wow! This person was hugging your new stylist when you walked in?"

Apparently.

"It's like God fills the world with the kindest spies," I text back. "I'm blown away."

"That is incredible," TJ writes.

"I know," I text back, "There are good things at work for us even now. It's like this huge puzzle and I'm crying over one piece. It's an important, heartbreaking piece—and I should cry—but I think there are other pieces I can't see."

I get glimpses of the other pieces, though, when I read this message. When other strangers send me kind messages. When I don't know what to wear for Luca's funeral I'm surprised by a package from a dear friend: a simple, beautiful black dress.

And just like that, there is death, but there is grace, too. And I continue to be rocked by both.

* * *

I'm home now, in Pennsylvania. As we were packing, everyone told me, "Have a great trip!" And of course they meant well, but I came home to bury my son. That's why I'm here. Everyone says how nice it is to do it on my family's land. It is nice—I know what they mean, and I love them for it—but it's so very horrible, too.

My parents keep talking to me about picking the spot, but I don't want to pick a spot, because I don't want to have to do this. It's not that I don't want to bury him in the grove or in front of the hollow tree at the bottom of the hill where my mom hid our Easter baskets when we were kids. It's just that I don't want to bury my son *at all*. I want to hold him, not bury him, and everything feels wrong.

It is hard to feel constantly terrible being back in the place where I grew up, though. Even grief has to agree with the beauty that lights up the night with fireflies. Charlee looks at them in wonder, because the world is finally as sparkly as she wants it to be.

I love what makes her happy. Extra points when it's not plastic or on sale for $9.99. I listen to my sister explain how the fireflies shine tiny flashlights with their butts. Their butts! I watch Charlee comprehend that fireflies are not only sparkly, but they are also funny! One day she will realize they poop as well, and the toddler trifecta will be complete.

Tonight, we sit on a porch while a summer storm sparks new conversations. We eat the kind of perfect peaches that make you wonder why you ever bother to eat anything else at all between June and September. As much as winter is for stew, summer is for peaches.

It is strange to be alive when someone you love is dead. It is, of course, profoundly sad. And it is also profoundly strange. I am not haunted by Luca's ghost; rather, I am haunted by all the questions that would be answered if he were simply here. I am haunted by the things I don't know about him and by what should have been. I think, *what now?* with enough repetition to warrant rosary beads so I can keep track of my desperation the way a devout Catholic keeps track of their prayers. Only I run out of beads before I run out of questions. *What now?*

You dig in. You do what's in front of you. It is strange to be alive when someone I love is dead, but there it is: I am alive. *What now?* is answered tonight by the sound of rain hitting the roof of the porch. It is familiar but also new, because I know the sound of rain, but not this rain—not rain heard through the blanket of grief. So I listen. *What now?* I look down at the peach, sweet and sticky and messy, and take another bite. It's good. Despite everything—or maybe because of everything—I savor how good it is.

Chapter 24

Back Where I Grew Up
(two months after)

I bought TJ a bathing suit today. "Why?" he asks. (Why does anyone ever buy a bathing suit? Perhaps there will be swimming in their very near future. I mean, maybe.)

"Because we're going to the beach tomorrow and you didn't bring yours." I found one that's red, white, blue, and 30% off, so like, perfect. Everyone is so happy about this holiday weekend, so the least we can do is put on some bathing suits and play along like we care, too. In fact, let's put on patriotic suits and really fool 'em.

My mom has given me three books on grief and pregnancy loss in the past six weeks. If her research cured my pain, Snoop would wonder what I'm smoking to make me feel so good. My mom is a superhero, and her power is an entire library's worth of information on whatever is threatening her kids. She reads everything she can about it, then summarizes her findings: You're going to be fine, and this is how we'll make sure of it. She also prays so well that one of her counseling clients never leaves her office without making sure my mom prays for her. The client is an atheist, but she likes the peace it brings—and I can't blame her. I will walk a long way and believe a lot of things for some peace.

TJ and I sit by the pool. We talk sometimes, or I read my book about pregnancy and loss. I trudge through all the ugly medical terms that describe The Things That Can Go Wrong While Pregnant, finally just skipping the last few pages of the chapter, because man. It's starting to feel like it's much harder for things to go right. I go to the next chapter, hoping for better news. I'm determined to find it, no matter how many chapters it takes. I can't help it.

When I was a little girl, I read Cinderella for the happily-ever-after part just about every day. I read it like you take vitamins. I'm still that girl, despite the things I've seen. And the fact that this is not a happily-ever-after kind of thing only solidifies my belief that we're just not there yet. It's not the end of the story.

We're at the beach surrounded by family, so that's good. But I keep thinking that someone is missing, so that's hard. When things feel bad, that's what I say: It's hard.

"Thinking about you, Jessica," my friends text.

"Thank you. It's hard," I reply.

I don't tell them that my insides have turned to water, that my skin is a thin layer between a whole storm inside of me and everyone else out there. That I smile and I'm scared. That I smile and I'm sad. That I smile when my brother explains to Charlee how to spot the pregnant sand fleas by the orange eggs they carry. I let her hold it and tell her to be gentle with this little mama—and inside I'm like, *God. Even the sand fleas hurt me. Even the f***ing sand fleas get to be pregnant.*

I think of that word sometimes now. (I know you don't think I mean sand fleas, either. That's technically two words, anyway.). It's a rebellious act of mine. I feel like my toddler when she looks at me and hits whatever inanimate object is in front of her. She smiles as if to say, "Somebody stop me." I love her so much. I love her when her big feelings make her hit chairs. I think God loves me so much. I think He loves me when my big feelings make me think of words we're not supposed to say.

I smile at TJ while we hide from the July sun under an umbrella. My family is loud and wonderful, and I am quiet and tired. "It's hard," I whisper, as the crash of the waves and the five conversations my siblings throw into the air at once mix with my own two words.

"You've got me," TJ says back to me. And I do.

My mom sends us out, acting like it's TJ and I doing her a favor, watching Charlee while we sit at a bar and eat dinner. While waiting for our meals, we talk about our favorite moments with each other.

"Remember the time I told you I wanted to be with you forever?" I ask, a smile spreading across my face. It was in Brooklyn, and I stopped talking afterward—for what felt like forever. I couldn't believe I'd blurted that out. I figured I'd need at least a month or so of silence to make up for that kind of revelatory noise. I didn't think that either of us were ready for it. TJ asked what it meant, and I couldn't answer because we both knew what it meant. It was too scary to explain. And then TJ said, "I know what you mean, and I want that, too." TJ was sitting next to me happy I'd said what I said, actually. Happy I'd basically proposed, in so many words, by cavalierly using words like 'forever' in the context of our relationship. Because he'd like to make me his wife, and then make me a mama. He said he'd like to do everything awesome together, and that even the terrible things would be less terrible because we'd do them together, too.

TJ smiles about that memory. It's just what we've done— even the terrible things have been less terrible because we've done them together.

Chapter 25

Turtles in Heaven
(two months after)

"Was his funeral what you wanted it to be?" my brother asks. I stare at him and think, but do not say, *I can't believe you didn't go.* Over the phone, he had explained that his kid had a soccer tournament, so he couldn't make my son's funeral. I told him I didn't understand. He explained again. I told him I understand what he's doing, I just don't understand the choice he's making. Now we're at the beach and he's catching up on my son's funeral and I am trying not to be bitter. I think about his question. It's not an easy answer. I didn't want it to be at all, so there's that.

"We're burying him on the land where I grew up," I tell my midwife before we leave.

"That's nice," she says warmly.

"No, it's not. It's terrible that we have to."

"No, it's not. It's terrible that you have to," she agrees with the same warmth.

I wake up the day of his funeral wondering if I can do it. The answer is I have to. Charlee is happily playing with family, so I lay in bed, crushed. I've never been this low. The very act of greeting people—standing up and smiling. Finding enough breath to push out words that are a pretense ("Hi!" "Thanks so much for coming!" "I'm okay, how are you?")—feels unfathomable.

Grief is so pervasive that not a cell in your body or thought in your head is unaffected. Grief is physical. You realize your ribcage is not only there to protect your heart, but also there to make it stay. It is there to keep it from sinking down so far that it slips from your body entirely. It is there to keep you from fully becoming a ghost, a shadow, a hovering breath of yearning and missing and sadness that still must wake up and try on life like it's one size fits all (but it no longer fits). When the truth is, you've drained away. The truth is, you've lost the ability to fill out the mornings, to wear Friday night like the sexy, curving, beckoning thing it is. Now life hangs awkwardly off your sharp, raw edges the way your mother's clothes hung from your five-year-old body when you played dress-up in her closet.

When the pain becomes too hard, grief is there with a handbook. You must do the decent thing and leave that broken heart somewhere safe and out of the way, it instructs. Perhaps you leave it under your bed or next to your toothbrush in the cabinet above the sink—but you simply cannot function with a heart still inside of your body, not when it has you feeling like this. Maybe last year's heart, but surely not this one.

But then there's the problem with the ribcage. It is what stands between you and the ghost that walks around, never committing to really being anywhere again. The ribcage keeps you human and feeling, even here and now, when you are as low as the shore being pounded by the waves every day of its life without doing one thing about the pounding. Even now. Even burying your baby, giving him to the earth. Doing exactly what a mother should never have to do, putting her baby down forever. At least on earth. *God, I cannot do this.*

I stay in bed so long that morning. I give in to all of it. All the apathy that has threatened to invade the rest of my life. I never need to get up or do anything again. Let the world stay busy and tend to its needs, and I will stay here, for I have none. Let my teeth rot in my head, for brushing them seems suddenly nonsensical: who cares. Grief has taught me these things don't matter. Nothing does. I reach for my heart one more time. Maybe the ribcage will slip, maybe I can grab my heart this time. Maybe I can finally remove what hurts so much.

"My plane is delayed," TJ texts, and I realize things still matter. TJ needs to be here today, especially.

And then it is delayed again. And then one more time.

I call JetBlue.

"My husband is flying in from Boston for our son's funeral," I tell the lady on the other end. "He needs to be here." My voice sounds small as I ask her, "Can you please tell me he'll get here?"

I might as well ask the sun not to rise, can it please just delay for a while? For all the good my conversation does with whoever answers the phones for JetBlue, but still. I have to do something.

My brother asks me which verses of 'How Great Thou Art' he should sing. I blink back tears and make a decision. My parents ask me where, exactly, I want to bury Luca. My heart gains a thousand pounds, and I make a decision.

TJ finally makes it to Pennsylvania.

On the day I bury my son, I spend hours lying in bed, crying and deciding I cannot do this. I feel like we tell each other we spent hours cleaning or working out when, in actuality, we folded a little bit of laundry and mostly checked our phone or did a plank and mostly texted our friends (or probably it is just me—carry on, then, with all your honorable hours of dedicated activity). But the hours I spend crying on the day I bury Luca is not an exaggeration. It is, in fact, hours. Round segments of time packed with sixty minutes of laying down and crying. Lots of these. Today is marked by rare moments when I'm not crying, rather than the other way around.

Strangely enough, I keep thinking of little Jessica growing up in this room where I lie now. I'm thankful nobody ever told her that one day her baby son would die. I don't think little Jessica could have grown up under the weight of that terrible knowledge. And today it is too heavy. It is also here, and it's also mine. My son. My son's death. My son's funeral—it's all mine, so I get out of bed. I brush my teeth and brush my hair and put on a black dress.

All through my parents' house there are pictures of me growing up. I look happy in these photos; most of them are of me on a stage. I feel sad for the girl in the pictures I study. I want to tell her I'm sorry this happens. I'm so sorry her son dies.

We all gather. I see my family and am surprised that it is not as hard to say hello as I thought it would be. Other people seem fairly normal. They are all talking to each other, and I am not under as much scrutiny as I feared.

Grief makes you feel like you're in a fishbowl. You feel so other, that you can't imagine people not staring at you when you enter a room. But most of the time, they don't. Most of the time, life just keeps happening, and you can enter it as much or as little as you need to in the moment. You can hear a conversation happening around you and choose to just listen, and most people are okay with that choice. You can draw a little bit of comfort from how the world keeps going. Your siblings still laugh and talk, and your parents are still busy walking three huge dogs and asking each other if they were fed today. Maybe it's like walking into the afterlife expecting to have to learn a whole new culture and language because you assume everything died when you died. But instead, you walk into a world where you see people you know and love and see familiar streets that you know how to navigate. You realize that *feeling* lost and *being* lost are not the same.

I guess what I am trying to say is that the anticipation of seeing people in real life while getting ready to bury my son felt horrible. Like it's too private a thing to include almost anyone at all. But it's a relief to see our families there, being themselves. They are sadder and quieter, and they are themselves too. And I am grateful we are doing this together.

It makes me think of our wedding. *(But Jess! How in the world does Luca's funeral make you think of your wedding? Aren't they opposite things?* Dear Person Reading: First, thank you. To pick up a book that has anything to do with grief and read it on purpose is brave. To do this when you're not even related to me is very encouraging. Again, thank you. Now, as for the question I forced you to ask. I think a funeral and a wedding can be two sides of the same thing: Love.)

When TJ and I were getting married—with a whopping engagement that lasted eight weeks—we had a wedding on my parents' land with one hundred of our closest family and friends. It wasn't the fanciest thing, and we planned a lot of it ourselves—with the help of very talented and generous friends. Once the wedding was over and TJ and I were in bed, exhausted, he told me, "I get it now. I see why people have weddings. It's incredible to have all your loved ones in one room with you, watching you do something as important as marrying your person. I wish I could do it again tomorrow."

Of course, this funeral is different—that much is obvious. But community means we rejoice with each other, and we grieve with each other. It means we don't walk through life alone. Not when we're telling the world, "This! This guy is my forever human!" and certainly not when we're doing the unthinkable and laying our child into a hole in the ground.

Both weddings and funerals involve other people standing with us. They are a tangible glimpse into our reality—that we are not alone and that we are loved. Both are empathy showing up. We care about each other's wellbeing. Therefore we are happy with each other and sad with each other. They are showings of how humanity depends on communication and collaboration—not just in making things happen in the physical, like building a bridge or voting in an elected official—but also in the emotive, soul spaces. Like looking up at your son's funeral and seeing every single person crying, too. Like feeling as if you can no longer face your thoughts and feelings alone, so you call someone. You give that person a glimpse of your inner dialogue, and they tell you the truth and take care of your heart. They encourage you so much that you hang up the phone feeling courage.

We need each other. Weddings and funerals are a physical statement of what is already true: We are connected, right now, in this deep sadness or deep joy. We need to feel and see and hear and know that this connection is intact.

We walk down the hill toward a hole in the ground in the woods. TJ and I hold hands, quietly trading words. The world is very small and very sad, and we are also very much together. This makes me feel less small, albeit still sad. We leave 2-year-old Charlee with a family friend, playing and swinging and laughing and entirely unaware of what's happening at the bottom of the hill.

I had asked my Pop not to sound too formal. "Please, just speak like yourself, not like you're conducting a funeral." I stare ahead as he begins the service, not focusing on anyone or anything. While my mom speaks, she says, "Satan comes as a stealer..." I hear my pop correct her under his breath, "...thief." He says this so quietly that most would miss it, I'm sure. But the former English teacher cannot help himself and must correct the word choice. He must do this even when it's his own wife speaking at their own grandchild's funeral. I steal a glance at TJ to see if he heard it, too. The twinkle in his eye confirms it, and we both work hard to keep an actual smile or, God forbid, laughter from manifesting. The whole thing takes maybe five seconds, but I find it oddly reassuring. Like walking into the first day of school and being surprised by a familiar face in an otherwise room full of strangers.

We are still us. Life is painful and life is funny, and I can't help but notice both. There were a lot of beautiful, valuable things said during Luca's funeral. I have a hard time remembering them all. I will never forget my pop correcting my mom's word choice with a whisper into the universe and how strangely comforting it was to recognize that both TJ and I found humor in it. Grace shows up in many ways and, though I never would have guessed it, this was one of them.

Oh, and my mom looked it up: *Stealer* is a perfectly fine word to use in the English language and warrants no correction.

★ ★ ★

I speak at my son's funeral. I knew it would be humbling. Talking surely would not keep me from crying. But the part of me that knows things—in my spirit, in the way my bones ache when the weather gears up to do something big, in the way I tell a friend she will be okay and, though I have a hard time believing this even for myself, I deeply know if for her—something told me I had to do this. I'll never get to read Luca bedtime stories, but I read my letter to him that day.

Our family makes a semi-circle around TJ and me in the hot early afternoon July air as I read my letter to my son's ashes:

Dear Luca, I say aloud, my voice quiet and steady and crying and talking over a lump that makes this hard thing harder.

Everything about your funeral feels wrong. It's hard to find words to describe the hole you left when your beautiful spirit took flight, but the thing is, I'm your mama. And as your mama, it is an honor to do anything at all for you, even writing these words to accompany your burial. I think about the hole we dig and the earth opening up to receive you, and I don't understand why the earth gets to hold you while I, your mama, do not. I think you would have liked it here with us, Luca. You have a dada who is the absolute best at taking care of hearts. Part of my excitement over you was getting to see the two of you fall in love. He's so amazing, Luca. And I don't know how he does it, but he can trim the tiniest toenails without a hitch. I can't say the same. I've accidentally hurt both your big sister and Luna—our dog you would've loved—and have therefore been banned from ever trimming a nail or claw again.

You have a big sister who is as wonderful as you, you know. She would have taught you the lessons that fascinate her; how people have favorite colors and how stories belong to each of us, but also need to be shared—like a fingerprint that is better for having been left all over the world. She'd teach you about shadows and how they appear when something blocks the sun from the earth. But what she doesn't know because she's only two, see, is that I was blocked from the sun the moment I realized you were gone. I didn't just see the shadows on that day, either; I became the shadows, I think. But because stories are better when shared, I need to share the story that gives me back my breath and bones and flesh.

Death is the hardest thing to endure here. And when death comes, it tries to leave a feeling of finality. Death is a thief, and all it knows to do is steal. But there are some things that cannot be stolen, and that is your precious life, Luca. The life that your dada and I made and anticipated and lingered over with our dreams.

Now, if death was the final word, I'd have to live among the turtles. I'd study their ways until I, too, grew a shell. And this shell would both protect me from the joy and pain of getting too close to others and provide a home only big enough for myself. Are there turtles in heaven, Luca? If so, I imagine the snappers only use their considerable and notorious skills to cut down long, but otherwise perfect limbs into just the right size for roasting marshmallows. In heaven, even the snapping turtles use their power for good.

But death is not the final word, so you won't find me with a shell like the turtles. Death lost its victory when Jesus won his, making it so that no, you're not here, but you're not gone, either. The reason I can sleep at night and not be afraid to keep loving your sister so well is because I know where you are, and I know you are well. The God of heaven not only made you but knows how to keep you perfect. I don't know what that looks like, having never shed this cage of a body myself, but I know you aren't sad. And if eternity and hope have a sound, I bet you're singing songs that sound like that. I bet those songs fill all who hear them with something that is stronger than the longing that accompanies us at birth.

I miss you every moment, Luca. It hurts to look at baby feet and double strollers and the tiny clothes you were going to wear. But this pain stands for something better than just the pain itself. This pain stands for love and I'm grateful to love you. From where I'm standing, it feels like a very long time until I get to see you again. One day would be too long, but this lifetime can feel cruel without you. But I know things are different where you are. I bet you'll finish that beautiful song of yours and you'll look up and suddenly we'll all be there to sing it with you next time around. Surely by the second chorus, we'll all be there together. Your mama loves you so much, Luca; and I can't wait to tell you that to your face someday.

I stop talking. I finally look at our family, and they are crying, too. We all hold hands, the circle we form dispelling the feeling that I am alone; we sing and pray to a God who binds up our broken hearts.

And somehow, during all of this, the crushing weight lifts. Not all of it, but I no longer feel the way I did when I was in bed that morning, dwarfed by grief and the impossible task of Luca's funeral and the also impossible task of living the rest of my life.

I can't tell you how or why, but Luca's funeral remains a blessing, of sorts. Terrible sorts, if one were to rank them, but a blessing, still. A reminder that this grief is not just mine. It is also our family's. The realization that you are not as alone as you thought can be the difference between making it or not. Luca's funeral is another reminder that we will make it. It is beautiful and peaceful and so profoundly sad.

We walk up the same hill, but it's different. It doesn't hurt quite so much to be here. I feel acutely aware of how precious life is. I can breathe. We all eat food in my parents' house and small talk happens. Life does that strange thing where it just keeps on going no matter what. People laugh, and I guess even I do, too. People hug me, and it's not as terrible as the long hours of the morning in bed had convinced me it would be. It's surreal. It's still awful. It's okay. I'm sort of okay, and I manage to fill my plate and eat and thank people for coming. It's pitiful to also be polite in addition to a grieving mother, but what else do we do? We cannot control who lives and dies, and we cannot keep our babies here. But we can say thank you for coming, so we do.

Chapter 26

Grief and Words and All Our Stories
(seven weeks after)

You have a child, and you're changed. You bury a child, and you're changed. Hard things are done to and by you; good things are done to and by you, and you're changed. It's a lot of changing, and it's tiring but necessary. Just like a doctor is concerned if your baby isn't changing with the weeks, time has a strict rule: You either change or you stop. So, in that case, I'm grateful for change. No matter how badly it can hurt to keep going, I don't want to stop.

"I need to talk to you, Jessica," says a missionary to West Asia who just happens to be at my parents' church the same Sunday as me. "My first daughter was stillborn—" Just five words is all it takes, but God, what words to speak; what words to have lived. It's strange to me that it's all just words. Like, we order sandwiches and root for sports teams and tell each other our child has died—all with words. The same door reveals both the most important thing and what's for lunch. The same pockets carry our most precious belongings as well as our trash. It is wild.

When you're grieving, you can't stand the trivial. Not when your words come with the price of the tears that transform your bed into a river at night. Not when your words drop to the ground with an unbearable weight—and the only weight you want is your baby in your arms. Our words have no place among those used to describe what doesn't matter. Our words that share grief don't belong among the words that describe wine tastings and poor service at restaurants and backaches and kids that complain too much.

"How do you deal with your toddler all day long without losing your sh*t?" I read in a mom's group on Facebook. The comments are filled with suggestions. I don't post mine: *You realize your kid is alive. Period.*

This beautiful missionary tells me a story that runs deep. We cry as she reveals her grief with some of the same pricey words I've been using lately. "I didn't name her," she says, quietly. "Nobody told me to—not until fifteen years later, when I started counseling with your father, and he suggested I finally give my firstborn a name." More words, this time a name. I wish that I could say my baby's name all throughout the day; I wish life gave me more of a reason to than simply in remembrance. I love the name Luca. It means "bringer of light." I just thought the light would come from his life here, rather than his death.

* * *

We have a tiny dinner table. I am not exaggerating, just ask anyone who's ever eaten dinner with us. We bought it when we lived in a studio apartment in Brooklyn, and it made the move to Boston with us. It is maybe 3x3 feet, and we can manage to seat four people at it if our drinks are on a nearby ledge, but not actually on the table. I love this table, and, late into the night when Charlee is asleep, I do my writing and sketching here. I feel safe and free—like the things that have happened to me are not nearly as much of a life sentence as the things I choose. I write words down and feel better. I concentrate and sketch stuff—silly stuff, like manatees in tutus—and feel better.

There is a great pull toward isolation. This is not to elicit pity or more invitations to birthday parties; it just is. There are not enough birthday parties in the world—complete with an invitation to every one—that could keep me from feeling this way. I know I'm included; I know I'm loved. I also feel very different, which is isolating.

Winston Churchill referred to his depression as "the black dog." So very whimsical and British of him. Even in darkness, he can paint a picture with his language. I, too, live with a black dog, but her name is Luna and she's an actual dog (I'm American and so, you know, literal). But I can feel Churchill's black dog hanging around, too. I don't think I feed him. Even when I lay down and cry because a friend had her baby, I don't think that's what that is.

Therapists call it *processing* and *grieving*, and I call it just on the edge of unbearable. Which is the layman's term for all the above. Every so often I come across an article that holds up a mirror, and it's like, *Oh. So, I'm not the only one. That person couldn't remember a thing after their loss, either.* I remember the big things—the things that hurt, yes—but the details fade. If I'm no longer holding something, I don't remember where I put it, even if I had it a minute ago.

"What was that person's name that we met tonight, Jess?" TJ asks. I don't even bother searching my brain for the information; it's completely gone. Unless the name is Luca. I'd never met anyone with that name, but in the last seven weeks since his death, I've seen a restaurant and met two humans named Luca. I remember that.

It's strange to be reduced to a conversation between other people. Among others, I am the girl who lost her baby, and isn't that just terrible? Even to those close to me, I am a sad conversation, a quick check-in to make sure I'm not feeding Churchill's black dog before they go on with their day or vacation or attend to their many living children. I don't resent any of that—I get it—but I feel different, because I can't just let this problem go and ponder fish or chicken for Wednesday night's dinner.

How do you let go of the fabric of your life? You don't. You weave the chicken or fish question right into the tapestry, right into the grief. Right into all the other questions that have become nomads, searching for a home—an answer—but finding none this side of heaven. But I sit down at my little table. I write out answers that don't look like answers at all. They are sketches, prose, lyrics, stories, and poems, and they're all I've got. Some nights, they are even enough to rock me to sleep in some kind of peace, at least.

Sometimes I want to pack a bag
With fifty less outfits
Than I think I need and just go.
I'll take my people with me
And we'll listen to songs
With lyrics that come easy;
Melodies that trace our scars
And remind us that love
Was a good choice.
(It always is.)
We'll get tired and grumpy
Because it's real life;
But we'll get a lot
Of other things, too.
Good things—
Like memories instead of deadlines;
Like our faces buried in wonder
Instead of in our phones.

Chapter 27

Conversations That Preach
(one month after)

"How are you?" a neighbor asks.

I hesitate, unsure how to answer.

"Listen...I know what happened, and I'm sorry," he says, putting me at ease. It's a relief when people already know, and I don't have to tell them.

"I'm...okay," I say, which is how I describe the tears that come at odd moments, the long nights, the anxiety that shortens my breath, the laughter and joy I still feel with Charlee and TJ, how much I miss my Luca, the blessedly razor-sharp focus I find when I create anything these days, the comfort that comes in words that are hopeful and good, kind and true, filled with faith, the way every instinct is heightened when a beautiful pregnant woman walks by. I can't really describe all of that easily, least of all casually. It's like asking someone to tell you what color the rainbow is. So I say I'm okay and ask how he is, because it's much easier to talk about others.

"You know," my neighbor continues, ignoring the question, "John and I were in New York City during the AIDS crisis in the eighties and nineties. We watched many of our friends die. There aren't any words to describe it. In our grief, we stopped making new friends. We never said it out loud, but I think we were both just too tired to say goodbye to yet another person we loved. So, our circle got smaller and smaller. It wasn't until we moved up here that we realized we hadn't made a friend in twenty years."

I'm listening hard now. This is real talk, and whenever you're a witness to it, you take note.

"Don't do what we did, Jessica. Don't close your heart. It's never worth it." It's amazing how preaching happens in so many more places than church, how God loves us enough to speak to us. We think we're just taking our dog out. We make the trip as fast as possible to get back to a (somewhat) controlled environment, that safe space called home.

But nothing is "just" anything. Not when your pain and brokenness is an SOS that reaches out to others without you realizing it—causing healing and courage to show up in seemingly random conversations, the books strangers send, the words of your two-year-old, the carrying that strangers, friends, and family alike continue to do with your grief, your gone son, your heart.

Chapter 28

God is Here (Even When "Here" Is Awful)
(seven weeks after)

Sometimes I let myself wonder what God was doing when Luca died. Oh, hi. Were you expecting something lighter? I just got back from New York City—perhaps you expected something about the views or the food (both were glorious) rather than meditations on God and my dead baby? Maybe tomorrow I'll write more about the greasy slices of pizza I ate or the streets radiating excitement—rows and rows of apartment buildings side by side with corporations reaching for the sky. But not right now.

I recently saw a post on an online moms' forum soliciting advice on taking a toddler to an ultrasound. There were lots of comments advising her not to do it, mostly because it could be bad news. But the day Luca stopped moving, I had to take Charlee to the hospital, because we were the only ones home. She was with me when they couldn't find his heartbeat—literally squeezed in next to my hugely pregnant belly on the gurney, because she didn't want to sit on a chair by herself while they tried to cajole his precious and baby-fast heartbeat to sound again.

We went together to the ultrasound, me in shock, holding her while she smothered me with kisses. Charlee doesn't usually do that. I mean, sometimes I'll even bribe her to kiss me (I'm above very little these days).

I wasn't even crying, either, just resolutely walking in somebody else's body—somebody else's life—to the ultrasound room. And still she kissed me repeatedly.

The picture of Luca was too still. Horribly still. The doctor was too matter of fact. Horribly matter of fact. But the midwife on call—though not my midwife—was weeping. I'll always love her for that. When TJ arrived, she told us, "I know you guys. I helped deliver your daughter. I'm so very sorry." She was crying as she spoke, her tears adding the weight of empathy to her words.

There is more, but tonight when I think about where God was on that day, I see Him in the kisses with which Charlee anointed my face. I see Him in the tears that streamed down an almost-stranger's face; tears that softened my heart even then, even when the world was telling me it should probably harden for good.

May I never hide my tears for another's sorrow; may I never deprive them of the balm it is.

★ ★ ★

Ten days after Luca died, TJ and I shared a meal at ABC Kitchen in New York City. Yesterday, we ate there again. Just shy of three months later, we were seated at the exact same table. I went into the bathroom to snap a photo in the mirror. I'm trying to document growth. My parents' house has a wall marked with all our heights—from the time we could stand until years later, when we were done growing. It tells me that growth matters, and I agree. This is my version of that wall, I guess, because I have done some growing since I was last here. I wish I could have grown with Luca in my arms, but instead I'm growing with him in my heart. It's painfully different, but it's still growth. And like I said, growth matters.

"Remember how I told you that I've prayed every single day since our wedding that God would bring us closer to each other?" TJ asks as we lay next to one another.

I silently nod in the darkness.

He continues, "Well, I've been thinking about it. I've never felt closer to you than these past weeks. Never felt so close to you as I do right now. What if this is a gift not only from God, but from Luca?"

The thought makes me smile. It's the first time we're talking about Luca the way we talk about Charlee. Like proud parents sharing an almost-normal, look-what-my-kid-did! moment. It's the way I feel when my sister brings Charlee back from the park and tells me she shared her toys with the kids and handed out stickers like a champ. I never thought I'd get to feel this way about Luca, too, but here I am feeling it.

"There will come a time when thinking about Luca will make you smile," my therapist told me in one of our first sessions. I didn't understand it then, but I realize it's happening. I don't want to write these words too soon. I don't want to confuse a world that already constantly bangs on the door of the hurting, asking if they're better yet. I am sad; I am not better. At least not in the way that someone who used to hurt when they walk is now pain free. I'm not that kind of better; it still hurts when I walk. But I also recognize a gift when I see it. Especially when it comes from Luca. It's grace and it's light, and both of those show up bright as daylight when your world has dimmed considerably.

Now it's 3 AM and Charlee is awake in her crib, crying for mama. I get out of bed, grateful that she's here to mother. I tell her everything is okay and hold her hand as she settles back down to sleep. There is no rush in me now. I'm content to be with her as long as she needs. A little less sleep because of it is no big deal.

I think about what TJ said, and I realize it's happening again. Another gift from Luca: Charlee gets a better mama because of him. I hold her hand, and I am grateful for Luca. This is not poetry; it is fact. It's a very bright star indeed that leaves so much light even after it's gone. Just like his name, Luca—bringer of light.

Chapter 29

Grief and Anxiety Intersect Inside of Me
(two months after)

When you're pregnant, the pigmentation of your skin darkens in spots. So, during a routine visit today, I tell my dermatologist that I gave birth eight weeks ago and ask if she thinks the spots will fade.

"Congratulations!" she beams.

It's a normal reaction. I'm not offended.

"Actually, he died," I say bluntly, not knowing how to soften the truth. "My baby was stillborn. It's hard."

"Oh God," she says, "I'm so sorry. How far along were you?"

"Nine months."

"Oh God."

"I know," I say, "It's devastating."

"Were you checked regularly through your pregnancy?" she asks.

I get this line of thought. When I read about a tragedy, I immediately and even subconsciously reason that it would never happen to me because I do things differently. I was gripped by the story of a family watching a movie on a Florida beach when their toddler went to the edge of the lake to play. The dad was right there when an alligator took his baby away. I couldn't stop reading about it. I comforted myself by deciding that it wouldn't happen to us because I'd never let my child in any Florida water—though I am sure that family was also doing what looked safe and never thought this terrible narrative would be theirs. These little mind tricks of ours are ways we try to control what is never in our control. A way to shield ourselves and our loved ones from indescribable tragedy and the grief that follows.

So, I get why people look for reasons why this won't happen to them (and it most likely WON'T—it's rare) because they'd go to all their appointments (I did) or be vigilant with kick counts in the third trimester (I was very aware of how much he was moving; he moved well until he stopped). I tell her my pregnancy was wonderful right until he died. We talk for a while, and she is truly compassionate—a healer in more than just the physical sense.

I show her spots that worry me, and she shakes her head. "You're fine. Let's just keep an eye on this," she adds, pointing to a small mark on my arm.

"If it changes, let me know."

Cue: alarm bells.

"So, there's a chance this could be dangerous?" I ask.

"It's not now, but yes, if it starts to change, then it could be." She looks at me, then offers: "But if it will give you peace, I will take it off right now."

I tell her I struggle with anxiety now, particularly related to death. I don't like relying on chance. The thought, *Oh that could never happen!* no longer applies to me. She listens and sets up her tools. I go home with a band-aid—a reminder that I want to be here. A lot of times the worst doesn't happen, and the best doctors are the ones who listen.

Chapter 30

Relating to a Non-Grieving World Is Weird
(three months after)

"I'm not sure I ever want to have a baby," the woman giving my hair a blowout is saying. "I just don't want to get fat."

I nod and tell her I understand, even though I don't, really. I'd get anything to have Luca. Definitely fat.

"You look okay, though," she goes on. I try to refrain from swooning over the compliment. Who doesn't dream of looking okay?

"How old is your baby again?" she asks.

Keeping it light, I answer that Charlee is two.

"Do you feel like you got your body back?" she asks.

The truth is, I haven't. It's not quite three months since I gave birth to my baby after having been pregnant for just about nine months, so it makes sense that I wouldn't have yet. But I tell her that sure, I guess it's mostly back. I change the subject, ask what the weirdest thing she's experienced is, since her job takes her into strangers' homes.

"I've seen new moms breastfeeding," she answers. "That was weird."

She has no idea she's batting a thousand with this conversation, and I have a very strong idea that we live on two different planets. My loss, my motherhood separates us like the Berlin Wall. She can't even see the wall, though. It's invisible to most but me, and that's okay. I'm also not sure this one will ever fully come down. I'm sure neither of us can climb it today, so we'll just keep talking over it.

She tries to sell me hair extensions. I politely take her number, tell her that I'll call if I decide to do it, knowing I never will. The need to be polite generates so many words, it's a wonder there's any room left over for the truth. She has no idea that everything is enough already. The showers I must take. The meals I have to make because people around me are hungry all the time, like, over and over again. The long slow march through grief. Shaping the future with my thoughts, doggedly arranging them in a way that gives me hope until I just can't do it anymore.

Until TJ tells me I need to write. Writing lifts the stopper and drains the despair. TJ knows this, so he reminds me to do it on nights I'm out of sync with hope. All this to say, I'm tired enough without another foot of hair tied to my head to deal with.

I look at my new yellow dress. It hangs next to TJ's suit in anticipation of the wedding we're attending. "In the Chinese culture, yellow is the color of both mourning and heroes," a friend writes me, lending me meaning.

"It's always been my favorite color, actually," I reply, "but now I love it even more."

★ ★ ★

It isn't so bad to see people. Boston feels like a small town, and I run into people I know just about everywhere. It doesn't hurt so much anymore to answer their questions. Yesterday I called someone other than my mom for the first time in almost three months. That's something, I guess. The kind of thing that makes my therapist exclaim, "You are so incredibly functional, Jess!" High praise from your shrink. Not being sexy or particularly fast when you run could be disappointing, sure. But let's face it, without those things, you could still at least make it in life. But finding a workaround to being functional would be just about impossible.

Our good friend is a math genius professor with a Ph.D. from M.I.T. He does stuff to our computers that makes them so much faster. I am not sure what, but he takes them when they are very slow and gives them back when they are very fast. The first time he looked at my very slow computer, he opened it, waited just about forever for it to load, and finally said, "Oh, this is not functional. It's not at all usable." All this to say, I am grateful to be functional. Really entering into life and calling humans. I'm functional—just like the kind of computer a Ph.D. from M.I.T. brings you.

I'm also afraid, but I don't know how to magic that away. I can, however, judge how valid the fear is and decide if it's a voice to act on or not. It's almost never valid.

When Charlee sleeps past 6 AM, I stare at the monitor, wondering if she's okay. My rational voice says that she is. Pro-tip: When you invite me to a party, make sure it's the rational voice you're inviting. She's the one who is polite and quiet and answers exactly how you think she will. You see her at the gym, living her best life while working on her lats, and you'd have no idea she just pushed out a baby and then buried him in the ground.

My emotional voice, however, is a mess. Drunk off her sorrow, she is somewhat unpredictable and doesn't shower as much as she suspects her friends do. She's weepy. It's not just something she does, like cries a lot; it's a constant feature of her personality—something that she IS. She tries to assuage her anxiety with Google, but it's like catching water in a sieve. It never works. Google simply cannot tell her she'll be okay, that everyone she loves will be, too. She is no better or worse than you or anybody else. She is just hurting.

Though she's going through it herself, she still finds it unthinkable when another mama tells her about the time her baby died. It's that bad. It's a thing you can't get used to. It's like getting all your limbs chopped off, except it's actually your heart, so you're not sure what you're left with.

But if there's one thing my emotional voice is great at, it's therapy. She knows how to share; her heart is as impossible to hide as the ocean. And she loves Jesus like that woman who loved him long ago, who came to Him with just her own tears to wash his feet, using her own hair to dry them.

So I need her. And I need a balance between the two voices, constantly talking over one another, day in and day out.

Chapter 31

Clues That I Will Be Okay
(four months after)

I've been changing my prayer lately. Instead of asking for blessings, I ask for eyes to see the blessings. Charlee is fascinated by butterflies and points them out all the time. Like blessings, the butterflies are here whether I notice them or not. I could miss them entirely, but she makes sure I don't. It's a gift to live with someone who regularly points out the butterflies.

Speaking of butterflies, while going through my divorce, I'd walk in the woods near my parents' home every day. That's how I noticed, one day, a stunning blue butterfly perched daintily on a huge pile of horse crap. I stared at the butterfly like it was a revelation. Like God himself was saying: *It's okay to be surrounded by crap. It doesn't change the fact that you are a butterfly.* I walked home that day thinking that, while I may be losing the house, his last name, and a piece (all?) of my heart, maybe I won't lose myself after all.

There is so much crap. We all know this. But it doesn't mean the butterflies become reduced to crap, too. They stay beautiful, luminescent, despite what's next to them or even despite what they're standing on. Twice now, things have happened to me that "only happen to other people." So now I'm guessing that there are no such thing as other people; there are just people, and we are them.

When my first husband gave his heart to another, I went to bed and tried to sleep forever. But every morning I had to wake up and remember that I, too, was getting a divorce. That I was no better than the fifty percent of married couples in America who end up doing this. That they all deserve grace just as much as I do, and there's no trap door that allows the special among us to skip suffering. I awoke to that realization so many times that eventually it became normal. It's both cruel and comforting what the human heart can call normal. It's a testament to the resilience that lines our spirit the way marrow lines our bones. We are not made for defeat; we are made to follow the instincts of survival and the will to hope.

We think we will break, only to discover that we bend into a shape that is as beautiful as it is strong. We embrace the pain only to find it's fire that purifies gold. This sounds lovely and poetic, but what about when all we have is fire; when the faint promise of gold is nothing compared to this raging pain? I'm not sure. I know I sleep a lot and eat less. I write like I'm Scheherazade, and the stories I weave are the only guarantee I have of survival. I don't realize that the stories are so much more than survival. I don't realize they are my small dose of meds that, when taken every single day, build up until I'm doing something wild: Healing.

I keep thinking about brokenness, and I'm convinced it doesn't have to be a bad thing. The clouds break to reveal the sun. When a bottle of perfume breaks, the fragrance is shared with the world. A bone that breaks and then heals is stronger than if it had never been broken at all. Grapes that are crushed and broken are made into wine. The ocean's shore is comprised of thousands of rocks and shells, all broken. And my favorite: God is close to the broken-hearted.

I'm wondering what comes of this brokenness. There are so many stories that point to healing, to better things, to joy that is so very precious *because* sorrow lives here, too. You can close your eyes and be back in the delivery room, back in the nightmare, back in the hello and goodbye and God-not-my-baby! all at once. It's never far below the surface, taking your breath away, leaving you speechless when someone asks how you are. It's dark, but it's also birth. Your son, your grief, the emergence of a newly broken heart, and this life now—it was all born that day. Eyes that see clearer, a heart that quietly thanks God for every single good thing still here, and a deeper understanding of the value of this life compounded by its glaring transience. It was all born that day.

Chapter 32

The Work of Grief, The Work of Hope
(five weeks after)

"Do you think you need to get tested for Lyme disease? You seem very tired," TJ says, breaking the silence.

I think about the work of grief, the high alert I'm on every time I step out of our apartment. I see someone familiar and immediately register them as Someone Who Knows or Someone Who Doesn't. Then there's the next layer: Someone Who's Acknowledged It or Someone Who Hasn't. Based on this data, I mentally prepare myself for the ensuing conversation; or, if possible, I simply about-face and avoid the situation altogether. This all happens in under a minute.

The first time I got a massage after delivering Luca, I spent the whole sixty minutes anticipating the therapist asking about my baby, because he knew I was recently postpartum: I'd written it on the intake. I wasn't cold, but my teeth uncontrollably chattered. I was so anxious that it was a tangible, physical thing. The massage therapist never did ask for details, and all that teeth chattering was seemingly for nothing.

There is some respite when I'm home, in a controlled atmosphere. But the grief doesn't leave; it simply morphs, a shapeshifter making sure I am never alone. The anxiety gives way to a sadness that seems vascular, flowing through my veins and arteries and grabbing at my laughter, cutting it short from within.

It's a different kind of work at home. Less vigilance and more sinking, while I work harder to reach beyond myself for encouragement and truth, for words that weigh more than the trite words of advice others give me like they are prescriptions with no pharmacy to fulfill them. Also, at home there is less distraction. It's a table for two, and I am sitting right across from grief.

Maybe it's good work. Work that, in a way, I'm grateful to do, as grief is a measure of love. So, I cry for my boy and know that tears are born of love, not just tragedy. And the only reason the tragedy hurts like this is because love was here first. And is here still.

Charlee is two and has questions that outnumber my answers. There are voices I must use for her dolls and stories I must tell for her peace. It's so good being her mama, and it takes every bit of me to do it well. She wakes just after 5 AM most days, after I've stayed up half of the night before writing down all the reasons I should not be afraid after googling all the reasons I should. I think about what TJ said. I am often tired, but it has nothing to do with ticks.

"I don't have Lyme, TJ," I finally say. "I don't need a test."

★ ★ ★

This afternoon TJ charges into an apartment of chaos. I've got squares of material all around me, and I'm sewing hard. Charlee is playing even harder. Basically, everything that can be strewn about the floor is. Even Luna's toys are haphazardly thrown all over the rug, like a trail of clues hinting that a dog lives here, too.

TJ is fresh off a successful solo trip to the grocery store, feeling empowered with cherries in one hand and the replacement for Charlee's body wash we'd just run out of in the other. "We're not cursed!" he says with real joy as I look up from ironing a square. I hope that he takes the way I start doing it with a little more vigor as the sign of solidarity it is. "We're blessed!" he continues, the cherries and body wash flailing around with his excited gestures like they're nodding. Nine out of ten cherries agree that TJ and Jessica are not actually cursed—they're blessed!

"God says it, Jess, that we're blessed. I can't help but look around and see Charlee and us together—and Luna, too, obviously—and I can't help but think our life says it, too. We're blessed. And I think we don't need to be afraid that we're cursed anymore, because we're not. We're meant to do a lot with these blessings. Even Luca is a blessing. It's a tragedy that he's not here, but I think God will bring blessing from it. I think he already is. And, no matter what, it's a blessing that he's ours."

I iron and measure the weight of our dead son against the weight of TJ's words. It's amazing what we ponder in our heart while our hands do the most menial tasks. We are magicians, hiding our ocean of complex thoughts and emotions behind vacuums and iPhones and a GPS that takes us everywhere and nowhere all at once.

TJ is either totally insane or he's right. Perhaps there's so much more to death than what we see here and now. My heart knows that he's not insane; it, too, sees the blessings. My heart also hurts immeasurably. My heart is a very busy place, and as you can see, I'm tired for more reasons than my daughter getting up at 5 AM.

"I know," I finally say. "We are blessed. I believe that there are good days—better days than we can realize—ahead."

Outwardly I keep ironing like nothing has changed, but inside, I feel a little less afraid of the long nights stretching before me.

★ ★ ★

The next day, I walk into my therapist's office and talk for an hour straight—unless I'm crying.

"Is this getting too sad?" she asks. I shake my head, because it's always sad. What even is "too sad?" Whatever it is, it's already happened, and nobody asked me that question at the time.

"I did something yesterday that made me feel alive," I say.

I made Charlee a quilt while I was pregnant with her. But I didn't get to do this for Luca, since—well, I had Charlee with me, and the precise kind of sewing and cutting you must do for a quilt doesn't go well with mothering a toddler. Plus, I was just so very tired working and Charlee-ing and growing a baby inside me all at once. When I think back to that time, I remember treading water, and you don't hear of many people who tread water and come out of it having made a quilt. If they even come out of it at all, they've simply survived, nothing more.

"I never got to make a quilt for Luca," I tell my therapist. "So, I started making a quilt yesterday."

She nods in that encouraging way I do with Charlee when she tells me she can jump so high and then proceeds to get maybe two inches off the ground. Any jump my two-year-old does IS amazing—she's two. Just like anything a newly grieving mother manages to do is amazing, I suppose.

And I think all of us—Republicans, Democrats, people who are neither—can agree that making a quilt is overall a net positive contribution. The world could use a lot less passive aggression, tweets, and soda, IMHO—but the world can always use another quilt.

"When I finish this quilt," I continue, "I'll give it to the hospital—to Labor and Delivery—for the next mama who has to go home without her baby. I just want her to know she's not alone. From one mama to another, she's not alone."

My therapist is genuinely smiling now, her eyes lit up. It's the same light I know my own eyes shine with when I work on the baby quilt. I don't say a word while I stitch the pieces together. I simply listen to the hum of the sewing machine, comforting and constant. It gives a rhythm to the prayer that fills the empty space in my heart as I think about the stranger who will someday hold this same material in her hands. I know it sounds nice, but it's not. It's still awful—but the thing about death, is that it feels so final. And those of us left in its wake would like something to do about it, see. And, in my own small way, making this quilt is something tangible I can do about it. It makes me feel like I'm doing something for my boy. Like maybe death didn't take away my ability to do something for him after all.

Chapter 33

A Chimera

(seven weeks after)

Sometimes being a baby-lost mama is expressed better by what you don't say. It's hearing someone refer to a mom and her *two* kids. But you know that family. You know the mom had a third child, a stillbirth. A short while ago, this offhand mention wouldn't have even made you blink. But now, you correct it in your mind. *Three kids*, you think. That family has three kids. It's important they have three kids—that the dead kid still counts— because that means you have two kids, that Luca counts, too. That means that Luca was here, that Luca is significant. It means the faint brown line you see when you unbutton your jeans is still the X marks the spot on your belly where, not too long ago, you got to hide treasure. And the fact that treasure is found and then lost does not mean it is no longer treasure.

I read an article that tells me what I already know: that Luca was here and his presence changed me for both the good and forever. The article says this is true, scientifically, and tells me it has a name. It's called *fetal-maternal microchimerism*. Those big words mean that with every baby a mother grows inside her, their cells mingle, changing the composition of each other. So a 70-year-old woman who once grew a baby boy—be it a fleeting or full-term pregnancy—is found with male DNA in her brain. Her boy lingers forever, no matter if he grew up and moved far away or never grew up at all. And if a mother sustains a heart injury, these cells from babies past gather around the heart and aid in its healing. It's incredible to read that science agrees with what you instinctively know. That scientists are uncovering in cells what is already written on every mama's heart: that your tiny babe is a part of your life forever.

To better understand what *microchimerism* means, I look up the word *chimera*. My heart skips a beat as I read the definition: A thing that is hoped or wished for but in fact is illusory or impossible to achieve.

Oh God.

I wonder if this hints at the hope of all mothers—that their babies could stay safe and with them forever. That is, of course, a chimera. My mom still cries because I live far away. I wonder if this word simply refers to me and Luca being together on earth, the way we were supposed to be: a chimera.

I come back from Luna's walk and mention to TJ that the hyper-aggressive bird was out again.

"Did it get Luna?" he asks.

"Literally swooped down and pecked her butt right as she was pooping," I say.

"Did you freak out?"

But now we're both smiling, so he answers his own question with, "It's kind of funny, isn't it."

It's a statement, a true one.

"Yeah," I say, "But only because she's always okay afterward."

And the thing that's shocking right now is that there are still good moments. Grief doesn't put life on hold. It's perplexing, because it feels like it should. But people still invite you places and go on and on about their broken foot and celebrate birthdays; they even still want to celebrate yours. All of life still happens.

But grief is a magnifying glass that brings whatever's already there sharply into focus. So the good is precious and the funny is hilarious and the meaning is deep and the sadness is a black hole I fall into and can't remember how to find my way back out. I miss Luca. I one hundred percent lost my child. I think about how the nurse at the hospital told me he looked just like me. He looked like his mama, and I am that mama, and he isn't here anymore.

I think about Luca when I take a spin class because you only do one thing in that class: pedal. Your mind wanders wherever it wants, because your legs don't need reminding to do something so simple. I used to like this aspect of spinning. Now it's hard. It's emotional. I had only wanted a quick workout but now I'm crying. I one hundred percent lost my child, and I feel it more when there's less distraction.

But then there are the normal moments. TJ and I talk about our dog being pecked by a literal angry bird while she's pooping, and we laugh. We can laugh easily together, more easily than among others, because we both lost a child and understand that laughing doesn't mean we aren't grieving. (I am hesitant to laugh in front of others, for fear they will take it to mean I'm better.) I get into the car and find a card from TJ. I one hundred percent lost my child, but reading these words fills my heart. My heart is shaped by this love. I inhale and exhale and think how I've lost much but still have so very much right here.

I one hundred percent lost my child, and (not but; and) I one hundred percent have this full life that demands not only the best of me, but all of me. Love, of course, demands all of me— and we go to the altar of love and happily lay down our hearts.

We don't often know what an altar is. We don't realize that here is where fire comes and burns up what it finds. We don't know that out of this fire comes grief. That it is not only born of love; it IS love. And both love and fire don't really discriminate: they always demand all. Somehow, I can be the girl whose son died and the girl whose life is full. Somehow, I can grieve him with my whole heart and live life with my whole heart. Together, at once. I have to. Sometimes I don't see a way forward at all, but when I do—it is this way. Not leaving either grief or the notion of wholeheartedly living behind. Perhaps certain hours or days or even months will feel slanted towards one, and that is okay. Perhaps I find that grief and wholehearted living aren't diametrically opposed. To do either authentically (or at all), one must first be willing to do both.

★ ★ ★

I am laying in the dark with TJ sleeping beside me, trying to come up with something profound to write. In the meantime, I'll just say this. The lyrics to the popular animated movie Moana's soundtrack keep running through my mind. Especially the self-actualization of Moana; when she realizes exactly who she is. You hear it in the swell of the instruments, the perfect crescendo as she declares: I AM MOANA!

It doesn't matter how many people tell her she's the daughter of the village chief, or that she is brave and resilient and can do hard things. None of that matters, really, until she believes it herself. Only then can she face a monster and restore it to its true self with kindness and compassion and considerable bravery. Importantly, she doesn't do any of this until she has to. Sometimes grim circumstances get us to reach heights that would otherwise be unattainable, ones we never desired to reach in the first place. I know there is a lesson here.

I don't feel strong or brave or sure. Often, I feel the opposite of these things. I wonder what to do next. But on nights like this, when I ask God for help—not just to make things easier, but because, otherwise, I don't know how to keep going—I close my eyes and try to rest my feelings on facts.

I think about how the prayers of my parents raised me. Maybe these prayers are like the falling leaves that reach the ground and become carbon dioxide and water. In time, these leaves become a protective blanket, a sponge, absorbing the morning dew, the evening rain. They remain a source of food and water for the tree through the long winter months. Perhaps it is the prayers we blindly and desperately cast—along with the prayers of those who love us—the words and faith and hope knit together, bound like chain-link around our own beating hearts... the prayers we see as useless, simply falling down, meandering to the ground as if by mistake, actually become—like the fallen leaves for the tree—our sustenance. Our food and water through the long winter months. Having fallen to the ground quite on purpose, they are doing exactly what they set out to do.

I think about how the prayers of my husband, who signed all the papers and talked to the funeral home and made all the horrible arrangements for Luca so that I didn't have to do a thing beyond grief—carry me. How TJ continues to make plans, continues to anticipate the good that God has hidden in all the days to come. How talking about all this with him saves my soul. Reminds me that life is worthy of our attention. Even in grief, even after burying our son.

I think about the prayers that are said on my behalf, and I lift my head a little higher, because all those words born of faith and hope might not be wrong. They are worth considering now (especially now). They might bear wings and, in their flight, lift me up. They might be leaves, and in their falling, help me stand. Tonight, I choose to agree with them. Tonight, I choose to be carried by them. Tonight, I will think about how brokenness can be the prelude to healing. And someday when I can, just like TJ is doing, I'll make plans too.

Chapter 34

On How to Grieve
(five weeks after)

I'm sitting with Charlee on the couch. We sit close—the kind of close you sit with the people who are yours. The kind of close where one of you laid inside the other's belly long before you laid side by side on the couch. Long before this particular Monday morning. Charlee is "reading" her Kindle, and I'm reading a collection of personal stories on stillbirth, called *They Were Still Born*, given to me by a friend. It's a beautiful book, even more meaningful because I understand the terrible price each contributor paid to write it. The price they still pay.

I read about a mother who laid her stillborn child to rest in the earth. She'd been told not to cremate him, not to keep his ashes with her. It would be unhealthy for her other children to be faced with it every day, people said, while their mother exists under the shadow of the great mountain her child's death has borne. It is years before she realizes that she can grieve the way she needs to. Finally, she has her baby's grave dug up, cremates his body, and chooses an urn. She places the son she has always missed exactly where she wants him—at home with the rest of her children—and finds great comfort in the act.

I remember a conversation I had years ago with a friend about a funeral in her family for a stillborn baby. She told me the parents dressed up the baby and laid the child out; we both decided it was creepy and strange and entirely unnecessary. I cringe now, remembering. I had no idea.

Grieving is an act of love, the soul's receipt for the price of love, and far be it for anyone to tell another how to love and, God forbid, grieve their child. I used to think that grieving is dark and does not belong in the light of the life we still have here. I didn't know what it really is—sacred and holy and incredibly necessary. It is as personal as your thumbprint, as utilitarian as the thumb itself. There is no right or wrong to it. I have to give myself grace. I didn't know any of this. And I suppose we cannot know before we do. In the words of the modern poet, The Notorious B.I.G., *And if you don't know, now you know.*

There is a sacred act called grief, and the only true and universal thing about it is that we do it. The how and why is secondary and belongs far away from the judgment of others.

A friend who also lost a baby told me that healing is not forgetting—it is remembering wisely. Which is good news, because forgetting the child you loved and who is now dead is something we can't do. I cry as I read the book, because I understand every word. I hold Charlee close and tell her that she is my favorite girl I've ever met.

"You're the weirdest mom I've ever seen," she says, and we both laugh. Here I am, crying for Luca and laughing with Charlee all at once. Here I am again, trying to describe the indescribable.

* * *

Sometimes I sit down to write, and I think: *Okay. Today I should write something happy.* And then I wrack my brain for something—anything—that fits. And there are things, small things, that pop up.

TJ texting me throughout the day, saying he can't wait to see me. Charlee and I searching for baby animals in the pool (you'd be surprised how many baby bears, deer—even dinosaurs—are in the water when an imaginative three-year-old is helping you look).

These are happy things, and I spend a lot of my day responding to them. But when I am alone, my story overwhelms me. So I carefully arrange a piece of it with words. Something calming happens as I place periods and semicolons and spaces around the letters I choose. It's a miracle. I'm not parting the seas, not creating wine from water, but right now it's my miracle, and I'll take it. Writing down how I feel is a solvable puzzle I can hold in my hands whenever I need to.

After I delivered Luca, the social worker told me to do things that would help relax me: "Drink a glass of wine and eat the food you couldn't eat while you were pregnant," she said. But I don't want to get in the habit of drinking when I'm sad—otherwise, I'd be drinking a lot right now. And call me crazy, but I don't feel like celebrating no longer being pregnant by eating a plateful of soft cheeses and processed meat. I don't feel like celebrating no longer being pregnant at all.

What helps me, though, is writing. It helped me when I was a girl, a young dancer anxious about the soon-to-be-posted Nutcracker Ballet casting, and it helps now as I grieve my son. I write and write and write. When I want to lay down forever, when I get the urge to call a friend but don't feel ready for the confrontation of a conversation, when I want to cry, I sit down, and I write. I am Scheherazade, preserving my life one story at a time, night by night, until I have told a thousand. And then, perhaps, like Scheherazade, I shall be allowed to live.

$\star\;\star\;\star$

I am staring at the last photo I took with Luca inside me. In it, I'm taking a photo of my reflection in the mirror, smiling. If I could talk to that girl, I wouldn't tell her she's right to worry about her baby. I wouldn't tell her that in a few hours she'll go to the hospital and find out the worst. She'll be stuck in the waiting room with a toddler and one pack of stickers that will be stuck and unstuck repeatedly for what feels like a very long time, reassuring herself that her baby is fine, waiting impatiently to go resume her life for the four weeks until he's due.

I wouldn't tell her that it doesn't happen, she never gets those four weeks. I wouldn't tell her because grace is never on its way—it's always here. It's magnificently present tense. When the pain arrives, so does the grace, strengthening you to live through the worst. If the pain hasn't come yet, the grace hasn't either. After all, you wouldn't get stitches for a wound that hasn't yet happened. I'm not saying that grace makes this easy; God, at times it is unendurable. It's a double-edged sword; the pain that brings the grace cuts so deep. But it eventually lessens while the newfound strength stays. So maybe grace cuts even deeper.

Last night I was decadent with my time. I spent four whole hours reading a novel about a small-town florist. It was lovely, just a little story to get lost in, and no babies died at all in the narrative. What really stood out to me—what kept me turning pages—is, believe it or not, discovering how flowers bloom. Listen: It starts with instability (which sounds a lot like something is wrong). Certain cells become longer than others— so much so that I wonder if the flower feels like it's in crisis. (If the flower is smart, at this point it goes to therapy.) Then, there's rapid growth, which causes such strain on the soft tissues that, eventually, they bend. It looks like breaking, but scientists call it maturity.

We call it blooming.

Every blooming flower we see has gone through a lot. The petals are so heavily strained that they finally break. They unfurl, letting the world see what's inside. It's worth repeating because it's powerful: The very thing that breaks a flower is what causes it to bloom.

And somehow, I find a connection between this final photo of me—looking pleasant in front of the mirror, not realizing I am pregnant with a baby who has already flown—and the story of how flowers break in order to bloom.

★ ★ ★

I meet with my therapist in an old building that has spiral wooden stairs. I climb the stairs quickly, not minding the lack of central AC or an elevator, not really minding anything at all. I like even being in proximity to her office. I always come early with a book and savor my time reading outside her door. There is a fan next to me, but I don't position it towards me, because it feels weird to be caught like that. Hair blowing wildly at the mercy of a jet stream is not the way adults greet each other. My therapist would say hi, and my return greeting would be in that robot voice every kid joyfully discovers when they first speak right into the fan.

I think I'll just stay hot. It's better than the three months of indoor frigid air that large buildings in summertime sentence us to. I imagine the thermostat in these buildings with the setting: FROZEN TUNDRA. I don't know why they see us in our tanks and shorts and think this setting is a good idea, but I don't understand a lot of things. Because of this setting, and despite it being ninety degrees outside, I find myself reaching for a cardigan every time I leave home in the summer.

My therapist and I talk about my belief in the goodness of God and how I'm reconciling it with Luca's death. I understand I'm not the only one hurting. I understand that life is not fair and that not everything that happens is a direct result of God's doing. I also understand that the bad is very bad, but man, the good is so wonderful. I'm aware of the goodness, and I'm grateful that not only is it still here, but that I can see it. Those two are different, and I'm grateful for both. I think about how someday I'll say that God is good because he healed my broken heart. It's not the healing I wanted, but it's the kind of beauty the world both relates to and needs (myself included). I try to explain this to her, and she seems to understand. She asks how TJ and I are doing.

"Oh, well, I kind of went crazy and popped off on him when he suggested Charlee might be eating too much sugar," I say, remembering.

"Have I told you that grief and anxiety and irritability all intersect?" she asks.

"I don't think so," I answer, but just her saying it is a mirror in front of me, and I exhale seeing it. It's a beautiful thing to go somewhere and hear that the feelings at war within me are not only normal but are also *not* here to stay.

★ ★ ★

"Can I stick my nose in the chocolate icing, Mama?" This is the fifth time she's asked; when I tell her no, she cries.

I know, baby. It's hard to not get what you want. And even harder when what you want changes from icing on your nose to something deeper—something that stems from the anchor in your soul called love. It's hard when we don't get the good things we want. Hard when others say, *Look how good God is: He gave me this beautiful baby.* And you can't help but think, *Look how good God is: He gave me a fresh grave.*

And all the work is hard. The anxiety and grief and mourning and answering people day after day when they ask how you're doing, but the truth is you're doing the same. Perhaps, instead of how, they could ask what you're doing, and then your answers could show progress. Like, *I'm getting Charlee ready for the pool!* And if they ask what you're doing again thirty minutes later, your answer is shiny and brand new: *I am at the pool with Charlee!* And they will be so impressed with your progress in life. There is a lyric in a children's song I love by Sweet Honey in the Rock that goes—*O my goodness, look at me: growing up positively.* This line could be my anthem as I continue to do things that mark progress. I didn't have sunscreen on ten minutes ago, but now look who's sporting that thick white chalky glow!

It reminds me of when I moved back into my parents' basement. I was going through a divorce and didn't have a job, and all my friends were, as the Internet likes to say, *literal goals* and *crushing life,* while I was actually *being crushed* by life.

I'd read the newspaper every morning. My parents still get a hard copy, and I love them for that. I'd eat cereal, skimming the pages, and my pop would walk into the kitchen and say, "What's new, Jess?" He asked every day. It was a part of a morning ritual that I grew to dread. Finally, one morning, I was done.

"What's new, Jess?"

"Absolutely nothing, Pop," I said, laying the paper down calmly next to my cereal bowl. "I'm still living in your basement. Still going through a divorce. Still not working. And I'm still crying myself to sleep most nights. I'd love it if things had changed between yesterday and today, but, depressingly, they have not," I concluded, emphasizing it by shoveling a giant spoonful of Raisin Bran Crunch into my mouth.

There has been a lot that is new since then, thankfully, and now we joke about that morning. But my pop never asked me that question again, God bless him.

* * *

There are 86,400 seconds in a day. I didn't even google that. I used a calculator. Which is something I didn't do my entire college career (thanks, art school). But that feels like more seconds than I have energy to hope. I feel good for several of them—like hundreds and hundreds, even—but 86,400? How can anyone keep up with all this time?

Now, I know, I *know*, one second at a time. I tell people these vague self-help-ish sorts of things myself. And actually, that is the thing to do. Stay present, and you'll find you can put one foot in front of the other. You'll eventually be on top of the mountain you swore you couldn't climb when you first saw it looming. I mostly have great faith in our ability to get there, in God's ability to help us get there. Because even the painful moments are just that: Moments. They pass like every other moment we've ever experienced. Sunday still folds into Monday, and Charlee and I go to the pool like every other mother-and-daughter team. Would you believe me if I say we go happily? Because we do. But you'd never guess there's also this inner monologue constantly telling the world that my baby died. I just don't usually say it out loud. I say *Thank you!* and *The weather is lovely, isn't it?* And *Charlee, baby, you must hold Mama's hand right now.* But I'm thinking it all the time. *My baby died, my son died, he's dead.* And I quietly listen in wonder while TJ tells me how awesome it is to live with his best friend.

Even though your best friend's baby just died? I think. But I know the answer. He says it by the way he keeps living life, our precious life, like it's worth doing. And I agree—it is.

But that doesn't mean it's easy. All those seconds every day are daunting. Such a large canvas that I'm trying to fill with hope, and I'm tired. And scared. Sometimes I wonder if sadness will become so familiar, that it will be the place I come home to. Like the time my ex and I moved from our first apartment to a townhouse. After his shift would end, he'd automatically drive back to where we used to live. We'd laugh about it, but sometimes what's familiar has a way of pulling you back again and again. And right now, this scares me. Right now, sadness is so familiar.

But in all the ways a human can communicate with another (and we've invented many; God forbid we look at one another and talk), I keep hearing the same thing: *I'm praying for you. I'm thinking about you. I care.* And that fills the seconds with good things, too. It helps. I'm alone, but I'm also definitely not alone, somehow, both at once. What a strange, hard, terrible, and sometimes wonderful place to be.

★ ★ ★

I'm at the pool, thinking about how I was so looking forward to having a summer baby. Not to have to wrap myself, my newborn, and my very particular, incredibly clothes-averse toddler in every available layer of warmth before exiting for the day. Not being worried that my baby is cold. Not to have to bundle him up while walking our Labrador in the middle of a blizzard also sounds nice. "Just the tip of the nose or a fingertip isn't a true reading," our pediatrician had assured us about days-old Charlee, who was born in a New England December. "If the middle of her belly is cold, THEN you can worry." It's hard to feel the middle of a belly, though, when your baby is wrapped in a thousand things for the Boston winter.

When Charlee was only weeks old, we were slammed with the three blizzards in a row. TJ was sleeping at the radio station to ensure he'd be at work in the morning. Our dog Luna had to go out, so I thought about the Eskimo women with their babies and pretended to be one while I bundled up myself and brand-new Charlee and stepped out into a blizzard. Eventually the Eskimo women inspiration wore off, and I found a lady in my building named Ping who would take Luna out for twenty bucks. Ping showed up, tiny and smiling, with a competent knock at the door. I wondered briefly if Luna weighed more than her before handing over the leash and a very cabin-fevered dog. They were gone for ten minutes, tops, before coming back covered in snow. "She did her business," Ping told me. I could've hugged her. It ended up costing two dollars a minute, but I would've given her double.

I don't know why I'm thinking about those blizzards during the early, overwhelming days of parenting while I stare at the pool in 80+ degree weather. I guess I was thinking about how nice it would have been to have a summer baby (*nice* isn't really the word). What I hadn't thought much about was the postpartum body in a bathing suit combination with no baby to show for it. Under the circumstances, though, my feelings about the shape of my body pale significantly compared to the shape of my heart.

Also, God bless the nearby elderly lady happily sunning herself in an eye patch and bathing suit. One lounge chair over from me, she has the kind of no-judgment vibe that fitness gyms over-promise and under-deliver and, so, sure, I'll take my cue from her.

⋆ ⋆ ⋆

I'm sitting in the car outside the grocery store with a list of things I need to buy that I'm doing a great job ignoring. It's raining so hard, like the sky is angry. I get it. The rain is pounding down on all of us staying dry in our cars; the harder it hits, the harder we hide from it. Eventually I will go in and buy bananas and milk and almond butter—all the necessary things that fill our pantries but not our hearts—but for right now, I will listen to the inescapable sound of another part of life I cannot control. That sounds bitter, but I don't think I am bitter. My therapist tells me I'm not. She even gives me permission to be unapologetically angry.

Being angry feels horrible to me, and I work hard at not being anything horrible. I also apologize easily. If you bump into my elbow on the street, *I* will say sorry. But my therapist says that no, simply feeling anger is not something to apologize for, that it can be entirely appropriate. I guess if one must be something, "appropriate" isn't too bad. Not that exciting, either—I mean, nobody ever says "I just met the dreamiest guy. His name is

Francis, and he's just so...appropriate." (I guess not many people say they just met the dreamiest guy whose name is Francis, period. My apologies to all the sexy guys named Francis. Not that you need it, but you have my permission to go ahead and prove me wrong.)

Grief is a ninja hiding behind corners. You never know quite when you'll turn a new one and find him again. Grief is also your neighbor's annoying cat who sits on your lap demanding attention when all you want is to borrow some milk. And you're allergic to cats. But you look back someday and see that the ninja and that dumb cat were part of this sneaky movement to eventually bring you peace. The ninja had to be confronted; the cat had to be petted. (Pet? Petted? Two English majors for parents, and apparently that's not enough to know how to write about petting a metaphoric cat.) In doing things like this more times than you ever wanted to, there's a measure of healing. In the meantime, I'll be having breakdowns in front of my dog walker, but otherwise blend in with the world as I run through the downpour to buy groceries.

Chapter 35

His Due Date
(three weeks after)

"Tell me how you think his due date will feel," my therapist asks me. "Hard," I say, "but all the days are. Like, I'll get through it. I'll take Charlee to the park or pool, and she'll drink enough milk throughout the day to make me wonder if I should let her have that much. It'll be Monday, and I'll be busy."

Which leads me to today, his due date. I never believed he'd actually arrive on June nineteenth. I always thought he'd come early. And I was right; he just didn't stay. I get an email from MGH today, notifying me of a new test result. I don't remember any recent tests, so, curious, I open it. I see the date—Luca's actual delivery—and then the words "fetal demise." There are more words, but it is all in very clinical terms that seem to include zero consideration of the fact that this is my son we're talking about.

It reminds me of how a mechanic might give a client the run down on their totaled car. The client might think it's a real bummer, but then he will go buy another car and maybe even a pizza to celebrate his new wheels. But this isn't a car, and there is only one. And this is one test result of which I am already aware. His unused clothes are still in an ugly plastic bin in my bedroom. I don't know what to do with them.

I'm going to therapy. My family keeps coming back, taking turns and trading places. Like the changing of the guard, only the prison is grief and rather than locking me inside, they're desperately trying to find any key to get me out.

My point is, I know what happened. It's changed everything. This particular test result is so superfluous, it's ridiculous. I stare at the words on my phone and think how strange it is that this is normal enough to be an email I open and read. It sits in my inbox, right next to a twenty percent off coupon from a makeup company. I think, too, that grief and technical terminology don't intersect well, that MGH has terrible timing, and that I can't wait to mention the irony of it all to my midwife. I will laugh, and in so doing, give her permission to find the humor in it, too.

Look! It's 11 PM. There's just one more hour left of June nineteenth. Tomorrow brings more milk for Charlee and more family to fill our apartment with all the glorious distractions a grieving heart could want. I am making it, one slow second at a time. Also, this really sucks and hurts so much.

Chapter 36

When Someone Else Goes First

(six weeks after)

Last weekend, TJ and I had breakfast with someone who is going through a lot. I won't share details; the story is hers to tell. But I will say that, at times, life asks too much.

Grief is like an ex-boyfriend who knows you too well. He knows all your favorite hiding spots, so even when you want to simply find some peace alone, he shows up. As if to prove that sometimes life is less about what you want and more about what just painfully is. Grief invites himself in close. He reminds you of what was, incessantly talks about what should have been, and you eventually stop trying to shut him up because you agree. *That is what should have been,* you think.

"Like, now I feel pretty okay," I tell my friend, sitting in front of a harmless pancake in the bright light of day. "But last night I didn't know what to do with myself. I felt so bad."

"Me too," she said.

Two small words—but man, what a startling gift to give someone. There aren't a lot of people who can say those words to me right now. This is okay. No, this is good. While I don't want this for anyone, of course, most of our lives are spent looking for a group of people who can say "me too."

First, it's family. *Who lives in the geodesic dome house in rural Pennsylvania?* And the other six of us raise our hands, say, "Me too." Then, *Who takes ballet like it's your job, even though you're only twelve?* I raise my hand, and my two best friends say, "Me too!"

But then it gets harder. *Whose heart shattered when their husband left?* I raise my hand, and I find less people to say, "Me too." But there's one, and we meet at the Cheesecake Factory and tell each other our stories over pieces of cheesecake we can't finish.

And now, God, this: *Who lost a child?*

I raise my hand, and there's my husband with his hand up, too.

But there are others, too. They tell me quietly on the Internet. They tell me in church, and I hold my breath, because I never knew. They email me and press send on the story that broke their heart. I'm so sorry to see all the people who say, "me too." I'm so sorry, but I guess there's something that lends strength and courage, even in impossible places, when you're not the only one.

* * *

"I hope you don't mind the random roll of toilet paper," my therapist says the first time I meet her. She's holding it high in one hand, à la Lady Liberty with her iconic torch, saying, "I ran out of tissues."

I look at the toilet paper and the way she speaks through a smile, a genuine one, nothing like the kind of tight-lipped smile the host of a posh South End restaurant wears while saying, "The wait is currently 2.5 hours, do you want to leave your name?" (So, we'll be seated right when we're due home to relieve the babysitter, how perfect.) I take in the big curly hair I've only ever dreamt of having myself and once again eye that single roll of toilet paper on my new therapist's desk.

I think we're a fit, I decide.

She tells me she isn't worried about me. Not like the kind of worry you have for someone you're not sure is going to pull through, at least. She says it looks like I've been showering (a few times, actually). She says she is reassured that I left my apartment alone (sure did), and that I'm functioning (takes bow).

Apparently, all of that bodes well. And in all seriousness, I like so very much that I like her so very much. It's also reassuring to hear from a professional that you're doing okay, when it's so hard to tell yourself. Still, it's weird to be considered doing okay when you're not. You've never been less okay than now, actually.

"Are you feeling okay today?" TJ asks me.

"No," I say as I pull the blankets around me even tighter, as I pull my sadness around me tighter.

"Are you feeling better than you were yesterday?" he asks, gentler this time, like your mom tried to be when it came to the delicate but necessary work of waking you up each morning for school.

He moves in closer, maneuvering the blankets so they are pulled tight over both our bodies now.

I shake my head a definitive no.

"What about two weeks ago? Are you feeling a little better now than two weeks ago?"

I can feel him wanting me to be better, because he deeply loves me. I can feel myself wanting to give him everything. But I can't give him that. Not yet. Not never, I hope, but not yet.

"I'm just more used to it now than I was two weeks ago, I think," I finally say.

He holds me, and I let my body relax into his. I let my grief lean hard into him. And I'm grateful for him, for us.

Chapter 37

My Not-So-Terrible Terrible Birthday
(two weeks after)

For the record, Charlee picked out the following birthday gifts for me: a Peppa Pig robe, Peppa Pig towel, new Play-Doh, and a Paw Patrol doll. She wrapped them with TJ, unwrapped them with me, then promptly asked if she could borrow them all.

"Would you just like to have them, Charlee?" I ask.

"No, just borrow them, Mama."

Sure, baby, girl. Sure.

People call to wish me a happy birthday over the phone; I don't pick up. The thought of having to respond with some sort of happiness in my voice is exhausting, and I am not up for it. People text, too, and this is much safer. I can text back an emoji heart or a "thank you" and leave it at that. I can cry while texting, and nobody knows the difference.

A neighbor asks me how I'm doing, and I reply with a blank stare. They quickly say, "I mean, other than that..." But there isn't anything other than that. It's consuming. Yes, sometimes I can talk about it calmly and can even enjoy sipping Pellegrino across from TJ while he drinks black coffee, but then I remember that on my plate in front of me is a thousand pounds of grief. I can push that plate away again and again, but over time, I am hungry for life. This is the only plate that is mine, and it doesn't matter how many people around me are happily eating the best life has to offer. This is my plate.

It's like when I was a kid, deciding I'm full the second my mom puts tuna fish casserole in front of me. After moving it around my plate, I get up to play but come back an hour later hungry, hoping for a snack. But she pulls out the same plate of tuna fish casserole and says if you're hungry, this is what's available. No tasty snacks, nothing really palatable, just the same awful meal I pushed away the last time I was here.

I take a small bite and chew and it goes down like cement. I hate how it makes everything heavy and all my steps slow and how even my hard-working lungs just aren't expanding as much. But the only way all this grief piled up in front of me will get eaten is if I open my mouth and take it in. So I do. It's the bitter herb that heals us. I hate it and I need it. And look, it's on my plate no matter what. It is here until it's not, and I have no idea when that will be, but it's not today.

Today I felt like breathing and walking and I smiled at a lot of strangers. I felt brave. Then I got home and looked up where the heck you even buy gravestones and felt pretty terrible. Do you know Etsy sells them? Do you know Etsy sells a ton more pet gravestones than ones for, like, humans? Do you know how weird it is to peruse gravestones and find one that looks okay and not too cheesy so you click on it and consider it only to realize it's for a cat? So then you press the back arrow really fast and think, *I almost got my son a cat gravestone.*

There is a special photographer who I'd excitedly booked for my maternity shoot. I had screenshot all these sacred photos of hers and sent them to TJ with the words, *Can we get her? I mean, look at these photos*! But then she was just one more person we had to tell. One more departure from the life we expected. So, TJ told me on my birthday that he re-booked her. "I know you love her photographs, and I think our family is still worth documenting." And it is. All of it. Our joy and our grief and all the moments in between are worth documenting. Our life today—our togetherness still—is worth documenting. And grieving Luca—this is certainly worth documenting.

★ ★ ★

"I'll take you shopping for new clothes, Jess—anything you want," TJ tells me later that afternoon. So we walk down Newbury Street looking for denim shorts.

"What size are you?" the salesman asks.

"I have no idea—" I answer before I shut my mouth to keep from telling him I just had a baby.

The body is a wonderland, yes, but the postpartum body is a wonderland of change. And I could be wrong, but I doubt John Mayer was referring to the first few weeks after giving birth. Anyway, that's why I don't know my size. *Congratulations!* The salesman would gush. And then he'd recite all the happy questions about the baby's sex and name and birth order, etc. And it would be a parade of ill-fitting and terrible answers, because it's a birth, but also a death. So you see the problem with small talk this presents? And then I'd cry or at least make the conversation intensely awkward with the truth. So I spare him the details and squeeze into a garment with no stretch.

It's hard, but I do hard things every day, so I'm unfazed by that final reluctant button, and bam! They're on. Which means the shorts fit, as far as I'm concerned. We walk out one pair of shorts and a whole swallowed-back story heavier. It's amazing to me how many people I come across who have no idea my baby just died. I smile at cashiers and talk to waiters about how wonderful it is that the sun is shining, and none of them know that I'm merely paying lip service to the art of being normal. It's a fun game, and I'm winning because they don't seem to suspect that I don't care about what they're telling me.

Shopping might sound like it doesn't matter, but this next part matters to me. Let me tell you why. I touch an olive-green tank that says **PEACE** and notice it's trendy and distressed, which is a fancy way of saying it looks beat up. It's the kind of shirt that a dad-like person would see you wearing and quip, "I hope you didn't pay full price for all those holes!" It's ripped; there's no pattern to the holes. They are random, like someone was wearing that tank top while clawing out of prison or climbing a wall full of splinters. All the while displaying this great big, beautiful idea: *Look: I am in hell AND I am at peace. I am hurting AND I am at peace. Life is not perfect AND I am at peace.* That's why there are holes in my shirt and peace in my heart.

I refuse to live in a world where you can't have both. I know pain is unavoidable; I hate it, but here it is, no respecter of persons—but peace! That's something that happens, so why not in my heart, too? Why not right here and now, when I need it the most? Peace is not something for the lucky few whose lives are coming along beautifully. Peace is for the bruised and broken and gasping-for-air among us; it's the salve that makes the wounds bearable.

Considering how messy life is, peace is a miracle. It's God's way of saying, "I am here. Despite what you see and hear and fear; put your hand over your heart and take a deep breath and remember that I am here."

Peace. I'll wear it on my shirt for a thousand days if it helps me practice it a little better on day one thousand and one. The saleslady probably just thinks I like it; she has no idea I'm hoping it's an oracle. I buy the shirt and walk out of the shop.

Chapter 38

Inside My Head
(three months after)

My therapist is generous; yesterday she gave me 90 minutes. Either I need it or she likes me or both. Afterward, I drive home slowly through the rainy clogged streets of Boston. I don't turn anything on—no radio, no podcasts, no noise other than my head sending my heart notifications. Like my brain is suddenly the tour guide of my life, but instead of pointing out statues of Washington or Paul Revere, it's letting me know when food tastes good and when the dishes are piled up and when it's probably time to shower again. And my heart is like, *Oh, thanks, I hadn't noticed.*

We grew up in a large house, and after my older brothers had moved out, we sometimes lent our extra rooms to people who needed them. One night a friend of a friend stayed over. He was kind and articulate and interesting and he also had no arms. My parents and I talked with him about lots of things— God, and our country, and the differences between New York and Pennsylvania. A few days later, I reminded my pop of that particular guest for some purpose of conversation.

"I'm not sure who you're talking about," my pop said.

Getting very specific, I point out that he was the only guy to ever stay with us who doesn't have arms.

"Oh—wait. Bill from last week?" Pop remembered, and I nodded before he added, "He doesn't have arms? I never noticed."

You could say my pop is either the kind of person who only sees what matters, or the most unobservant person on the planet, or wasn't wearing his contacts that day. Probably all three. I bring up this story because I feel it. I don't care about things that don't matter—I barely see them—and the margin for what does matter is slim. I only want to hear things that are true— and even beyond that, encouraging. I'm not busy, at least not in a conventional way (okay, I have a two-year-old, so I'm totally busy. But I have no deadlines outside our home right now), and I'm also not available. It's a strange, necessary time, this grief. Those who love me check in; I sometimes respond with words and sometimes with a heart emoji. God bless the heart emoji, making room for those of us who are too tired to say more.

Chapter 39

Thanks, That Helps
(two months after)

Someone asks me, "What's the most comforting message you received after Luca died?" But there isn't just one note or meme or thought that helped. It was a combination of factors. It was community, yes. And it was me by myself, writing everything down. It was therapy, and it was faith in God's kind plan for me and my family—which, I would say is the umbrella everything else falls under. I think in grief, in our desperation, we become like the gang who finally meets the Wizard of Oz. We want him to say something that makes it—makes us—better. Say that I am what I'm not, that life isn't what it is. Instead, he says what has been there all along.

Grief does this, too. It changes nothing outwardly in the sense that people who see us with a limp know something is wrong. But emotionally, on the inside, it emphasizes what is. Every single moment of what so terribly is. And what so tenderly is.

My divorce was a wildly polarizing time, because I'd never felt so hurt before and, at the same time, had never felt so loved. I'd been rejected and abandoned by the man who'd married me—and yet, family and friends and even acquaintances in my community stepped up to show me I was loved. People would drop off food and money and even a whole bag of skin-care products "to make sure I don't forget to still take the time to care for myself right now." Some of these people were little more than strangers. But they made it hard for me to believe the message my ex-husband's actions conveyed—because clearly, I was loved. Clearly, I was worthy of love. I've learned that the point of community isn't simply to celebrate birthdays or holiday parties. We also need community so that we are not alone when we suffer.

We need others to remind us of who we are, despite how we feel. We need to let others close to us so that we have their care to pull us back from the urge to simply sink into unrelenting despair. Or, as Angelica sings in Hamilton's perfect song chronicling grief, *It's Quiet Uptown*: "It feels easier to just swim down ..." And it is. If not for the care of others reminding me I could also continue to swim, to fight for breath, that my life was and is worth it, I am not sure where I'd be today.

* * *

Grief reinforces what's inside us the way scalding water turns dry leaves into tea. Grief is hot water. Grief is the Wizard of Oz igniting what is buried in our hearts to meet the world. I don't want grief. But I think—or rather, I wonder—if grief is what love leaves us. Maybe it's a terrible gift that I will try to give back every time. But maybe life without grief would be life without love. So maybe grief is a gift. And I am left trying to figure this out.

When my pop comes to Boston after Luca dies, he says something simple and profound. My pop is a pastor, but he doesn't pretend that faith and hope aren't often grown in a garden of pain and desolation, which is where we are now. He doesn't pretend that mystery is a happy surprise party. Surprises aren't always good. Sometimes it's your marriage ending, your child dying, your life not being what you dreamt. Yet somehow mystery is not a weed that chokes out faith. Faith is one of the most beautiful things I've seen in this life—and without mystery, there would be no need for it.

My pop talks with me and TJ. We are sad, and we have questions. We will be okay, and we have questions. My pop has questions, too. He is also sad and will be okay. He is the Great Wizard of Oz, telling me what has been here all along. Over bagels, he looks at me and says, "You're still you. You're still Jess." He says this with relief in his voice. Like he was wondering if I could still be me after Luca has died. But seeing me face to face has assured him. I am not so sure. I have always liked being me. But now I don't know if it's possible for my son to be dead *and* for me to be me.

But TJ keeps bringing me back from drowning in my questions. He loves me—even in—especially in—grief. At night in bed, he pulls me towards him; his hands and his words reaching toward me with enough confidence to make me believe in our closeness, in our ability to do anything. Even grieve our baby and live well. He still makes me laugh. He does it in our bedroom, next to the bin of Luca's clothes I don't know what to do with yet. He makes me laugh here and now. It's a miracle, and I'm on my knees believing because of it.

And my pop calls me back to myself at lunch. "You're still you, still Jess," he says with a note of surprise in his voice.

★ ★ ★

I'm sitting at a coffee shop across from TJ. We're drinking tea and writing, respectively. He keeps a journal with an actual pen and paper. It's timeless and lovely, but I don't have the patience for it, myself. I write on a phone or a computer—something with a delete button handy, because I edit so much.

This reminds me of the first email I ever wrote to him—the one time I didn't edit enough. He interviewed me at his previous radio station after a stranger uploaded a YouTube video of me performing on the New York City subway and it went viral. I left TJ's building wondering if I'd ever see him again, and by the next day, I realized I'd like to see him again. So, I wrote him an entirely-too-long email, essentially asking him to be my friend. I went on to specifically say, "just friends, though," because "I've had a rough time already and am not looking for a relationship."

Dear people, I write this simple ask in way too many words that equal, like, multiple paragraphs of an email. Then I hit send before I can chicken out (Is this offensive to chickens? Will chickens not buy my book? Not even grieving chickens?). TJ got that email, read all those words and protestations, and immediately decided, "She likes me." This still annoys me, because I guess I did. But I honestly thought I just wanted him as my friend. I'd never met anyone so kind, funny, and interesting before, and who doesn't want the most kind, interesting, and funny human as their friend? (Or their husband.)

I'm so glad we became friends, so glad he became my boyfriend, so glad he's my husband. He's all three of those things to me still, and it's daily medicine for my soul, my heart, my brain, even the backs of my knees feel better with him close.

* * *

"I spoke with your husband for five minutes on the phone—just about insurance—but I could hear it," my therapist says. "The way he loves you, Jess. I didn't even know you yet, but it warmed my heart to hear how willing he is to do whatever he can to make sure you get the help you need right now."

I nod. "I know," I say simply, smiling, despite the reason I am in therapy. Despite what feels like everything. TJ is proof that God cares about me and that the grief I've known and know now is not the whole story.

* * *

I step into our elevator with Luna on her leash. A woman next to us looks vaguely familiar. A neighbor, but I don't know her name or her story.

"How is your baby?" she asks.

I stare and blink. I'm not sure who she's talking about. Is she talking about the baby who was so recently in my belly? Does she know about Luca?

"Excuse me?" I finally say.

"How's your baby?" she asks again, not helping.

Seeing my confusion, she clarifies,

"Don't you have a daughter?"

I exhale, relieved. This is an easy question to answer. "Yes! Yes, I do. And she's doing great!" I reply over my shoulder as I exit the elevator. I walk the familiar path from the elevator to home. I think about how I have two children. I think about how there's nothing normal about getting to bring one baby home and not the other. I take a deep breath, open the door, and drop to my knees so Charlee can almost knock me over with the force of her hug.

* * *

I step into the elevator again, this time with groceries. Three men and a woman with a daughter a few years older than Charlee join me. Our kids have played at the same park before, but otherwise, we are strangers. I figure she remembers how pregnant I was, so she'll ask if I had my baby. I feel sorry for the crowd, dreading the impending awkward conversation.

"Can I hug you?" she asks quietly, empathy in her voice.

I set my groceries down, confused.

"I figured out about two weeks ago that TJ is your husband. I listen to his radio show. I...I... know what happened, and I'm so very sorry."

Now we are hugging. The rest of the people in the elevator are forgotten; I am hugging this woman and warmed by her kindness. And I know it sounds strange, but it's comforting. There is grace in the fact that she already knows. I won't use the word easy about any part of my life right now, but I will say that this makes things easier. And I will take easier. She tells me her unit number, her name, and her daughter's name so we can make plans for Charlee to play with her. "We've been thinking about you guys so much," she finally says, "Every day."

It is not the interaction I was expecting; it is so much better. That happens sometimes. Life is sometimes better than we expect or deserve.

* * *

"I may never do anything ever again," I tell TJ, not for the first time.

"That's okay," he says, "But I don't think that's true."

"Well. I may never hang out with anyone ever again."

"That's okay, too," he repeats himself, "but I don't think you'll feel this way forever."

"Maybe I will, though."

"Maybe you will."

"And that's okay? If I do?"

"That's okay if you do."

Part of it is that people invite me to do something, and I just wonder if they even know who they're inviting. Like, it's not just me anymore. It's me and all my grief. And my grief is invasive, somehow filling whatever space it's in. It doesn't matter if we're in a closet or a stadium; my sadness occupies the space along with me, leaving no room for anything else.

When I moved back home in my twenties and was going through a different kind of grief with my divorce, my parents' dogs had puppies. I'd sneak one pup out of the whelping box and hold it, thinking, *This is therapy.* One by one, the puppies went to other homes, until there was just one left. We named her Willow. She was inseparable from her mother, Arwen. For weeks, they discovered spring together—Willow the pup, for the first time ever, and Arwen for the first time as a mother.

Then finally, someone came to take Willow home. I'll never forget Arwen in the following hours. She ran from room to room in our house, crying, looking for her puppy. The sounds she made came from some deep, visceral place—one that I recognize now. She didn't want to fetch or swim or eat or laze in the sun with my parents' other dog Strider. She was desperate and so, so sad—trying to make right a world that had suddenly gone terribly wrong. Her baby should be with her. And now everything she has ever been was replaced by this one thing: Grief—a desperate sadness because her baby is gone. She wasn't this way forever, but she was this way until she wasn't.

Chapter 40

Life Goes On
(four months after)

"Do you think we'll ever even fight again?" I ask TJ the day we get home from the hospital. We laugh and agree that probably-maybe-definitely we'll fight again. But in the days right after Luca's death, all of life equals the fragility of our baby in my belly, who for just shy of nine months was well, and then in a moment was gone. All of life is too weighty, too fleeting, too hard and uphill to spend any time or energy fighting. But then you start being a little bit normal again. You don't want to, really; but you have to. Time demands it. The cold rainy Thursdays demand it. You're stuck in traffic, your daughter is crying, you're hungry, and you're just so profoundly sad. So you're short with each other. You forget that this is a hard climb for him, too, and that the thing you're most honored to do in life is to make his journey a little easier, a little more grace filled, a little lighter, and a lot less alone.

Evening always comes, keeps coming back, again and again. And when the precious girl you get to raise is finally asleep, you are sitting together on the couch with a thousand hopes and fears between you. The fears are paralyzing, and there's an ugly voice trying to convince you the fears are the facts after all.

But here's the best part: TJ, my husband, chooses hope. Sometimes it's a harder choice than others. Sometimes it takes many moments of raw struggle, but, lately, he always lands on hope. He does it with the fears I've nursed through the night about our daughter; and through the silent-as-death first moments with Luca in our arms, he chose to hold onto hope then, too. Maybe it's because he senses my fear. It's like when you're with someone who's super afraid of the noise you both hear in the dark, you must be the brave one, whether you want to or not. The role of Super Afraid Human is already taken, so you jump into what's available, grab the flashlight, and pretend to be Super Confident Human while you walk into the dark.

It doesn't always make sense, but I'm not in it for the sense. TJ's hope in the God we trust and the life He's given us coaxes my soul to join him there, too. Even on the cold and rainy Thursdays. Even with a broken heart, TJ reminds me that something must still be working, because look, there it is: my own little wick that can't help but join his beautiful flame. It can't help but be bright, too, standing so close to his fire.

Chapter 41

Small Fumbling Steps
(three months after)

So many little things pile up and take your heart places. I open my calendar to a highlighted date.

Luca's due date. *Oh God*. I shut my phone and busy myself with ordinary tasks that don't hurt me, like cleaning. Give me a job that I can accomplish in one hour. Great. So wonderfully definitive. So unlike grief. That task is daunting. Existing in two universes is tiring work. I'm saying hello to people, talking about mundane things and reminding Charlee to wash her hands. I'm also in our bed, quietly telling TJ that I can't believe our baby died. When he suggests a restaurant, I tell him the last time we were there I was pregnant. I go through our stored clothes and see the matching outfits I bought Charlee and Luca. I tell myself I'll be okay and don't really believe it. At least cleaning is satisfying and finite. I know what to expect.

After getting my wisdom teeth out, there were complications that landed me in the hospital for emergency surgery. Afterward, I could barely open my mouth, so the surgeon told me to stretch my jaw.

"For how long?" I wanted to know.

"For as long as you can stand it."

"How many times a day?" I asked.

"As many times as you can stand it."

I was trained as a dancer, so I don't mind hard work. But endless and immeasurable hard work is a different story. The amount of work I needed to do to get my mouth around a sandwich again felt infinite. *Do everything all the time (Oh, just that?). Oh, and don't ever stop—that is, if you want to get better.* This is what grieving feels like. And nobody can tell me when I'll feel better. What they can tell me is to feel what I feel.

How many times?

As many times as you can handle.

For how long?

For as long as you can handle.

This is why grieving people are so tired. There is so much constant invisible work we are doing.

This is also why, strangely, I love washing dishes. In the length of one Peppa Pig episode, those dishes end up clean. The cause starts with me, and the effect is clean dishes. That feels safer than when the cause is something I can't control, and the effect is me silently crying during a massage because I'm terrified that the therapist might ask me about the baby I just had. But cleaning gives me no anxiety. I see the progress, it is measurable, and that's encouraging.

Perhaps I will start a cleaning business and be the most fulfilled person you know. Perhaps the people we know whose homes are spotlessly clean are doing it for more than just appearances. And I don't know, perhaps I should clean my own apartment, like, a lot more.

* * *

I don't think my therapist even expects me to mention it, but she asks how me and TJ are doing, and I say, "Great. We're having really great sex."

"You're intimate? Already?" she asks with surprise in her voice. Already? It's been over two months now. Does that warrant the word 'already?' I spent so many years not having sex. And I don't regret those years—I chose them consciously. They number all the years I've been on this earth unmarried. So now that I can have sex with a husband who loves me as well as TJ does, I want to do it. Even now. Even after our baby has died. I want to be as close to TJ as I can be in as many ways as that is achieved.

We take long rambling walks past the same stretch of the Charles River every day. We hold hands and talk honestly, and I tell him again how sad I am. I constantly look for new words to explain it. I tell him who has made me feel awful and who has said the wrong thing today. I tell him who has made me feel seen and loved and he listens and says, "That's wonderful, Jess."

We hug a lot. Growing up, and in a lot of settings still, hugs mostly feel like things to be endured before you get to do something you actually want to do—like talk or eat appetizers or just sit and listen to music. But hugging TJ is a place where my grief can sit down and rest. My body is no longer on lookout duty. My mind climbs down from its vantage point, scanning for the possible conversations or situations that will make me hurt even more; always on guard for what to avoid. When I hug TJ, I am just all in one place, doing one thing. Being here, present, feeling held by someone who loves me well. Anyway, all that to say—I don't want to go to birthday parties, but I do want to have sex with TJ. (I definitely don't want to have sex with TJ at a birthday party, just for the record.)

I nod and my therapist says, "That's WONDERFUL!" She says it with caps locks and exclamation points and everything. Like what I say to Charlee when she tells me she's decided to like chicken. A BIG! DEAL! RESPONSE! is warranted when my two-year-old decides to cautiously try life on the other side of macaroni and cheese.

We run out of time, because that hour every week when I'm in her office is always a time warp. I sit down and tell her all the reasons why life is painful and hilarious and wonderful and how badly my heart hurts today, and before I can even take a second breath, she looks at the clock and tells me we need to wrap it up.

I think I will start doing that when I meet my friends for dinner. That way I can always just come back home after an hour. That doesn't sound too daunting. One can do almost anything for an hour. And I will strictly adhere to it. Even when they mention how good it is that it's Friday, or that they got a promotion, or that their dog can drive a car, I will tell them that's wonderful! But that it's time, so I will see them next week, and then I'll ask the waiter if I can have the bread sticks to go. He will say yes, and I will once again say that's wonderful! Then I will go home and spend my night googling all the things I'm scared of.

"Why are you so tired, Jess?" people will ask. "Is it grief? Is it having a toddler who wakes up at 5:15 AM?"

"It's Google," I will say.

* * *

When TJ and I are close, it's unlike anything else. The whole world becomes small and safe, just he and I, and finally my mind calls back all its wandering thoughts to be here, to notice right now. All the possibilities of what else could go wrong—the shadow in which I live these days—are eclipsed by what is right.

The two of us, close.

Like dreamy-grief-induced close.

Like grabbing-onto-one-tiny-lifeboat-big-enough-for-each-other-in-a-storm close.

It is good, purely good, and I am grateful.

While we lay next to each other, hearts full and bodies having been quieted, I cry a little bit. Grief invades every space that I inhabit, even this one. I miss the boy we made together. And it feels like different shades of the same thing—missing Luca, loving Luca, grieving Luca, making Luca. All of this, together. All of this is love, and it's a deep well I haven't been able to tap the bottom of yet. Not even with my foot when I go limp and let the air out of my body and decide sinking isn't so bad when I feel so bad.

This love is the best gift I've ever received, the one I hold with trembling hands. More than ever before, closeness with TJ makes sense at a time when a lot does not. On our walks, we check in with each other. I cry and ask if I will always hurt like this. Our words convey our emotions that mingle in the air. They hang and shimmer in the space between us and we see each other. It is unbelievable, really, to see each other. I cannot see the future so well anymore. But it helps to see TJ. It helps to see him in my tomorrow, too. It gives me an escape from the terrifying thought that my grief alone is waiting for me in the future. TJ is waiting, too. Our closeness introduces another player to my story, my heart; it's something other than suffering. It is healing for me to embody this moment, right now, with one other person who sees me—my pain and brokenness and grief—and finds me worthy of all his attention. And I can't think of much that the broken need other than healing. The truth is that life is not ever all one thing. This is disappointing when we are mostly happy, but this is a lifeline when we are grieving.

★ ★ ★

The idea of complicated grief scares me. I see it in the stories written by mothers who lost their babies, too. "I am fascinated by their stories," I tell my therapist. "I am compelled to read them, actually—it's almost like I don't have a choice." For each one I pick up, I have to get to the end. I have to find out if they end up okay eventually. I silently beg these women to find peace and joy again. I root for them so hard, probably selfishly, because in doing so I am rooting for myself. If they get better, then I will, too, I tell myself.

"But their grief ..." I search for the right words to tell my therapist, "... it's consuming. They are changed forever. And I know that I, too, am changed forever—but I am determined that it will not be for the worse. Right? I mean, can't that be my story?"

She smiles and nods. "You've said it so many times, Jess. These women's stories are not yours. And there is a difference between complicated grief and the grief you are experiencing. Complicated grief often makes a person completely unable to function. That's not you. You are mothering Charlee. You are doing things, leaving home. I am not worried about you,

Jess, the way I would worry about someone showing signs of complicated grief. You are not okay now, but I am confident you will get to a place where you are."

I love this diagnosis. I will be okay. I think about tattooing it on my body, but there is not a single spot on my body I look at enough to match the times I need to read this. I decide to tattoo it in my mind, so I can read it the moment my mind is active in the morning and before I drift off to sleep at night. So I can see it repeatedly, until the thoughts that shape a terrifying future aren't quite as loud as this one true ringing statement: I will be okay. I am not okay, but I will be okay. And maybe in time I can read stories by other women who have lost babies and find they are not the mirror I fear they are.

Chapter 42

Tired Little Heart
(five months after)

I remember when I first felt him move. I was lying on the couch. I'd get more specific about which couch, because details matter, but we only have one couch. We live in the city; every square inch of our two-bedroom apartment is prime real estate, and what do you take us for? A two-couch family? I mean, I am flattered, but no. (If you're keeping track, though, along with two couches, I also dream of two ovens. And then I will throw grandiose couch and oven parties, and all of Boston will be so comfortable and so well fed that world peace will happen simply because a whole city ate a great meal and then took a nap.)

I felt Luca move, despite it being too early. It was just the beginning of the second trimester. I didn't tell anyone but TJ, because who wants to be the crazy pregnant lady who feels her baby move before it's normal for a mother to feel it? I didn't know at the time that feeling him move inside me would be the only way I'd ever feel him, earth side. (Talk about depressing, guys. These are the kinds of sentences that really bring down a room, I know. This is technically a book about grief, though, so I really think they have to be included. How about I promise a joke book next?)

We can be aware of death, appropriately sad when it touches our friend's neighbor, discussing it over a beverage with sad faces and hushed tones. But we finish our beverages and remain comforted by the fact that these things don't happen to us. We eventually talk about other things because we're not morbid. We know to avoid the shadow it casts; we certainly don't want to build a home in that shadow, anticipating the time it chooses us.

I mean, I've now experienced the death of a marriage and the death of my first son, and I still don't really think it's coming for me. I'm still surprised this is my story. Humans are strangely resilient, believing against the odds again and again, even when we bear the scars from when the odds came bearing our name. We are a bit insane, I suppose, continuing to do the same thing repeatedly—living our lives—and expecting different, better, results. But please don't change. Stay insane with hope. Stay insane with me. Those are the people I prefer. Those are the people I will invite to my couch and oven parties. And let's write grief books and joke books and cry and laugh together as much as we need to, if you don't mind.

* * *

I find my friends holding back, reticent to tell me what's wrong in their own lives. But I don't want that. There's got to be a balance between an acquaintance droning on about her broken foot, making this the "worst summer ever," and a friend glossing over the very real trials in her life that don't stop for anyone else—not even me, despite my heart being consumed by the loss of my son.

I text friends, "How are you?"

"Fine," they say.

I suspect they're not, though, because who is consistently "fine" for three months now?

"More importantly, how are *you*?" they add, quick to place the spotlight back on me.

But everyone knows how I'm doing, mostly. I'm Jessica, I'm TJ's wife, I write about everything, I live in Boston, I lost my son, I lost myself, I'm grieving. The facts are out there, and I miss my friends. I miss them telling me about themselves. I walk around with alarm bells constantly sounding. They go off when a beautiful pregnant woman walks by, when I glance at Luca's tiny shoes, when a family with a toddler girl and brand-new boy comes into view, when almost anyone wants to talk. They've become a ringing in my ear, and I'm accustomed to the sound. But it's nice to hear something different occasionally, too.

"But how are you REALLY doing?" I try again, trying to convince my friend that I can be sad about my life and care about her. That I can need empathy and give empathy. That the human heart knows no bounds—maybe Luca is teaching me this, too. That we are meant to take and give, meant for both.

"I'm lonely," my friend finally admits.

"We got bad results from the doctor," another tells me.

"I had a miscarriage," says another.

Slowly, my friends are coaxed out from behind the walls they kindly built to protect me. I love them for the walls, and I love them for removing them. And now my prayers are no longer a solo—a single thought—a search for a lifeline big enough for just me. Now they are a choir of hope, looking for the rescue boats to float us all above the angry sea. There is harmony, the sound of many voices and textures blending into one. I'm grateful to have my friends back.

Chapter 43

Normal Things
(four months after)

Tonight we are out to dinner, just TJ and me, and everything feels pretty ordinary. At least, the kind of ordinary it's been since Luca died. The "new normal"—as people like to say. As if it's not an excruciating change; as if they're not just painting a turd and calling it worth keeping.

TJ is eating carefully around the parts of bread that he's touched with his fingers while holding it—like he does. I'm mentioning how hard it is right now when our friends have babies—like I do. You know, ordinary. But then as we drive home, TJ pulls over at the Public Garden. "Do you have to be anywhere tonight?" he asks before we get out.

I smile because I never really have to be anywhere, lately. I'm full-time grieving, mama-ing, and writing. As long as Charlee is taken care of, I could go to the moon, and nobody would wonder why I'm not somewhere on earth at a certain time. It's a weird thing to exist without the boundaries that appointments provide. It's a weird thing that, two weeks ago, I told the boutique fitness studio where I'd worked up until Luca died, that I'm not coming back to teach. I've become the girl who my former clients will remember as the one whose baby died and then just never came back. It's strange, the roles we play in other people's stories.

"What are we doing?" I ask.

"Making a pit stop, so I can focus on you," TJ says.

We walk arm in arm through the garden. We stroll slowly, with no hurry, the way you do when you're dating and realize that sometime in the past six months you've fallen in love. The revelation creates a physical reaction in you—slowing your steps, because you suddenly know that wherever it was you were going is now no longer nearly as important as the person who is going with you.

It's just past the golden hour, when sunlight and dusk mingle, one last dance before the light is gone. It's when our shapes are darker, too, like God himself has drawn us with a fine black pen, the outlines more noticeable as the sun sets.

"I'm going to tell you three things I appreciate about you," TJ says, "for no other reason than that they're true and you need to hear them tonight."

I smile and listen. He tells me beautiful things, and I feel my heart settling, like the deep breath you take when you crawl into bed at the end of the long day, signaling to your body and brain to let go of the never-ending to-do list and finally be at peace. It reminds me of my first baby, my Charlee, when she is tiny and angry at the world whenever I dare put her down. She won't sleep anywhere but in my arms, despite all my attempts to lay her in her crib and steal away, a bathrobe-clad ninja stealthily exiting her room. (All mothers of babies are ninjas. You may be fooled by their milk-stained pajamas and dirty hair, but just try to hear them leave a room with their sleeping baby in it— you will not. They are silent and calculated. And the only thing more dangerous than a ninja is a desperate ninja—which is what sleep-deprived new mothers are.) Inevitably, ninja or not, Charlee wakes and cries, and neither of us can really settle until she is laying on my chest. Until she sighs the kind of contentment that spans all of us, whether we can describe it or not. It's that understanding that you've come home. It's the steady diet of wanting swallowed up by the sudden and startling revelation that you are content. It feels purely good, and after you find it, you'll cry whenever you're anywhere else, newborn or not.

TJ walks me around the garden and I, like baby Charlee, sigh because I'm safe and home. It's good here. It's still hard here, but it's also good here. I never knew that life could be both. But it can, and it is.

Chapter 44

Lily of the Valley
(three months after)

A stranger sends me a gift after Luca's death, a lily of the valley brooch. If you don't know what a brooch is, read a book starring an 18th century heroine; she always wears one. If you haven't got time for the Brontë sisters, just imagine a fancy, grandmotherly pin. "Lily of the valley is May's birth flower," the stranger writes, explaining the brooch. Intrigued, I dig deeper. Its scientific name is *majalis*, meaning "belonging to May." I've stumbled upon clues to my May-baby—the boy I didn't know nearly long enough, the boy I will know forever. I read: *the lily of the valley represents Eve's tears after she and Adam are banned from the Garden of Eden.*

Yes, I see these tears. I understand how it feels to know exactly how life should be and crushed by how different it has turned out. The Garden of Eden exists in my heart; it's my whole family here, together, the first plan. Before the tragedy. *The lily of the valley represents the return to happiness*, I also read. Wait, what? Happiness? How can Eve find happiness after being banished from Eden? In addition to the loss itself, it's like I've been diagnosed with an incurable disease called grief.

"I'm sorry you're going through this pain," the woman who sends the brooch writes. "I can't imagine. Also, it will never change."

I hear variations of this painful conclusion from others, and I cannot help but wonder if maybe my interior could change— even if the exterior does not. Surely God heals. Surely TJ and

Charlee deserve a wife and mama who isn't forever emotionally limping. And the very act of continuing to be alive means change. I've changed all my life—and while growing pains never get easier, they are always necessary. Why would I stop changing now, of all times? How could I possibly stay still in this grief forever? I think the stranger is wrong. No one else gets to say when I stop changing, growing, evolving, healing. They don't get to label this tragedy as simply bad and tell me I'm doomed to live within it, navigating this forever unhappiness, in perpetuity. I carry Luca in my heart always. I dream of a place where death is relegated to the nightmares I had as a child, to boogeymen that don't really exist, to the shadows that look threatening until the sun shows me the truth. Now I know what death really is— but it doesn't mean I have to live within its shadow forever.

I think of Luca's lilies, thriving in the depths of the valley, in the shadow of the mountain. Winking up at the sun. I wonder if life is so big that it can hold both sorrow and a return to happiness—and not just once, but repeatedly, as many times as we need it.

★ ★ ★

I'm not totally sure when I'm supposed to get my period these days. I download an app—something I never used in my previous pregnancies—to track my cycle. There's a whole community you can join, notes to compare with others who are also TTC (trying to conceive), but I stay out of the chat rooms. I'm sure many find it a good support system, but I don't need more chatter. I don't need more stories to scare me. "Would you like me to connect you with my friend/mom/sister/cousin/

dental hygienist who also lost a baby? Would it be helpful to talk with them?" so many people kindly ask me.

I hesitate. I try to ask as tactfully as possible how they're doing now. If they're depressed, a shell of a woman, someone stuck in complicated grief, then I am scared to know them. I'm scared they're an oracle for my own life, and I don't want to look. "Are they whole? Did they fully re-enter their lives? Did they have another child? Did they want to?" I ask for too many details, and if the answer isn't a big collective yes, I say no, I don't want to talk to them. Because these women terrify me. Because there, but for the grace of God, go I.

It's not that I isolate myself. I speak with friends who've had stillbirths (remarkably and tragically, I know three of them). I make close friends with another who's on a similar journey, as she lost her twin boys the day before I lost Luca. We met through Instagram, and we've spent the last few months being honest and unafraid as we write to each other. We find solace in the fact that it's always met with some form of "me too." But I don't want to be haunted by the Internet's worst cases. (I spend enough time googling random medical conditions; I don't need more from my fertility app.) And I don't want to see myself in the stories of people who are never whole again.

So, I stay away from the chat rooms. I use the app halfheartedly, not convinced I need it. Not convinced that acting on the desperation I feel inside and downloading a bunch of apps is the best step forward right now. The truth is these apps won't give me the control I really want.

My dear friend here in Boston who is pregnant and about to have her daughter—we were pregnant at the same time for a while—offers me her ovulation test strips. I've never used these before. I say no, and then I go home and order some on Amazon anyway.

* * *

I take a pregnancy test exactly four weeks after my last period came. My cycle is still not quite regular, so it's hard to anticipate. But it's always been early since I lost Luca, and finally it's not. "Please pick up bananas, yogurt, and a pregnancy test," I text TJ.

"Really?" he asks.

"Really," I say. "We're out of bananas," I add, because I am incorrigible.

That night I take the test, and it's negative. I am surprised by how sad I am; I feel crushed all over again. All the days of doing better don't matter as I stare at the single bold line, a STILL NO to the baby I want so much. I glance at the clock. It's only 8:30 PM, but I'm so heavy with sadness that I just go to bed.

Three days later, my period has still not come. I take another test. I wait the three minutes it takes to predict the next nine months—the next lifetime, really—and see two distinct lines.

I'm pregnant.

Almost four months since Luca died, I am staring at a positive pregnancy test. In that moment, I am not even scared, just happy. Yes, happy. A word I haven't owned in a long time is finally perched inside my heart. I know these fragile little hollow-boned birds fly away easily—I know this painfully well—but while it's here, I cannot stop staring at the wonder it is. I try to be careful; I try not to scare it away. But it's hard to be cautious when I'm so very proud of its gorgeous feathers and the whir of its wings in my ear. I must tell TJ; I must tell him this little bird is back. TJ is hosting his radio show, but I call him anyway.

"Hello?"

"I'm pregnant!" I shout into the phone.

He is quiet, but I hear the joy through his whispered I'm-at-work-on-a-commercial-break tone of voice.

"Really, Jess?"

"Really!"

Oh God, how I love to bring good news. How I love to talk about this little bird that sits inside my heart once again. I am not nearly so afraid of others when my quiet little bird is here.

"I am happy, too!" I think, as I greet a non-grieving world.

"I am pregnant, too!" I think, as I greet what seems like just about every woman between the ages of 18 and 50 in the city of Boston since my Luca died. Since the little bird of happiness flew. Since everything changed, since I began to wonder if I'd ever be happy again. But today, I discover something new. Isn't that just like life? This is why we keep getting up and brushing our teeth and doing all the normal daily routines that frame the epiphanies that distinguish the days from each other. Today, I learn I can be happy again. That my crushing grief and ecstatic happiness can somehow coexist side by side. I suspect this every time Charlee is close, being her two-year-old bundle of huge emotions and the softest skin and adorable baby belly self. Experiencing both her fierce independence and her "Hold me like a baby, Mama!" cry in the early mornings when I gather her from her crib, makes me think of the lily of the valley, the return to happiness. I am happy at these times, yes.

Charlee is always enough. She is always one hundred percent my daughter; making me one hundred percent a mama.

And I am happy with TJ. When he draws me close to him at night, when words are not enough, and he has to tell me he loves me with his hands and his embrace and his mouth covering mine. When he tells me that I bring him so much joy and I think, in that moment, that maybe all that joy is enough for both of us. I am happy then, too.

But now, today, I am happy all by myself. I am happy just staring in wonder at a plastic stick that tells me I get to bring another baby into the world, and that everything that went wrong with Luca now has a chance to go right with this new soul—Charlee and Luca's little sibling.

This baby's due date is days away from Luca's birthday. Talk about redemption; perhaps, unexpectedly, the month of May will bring more than just dread. I am in awe of the way God works, coaxing life from the areas every one of us leaves for dead. I am in awe of the lily of the valley, how it seems to live up to its title: a return to happiness, indeed.

Chapter 45

That Little Bird Flew
(thirteen weeks after)

For one whole week, I have this secret life inside of me. We tell some trusted people: my family, TJ's parents, a few friends. I text my midwife about it, who replies immediately that she has tears in her eyes.

"Me too," I say. "Finally, I can text you with good news!"

It feels incredible. It is a gift not to feel like the one for whom everyone feels sorry. The one people look at and are reminded to count their blessings. Exactly one week later, TJ and I are at dinner—a Mexican restaurant that is so cool that its sign has only a star on it. No name needed; it's the dining equivalent of Cher or Madonna or any of those divas whose last names are unnecessary. It's loud and mostly a bar, and their Mexican street corn is perfect. I am happy that I decided to wear maternity jeans already. My non-maternity jeans are still tight, and I've spent so much of these past four months intensely uncomfortable—in every way a human can experience discomfort—that it's nice to at least wear comfortable pants. (Not as nice as feeling happiness again, but still pretty good.)

I wake at 3:45 AM to a feeling reminiscent of my water breaking in the beginning stages of labor during Charlee's delivery. I think I know what it is. Heart sinking, I run to the bathroom and turn on a light. I'm bleeding. I'm bleeding so much. Not the kind of spotting that makes you hope everything is okay; it's gushing. It's clear that I'm miscarrying this baby. I automatically go about cleaning up. I wash out my underwear because it's my favorite pair—those gray Calvin's—and, ridiculously, I think about how I don't want to ruin them. Otherwise, I am numb. I wonder if I should just pretend I'm having a heavy period and erase it from my mind. I wonder if I can trick myself out of more sadness.

I wake TJ up. "I'm miscarrying," I tell him, his eyes squinting with sleep.

"NO," he says, plaintively. Like enough is enough.

But there's no such thing. Enough actually isn't enough. Too much isn't even enough, it seems. Life isn't like insurance, where you hit a quota and suddenly you no longer have to pay out of pocket. We keep paying dearly for loss. I am bleeding out another baby—this one in a very different way. All the hope this new life brought is now in the toilet.

I don't flush the toilet, for fear of waking Charlee, whose bedroom is separated from us by one sliding door. So I just keep returning to the bathroom throughout the night, filling the bowl with more blood. Once, I peer down and see something floating in the blood. I look closer, and I think I see my baby. I remember that at five weeks, a baby is only the size of a poppy seed. I am relieved that I am not seeing the shape of a baby in front of me; rather, I am seeing the tissue the baby grows inside—would have grown inside, if the baby had stayed. It's terrible to see it this way. I finally flush it down the toilet, crawl back into bed, and lay awake crying.

People tell me to rely on the dawn always breaking, but here in the dark, feeling the deepest darkness, I dread the sun. I think about the small handful of people who I now must break this news to in the morning. *Remember that baby I told you about just last week? The one that everyone called redemption? Yes, well this one died, too.*

Too. Yes, I thought this one was going to work out, too. Yes, it's hard, but of course I will be okay. I always am. Finally, the weight of the bad news I carry becomes unbearable. I can't wait another minute. I pull out my phone in the dark and compose a short email saying that I miscarried. I send one to my family and one to my friends. As the world wakes up, the responses come.

"No words," a lot of them say, "We have no words." This is a problem for me. A wave of anger washes over me. Well, do you mind at least attempting to think of some? I am the one lying in bed, bleeding out another baby—maybe you could tell me SOMETHING encouraging. Even if you have to make it up and don't believe it for a second, feed it to me, because I'm starving over here.

One friend simply writes, "Oh Jess ..." I wait for the bubbles to show up on my phone, indicating that she is composing a much more expansive note, filled with encouraging thoughts, but it never comes.

Why the ellipses? I think, irrationally. *Why the effing ellipses — why "OH JESS ..."? OH JESS — WHAT? I think but do not say.* Nice Christian girls don't voice these things, and they certainly don't say "effing." *

*Between you and me, I don't regularly use curse words, they aren't part of my vernacular, but I do think curse words can help express a feeling. When we weaponize our words—all of them, curse words included, but not exclusively, we use them to tear each other down. This is ugly. But I suspect this is different from using an occasional curse word to express a depth of emotion. I remember the day I heard my pastor mom say she was pissed off. It was probably the first time I glimpsed her humanity. Her working-mom-raising-five-kids vibrant humanity that needed a little color in her word choice. And then there was the time my first husband broke all his vows and left. Other than quietly wasting away in my parents' basement while my pop tried to entice me to eat sandwiches—"Please, you look so skinny, Jess!"—I didn't know what to do. So I wrote a song that called him a bastard. (My ex, that is—not my pop. I will never call anyone who plies me with sandwiches a bastard.) It felt deeply true when I sang it. I remember my lips forming around the B—how satisfying that felt—and just spitting out the word like it was a toxin that needed to go. My mom who really prefers all of us not to cuss at all—and will probably ask why, in my book about grief, I felt the need to reveal that she was once pissed off and even mentioned it out loud; like how in the world did that make it through the 75 rounds of edits, Jess?—never said a word about the new bastard song. I think deep down she just knew it was true, so why even argue with it. Basically, if you're only going to walk away with one thing from my book about grieving my son, it should definitely be that my first husband acted like a real bastard, and so I sang about it.

* * *

I've learned that grief likes to tell you over and over again, in as many ways as possible, that you are alone. This is why it's so important for our community to surround us and show us otherwise. Write the text, send the food, offer to come over—do whatever it takes to show a grieving person that they are not, in fact, alone. Nobody is expecting you to be perfect or have the perfect words. Nobody expects you to sound like a therapist or be able to explain why this terrible thing has happened. Sometimes a grieving person just needs someone to be there—someone to say I don't understand, either.

One nice thing about miscarriages (which is a ridiculous sentence, because there is nothing nice about miscarriages. Let me rephrase that: one thing that is comparatively nice about miscarriages), is that the whole world isn't privy to your devastation. I can go and meet with a client, and they aren't looking at me with a mix of pity and compassion, telling me that they're sorry, that they don't know how I do it, that I'm so strong. There aren't a lot of horrible conversations, which is a blessing. Nobody is telling me that God only gives us what we can handle (grateful to be able to handle all this—truly #blessed). Nobody is avoiding me awkwardly because they can't deal with my grief. My family and close friends know, and their sadness weighs on me enough.

My parents are devastated for me; they call and there is lots of silence, because nobody knows what to say. They send a fruit basket. I am terrible and text them that, with every bite of fruit, I feel better about another baby dying. I also thank them for their love and tell them I will be okay. My parents are wonderful, and it is hard for me to bring so much sadness into their lives. My cousin texts that her heart has been ripped out. I can't handle this. I silently ask her to put it back together. My own grief is too much to handle; at this point, I cannot also handle our families' grief. We decide that we will not share the news of a subsequent pregnancy until it is obvious that I am pregnant. It's too much to deal with their pain and sadness and ripped-out hearts. I need faith and hope around me, not an echo back of what I'm already feeling.

I am not saying our family is wrong. They aren't. This is what we do: we rejoice with each other, and we mourn with each other. We support each other when one of us cannot stand. I just feel too raw. And this is all too much. I want to give people good news and not have to take it back soon after. Period. At this point, I think this means that TJ and I keep a subsequent pregnancy just between the two of us for as long as possible.

I mean, I don't really know. I hope this will protect my heart, but really, it won't. Really, I could lose another baby. And there is nothing I can do to protect my heart against this. But at least now I can go teach a class and not be the weird, newly grieving one. It's a relief to walk into a Pilates studio and get ready to work out and escape from my sadness because nobody there knows about my latest loss. And if nobody knows about it, I can pretend it's not there. At least for the fifty minutes I'm teaching a class, anyway.

The Monday after the weekend I miscarry, this is not the case. Because I've been training with a lovely Pilates instructor, Samantha, I had told her about this pregnancy. There is less of a focus on your core when you're pregnant—both to prevent injury and because there's no way you're getting your six-pack back in the next year. During our last session, I had to tell her that I miscarried, that I'm no longer pregnant. As I walk into the Pilates studio, about to teach a roomful of students, her husband is there, working at the front desk. I don't know him well, having seen him only a handful of times over the years I've been working here. He asks me how I am, and I quickly say I'm fine.

"Samantha told me your sad news," he tells me over the desk. I'm confused but figure it out quickly as he continues. "I know she wasn't supposed to, but she did. And I'm sorry about the miscarriage," he says in a sing-song voice that makes me feel too vulnerable, too exposed, too-obviously-can't-grow-babies-well here, in a fancy downown Boston Pilates studio. I am shocked. I didn't think I'd have to hear more condolences. At least not here, right before I teach a class. I am bleeding, I am deeply humiliated, and I don't want to talk about it.

"Okay," I say quickly, not even looking at him, while walking past him into the studio. Once inside, people are quietly warming up on their mats. One client I haven't seen in a while waves me over.

"I never heard—what did you end up having?" she asks warmly.

"A boy," I say right away. "He died."

A look of shock crosses her face, like she's been slapped. I am so tired of making everyone upset; so tired of being upset, myself. I am tired of explaining my sad story and it being a juggernaut that no casual conversation can sustain.

I text TJ about the terrible conversations I've had in the last few minutes. He says he's sorry; he says to write it down, that my narrative is powerful. I think about what I'd write in this moment. A curse word comes to mind, and I think that covers it.

I don't cry; I breathe deeply at the music console while I choose today's playlist. I plaster on a smile, ask everyone how they are, and introduce myself to the new students. I am bleeding, and I am pretending to be fine. For the next fifty minutes, I focus on everybody else, and it's a reprieve that is good for my soul. As people thank me after class, I have peace. My insides feel less like water. I realize that, once again, I am going to be okay—eventually.

* * *

I have a pair of gray Calvin Klein underwear that used to be my favorite. But I've avoided them since I miscarried while wearing them. Basically, this year is that scene in *Of Mice and Men* when Lennie plays with his puppy and then gets too rough and then never stops and then the puppy dies. (Hint: I am not Lennie; I am the puppy). I recently tell TJ I haven't worn this underwear since that day, thinking he'll say we're not superstitious people. That if I like the underwear, I should just wear it.

"That makes sense, Jess," he tells me instead. "I think you should throw them out. Buy new underwear that doesn't make you sad."

Oh. Yes, of course.

Being brave doesn't always mean you do the hardest things. Sometimes it means you're honest about how hard things are already, and you avoid the hurt that is unnecessary. A dear girl I recently met lost her baby this year, too. "My friend is having a baby shower—do I go?" she asks me. "I think it will be hard, but she's a friend."

I don't tell her what to do, but I say that now is not the time for me to attend baby showers. It's just too hard. I'm already working hard with therapy and making room for both honesty and gratitude and grief while navigating the complex relationships with friends who are having babies. I can skip the parties.

And I can get rid of the underwear that makes life even a little bit harder. I think it becomes a more natural thing to be compassionate with others when we are also compassionate with ourselves. I think it's the kind of thing that, like love, multiplies once we practice it even a little. Also, please don't feel devastated about this miscarriage for me, dear reader. We are at peace and feel grateful for the good that is here. Oh, and no condolences. I reached that quota a while ago and won't be accepting any more this year. I am just tired of being the girl for whom everyone is so sad.

Things to say to me instead:

Cool, I wear underwear, too.

I read *Of Mice and Men,* and all I remember is they talked a lot about rabbits.

I know someone who miscarried; she's super hot and hilarious.

I miscarried; I'm super hot and hilarious.

Chapter 46

The Magi and the Miracle
(fourteen weeks after)

A lot doesn't matter now. This belief probably has something to do with how my nails look (not manicured) and the long gaps between hair appointments. Last week I took a dull pair of scissors and, in an act of desperation, cut my bangs myself, like I went to the Aveda Institute instead of the University of the Arts. My bangs are currently all different lengths, and I run the risk of disappointing my magical-human stylist when I finally make my way back to him, looking as guilty as my dog when she ate every single Christmas cookie I baked one holiday season. I'd made them for TJ's office the first year we were married, but none of them got to the office, not even to TJ. Side note: Did I say Luna looked guilty? Because what I mean is that she SHOULD have looked guilty. How she actually looked was triumphant. She sauntered into our room with the now-empty basket I'd packed the cookies in dangling from her smiling mouth/nose (does a Labrador have a mouth on their nose or a nose on their mouth?), as if to say, *Christmas came early for this pup!*

But, back to my hair: I can see again now. And they are bangs. You know, just hair. Totally fixable. Totally cut-able, blunt scissors and all.

I like to think of the gifts of the Magi. Yep, in a month other than December, way before we're ready for Christmas, I rebelliously think about them anyway. Because Mary's pregnancy, giving birth in a manger with dirty animals—none of that was Plan A. And I imagine it probably scared them a lot more than we represent in Christmas pageants, with grandparents smiling on as we dress our toddlers as sheep and tell them to *baaaaa*! I think there's something about that messy, not-the-plan part of the story that ushered in the gifts from the Magi.

The Magi is a fancy word we use to describe the scholarly, mystical men who showed up after the birth of Jesus in a very unexpected place for Magi to appear. But they came to witness the miracle and to bring gifts to this baby King. The miracle took place in a dirty manger with unkempt animals all around, but they wanted to be where the miracle was, so this didn't faze them. They brought gifts that were valuable, much more than simple Mary and Joseph expected to see in their lifetimes. That's what the Magi do, I think; they show up when God's plan leads us to an unfamiliar, scary, messy place.

I think about the Magi showing up here, with me too, because they want to see the miracle that God is bringing about. I hope so, anyway. It's like they've handed me a scale with the title WHAT MATTERS, and it holds a lot less than I thought. But what's on there is valuable, more than I ever expected to see in my lifetime. As I look around at my own certainly-not-Plan-A— this messy, dirty place called grief—it makes me wonder about a miracle. I have the darkness, a perfect place for the light to show up.

Chapter 47

I Might Be Pregnant
(fifteen weeks after)

I am sitting in a Starbucks in downtown Boston on a rainy Thursday morning. With apologies to Amy Schumer—whose charming book I just read and found "people who write at Starbucks" on a list of things she hates—I am writing. However, were I to explain to Amy that this is not a regular thing, that it's simply right next to the salon where I'm getting my hair done in thirty minutes, and I need to write, I'm confident she'd understand. (Thanks, Amy.)

Charlee woke up at 5:15 this morning. I don't want to be a mom who always talks about how tired I am because of my kid—because come on, I chose to have this kid and therefore everything that comes with it. But, well, I am tired today. I also might be pregnant. I could probably take a test now—it's been almost five weeks since I miscarried—but I just don't do it. I have one; I know exactly where it is in the cabinet above our toilet, but I keep ignoring it. A part of me would rather not know. I think I would rather just bask in the potential that I could be pregnant, rather than knowing definitively that I am not. But if I am, I will be cautiously happy, and TJ and I will tell nobody. Well, by nobody, I mean I will tell my therapist. But nobody else.

If I am not, I will tell myself I am fine, but I won't be. I will be disappointed; I can't help it. To hope, to dream, is to open your heart to the bitterness of unrealized dreams. But the answer is not to stop hoping, not to stop dreaming. I'm not actually sure what the answer is. There is no formula, nobody to tell us to do such and such for this long and then life will make us feel okay. I have found that there is some eventual peace when I realize that there are no bad emotions, just the bad—or great—things we choose to do with them. I have found that there is some peace in being here and now, when I let myself feel how I feel, without the word "should" providing judgment in my mind. I have found that there is a wholeness to my being when I tell my story. When I believe that even though I hurt, I can also heal. I can believe that God has even better things ahead than what I've left behind. Well, okay—when you've left behind a child, I am not sure that cliché applies, because what is better than your child? But surely there are way better things ahead than experiencing the loss of my child. Surely Luca is in my future, too; my faith is a constant Sunday school lesson that says, Dear heart, trust that you will see him again.

I try to do the hard work of believing for good things. Like carrying Luca in my heart in such a way that it doesn't make me cry from the pain of it every single day anymore. (And if it does—that is okay, too.) I continue to open myself to everything—for the human heart is a wide net, and it catches everything. I hold onto this steely hope that the beautiful outweighs the tragic. That there is even beauty in the tragedy. There is something sacred in grieving those we love, as we continue to create space for them in our hearts. There is something brave—whether we feel it or not, whether our tears are permanently caught in the creases of our smile or not—as we navigate this life without them here in the way we want. There is also faith—a belief that I can look forward to Luca (that I can look forward at all). That we will be together again. So perhaps this is why I can peacefully say the best is yet to come.

Okay, I do it. I take a pregnancy test. I keep telling myself it does not matter if a second line appears, but my body says otherwise. I am so shaky and nervy—all my insides feel like someone gingerly standing on a pile of quicksand, not shifting their weight—and it matters, it does, no matter what I keep telling myself. Usually when I take a pregnancy test, I leave the room for the three minutes it takes for the magical stick to either show two lines or one. It's like I give it privacy or something while it makes up its mind about me. (God forbid it feels pressure from this desperate woman and so, in irritation, decides to withhold good news.) But this time I am so over it that I just stay in the bathroom and brush my teeth in quiet. I irreverently pretend indifference to the stick that is acting as an oracle on the toothpaste-stained counter to my right. I am right there for the whole three minutes. *Suck it, pregnancy test,* I rebelliously think, as I pretend the minutes are just flying by and I'm fine. Has it been three minutes? Oh, *I hadn't even noticed.*

What if I ended the book here? Hahahaha and everyone was like, BUT THIS IS SO MEAN! and I'd be like, WELL, MY BABY DIED, SO I CAN DO WHATEVER I WANT! And then I literally never wrote another word for the rest of my life. Not even in like five years, to sign a permission slip for Charlee when her school wants to take her to the nearby farm to see where milk comes from. (Okay, okay, I'll keep writing things down. I'll sign that permission slip and everything. I won't end the book here.)

I'LL END IT HERE! (Jess, this gag is getting old. Just tell us what happened, please.) FINE, TWIST MY ARM!

Two pink lines.

Two pink lines happen.

I put my toothbrush down and stare. I am so jittery inside. The way the orchestra sounds while tuning up is the way I feel as I stand in the bathroom with a positive pregnancy test. I never get my period after I miscarry. It's still early—I am just past five weeks—and we aren't telling anyone this precious news. In my mind, I am wondering how to feel. I mean, I feel grateful. But I'm also so scared that I will lose this baby, too.

Too. It's a hard word to write. A stillbirth, then a miscarriage. (I hate the word "stillbirth," because it sounds so impersonal. His name is Luca. That's who died. He's my son; that's who died.) It's a lot to carry around inside a mind that remembers the terrible things so well. Turns out miscarriage is traumatic, too. I have a visceral memory of how it feels to bleed like that. Such a gush, so much blood. My underwear soaked, could-be-wrung-out-over-a-bucket wet. It is so sudden that it wakes me up. It is a staggering amount of blood. When I call a nurse the next morning, she tries to offer me a seed of hope: "So you think you're miscarrying?" There is a finality to all that blood when you're so very early in your pregnancy.

"No. I know I'm miscarrying," I say flatly. It is exactly as bad as it seems, and there aren't sufficient words to describe how badly I don't want this to happen again. Just like I don't ever want another stillbirth. I just want to bring this baby home. And I have no more control over this than I did with Luca, my miscarriage, my first marriage—really, anything.

Chapter 48

A Friend and a Miracle

(five weeks after)

Every day I wake up and think, "Today I am pregnant." I feel afraid, and forty weeks feels like a really long time. Sometimes I let myself imagine bringing home a living, healthy baby again, and for those moments, I feel fleeting, dangerous joy. Like little Mary Lennox unlocking the door to the secret garden in the book with the same title, gazing at the forbidden beauty anyway. I guess those moments, those glimpses, keep me realizing that all this uncertainty and risk of further loss and devastation is worth it. The secret garden is beautiful, you know? It's worth a glimpse, forbidden or not. Sometimes I close my eyes and see it. I don't move or blink or sigh or anything for fear it might go away.

Something happened this week that I want to share because it's a miracle. I sure do write about the hard stuff, so I want to describe the miracles, too. My dearest friend in Boston became pregnant with her first baby four months after I became pregnant with Luca. Perfect, right? We are already close friends, and now we get to be mom friends! It is ideal. Until, of course, it's not. Until my baby dies and I go home to a world where everything else is the same except my own shattered heart and the box of his tiny clothes, still stiff and unused.

I wrote about Joanna before. How I run into her in the parking garage shortly after delivering Luca. I see her burst into tears as she's walking up to us, and she can barely get the words out to say how sorry she is, and how she cannot understand how such a terrible thing can happen to me and TJ. She is kind and compassionate, and her tears mean a lot. I tell her that we will be okay, and she is apologizing for crying, saying she should be strong for me. But crying right now is one of the kindest things she can do. Sometimes tears are the only appropriate reaction to tragedy.

* * *

Joanna continues to get larger with her child as the weeks pass. I train myself to look her in the eyes. I try not to fixate on her belly and how much it reminds me of Luca. My feelings are raw, and it is complicated being her friend. But she and I are honest with each other. I tell her that I am sorry I cannot be the friend I would like to be to her. We go on walks, and I don't ask about her pregnancy. The words just won't come. We talk about our dogs instead. She tells me that she cannot imagine what I am going through; that she is afraid she is torturing me with her belly. She is not torturing me; also, everything is torturing me. She doesn't give me pregnancy updates, and I don't ask. I am so grateful for Joanna. She is not afraid of my grief or sadness and is constant with her communication to me.

"How are you doing, dear?" she texts me often, day after day. "I am here, if you'd like to get together," she says. "No pressure," she adds. Joanna is a friend I do not want to lose, even though she is pregnant. We talk about this. I tell her it's complicated, and she understands. I tell her that everything is complicated for me right now, and she gets it. She is a true friend.

Let me tell you how good of a friend. It's a few weeks after Luca died, and TJ has taken a day from work. This is something that is unprecedented for him. We have been married for four years, and we have yet to go on a honeymoon (though he promises me it's coming!) because we got married on a Saturday and he was back on the radio the following Monday morning. He told me he planned something special for me and Charlee on this day, and I feel something close to happy about it. I like the idea of being together as a family, of TJ being home on a Friday morning. I am tired of being tossed by the waves, and this idea feels like the shore.

Finally, it's the time he's set for our surprise, and I hear a knock at the door. Joanna walks in, and TJ announces that he has arranged for my dear friend to take me to get a pedicure while he takes Charlee to Target. Both TJ and Joanna are smiling, anticipating the reaction I would have given a few weeks ago. But everything is different since Luca died. I try to smile and halfheartedly say thank you. Then I excuse myself to the bathroom where I burst into tears. TJ finds me there.

"I misread what you wanted, didn't I?"

I nod, tears streaming down my face. "I don't want to leave you and Charlee. I just need to be with you guys, as a family; and I thought you were planning something for us to do as a family. I'm sorry, this would've been perfect just a couple weeks ago—but it's just not right now."

We walk out of the bathroom and TJ explains to Joanna that he didn't realize that I'd just want to be with them. I apologize at least six times while we walk her to the elevator. I tell her how sorry I am and how the last thing I want right now is to hurt her feelings.

"Jessica, you are going through so much. All I want is for you to get what you need right now—whether that's with me or with TJ," she tells me sincerely.

She's present but not overbearing, never taking my unavailability personally, and remaining a good listener. Also, she tells me things about her life, her struggles—something I've noticed a lot of people don't do when you're going through a tragedy. They think all their problems are nothing in comparison, and therefore always just tell you they're "fine." But the thing they don't realize, I guess, is that it's a welcome break to think about somebody else's life and difficulties occasionally. Plus, it helps bring some semblance of normalcy when you can once again just be a friend who listens, too.

Finally, Joanna's in the hospital, and her baby girl arrives. Joanna is not American, so her family and closest friends are an ocean away. Weeks ago, I'd asked if she had anyone planning to visit in the hospital. She said no; she was very stoic about the whole thing, like it was no big deal. I asked her if TJ and I could visit—if she would like company after a day or two.

"Jessica," she said, "You don't have to do that. I don't want to add to your pain in any way. I can't imagine how this wouldn't."

"I am your friend, Joanna," I said, "I may cry or something, but if you don't mind the possibility of me being emotional, I'd like to visit you in the hospital."

She left it up to me, and I still feel the same when she texts me that her daughter has arrived. TJ and I get dinner and drive to the same hospital where I delivered both Charlee and Luca. We walk through the lobby, and I tell him I have no idea how I'll be.

"I may be a mess," I warn him.

"You probably will, Jess, and that's okay—it's really brave that you're here." TJ grabs my hand and quietly prays for peace as we wait for the elevator. We get to their door, and it's shut.

For the first time, I ask TJ about the teddy bear that was on our door while we were delivering Luca. I'd never known this—I guess not many people do—but when you are delivering a baby who has died, they put a teddy bear on your door to let all the medical personnel know that this birth is different.

"What did that teddy bear look like, TJ?" I ask, "Was it ugly?"

"It was just a teddy bear, Jess ..."

"It's got to be a sad teddy bear, though, right?"

The door opens and our friend Gavin ushers us in. He's happy to see us, and I'm so happy to be happy to see him, too. Joanna is nursing her new baby, who is in the same kind of blanket and hat that both my babies wore when they were born, too. Joanna asks if I want to hold her daughter, and I do. I am so happy that I do. I hold her and rock her and stand when she gets fussy to rock her even better.

"Pro mom move, right there," Gavin comments, and I smile. It's okay that they have their healthy baby. It's wonderful, actually. I don't feel crushed or despairing in this moment, meeting a newborn. It would be okay if I did—expected, even. My own baby died five months before, after all. But here I am, feeling peaceful, hopeful, and so happy for my friends and their indescribable gift.

I know this doesn't mean I am done grieving. But it does mean my grief allows for more feelings than solely profound sadness. This is a relief. I didn't know I could be grieving my own baby, and peacefully hold my friend's newborn. So many people say there is no such thing as a mother's heart healing after the loss of her child. Maybe we don't fully understand the creativity of God. Maybe I can grieve and celebrate at once.

Maybe I can trace the forever-changed shape of my heart with one hand and the feet of my friend's tiny baby with the other. Maybe the depth of the human heart is greater even than the as-of-yet unexplored depths of the ocean. We are still discovering new animals down there; why can't we discover new ways for a heart to heal? Maybe the loss of my son is not the life sentence I feared; perhaps one of Luca's gifts is leaving me with a heart that has a greater capacity for depth and healing, for love and bravery. I am shocked that my own heart is okay holding my friend's new baby. I am shocked by the moments of okay-ness in general. My first onslaught of grief surely didn't hint at this coming down the road.

What is interesting is that we try so hard to crystallize and identify with where we are now. Like, when you're a kid, you feel like your whole entire identity is just that: a kid. But you're only a kid for a while. If we are anything, we are ever-changing. There are some immutable facts about us, sure. We are loved, we are uniquely created—none of us being exactly like another— we may have some preferences that stay the same throughout our lifetime (but maybe not; I only started liking guacamole after I met TJ. I spent many years completely ignoring it like the picky little close-minded-to-mushy-green-food-creature-that-I-was, sadly), but we are changing. We are growing and going and learning and discovering and, yes, grieving. We are also breathless with joy on the beach. Or we are laughing and crying at once until a friend pees her pants right in front of you, right on her mom's carpet (we still laugh about this).

My point is none of these elevated moments define us fully; they become integrated within our hearts. We take the meat and spit out the bones. We even do this with grief. And eventually, the plate is clean and something else fills it. We are creatures made for wonder and adventure, for life in abundance, for the whole, full, bursting use of the entire heart. And thus, we discover the highs and lows; and we also discover that we pass through them. We pitch tents, rather than build houses of stone here in the highs and the lows, because we are only passing through.

I have the same resources as you. I am made up of a heart, a mind, a spirit, and a body, just like you. I write about all this to tell you that miracles happen. I think one of the greatest helps to me while grieving has been people who believe the same. Who tell me that hearts can heal, and lives can be lived fully on the other side of loss; that loss is a part of a life that is blessed with love. And this night, while I peacefully hold my friend's newborn baby in the same hospital where I said both hello and good-bye to my Luca just five months before, leads me to believe they are right. If your people are not saying these things to you—if they are not surrounding you with hope and faith when yours feels dim—please, find new people. I promise they exist, and that their friendship is part of the healing too. And if your people absolutely cannot learn to believe in miracles, and, for whatever reason, you also absolutely cannot ditch them, then may they learn to make incredible casseroles and wordlessly, so as not to dim your own flickering candle of faith with their own unbelief, drop food at your door so that your belly at least can be full during your dark night of the soul.

Chapter 49

Stories That Have Nothing to Do with Luca's Death
(Intermission)

We're out at a restaurant tonight, just TJ and me, and everything is normal until it isn't. Until it's so much better than normal. I'm waiting by the entrance while TJ is in the restroom, and an older man is walking toward the door. He is limping badly, his body listing to the left. His hands are mangled—fingers rigid and crossed over each other in piles that must make it hard to do even simple tasks. Every part of his skin is badly burned, and he's missing an eye. Both a waiter and waitress catch up to him, the waitress getting there first.

"You got him, Mary?" asks the waiter as a young woman with short hair and a nose ring nods while grabbing a nearby jacket.

"James!" Mary says, smiling at the man limping toward the door, "You know you need someone to walk you and make sure you get home safe each night."

She deftly takes the jacket and puts James' arms through the sleeves. Standing in front of him, she affectionately closes each clasp, bottom to top. She is much younger than him, but it doesn't matter; in this moment, she is his mother, his sister, his friend. She is myself with Charlee. She is every person who has ever truly cared for another.

Mary pauses as she closes the snap under James' chin; she puts a hand softly on his chest. "Stay home tomorrow, will you? The snow will be bad, and nobody wants a frozen James."

Smiling, James limps out of the bar, and Mary goes back to her tables.

TJ and I walk to our car, and I tell him about what I saw. About James, a man who I imagine the world is not generally kind to. About Mary, who changes that story. Who, with kindness, care, touch, and love makes an ordinary bar in Cambridge an extraordinary place. I don't know Mary's parents, but I want to tell them they did it: they raised a human who really sees people.

"We have to give her something," TJ tells me as we get into the car. And now this is the part when I wonder what he means. I get just a little bit nervous because I see where this is going as TJ drives to a nearby ATM and withdraws cash and puts it in an envelope. "Go back inside," he says. "Tell the waitress how wonderful her kindness is and hand her this." I take the cash and think about it. Ugh. I really don't love walking up to strangers and disrupting their lives. Not even with cash. It makes me feel embarrassed and uncomfortable.

"Can't you do it?" I ask.

"It's gotta be you," TJ answers, shaking his head. "It'd be too weird coming from a man—she'd probably be suspicious of my motives—plus, you were the one who saw it."

TJ and I drive back to the restaurant. I spot Mary bussing a table in the back and walk up to her. We make eye contact and she smiles, expecting me to say something, because why else am I just hovering as she clears her table. "Hey," I say quietly. "I know this is weird because we don't know each other, but I just have to tell you how beautiful your heart is. The way you took care of your customer tonight—the man whose jacket you buttoned—"

"James," she adds, with a smile.

"Yeah, James," I say, smiling too. "It was just one of the most beautiful things I've seen in a long time. It really gave me hope. Thank you for being so kind and caring. My husband and I wanted to give you this, just—well, just because you inspire us."

I slide the envelope towards her on the table and walk away as she says thanks. I'm glad TJ turned my noticing her into us thanking her. I hope she sees who she is and how powerful she is. How powerful we all are.

Tonight, I'm thinking about Mary and James, about how unfair and hard life can be and how love somehow beats it all. I'm thinking about Jesus' words, "Blessed are the merciful, for they will be shown mercy; blessed are the pure in heart, for they will see God."

* * *

Hi. Here's something you may not know about me. (*But we know everything about you, Jess! You are so open. So wonderfully open. Okay, mostly wonderfully open. Sometimes it's a little much. Sometimes it's uncomfortably open. But still wonderful. Just also uncomfortable. But so is Christmas dinner with our relatives, and we still look forward to that, so I guess keep it up!*)

My first pet was a ferret named Snackers. He didn't have to be called Snackers (that was my choice), but he had to be a ferret (that was my parents' choice). Having grown up and shared many talks with other women since then, I've never met one other woman who had a pet ferret as a little girl. (Way to not conform, Mom and Pop!)

The Snackers story I'd like to share today is the time I took him to the vet after I found a lump on his ear. Since I was only 11, I couldn't drive. Even though I grew up in the country and my pop drives a tractor, I still had to wait until I was sixteen for a license, just like the suburban kids who are lucky enough to hear the ice cream truck on summer days.

My mom took me and Snackers to the vet, but being the pet owner, I went into the exam room by myself and explained the problem with the growth on my ferret's ear. The vet closely and seriously examined Snackers. I watched him grab the tumor between his thumb and pointer finger and break it off. I was surprised, but I've never been a vet, and am not up on the latest methods for removing lumps from small animal ears. The vet turned toward me and, continuing with the same serious medical tone, explained the situation: "Your ferret will be fine. A small turd got stuck to his ear. Try bathing him more often."

And that was it. I remember feeling hot shame fill my chest and show up on my face as I thanked him and grabbed my newly de-turded pet. I told my mom about the turd stuck to Snackers' ear and, as she laughed about it, I realized it was actually pretty funny.

So, there you go. Not everything is as it seems. Sometimes a turd is really good news.

* * *

Once while visiting my family, TJ finds a photo of me with Caspian the dachshund, my childhood dog. He snaps a picture of it with his phone, because "I like to look at the dog little Jess loved." This leads me to the story of Caspian.

With my eighth birthday looming, my parents ask what I want. "A dachshund," I say, "Just like mom had growing up."

"Anything else?" My pop asks desperately.

"No."

On my birthday, I unwrap a new board game. Guess how I feel about the board game not being a puppy? Right. My face falls. My parents ask what else I want, but I steadfastly refuse all other ideas for birthday gifts and go to bed sad. My pop wakes me with this news: "We're getting you a puppy!" That same day, we bring home Caspian.

He's a wonderful animal. Okay, so he's wonderfully loved. He has a snaggly-toothed underbite, never masters the art of being housebroken, and has an embarrassing attraction to a pink raccoon stuffed animal of mine, which, looking back, is probably my first lesson on sex education (and quite possibly my only lesson on sex education; shout out to my fellow homeschoolers). There are entire hours each evening when Caspian will bark and bark and bark for that stuffed pink raccoon high on a shelf and therefore out of his reach. He does this until he loses his voice. He's a wiener dog with laryngitis, his barks having turned into odd rasping sounds until I finally go into the room, grab the pink raccoon, and let him have his way. What's weirder is the pink raccoon is holding a baby raccoon in her arms; she is, from all appearances, a single mother. But Caspian has a strange thing for her, and I don't want him to keep losing his voice. So, I take her down from the shelf and close the door behind me while he gets to work humping the pink raccoon.

Now, please bear in mind, I am somewhere in the vicinity of 8 years old. One time I open the door before Caspian is done. I don't know how to say this, exactly, so let me quickly google some technical terms. Okay (deep breath), this is what I learned from Google. Apparently, the thing that protects the dog's actual penis... (I can write penis here, right? It does feel strange, but it's valid. It's the exact right word I need, so, buckle up, I'm using it. The word, that is; I am referring to using the WORD. Speaking of penis, one time two of my nieces were playing make believe. They were about two and four, respectively, and each of us had to pick a body part to be. I hesitated and they quickly assigned me to be a penis. I was like, "Is it okay if I pretend to be something else?" Very magnanimously, my older niece sighed and said, "Fine. You can be Hand.").

Back to male dogs and their anatomy: what we all mistake for a penis (perhaps I shouldn't speak for us all; let me rephrase that: what I mistake for a penis) is actually the thing that sheaths the penis, and it's called a prepuce. That's a strange word and if this is the only thing that sticks with you after you read this book, I think I will not have done a very good job writing a memoir about grief. But also, it is hard to compete with the what-we-think-is-the-dog-penis-is-actually-a-prepuce-bomb-of-a-fact, so I guess I wouldn't be able to blame myself (or you, dear reader). When the dog gets aroused, the real penis comes out. Some people refer to this as lipstick (if you've seen it, then you know). So basically, I walk in on my dog Caspian and the pink raccoon (and her baby clutched in her arms, how bad is that). I am shocked to see this long red thing coming out of his crotch and, even though Caspian is a longish wiener dog, the red thing is as long as his entire body. I scoop him up, red thing dangling while careful not to touch it, and run to my pop.

"Pop, look!" I yell, as I show him the alarmingly long red thing I'd never before seen protruding from my beloved dog. I wonder if it's his intestines. Pop stares, waits a beat, before finally saying, "Well, there's obviously something really wrong with him."

(Maybe you can tell, but neither of us are veterinarians.)

The red thing finally recedes, and Caspian seems no worse for the whole ordeal, so other than having that awkward conversation about how long Caspian's penis is, we don't do anything. I can imagine my parents had a good laugh about it that night, though.

The one time my pop shows an ounce of pride in this tiny wiener dog, he shouts from the garden, "Jess! Come quick! Caspian has a snake! And he's fighting it!" We tiptoe up to Caspian and the snake, and as we get closer, the dramatic scene unfolds. Caspian has a long white tube sock in his mouth that he relentlessly and mercilessly is shaking and wrestling. The good news is that he is winning. The bad news is that there's no snake. My pop goes back to thinking that, as far as dogs go, Caspian is a rather disappointing creature. Caspian keeps wrestling the sock, completely oblivious to the fact that he was *almost* revered by my pop.

Caspian is a real fan favorite with my family because whenever anyone comes over—just steps inside the house, really—his excitement triggers his toy dachshund size bladder. (Mistake number one, dog-breeder geneticists! Dogs are not toys and neither are bladders!) I am sure you don't need me to explain to you what happens every single time anyone walks into the house. You don't need me to tell you how he starts peeing all over the place (Caspian, not the guest—just so we're clear); how the visitor shouts my name while I race to pick Caspian up and hold him upside-down in an attempt to make his freely flowing urine drip onto his pink spotted belly rather than myself before I can put him down outside. All this to say, people come over a lot, my parents being pastors and all. So that's a good time.

One time my brother has a group from his high school over and Caspian is so excited that he flips onto his back and does a version of spinning and doggie-breakdancing so that his pee acts as a fountain, shooting up into the air and then out into the atmosphere. If it wasn't so gross, well, it would have been awesome. (Is it alright to admit that it's basically both?)

Another time my brother had made an entire plate of brownies to bring to his school the following day. Though the brownies are covered in tin foil, Caspian lives up to his hound heritage, hunting down the source of the smell, discovering the plate, and eating every last brownie. This is a seven-pound dog, guys, who eats an entire batch of brownies. Being so young and inexperienced with the care of animals (reminder: I am not a vet. I am also a kid), I don't understand how dangerous this is. (One time Luna, my Labrador, ate a piece of raisin bread, and TJ and I completely freaked out until we got her to vomit; my point is I care very much about keeping my animals from dying. I just didn't realize chocolate was something that kills dogs. Someone should probably have a talk with my parents about 8-year-olds and their sense of responsibility and ability to care for living things.)

No one else in my family seems particularly bothered by the thought of our toy dachshund eating an entire batch of brownies, either—there is no mention of a vet visit or any attempts to induce Caspian to vomit. It is more like we are all just kind of annoyed that he ate all the brownies. Caspian doesn't seem to care much either, other than being happily full. He never does get sick from those brownies. Thinking about it now, I'm wondering how that even happened. Caspian is white with brown spots all over his body—something that doesn't really fall under the category of any other dachshund's coloring I've ever seen. And now apparently chocolate doesn't faze him. Is this a sign that he is different? Otherworldly? *Is he even a dog?* Whatever he is, he is loved. (By me, at least.)

When I go to college, I begrudgingly agree that my beloved dog is better off living with family friends who adore him. Both my parents work, and it's not a good idea for Caspian to be home alone all day. He'll live with friends just until I'm done, of course. Oh, and he'll probably have a lot of fun, because these friends are clowns. I don't mean this as an epithet. They are actual clowns with an act and everything. They incorporate Caspian into the act. His stage name becomes "Pork 'N Beans" and they pull him around in a wagon at clown events. Life is wild, guys. So many things I can't predict. My first marriage ending. My son dying. My childhood dog having a second career as a clown named Pork N Beans.

At first, I get regular updates on Caspian. Months go by, though, and I realize I haven't heard about him. He's a busy performer; I get it, but I ask my mom how he is while we're in the car one day. Mom bursts out laughing and crying at once. I stare at her in shock as she emotes all over the place. "What? How? Is he? Oh no." I think with a sense of foreboding. She finally manages to get three words out: "He's dead, honey!" I absorb this news for a moment, then turn to her accusingly.

"Why didn't anyone tell me?"

"It happened months ago—we were all just hoping you'd never ask about Caspian again."

They just hoped I'd never ask about him again? Let's just say I'm really glad my family isn't advising the Pentagon when it comes to strategy. This is the end of the story of Pork 'N Beans, née Caspian. He lived a long life with a surprising career change in his golden years and was well loved. And apparently, he died doing what he loved, because—well, I don't know how else to write this, but he was accidentally run over by the clown car. The clowns/family friends felt terrible about it, and it took a long time before they stopped acting guilty around me. Every time I'd see the guy who ran him over, he'd just look sad. But I forgave them; after all, it was a true and tragic accident. Also, I don't really have normal childhood pet stories, I guess.

Chapter 50

(Luca) Thomas

(three months after)

While TJ and I are dating, he mentions that if he ever has a son, he'd like his middle name to be Thomas.

"Oh...I don't, like, love that name," I say, offhand.

A look of surprise and sadness crosses TJ's face. And then it dawns on me. "Oh my gosh!" I exclaim. "I'm SO sorry—that's your DAD'S name! I totally forgot!"

"Jess," TJ says quietly, "That's *my* name."

This is what you'd call an unrecoverable moment. Sort of like when my mom's friend showed her a photo of the time they went to the beach together, saying, "Look who finally got in the water!" My mom, assuming the photo was of herself, replied, "Ugh. I look like a beached whale!"

"That's actually me..."

The photo, of course, was of her friend. (They weren't very close after that.)

I apologize and tell him the name will probably grow on me. I cringe; I can't imagine that this is enough of an apology. But TJ. He laughs it off. He tells me it's not a big deal; it's just a name. He's not faking it, either. He doesn't get easily offended, and this has saved us over and over again.

I think I've stopped looking for balance. It might be a unicorn, it doesn't exist. There are passion and dreams and rest and work, and we dive deep into all of them all the time. What I do is keep looking for us, me and TJ. And the best thing I've seen is that we're here still. In joy and busyness and exhaustion and grief, in both our realized dreams and the ones still beckoning, in putting Charlee to bed four times in an hour—we're here.

I love when Charlee is asleep and we are not too tired to remember ourselves. We sit on the couch and talk, and it is another way to make love. Our words connect and expose and draw pictures that hang in the air between us, like after the fireworks disappear but their remnant shows for a glittering, lingering moment in the sky. Our conversation finds the hidden places that belong only to each other, and I'm not sure a body can do that any better, really. TJ's love is God's grace made evident in my life. It is my continuous reassurance of redemption, that there is something better coming—that pain can lead to life. I'm grateful for TJ. And I really, really, really like the name Thomas now. I promise. Enough to have named our very loved son Luca Thomas.

Chapter 51

Not a Normal Pregnant Lady (What is Normal?)
(five months after)

I am pregnant. Still pregnant. It is an exciting, terrifying, and wonderful secret that TJ and I share between us, glimpsed in the quiet conversations we have about what next summer will look like with this baby. We don't yet talk about names. I have ideas that I write down, but I don't say them out loud. I like to comfort myself with the thought that lightning never strikes twice in the same place. But this isn't true. I know because I googled it one night. In fact, Wikipedia informs me that, if given enough time, it is almost inevitable that lightning will strike the same place a second time. (Thanks, Wikipedia.)

I have friends who have lost two babies in a row—both stillborn. It is unfathomable, and yet it happened. The truth is, there is no way we can shield ourselves from the threat of more bad stuff happening. There is no quota; there is never a time when enough is enough. But I try to focus on what is. I choose to be grateful that I am pregnant today. I am grateful for the little baby we see on the screen who looks like a gummy bear, grateful for the ultrasound tech cheerily saying that everything looks normal.

I am not sure why we have to wait to go into another room with a nurse who tells us the exact same thing the ultrasound tech said fifteen minutes earlier, but I am grateful to hear good news. Sure, even twice. The nurse ends our little chat with, "Fingers crossed!" I smile and nod and keep my fingers uncrossed, because I have no control over this and I've stopped pretending.

However, I suppose I do my own version of fingers crossed, because I have yet to wear the pair of underwear I miscarried in. They are my favorite, but every time I grab them, I quickly put them back, remembering what happened last time. I guess I should just throw them away. Or maybe I'll keep them, and once this baby is born, I will wear them in a triumphant underwear dance of joy and gratitude. I'll be sure to let you know. Maybe I'll open with this scene in my sequel.

I sometimes let myself imagine how it will be going home for Christmas this year. I will be twelve weeks pregnant, definitely showing, as it will be my fourth pregnancy. I'll let my family figure it out. I will see how long they go without directly asking if I am pregnant. Finally, when they ask, I will just confirm that I am, and man, we will all be so happy. I hope, anyway. And that's something I continue to decide to do. Hope.

This child could leave me, too. And then what—I would be devastated. I would survive it. Some of the best stories are about people who survive, who even thrive with a kind of resilience that doesn't make sense from a distance. But they do (we do). And God, in His kindness, would continue to take care of me. I don't mean to sound casual. I understand that the storm comes and, when it does, it can be unrelenting. But I have seen life after the storm. I have even seen such tender care and grace during the storm. It doesn't mean you want the storm, but it does mean that God is here, caring for us as we weather it. And this is why I keep choosing to fix my eyes on that.

Fred Rogers famously calls it the helpers. "Look for the helpers during a disaster" is the well-traveled meme we've all seen. "There will always be helpers." We can continue to stare at the disaster, and that's all—or, in an effort to see the whole picture, we can take in the helpers, too. We can witness the grace God sets in motion the moment grief arrives. And it's easy to write these words in a hypothetical context, but also, I know I am risking my heart and also know it is worth it. Losing Luca has taught me this, because, see, I would not choose to have never had Luca. He's part of our family. In a terribly different way than I want—but he's still part of us. And all of the moments of feeling buried by grief—of wondering how I can ever stand before a well-meaning conversation with an acquaintance and keep up, for grief has rendered me too raw to be exposed to almost anyone but a very small, necessary circle—they are worth experiencing for the truth that Luca is part of us, part of me, forever.

This baby I'm carrying is alive today. This baby could be just like Charlee—born alive, filling the room with the glorious sounds that accompany that. Pregnancy, I am learning, is no different than a lot of things in terms of how much control I really have. Sure, I am healthy and I stay away from soft cheeses and don't let my daughter jump directly on my belly anymore— but I did all that with Luca, and he died. We simply don't control many outcomes in life, despite how profoundly the outcomes affect us.

My nurse is wonderful and kind and asking me all the right questions. "What do you need?" she asks this week. "If it's better for you to come in every single week to hear the heartbeat from now until this baby is born, that's what we'll do." It's good to hear this from the medical community. This is compassion and empathy, and it's what I need.

"Thank you. I ... don't think I need that, though" I say, softly. "That's an illusion of control—but that's all it is. I don't control this. I know that now more than ever. And even if I'd come in that often with Luca, he still would have died. I will do whatever my team thinks is best, but letting fear dictate how often I come in probably isn't the best."

"You're not high risk," my doctor tells me. "Physically," she amends. "We do worry about you psychologically, and we are committed to making sure every part of both you and your baby are okay."

I'm not high risk. Luca died from a cord accident, and there's no evidence to suggest it will happen again. It's like a member of your family being hit by a truck. It's tragic and terrible and there are no perfect words, but it's not like there's danger of this being a recurring event in your family. No more so than any other family, at least. But you will probably think twice before crossing the street. You might even stop crossing it entirely for a while or forever. Sometimes I feel like there is something so fragile inside of me—that because of Luca's death, this pregnancy is irreparably different, and therefore I cannot celebrate it like other pregnant women can.

I will be 12 weeks pregnant in a few days. Other than my medical team at Mass General, I still haven't told a soul. I am walking a tightrope of emotions: fear that this baby will leave, too, so maybe if I pay less attention to it, I will hurt less. But also, I feel so much joy and gratitude that I get to be pregnant. I hope to deliver a living child, give Charlee a sibling on earth, discover motherhood reflected in the eyes of one more human. It's a gift, shown to be that much more fragile because Luca is not here.

I think about the pregnancy announcement we will eventually make. It's a heck of an announcement. HI WE ARE PREGNANT AGAIN AND REALLY HOPING THIS ONE LIVES! #blessed #reallyreallyscared #youcanbeboth

I also simply cannot think about the pregnancy announcement I will eventually make without thinking about those it will hurt. I KNOW it will hurt them. Because I am still there—still in that space where pregnancy announcements touch something so raw inside that it's hard to describe the conflicting emotions fighting to rule one single event. I know that my senses come to the kind of life that occurs when you are in danger. I know that my breathing changes, my adrenaline shows up, and that Luca is dead all over again.

It's so hard.

And here's something hard that I have been trying to figure out how to even deal with. Because people don't want to hurt me by letting me see their general announcement along with the social media masses, I am now privy to private pregnancy announcements.

Yes, that's right. I now get these surprise Facebook messages or texts that come out of nowhere. Like, I am playing with Charlee on the floor, she's dictating to me where I should sit and how, exactly, I should make Candy Cat talk to Peppa Pig, when I glance at my phone and, so as not to hurt me with their big announcement, it's someone letting me know privately that they are pregnant.

And then there's the wording that feels so cold: "I understand how it feels when your attempt to grow your family doesn't work out the way you think it will." It didn't just not work out. Missing your flight is when something doesn't work out. You go to college, and your high school boyfriend doesn't work out. My son died. If you're going to allude to this, acknowledge that it's a big deal. That way all these crazy feelings I'm getting while reading your private message to me about your pregnancy feel somewhat normal, considering. It makes sense! My son died. No wonder I feel so many complex, uncomfortable emotions while reading this message. My family planning didn't simply not work out; I feel jealous and sad and alone and like my heart will continue this slow drain that began the day Luca died. What I mean is that I am a mother, and my son is dead.

I understand they don't mean it this way, but words matter. When emotions are ripe and big and hard to place because they are so heavy that everywhere you lay them down buckles under the weight of them, someone's ability to say something that makes you feel understood or legitimate for feeling this way is a gift.

And now I am silently crying and typing *BEAUTIFUL!!!!!! HOW WONDERFUL FOR YOU GUYS!!!!!!!!* All the screaming caps locks and exclamation points making up for the fact that it just plain hurts me inside. Am I happy for this person? Yes. I mean, yes. Do I wish it wasn't something I now know or have to think about? Yes. Would I have preferred to see this on Facebook, so that I could hurriedly click the like button or just keep scrolling? Yes. Is the message sender not trying to be a sniper and simply trying to be sensitive to me? Yes. Am I ALSO pregnant right now and shouldn't that make other people's pregnancy announcements less sad? Well, no.

There's no 'should' when it comes to how we feel when we grieve. There is logic, and then there is the wild, unchartered terrain of our hearts when we grieve. The two can intersect, sure, but in grief, they often don't, is what I'm finding. It's just so complicated. I really don't know what to tell pregnant people to do, short of finding a remote island and staying there forever.

And I *know*. I know all this is entirely hypocritical, because I am pregnant now. I belong on that island, too. I was pregnant with Charlee, and it was so incredibly perfect. I got to be pregnant with Luca, and even his birth was sacred—tragic, yes, but still sacred and beautiful. He's my son, and I got to carry him for over thirty-five weeks and deliver him, whole and perfect, though his spirit had flown. I don't want to rob others of the joy of making that announcement. Also, I wish I could just be away from them. It's just complicated. I wish it wasn't, but that's where I am.

There's really no "should" with grief and feelings. There's no way to convince our feelings to be something else. There is processing them and giving them space to be and maybe even describing them to someone we trust. And that all helps. But pretending or throwing up a great big measuring stick of 'shoulds' really never does help.

★ ★ ★

Now I am thirteen weeks and three days pregnant—yes, I am counting. Rolling the days back and forth in my mind the way I imagine a devout Catholic rolls the beads of a rosary between their thumb and fingers. Is it anxiety that causes one to roll over each bead, each day? Is it hope? For me, it's both as I walk back into Mass General, and smile at everyone I see. *I'm so normal*, I think to myself. *This is so normal—if it weren't, would I be smiling like this?* It's 7:30 AM, and I didn't sleep well the night before. So now I have a headache and am tired, and I suddenly realize that I am scared. And alone.

Why do I keep doing this to myself? Why do I keep scheduling appointments when I know TJ can't come because he is literally on the radio? Who do I think I am—a hero? What do I think I am—fine? I'm neither of those things. I'm back where I was when they told me Luca was dead. I hope this goes better, but what if it doesn't? How do I hope and also steel myself for more bad news at once?

"Jessica?" says a benign young blond lady from the doorway. I grab my bag and follow her. She is pleasant and neat, dressed in muted tones; if you looked into her wallet, you'd probably find an Ann Taylor credit card. She has long straight blond hair that is parted in the middle and a wide closed-mouth smile that I get the feeling she uses a lot. She's the genetics counselor, and she asks you all sorts of questions about your family, your baby daddy's family, and yourself to determine the chances of your baby being healthy. It's awful. I bet she uses that smile to try to balance out the awful.

I just went through the whole Family Tree of Health and Genetics while pregnant with Luca, so I am not sure why I have to do it again when there have been zero changes. It's not like we will suddenly discover a great aunt on a hidden branch of the family tree that clues us in on why Luca died or if this one will, too, but here I am anyway.

I glance at the lady's pen and notice it says GENETICS in large rainbow font. That's right, her pen says GENETICS. It's like going to an optometrist and seeing her hold a pen with the word EYEBALLS written on it.

I see her noticing me eying her pen, so I tell her I like her swag. Her wide smile opens up, showing even white teeth. This genetics counselor with her GENETICS pen is just doing her job, and I have a feeling that thoroughly filling out the branches of the genetics tree is very important to her. So far be it from me to say we should skip this part. I ask if she can see my record. I want to know if she knows my son died in May. She suddenly looks sad, her face answering my question before she can speak. We talk about Luca's death, about how it was a cord accident and how my doctor has zero concerns about a subsequent pregnancy.

"How are you doing, though?" she asks me, her voice quieter, more personal. I pause, because this is an overwhelming question. The answer is almost always more than anyone has time for, including me right now.

"I just hope everything is okay this time," I finally say.

She's a genetics counselor, and a big part of her job is to tell people that everything is not okay, so she doesn't try to tell me that she's sure it is. Nobody can tell me this. One of my dear friends actually does tell me this and I appreciate it, but even as she says it, I know she's just trying to give me some hope for another five minutes. Which is something, especially if it works.

The counselor nods and asks if I want to take the blood test that will reveal the gender. This time I want all the information I can have. I've had enough surprises to last me a lifetime. I say yes. She begins telling me that if there are no red flags, she'll send me an email, but if there are, she will call me. I must look increasingly more nervous as she's explaining this process, because she finally just stops her spiel. That very personal look comes over her again as she asks softly, "Would you like me to call you either way, Jessica?"

"Yeah," I say, "I would appreciate that."

I leave her office wanting her to call me right now and, at the same time, never call me.

When I grew up dreaming of mothering babies, I never thought of loss, sterile offices and nice ladies who tell you your odds of having a healthy baby after your baby already died. I never thought about all the fear that runs through your body like adrenaline over the course of the forty-week marathon of pregnancy, right alongside the hope that made you decide to get pregnant in the first place.

This stuff is hard.

I go back to the waiting room. Finally, an ultrasound tech with long, softly curling perfect pageant hair calls my name. I follow her into the dark room where she will examine my baby. It's the same room where they told me Luca was dead just six and a half months earlier. I'm not even just nervous anymore; now I'm scared. My palms sweat as I clutch at the arms of the chair.

God, whatever the news is, be with me, I whisper in my mind. I know He is. The part of me that looks at my life from a narrator's perspective realizes this prayer is redundant. God is always with me. *Maybe it's strength I'm asking for,* I think and then will myself to stop overthinking my prayer. I think about how I can do this. I've been here and heard the worst already; whatever they tell me today can't be worse than that, right?

The tech is quiet, totally opposite from the chatty woman who examined Luca at this stage of his development last year. She was going over his image and saying aloud how perfect he is. "Look at that nose bone!" she said, admiringly. "The perfect amount of amniotic fluid, too!" She was so reassuring, and I didn't even really need the assurance. With Luca in my belly, I wasn't thinking about the things that could go wrong. I remember being surprised when the tech told me Luca was a boy. At the twelve-week scan, it's supposed to be too early to really tell—plus, I had wanted to find out with TJ—but she bulldozed me over with the information anyway.

"I'm not supposed to say anything," the tech had blurted out, "But no girl looks like that!"—and pointed to what I could only assume was a penis. I was shocked. A boy! I hadn't actually hoped for one, but a baby brother for Charlee sounded perfect.

Today, my tech just quietly looks at my baby and finally says flatly, "I need to go see the doctor now."

I want to ask her if she sees something wrong, but I am too scared to say the words, so instead I just watch her leave. *Okay, yep*, I think, *This is serious*. The doctor will come back and tell me bad news. I will make it through this. I sit in silence and darkness and wait for the doctor to appear. I try to remember what happened with my beginning-of-second-trimester scans with Charlee and Luca. I try to remember what is normal. I decide this can't be good news when a doctor is called in.

The tech comes back in, "Everything looks great!" she says perfunctorily.

"What? Really?!"

"Yeah, really," she says, surprised that I sound so surprised.

"See, my baby died in May. He died from a cord accident at 35 weeks, so this is—well, just being here is hard, and I'm, uh, scared."

Her face changes and her voice softens. She is sorry, and we talk about Luca a little bit. She assures me that everything looks perfect at this stage and that she sees nothing to cause her concern. I walk out and text TJ immediately.

"BABY LOOKS GREAT!" I send him an image of our baby looking particularly cute sucking its thumb. I am so relieved. For now, at least. I thank God. I marvel at the joy of good news.

Chapter 52

When a Stranger Gets It Right
(five+ months after)

I walk into the bathroom on the way out of the hospital and an older British woman is there brushing her hair. She is open and friendly and accented, and I have a weakness for all three of those things, so we talk. She asks where I live and if I have kids. I tell her about Charlee and divulge that I am pregnant. She thinks the three-and-a-half-year age difference is perfect for siblings. She couldn't know that it was supposed to be two-and-a-half years, I can't help thinking fleetingly. She tells me that her name is Ann, that she lives on the water and MGH is a drive for her, but the staff is so good that it's worth it. She says that her daughter is a nurse here, one of the best in the business.

"Oh, I'm sure," I say, "They are all so wonderful here. What's her name? Maybe I've met her."

"Oh, I'm sure not, and I sincerely hope that you won't meet her ever." I am confused, so let her go on. "She works in oncology. But when a woman has a stillbirth here, they bring her up there after delivery so she doesn't have to hear the other live babies on the floor. Can you imagine how sad that is?" she asks. It's a rhetorical question, I know, but I don't need to imagine.

"Actually," I say, diving right in, "I lost our son this past May at 35 weeks. I delivered him here, and I recovered on that floor, too."

And then well-mannered, lovely Ann says just two words: "WELL, F*CK!"

265

Ann is a woman in her seventies with a British accent. She is intelligent and demure, and over the course of this short meeting, I can see she is a good conversationalist. And when I tell her about my son's death, she simply says the most powerful thing she can think of. Strong words reserved for strong feelings. And there is something about a woman who is probably the closest I will ever get to the Queen of England responding like that after I tell her about my son dying. It feels right—like she gets it.

The raw response she gives me in that hospital bathroom, hairbrush in hand, remains one of the most pitch-perfect responses to my son's death that I've ever gotten from a stranger, a friend, family—anyone. Appropriate for all audiences or not, her brutal, direct, and raw honesty in response to my story, to Luca's death, made a visceral sense to me.

Chapter 53

Hope + Fear Arm Wrestling
(eight months after)

I keep telling myself that I should be like all the other happy women in their second trimester. I'm at the point now that women as far along as I am have already made their big announcements on social media. Their news is public, they are thrilled, and they keep saying the kinds of things people say when they assume they'll have a baby to bring home come summertime. You know, blissfully ignorant pregnant ladies. It's how I was with Charlee. Luca, too. It's nuts.

TJ has a wonderful mentor. He teaches him about the Bible, is truly kind, and is generous with his wisdom. I tell him that Charlee is a total blessing, and if she is the only child I get to raise on earth, then I am one hundred percent blessed. (I never want my daughter to think she is not enough. She is. She is more than I could dream of). TJ's mentor listens before saying, "But it's okay to let yourself hope, Jessica. I fully believe that God has another child for you to enjoy on this earth. I think you can hold onto that belief, too." This leaves me here, holding onto a belief that seemingly contrasts with what Luca's death has taught me.

But that's not the real lesson in his death. Some days, I can see a deeper lesson buried in the excruciating pain: not to let go of hope. (And some days, I just see the pain.)

In a tragedy, the real and terrible lesson is to hold onto hope even more than before. Although, "lesson" is not the word to use. I don't think God is some great big teacher in the sky who decides that today's object lesson will involve killing my baby.

And I don't think a "lesson" could ever balance the scale after you've lost your child. Perhaps I should write: this is something I've learned while suffering. (That's better.) Hope becomes more vital. Now I have a baby boy who I will see again—or so hope teaches me. I am learning that hope isn't an extra layer we add to our pleasant lives. It's not a filter we throw on to make our life look more attractive. It's a backbone. It literally enables us to stand despite all the forces pulling us down. Hope is the steely, gritty substance that shows up when everything else has gone. It's picking your baby's gravestone and then joyfully tickling your toddler moments after you press "checkout" and put down your phone.

In the opening scenes of *Charlie and the Chocolate Factory,* we see the poverty in the home, the frailty in the family, and the bleak, everyday sameness for them. They find hope in the form of a golden ticket. It comes with a powerful kind of permission to dream about a way forward, up, out—being better, being elsewhere, finally having not just what they need, but an abundance. What's that like? They let themselves wonder for the first time. That golden ticket is hope. When they first find it, nothing has physically changed. Same shabby apartment, same frail family, same meager living, but this bright and flimsy, foldable thing changes the way they see the future. It changes them on the inside, and they can't help but see the outside differently.

Sometimes I cannot see anything but how hard it is to be here, a mother without her baby—to be her, this woman wrapped in grief, who hurts so much, surely this is not my destiny? But then I write and blink and breathe and there is a shift inside. A tiny golden ticket, just the edge poking through what I'd come to expect.

I walk along so many trees standing next to me, tall and ancient, pillars that hold up a sky streaked in pink. It is all so beautiful, and it is hard to say I am not meant to be here and affected by this beauty. Here, the trees and the colors and the living, growing things are loud. Loud enough to drown out the questions I have about my baby and my grief and how I am doing and how I will be doing and if I am better now and if better will ever come for me. The woods are loud with the sounds of living things still going about the business of growing and being. It is enthralling to see how life still happens, even now.

Grief doesn't seem to eviscerate me quite so much out in the woods, like it does at the mall with people who call me "ma'am" and take my credit card and make small talk and have no idea how much energy it costs for me to keep so many balls in the air like this. Perhaps it is life-giving in the woods because the trees, the squirrels, and the rustling leaves don't care at all if I drop the ball. Life just keeps happening, making it so obvious that if you're here, you grow. Even the leaves that fall simply reinvent themselves in the ground. I see this, and it is hard not to feel like there is hope. I don't mean to feel this. I come here to get away. But when I get here, I find I am arriving. And it is probably similar to how the character Charlie feels unwrapping that golden ticket. Finally, I am going somewhere better—there is more to life than what I see, after all.

There is hope.

Now I have a son whose name means "light," who left too soon. People tell me that simply reading about his short presence here has illuminated beauty in their own lives. Hope teaches me that he remains a light. That the light was not taken because his body left. Hope tells me that I now have a co-destiny with Luca, that the trajectory of my life has changed. It has become bigger, more specific, and more meaningful since he left so soon.

I read about Polaris, the North Star. It is 680 light years away from earth. Meaning, that when we actually see its light, it is long gone, 680 years long gone, to be specific. This makes me think of Luca. Of his light that still shines, though he's gone. I don't think his name is an accident—my light in the sky, shining still, from somewhere I can't see from here.

★ ★ ★

I walk through life tasked with the ordinary burdens that a lot of women carry. I'm raising a daughter and convincing her—sometimes unsuccessfully—to wear gloves in a blizzard. I am constantly forgetting that clothes need to not only be washed, but also dried within the same 24-hour period. Whenever I can, I am stealing away to write the things I find buried in my chest, ugly and beautiful thoughts that crowd me from the inside. I feel better for writing them down. I am writing down clues to a story that I am proud of. I am in love with a man who loves me so deeply that I now identify with every single love song I hear with the overwhelming thought: *I could have written this.* All these ordinary tasks are the gift—the perfect distraction—that carry me through the extraordinary task of holding onto hope and grief at once. I am both grateful for the people who fill my heart and terrified that they will leave me, too.

I often return to books about soldiers. It's not that I love war—I don't—but I just can't look away from the people who view a cause greater than their own physical life. I am currently reading about the Civil War—about Ulysses S. Grant in particular—and there is one theme I keep noticing. Both the North and the South are constantly recruiting throughout the war, but the generals speak about veteran soldiers with a reverence the new recruits haven't earned. Nothing against the new recruits. Maybe they'll get there. They have just as much a chance as the vets ever had. But the confidence a general displays when going into battle with experienced soldiers is something special. Sure, they need any soldier they can get, but what they want more than anything is experienced soldiers.

What sets a veteran apart? I think it's that they've fought battles, survived, and continue to fight them. That's it. Are they still afraid as they march toward enemy lines? I'm sure they are. Do they want the war to end so they can go home to their families? No doubt. Do these feelings disqualify them from being a veteran? Nope, because they've fought battles, and they continue to fight. And wouldn't it be ridiculous if experienced, battle-ready soldiers were ashamed of the battles they'd fought?

I have fought battles, and I'm sure you have, too. I wonder if God looks at us and thinks, *It's going to be okay; I've got my vets down there in this battle. They've held onto hope in dark moments; they've not stopped fighting despite what they've seen and felt. They've been tested, and I can count on them.*

Don't hate the battles you've fought. Don't be ashamed of them. That experience cannot be bought, nor can you read about it in a book and come away with the precious knowledge you now own. Those lessons cost your whole heart, but they give you back a new heart. A bigger one. A steady, battle-tested heart. A beautiful one. You are a veteran, the best kind of person to be by my side as I go into a battle I never wanted in the first place. You help the world trust it's going to be okay because you fought and not only survived, you thrived.

Don't envy the new recruits, the young and inexperienced ones. Don't be mad at the twenty-year-olds who don't quite get it yet. Who don't know to memorize their parents' faces because life is not actually a guarantee. Who don't know how fleeting and precious it is to love someone who you can see and touch and feel the rise and fall of their chest.

Their battles will come. And when they do, they will need you to show them how to be brave and how to do the things that seem impossible, like holding onto hope and forgiving and practicing joy for others when life is terribly unfair and dark with grief.

Chapter 54

Some News

(eight+ months after)

My cellphone rings—UNKNOWN NUMBER flashes on the screen—and I answer it.

"Hi, Jessica?"

"This is Jessica—"

"This is Kim from Massachusetts General Hospital Genetics. Do you have a minute to talk?"

I can feel the adrenaline doing its work, alerting my body of a possible fight coming. *THIS COULD BE DANGEROUS!* everything in me shouts. I don't show any of this with my voice, of course, not even my surprise that she's calling now. Oddly, I also remember her GENETICS pen. My brain is busy recalling things that don't matter, while my body reminds me how much this phone call does.

"Sure," I say, quietly, trying to project calmness, both for her and so I don't distract TJ from his business call in the other room.

"The results from your blood test came back, and they're good news."

Oh God, thank you thank you thank you, I think, exhaling heavily and sinking down onto the couch. There's nothing ordinary about good news, just like there's nothing ordinary about food when you're starving. My body stops its internal high alert; my brain signals the troops to be at ease.

"Everything came back negative," she tells me. "Your baby looks healthy."

"That is good news—really, really good news. Thank you for telling me."

"Of course. Do you want to know the sex?" she asks.

"Yes."

"You're having a girl."

I thank her and hang up. I stand quietly for a second, waiting for TJ to finish his call. I'm having a girl. For maybe the first time, I realize that I had subconsciously thought—hoped—I would have Luca again. That this time he'd stay. I realize that I was counting on this baby being a boy—as irrational as it sounds. I was counting on a second chance to have Luca, and getting to keep him this time. On opening up the bin of tiny boy clothes and getting to use them after all. I am ashamed because I am crying, and it is not entirely from happiness.

There is no wrong sex: I've said that over and over again, and I stand by it. I love my Charlee more than I could ever measure—but I was going to have a girl and a boy, and then I didn't. And then I got to be pregnant again, and I thought maybe I'd still get to have my girl and boy. I peek my head into the bedroom after I hear TJ end his call. I tell him that MGH called, that the results from the blood test are so very good, that our baby is healthy. Dear God, this baby is healthy.

"And we're having a little girl," I say quietly, gauging his face for any of the same feelings that are uncomfortably shifting around in my own heart as he processes this news.

"Another girl?"

"Yeah," I nod.

"That is WONDERFUL! We love Charlee so much—and now we get to have ANOTHER GIRL!" He is happy. He is only happy, I can tell, and that is such a relief to me. I agree with him; it is wonderful news.

"But it also feels like we're losing Luca all over again," I say hesitantly, my voice breaking.

"Jess, Luca will always be safe with Jesus. We know that. Even if you were carrying a boy, it still wouldn't be Luca. We're getting a sister for Charlee and another little girl for us. This is really beautiful news. And if you want—we can have another one after this one," he says, pointing to my round belly.

"I don't know if I can handle going through this again," I answer truthfully, tears running down my face. But right now, it doesn't matter if I can do this again. It matters that we get to have another baby girl, and that the news about this baby is positive today. Positive. Because there is no wrong sex, and my son died, and this baby is alive, and the possibility is growing stronger and stronger that I'll get to deliver a living child this time. A living little girl. Like Charlee Jane, but not like Charlee Jane, because she'll be all her own brand-new self, and I am letting myself become a little excited to discover her. (And, of course, sneak bows on her head before she's onto me and pulls them off).

Chapter 55

A "Normal" Parent
(nine months after)

I am talking to Nancy, my therapist. Aside from TJ, she is still the only one I've told we're having another girl.

"But I was disappointed when I found out," I confess to her. "I thought I'd finally get to have Luca; that I'd get to dress him in his clothes, at least."

She is gentle and kind and honest, like always. She isn't surprised or judgmental about my confession, and that feels good. I guess that's empathy—trying to see life from another's point of view and not only *not* being repulsed by it, but telling you the view is worth seeing. Nancy tells me what I already know, that Luca is with me but that I was never going to carry him again, not even if this new baby were a boy. And that it's okay to feel whatever I feel. That this whole pregnancy is emotional, and it's okay that not all the emotions feel good all the time. And also: they're just emotions. Feelings are fine, but they are never facts.

"Also, I now find myself getting worried that this little girl won't be as cute as Charlee, because Charlee is so incredibly cute! I KNOW how ridiculous this sounds—my Luca DIED! I mean, I'd take any baby—even an "ugly" one—so why am I so worried about cuteness all of the sudden? What is wrong with me?!"

Nancy just smiles.

"I know I sound crazy," I say.

"Actually, do you know what you sound like?" she asks.

"You mean, other than crazy?"

"I mean, do you know exactly what you sound like?"

"What?"

"You sound like a normal parent with normal concerns about a subsequent child."

She is beaming at me, like I'm the second-grade wiz kid who knows how to spell *rhythm* and wins the whole dang spelling bee.

"Oh," I say, taking this in. "But I'm not a normal parent..."

"You're not," Nancy agrees. "But these are fears that normal parents have, rather than the paralyzing fears that indicate trauma. It's—well—it's promising for you, Jess," she says, still smiling, because apparently, I still won the spelling bee (R-H-Y-T-H-M).

"I don't even believe in using the word ugly for a baby—or anyone—anyway. I'm sorry I used that word," I say after a while.

"I know. You didn't call anyone ugly—you were speaking in hypotheticals." She is doing what she does best: reassuring me.

"I don't think my baby is ugly. I don't think this little girl is ugly at all."

"I know you don't."

I leave Nancy's office a little bit proud of my normal-parent fears. I walk out of the building and into the cold Boston air, and I am smiling at strangers now. *Hi! Just a normal parent here, smiling, because I am so wildly normal. I hope this daughter is as cute as my other daughter, see? That's what you call normal. Not stuck in complicated grief. Not convinced this child will die too. Just, like, nervous about this kid's looks because her older sister is the cutest thing ever, you know?* I should probably start posting bump progress pictures and signing up for those awful weekly pregnancy progress reminders about how big your baby is now—the ones that would still come even if you lose your baby, so I don't sign up for them this time. But I'm so normal that I probably should.

But I don't. I don't sign up for those weekly emails. I don't post bump pics. But I do have moments of "normalcy"—they are still irrational and ridiculous, but not grief induced, so they are something to be grateful for. Today I am pregnant, and this baby is, from what the experts with their blood tests and machines can tell, healthy. Today I am normal, because I worry that this little girl won't be as cute or as smart as her big sister. Today I am not normal, because I don't dare sign up for anything that would still come as a cruel reminder if this baby dies. (Your baby is the size of an orange this week!) Today I am not normal, because I had thought that maybe this baby would be a boy, too, and that maybe he could wear Luca's clothes and maybe it would be like Luca hadn't left after all.

Today I am normal and not normal. Today I am grieving and grateful. Today I am here, fully experiencing life.

Chapter 56

Bouncing Forward

(nine+ months after)

My first job is at a restaurant called Grotto Pizza. I wait tables and there's really nothing worth mentioning until I clear dishes, when I meet the dishwasher. We're both teenagers. I am a waitress, so I wait tables; he is a dishwasher, so he washes dishes. He stands in front of a big sink and waits all night for people like me to dump dirty dishes in his soapy water. That's the only reason he's here. Every time I bring him dishes, though, this happens: he's surprised. Then he laments. "MORE dishes?" he says, emphatically—"Ughhhh!" This goes on through my entire shift. I don't remember much about that gig, but I will never forget the dishwasher.

I still think about him now. Like when Charlee is acting like a toddler and, at first, I'm surprised and even annoyed. Then I tell myself, *Jess, don't be like the dishwasher. You signed up for this.* When I signed up to have a baby, I signed up to have a toddler who also acts like a toddler. Which brings me to this point: when it's really cold outside in the middle of winter and I start to think longingly of summer, I remember the dishwasher. Nobody is forcing me to live in this beautiful New England city. I get to live here! Also: winter comes every year; don't be like the dishwasher.

My therapist and I talk like old friends now, so I interrupt our chatter about the girls and TJ to say something serious. "I've been feeling apathetic," I say quietly. "I don't really know why. I'm avoiding my email because the idea of responding to people is overwhelming. Also, I feel anxious. My parents' beloved dog is old and feeble, and they keep thinking tonight is the night for him to go. But then he rallies, and he's here another day. But the thing is, he *will* die. It's inevitable. And sometimes it feels like life is waiting around for your dog to die. Or your parents. It's terrifying."

I take a deep breath; it feels good to admit how awful I feel.

"You know, Jess," Nancy says gently, "Death is part of our experience here."

"It doesn't make it easier—"

"It doesn't make it easier," she agrees. "And it's an interesting dance to perfect—loving so completely and throwing yourself into a moment that will not last. Knowing loss, honoring loss, acknowledging loss—but not becoming its slave, allowing the fear of loss to dictate your life."

"It's really hard to be here." I say, and she nods.

"It's also really better than I thought it'd be," I say, and she nods before I add, "It's both."

"Let me ask you, Jess—has the unimaginable loss you carry—Luca dying—made you wish you weren't here? Does this grief make life lose its...invitation?"

I think about this question. Nope nope nope nope nope, I realize. There is so much good here, still, despite a loss that, at times, has felt unrecoverable. Not that I've recovered—I am not sure what that means. I have changed—but here is the miracle: the change isn't completely bad.

I first read about post-traumatic growth in Cheryl Sandberg's book, *Option B*, and it's a relief that this phenomenon is even possible. Something terrible happening to me and my family doesn't automatically result in a terrible life forever. Growth is an option. Growth! Can you believe it? This is amazing news for me. This is amazing news for all of us.

In an article in *The Atlantic*, Sandberg's co-author, Adam Grant, writes, "When psychologists started studying resilience, they thought there were two paths. One was to be broken by tragedy…to walk away with post-traumatic stress disorder, debilitating depression, and severe anxiety, and the other was to…return to the state you were at before the event. They were really surprised to discover…a third response, which is not just bouncing back but bouncing forward, and that's about emerging with some positive change from a negative event. That's not to say that the grief or sadness goes away, or that anyone is happy that it occurred. But alongside those negative emotions often come improvements in people's lives, where they're able to say, 'I'm stronger. I lived through that, I can live through anything. I'm more grateful'…"

"I'm grateful to be here," I admit to my therapist. "Grieving my son, doing life with Charlee and TJ, I don't want to stop greeting Monday and washing the dishes my family has eaten from and feeling alive writing into the night while everyone else sleeps. I'm grateful to be here for all of it. I'm grateful."

★ ★ ★

"I don't know how the details will play out, Jess—nobody does—but I imagine that this grace that has gotten you here will continue to do its work in every season," my therapist replies.

I realize again that while I cannot predict my future hardships, I can absolutely predict the grace that will carry me through them. I can't help but notice a theme: that good comes despite evil. Despite the worst.

In the Apostle Paul's letter to the church in Rome, he writes these beautiful words: "And we know that in all things God works for the good of those who love him..." (Romans 8:28).

The stalwart reassurance that line carries makes me feel like *safe* is actually possible. Also, it's important to note that Paul doesn't write that all things are good. They aren't. If you are an adult who is honest, has read history, or even has paid a little bit of attention—you know this. But God, in his creativity, is able to draw good out of brokenness.

I never watch TV at home, but sometimes I do in waiting rooms before I see a doctor, and I love when a cooking show is on. To a degree that is more than I ever suspected I would, I enjoy watching the chefs run through a run-of-the-mill grocery store, grabbing the mundane or downright strange ingredients they're forced to use per the rules of the competition, and turn things like Laughing Cow cheese, Wonder bread, and pickled cherries into a masterpiece of a meal. Honestly, I get so bummed if my name is called before all the final meals are presented. My favorite part is the magic of making something elite from whatever life has handed you. Something delicious from ingredients you probably would never buy on your own.

It's like in the book of Genesis, the very beginning of the Bible, when we see God hovering over the void, the emptiness, ready to create, call forth light, divide the firmament from the land, fill the ocean with fish and the sky with birds and variations on the color blue. Then He makes us because it's not enough to just create beauty and ingenuity, he creates relationship, love, the strength of hearts drawn to each other, His to ours, and then we get to reciprocate.

When I look at the vast crater that grief has made—my own empty arms where Luca should be—it helps to think about God hovering over my own emptiness, ready to call forth light again.

I will always want my son here—always—there is no "but" that will absolve this fact. And I cannot deny the closeness that grows between myself and TJ in the days, weeks, and months we continue to return to ourselves and each other in the darkness of our grief. Luca teaches me to love better, to love now, to even love how hard it can be to raise any babies at all, because the headline will always be that they are here to raise, and he is not.

Luca teaches me that the end is not the end—that not even death is the end. Growing up in Pennsylvania, I watched farmers plough fields. It is always the same. The dirt is cut into—broken—but that is not all (broken is *never* all). For it is into broken soil that the seeds go deep, deeper than if the ground had been left untouched. As a result of this cutting and breaking and exposing deep parts of the earth's insides to the sunlight and air and seeds, the fields feed whole towns. But first they are broken. So it is with our hearts, with my own. I hate the brokenness; I wish it didn't hurt like it does. But I am in awe of the growth that follows. I am in awe of the part when the world is fed.

"Also," my therapist adds, "It's February." She's lost me with the February thing, so I wait.

"Do you know how many people make extra appointments with me in the winter?"

I keep staring.

"The lack of sunlight and vitamin D, the cold, feeling trapped inside—these have an effect on our mood—and all this to say—" she takes a breath, "Spring is coming."

I cannot get away from it. The seasons. Fall is so vibrant, surely it will last forever—how can such blooming color not remain? You don't realize the leaves swirling in what can only be patterns of celebration is actually their last dance. Winter comes; it looks and feels like the end. It really does, but this is what life and God in His kindness continue to teach me: spring is coming. New life. Post-traumatic, post-winter growth. So winter is not the end. It's connected to spring, not even just symbolically, either; spring could never physically come without winter arriving first.

What if life's seasons of winter are not simply to be denied or even endured, but embraced. What if the lessons of winter are just as poignant as the lessons of summer. I want to be happy; I love being happy! But the raw, inescapable grief that I walk through leaves permanent, undeniable gifts in my heart, gifts that happiness alone simply cannot offer. I am a more patient mama now. I love better and am more mindful of being present. I am still afraid of tragedy, but I have seen that a broken, open heart grows joy again and this makes me able to say, like the poet Emily Dickinson, "I dwell in possibility."

Like a ridiculously stubborn bloom struggling out of a cracked city sidewalk, joy can grow from places we leave for dead. Also, I would have no resilience without the hard seasons, for there is no discontent in happiness that would compel me to search for it. Resilience doesn't come from reading books on pain or watching movies about pain or listening to podcasts on pain. It comes from walking through pain. That's it. Resilience is worth as much as it costs; and there are moments that feel like it has cost everything. Winter is hard and also good and necessary and eventually brings spring. All of it matters; all of it works in our hearts in ways that we need.

For those of you who are feeling buried and buried again by winter, I promise you: spring is coming. Oh, and by the way: don't be like the dishwasher.

Chapter 57

God Bless Mary Todd Lincoln
(seven months after)

Nancy, my therapist, works as a social worker for Labor and Delivery at Massachusetts General Hospital, as well as having a practice of her own. But now that I am pregnant again and under the care of MGH, I meet with her every week at the hospital. It's a strange thing to continue to go back to the place where I first confronted Luca's death. I realize that most people avoid this kind of thing, but the care here is so comprehensive—both physically and emotionally—that returning to this haunting place proves worth it. Plus, they know me. It's really nice to go where you're known.

I am reading about Abraham Lincoln and the complicated grief his wife, Mary Todd Lincoln, experienced. She grieved first for the death of her sons, the second of whom died during their White House years (later, a third son died, too—how does one bear so much loss?), and then she grieved anew after the assassination of her husband. There is no judgment here. God, there is absolutely no judgment toward the way a mother copes with the loss of her son(s) and then her husband. I lost a child, and I still cannot imagine exactly how a mother feels when she loses her own child. Especially one you've been able to know on earth even longer. It is simply unthinkable—even when you've been forced to think about it yourself, over and over again. There is no perfect way to walk through the crushing path grief takes us down. With grief, there is no hero who does it better; there are simply those of us who must do it at all. And there are all of us who have to do it eventually.

But in the case of her tremendous losses, Mary Lincoln didn't attend any of the funerals. As much as any one human can understand another, I get it. I didn't want to attend Luca's funeral. I hated the very thought of it up until we were walking down the hill with our families, to the place we'd chosen to bury him. I couldn't anticipate what happened there. I can hardly describe it now. But I know that it was significant and I was a different woman walking up the hill after burying his body. I was acutely aware of our togetherness—not only mine with TJ, who was also a parent burying his son—but with the people who stood with us. Luca's grandparents and aunts and uncles and cousins were grieving him too. They didn't stand exactly where I did at his funeral—nobody else could—but they could stand as close to me as possible, which is what they did. They could cry with us and promise to remember him, too. The fact that we all stood in a circle, hand in hand, praying and singing to a God who promises better things than death and loss, continues to mean something.

At the risk of sounding too simplistic about something that is complex, it makes me think about the end of Dr. Suess's *How the Grinch Stole Christmas*. The night before Christmas, the Grinch (the poor guy has no proper name—maybe this, along with his tiny heart and too-tight shoes, was part of the problem)—steals every single physical thing having to do with Christmas. So, the Whos wake up to bare walls and empty space where there used to be festively bedecked trees. The gifts, lights, and feasts are gone, too. The Grinch leaves early in the morning, satisfied that he's finally ended Christmas, sure he will no longer be tortured by hearing their singing from his cave high up on the mountain on Christmas day. Except, they still find reason to sing. They still hold hands and sing their songs, because they still have each other, and it turns out that this is something worth holding onto. Turns out, they discover this is enough.

Although at his funeral, TJ and I see a world without our son, we still find reason to sing and pray to a God who gives hope. Although Luca isn't here in the way he should be, I am grateful he isn't gone forever. Acknowledging both of these truths—along with the support of those who love us—proved much more important than I could realize before actually being in that circle on that hot July day, praying, singing, and crying with people who were doing the very same thing because my baby is dead.

And again, as much as any of us can understand the actions of another in crushing times of grief, I understand Mary Lincoln's choice not to face such a physical reminder of the deaths of both her son(s) and her husband. I get it, Mary, and I am deeply sorry that funerals happen at all. There aren't perfect words, but let me stumble through saying that it's not fair, and yes, it is too much for a mother and a wife to bear. AND (not but—*and*) I wonder if, by missing those funerals, she missed some of the comfort, the healing, the togetherness that speaks of better things than our solitary grief.

Mary refused to go into the rooms in the White House that had specific attachments to her young son, Willie. Again, in whatever capacity we are allowed to understand each other's journeys without being the one to walk them, I get this, too, and I want to say to a grieving mama: whatever you need to, do. It was terrible that she could not simply move and live somewhere new, that her mental health was judged, her grief picked apart and criticized by a public that was devastatingly unkind to her. But I also wonder if eventually letting herself visit the rooms that reminded her of her son could have helped her heal. It would hurt; but maybe had she visited the rooms, and had not cast aside this physical memory of her son, she would've seen that her experience with Willie was worth all the feelings that come from love and now grief. That the fact that he left didn't diminish her love for him—and that the pain she felt over his death was because of her great love for him. Could the pain, because it was connected to her love for her son, be perhaps sacred and beautiful, albeit awful and unwanted?

I think some pain—maybe even all—is the entryway for healing, if we can endure it. I don't mean to say, "You're grieving, so go do terribly hard things for doing hard things' sake on top of everything else. The more pain, the better." And I certainly don't mean to say go and do those hard things now. Some things are meant for now, some meant for later, and some meant for never. The wisdom to decipher these things is what I hope for all of us.

For instance, we go to my parents' home in PA to bury Luca in July and don't go back until Christmas. Every day during this past holiday, I think about walking down the hill into the plot of woods where he is buried. Every day, I decide not to. The emotional component of the celebration of Christmas in general (our first Christmas grieving Luca), being near Luca's gravestone (it is just down the hill, as opposed to our life in Boston, where it is a 7-hour drive away), and having a toddler who has suddenly decided she doesn't want to sleep anymore are already enough. When I burst into tears the moment TJ suggests we walk down to see Luca's stone, TJ wisely helps me decide that, actually, we can do that another time.

But I wonder if walking back to the place where Luca was pronounced dead—sitting there in the same waiting room, going to the same ultrasound room, this time with his little sister in utero—I wonder if that helps. Like it's another version of going into your closet with your parents and fully facing the monster you're sure is there. Only you find—what? That the closet is empty and your fears are far worse than reality. That you're not alone as you face them. That you're going to be much more okay than you ever thought at 3 AM in the dark by yourself. That the baby you carry doesn't die every time.

With this said, if you need to never go back to wherever it is that the loss in your life occurred, I understand. I am not here to argue with that very personal choice. As my father-in-law said to my mother-in-law (while leaving New Jersey to visit us in Boston in the dead of a cold January when she suggested he grab a coat), "You do you, and I'll do me." (Four hours later, he walked into our apartment obviously freezing, sheepishly saying that he had decided against his coat while my mother-in-law looked on in exasperation. Thankfully, we had a spare coat like any good New Englander should.)

I am here simply to say "me too"—over and over and over again, until you realize that, though your beautiful life is absolutely unique, you are not alone, and there are others who are hurting and healing, too. I say this to Mary Todd Lincoln, who endured more than I can imagine, and I say it to you, too.

Chapter 58

Today Wasn't Supposed to Be Terrible
(eight months after)

I tell my therapist that I'm seventeen weeks pregnant tomorrow, and I still can't feel this baby move. "Sometimes I'm afraid something is wrong—that this baby has died too." I expect Nancy to listen to me and agree that this is scary. I don't expect her to ask me if she can grab a nurse.

"Since I am not a nurse, doctor, or midwife, I think it'd be good for you to talk to a medical professional about what you should expect to feel right now." I am taken aback. She looks at me and adds, "And maybe the nurse can just grab a Doppler real quick and listen to the heartbeat."

I realize that most pregnant women would jump at the chance to hear their baby's heartbeat and be reassured that everything is alright. I don't know if I am surprised by this or not, but I don't want a Doppler. Not today. This was supposed to be an easy appointment. Just therapy. And in therapy, nobody was going to potentially tell me my baby has died.

"I don't want that," I finally say. "I don't want bad news today." Nancy listens. She nods and says that I don't have to have a Doppler. But could she grab her favorite nurse to have a chat with me?

"Yes, of course—and if I knew everything was fine, I'd say yes to the Doppler. But I don't, and that scares me, and today wasn't supposed to be terrible." Nancy says she understands before leaving and returning in a minute with a nurse. I recognize her immediately. "You gave me a flu shot last month," I say. "You told me you were so good that I wouldn't even need a Band-Aid!"

"Sounds like Sue," Nancy says, and now we're laughing. Jumping right in, Sue says, "Nancy tells me you're seventeen weeks and nervous because you don't feel your baby?" I nod.

"We don't generally worry about women not feeling their baby move at this point in time—but how about I put your mind at ease with a Doppler?" Why does everyone want me to potentially hear bad news today? I try to slow my nervous breathing as I give in and say, "I guess the baby is either alive or dead—and either way, I need to know, eventually. Might as well listen to the Doppler today."

I follow Sue out of the room, and we find an empty exam room. Nancy tells me she'll be nearby if I need her. "It might take me a little while to find the heartbeat," Sue tells me, her play-by-play both practical and kind. It's a few moments with the Doppler on my belly and my breath suspended and the silence terribly loud. Then, suddenly, woosh woosh woosh woosh woosh woosh … and it doesn't stop. My baby's heartbeat. I am breathing again and so grateful.

"Oh, thank God," I say quietly.

"That's a perfect heartbeat," Sue says, and I agree.

So I am not always the girl who finds out her baby has died. Sometimes it's different. Sometimes my baby is still alive—like now.

Sue and I walk out of the room, and I walk right into Jenny. She is another nurse, and I love her. She helped me deliver Charlee. I labored with Charlee for 32 hours before I could start to push—and 15 hours in, I was still unmedicated. Meaning it hurt beyond what I can really explain. There is nothing to compare it to (please don't say period cramps, because no). It is simply childbirth, and it feels like all of you is simultaneously lit on fire and ripping in half. (I don't mean to scare you; maybe labor will be a real walk in the park for you. Also, there are drugs, and they do make a huge difference. I learned this first-hand with my own blessed epidural. An epidural and my divorce from my ex-husband are two of the most compassionate things that have happened to me on earth.) Being in obvious pain, my nurse Jenny took my hand.

"Women have been birthing babies naturally for centuries," she said, "And they've also been in tremendous suffering for centuries. There is absolutely nothing wrong with taking advantage of the fact that your time to give birth has come in the 21st century and modern medicine is available. I've had three babies and three epidurals, hon. No need to be a hero beyond pushing this baby out today." My sister-in-law in Los Angeles was also sending me texts, encouraging me to take full advantage of the benefits of living in modern times. Plus, my body was in so much pain, and after fifteen hours of labor, I was only one centimeter dilated.

ONE. You are supposed to get to TEN before you can even think about pushing the baby out.

"Have you ever known a patient to become paralyzed because of an epidural?" I asked my midwife.

"No, never," she said.

I told her to send in the clowns. Okay, so actually it was the anesthesiologist, but he made me so happy, he might as well have been one. (No, no way—a clown doesn't even come close.)

Send in heaven, Jesus, hope, salvation, a break from suffering. Send in the anesthesiologist!

He came in quickly, and suddenly the lights were bright again and people in scrubs were telling me to hunch over. I would have offered to stick the needle into my spine myself, if it would have moved things along. I was in so much pain at this point, I don't even remember the feeling of the injection. But boy do I remember how it felt when that sweet medicine started flowing. Suddenly there was a coolness where there used to be fire. My body relaxed. TJ and I were laughing, and I was cracking jokes. My parents were in the other room, and I asked TJ to go get them. "They live so far away—we might as well talk, since they're here!" I called out cheerily.

The rest of Charlee's birth is wonderful. I even take a nap before pushing, since I've been up since my water broke the day before. I push for thirty minutes, and suddenly there she is—all red and hungry and loud and wonderful and ours. She nurses right away; having been placed on my chest, she opens her mouth wide like a flip-top and then clamps down on my breast with incredible urgency. TJ and I exchange a look that is probably not altogether unlike the look on Dr. Frankenstein's face when his monster starts walking and talking and owning an actual life. Anyway, God bless Jenny and her way with words. That epidural was really wonderful.

When Luca dies and I am being induced, Jenny is once again one of our nurses. Having walked with us through bringing Charlee into the world, she walks with us through bringing Luca's sweet body into the world. It is terrible, but she is there, and she is wonderful. It is strangely right that she is there for both of our children's grand entrances. She cries with me over Luca's death, holds my hand, is the kindest of souls to have by my side.

And now she is looking at me seventeen weeks pregnant, having just heard my baby's wonderful heartbeat. We hug.

"I might cry," I warn her.

"I might cry, too," she says, because that is the kind of nurse she is.

I tell her how I'm doing, and she is thrilled to see me doing better, thrilled to see me in a much different circumstance than birthing my dead son. We still haven't told many people that I am pregnant, but it's so very good that Jenny knows.

Chapter 59

Pregnancy After Loss is NBD
(except I'm kidding because it's really hard)
(nine months after)

I see her—the baby girl who lives in my rounded belly. We have the big scan this morning, the ultrasound where they take a close look at the growth of your baby. They examine the brain, kidneys, heart, etc. TJ and Charlee are with me, and, other than the anxiety-ridden dream I had last night in which the ultrasound showed my baby to be a small, oddly teenaged girl and not a baby at all, the appointment is peaceful. The ultrasound tech tells me that she remembers us. "I think I was the one …" her voice trails off, but I know what she's saying.

"To tell me our son has no heartbeat," I say quietly. "I'm sorry—I only remember the doctor from that day. I guess she came after your initial look. I just remember her because she was … so cold. That's the kind of thing that stands out."

"I'm so sorry," the tech tells me, "… for everything."

"Thank you," I say.

She says the baby looks good. "I'll go get the doctor now."

"That's normal, right?" I ask, even though I know the answer, "To get a doctor to go over what you see?"

"Totally standard. We always do it—doesn't mean anything other than protocol."

I appreciate the doctor who is now looking at the ultrasound screen and telling me things like, "As far as we can tell right now, your baby looks healthy and normal." The doctor who looked at Luca at his big scan told me with full confidence, "The dark days of pregnancy are over. We expect a healthy boy in another twenty weeks or so." I often think about how neither of us could anticipate just how dark the days would get.

This doctor tells me he is reassured by the scan. But he also says that nobody can really guarantee me anything. I nod my head because I know. God, I know. But there is wonder in this tiny dark room. Charlee is wide-eyed and staring at the screen as TJ holds her close and points out her baby sister's feet and hands.

"You know, Charlee," I say, "a lot of babies bring a gift for their big sister—what do you think about that?" Charlee's face is radiant and smiling as she walks right up to my belly and speaks directly to it, "Hi baby! Please get a present for your big sister. That's me, Charlee!"

TJ and I smile at each other, and it's as good as done now. This tiny growing baby will have a gift for Charlee when they first meet, no matter what. I am smiling writing this down tonight. It hasn't even been nine months since we were back in the ultrasound room, looking at the still heart of our son Luca, and I can hardly believe the joy that we get to have today. I think that it never does run out. As much as I've been convinced that the joy in my life is gone for good, there is still more to experience. I think I am finally learning this. I am shocked by it, too.

* * *

Social media is wonderful and awful. I sincerely appreciate how it allows me to write and share and connect with others. I value the updates and photos from family and friends. I even enjoy occasionally seeing what my exes are up to. (Come on, you do it too … right?) But then there are times when you are struggling, and it seems like everyone else is LIVING THEIR BEST LIFE! and ACCOMPLISHING ALL THEIR DREAMS! and HAVING ALL THE BABIES! And that's hard to see. It's triggering, as they say. You can be just fine and then see a pregnancy announcement—and suddenly you are hurting all over again. It takes a lot of discipline not to compare your life to the ones you see edited so perfectly right in front of you. It's easy to compare your everyday, sometimes very-painful moments to another person's highlight reel and feel like you got shortchanged. But it's not a true comparison, because we never really know what battles others are fighting. We're all fighting them—some are just more public than others.

One night when my brothers and I still lived in the same town, there was a meteor shower. So, we piled onto my parents' deck in Pennsylvania, far away from the city lights. We laid down on the wood floor and waited, because sometimes the only way to really see what's happening takes patience. The night felt alive. I've realized that this scares people who don't understand growing up in the woods. They think it's a quiet kind of living, because they haven't heard it themselves. But it's loud, so wonderfully loud. The electric buzz of cicadas, the bullfrogs, the owls, and the wind—they never rehearse and always sing with everything they have. Or maybe they always rehearse. Maybe the rest of the universe consists of tenants below and above. Maybe we're all in the same building, and everyone else is thinking, *Great. We're sharing space with Earth, the musician who won't stop practicing.* But there are those of us who hear the woods and the sounds of this beautiful world and think it's all really great.

Like the time I was living in upper Manhattan, and there was an opera singer living above me and a saxophone player to my left. When I heard them practicing over and over again, all I could think was musicians are some of the few people whose dreams can actually be heard out loud.

That night with my brothers was loud, too—woods-loud— and then suddenly the stars started falling out of the sky. But I kept missing them. One brother would point and say "There's one!" And another brother would say "Ooh—look over there!" I'd turn my head in that direction, but it was always too late. It was disappointing to be around something so spectacular but not see it for myself. In a deeper setting, that kind of thing can crush a person (I know). Like my brothers continuing to see the falling stars, but I don't. Like other mamas coming home from the hospital with their babies, but I don't.

So, I finally decided to lay there and wait. I stopped trying to catch sight of my brothers' shooting stars. And eventually, I saw my own. It was beautiful, and I'll never forget the revelation: to trust that my own path has what's mine and to focus on that. That the sky God made has more stars than people, and we don't have to worry that they'll run out.

Chapter 60

Their Pregnancy Has Nothing to Do with My Loss

(nine+ months after)

I am absently scrolling through social media when someone's post catches my attention. It's a confessional, a link to something she wrote about a recent miscarriage. I don't know her well, but I comment and say that I am so sorry she is going through this. I tell her I know it's hard and I am holding hope for the day she brings her baby home.

Something she writes strikes me in particular. I don't remember it verbatim, but the sentiment was this: "A lot of my friends are pregnant. And for a few wonderful months, we were pregnant at the same time. Now they are pregnant, and I am not. So, I see them and smile and repeat in my mind what has become my mantra: 'Their pregnancy has nothing to do with my miscarriage.'" I read that sentence again. I write it down to hold it better through the coming days.

And then I notice a pregnancy announcement from a dear friend I toured with years ago. We were dressing-room mates and had developed a special friendship. I can see how thrilled she is to make the announcement. I'm touched to see that she included her sweet mama in the photo she posts alongside the announcement. This is very special for her mom, a widow, now expecting her first grandchild.

For the first time, I think about someone else's pregnancy as having nothing to do with losing my Luca.

They are two different things—one joyful and one tremendously painful. And part of living a whole life with a heart that fully works is being able to meet each event with an appropriate heart posture. The Bible calls this rejoicing with those who rejoice and mourning with those who mourn. Therapists call it having empathy. Maybe there is enough space in my heart for grief for my son who I am not raising and joy for my friends who get to bring their babies home. Maybe our hearts are bigger than we ever first imagined when we were little—when we were sad, so life was clearly terrible, or when we were happy, so life was finally perfect. Maybe it is actually both, weaving between the two so seamlessly that it's never just one thing at all.

* * *

Also, speaking of comparing ourselves to others—well, something happened to me. (*Yeah, Jess, and we're all really sorry about that.* No, for once that's not what I mean, but thank you. Truly, thank you.) I mean, somewhere on this trail of grief, something happened to my heart. I'm not sure that it's good or bad yet, just that it's here. I think it might be good. Or like a lot of other things, even if it didn't start out good, it will eventually become good.

I used to see people doing something I wanted to do and get that prickly feeling inside. It was, I think, part motivation and part jealousy. I'd feel hot and sad, like someone else's success somehow took away my ability to succeed too. Like our world is so small, it's only big enough for their gifts. So I'll just sit on my gifts and hope they're an okay booster chair because I feel small when I think this way, like I can barely see past the dashboard— let alone see where I'm going. But then some suffering happened to me, and this started to change. And then more suffering happened, and the change sped up inside me. And now I see people doing what I love, and I root for them. I'm not worried about my place in the world. It's clearly here, I'm clearly here, and we're all just trying our best to keep our loved ones here, our hearts connected, and the laundry done.

Now I see people hustling and I'm like, *YOU'RE AMAZING! But if it's alright with you, I'll stay on the sidelines and talk about how I feel. Maybe I'll do this forever. Also, sometimes I'll bake.* Anyway, it's nice to not be preoccupied with my perceived place in this world. To not have to guard it. It's nice to be like, *Okay girl, go live your best life while I am busy acknowledging that life is stunningly hard. (Although, I'm not sure what living your best life even means, because it's got to be more than the gym and a cold-pressed juice and brunch on the weekend, despite what the Influencers say.)*

I suspect that our best life is the one where we show up for all of it. For the part that hurts, the part that's casual, and the part that takes our breath away. I suspect it is when we practice vulnerability and allow others to see us even when we're in pain, which feels particularly hard for me. It is when we allow others to help us, to let them make us meals and watch our kids and listen to the questions the world answers with silence. It is when we stop pretending. At least mostly. A little pretense is perhaps necessary; a little bit of saying fine when we're not, just to get through making a purchase at CVS—but to make sure we have our people with whom we do not pretend.

Our best life is when we admit that this is hard and find that we are resilient. When we admit that nothing looks worth rising up for, but our faith admonishes us to close our eyes and to rise up anyway. I love Anne Lamott's book title, *Hallelujah, Anyway*. I feel like both life and faith ask this of us over and over again. Our best life is so much deeper and harder and grittier and more glorious than brunch on the weekends and trips to the spa would have us believe. Self-care is so much messier than social media would have us think.

It's nice to trust that the right doors will open and that the locked doors aren't hiding things I really want anyway. They're closed for a reason, so maybe I can put down my crowbar. It's so nice to no longer carry a crowbar! It makes walking so much easier. And it's also nice to glimpse that life is actually much bigger than we ever suspected, with enough room for all of us and enough corners to surprise us with something good we didn't see hiding in tomorrow. It's okay that others see the good today—because surely, we will see some good tomorrow or the next day or even next year.

Ours is coming, too.

It may be hidden in deep places like our hearts, and you may never be able to photograph it and slap it onto Instagram with a filter, but it's coming eventually, and it is worth the wait. And we are worth experiencing the riches that life offers. Maybe those riches will never be a fancy car or title or vacation house; but maybe they will be revealed *in* us. Maybe we won't necessarily get to go somewhere more beautiful than here, but maybe we get to *become* more beautiful, more loving, more hopeful, more steely in our faith and kind in our words and thoughts. Maybe, like the Velveteen Rabbit, and our grandmothers who we adore, we get to become. And we learn that part of what gets us there is less about gobbling up the pleasure we love, and more about allowing the pain we avoid desperately to do its slow, deep work in us. So that we finally wake up, and gratitude compels us to say, "Hallelujah, anyway."

Chapter 61

This Glorious Life
(four months after)

I have a friend who was diagnosed with cancer. *(Dear Jessica, my dear reader might ask, Have you ever considered writing about puppies? Not dead ones, either; the* Of Mice and Men *reference does NOT count. Just normal, healthy puppies with sharp teeth and sweet breath. Not that we don't love the dead baby and cancer musings, of course, but enough is enough, maybe? Love, Your Readers. Dear readers—this is Jessica—please feel free to write about the wonder that is puppies and tag me on your social media posts. Love, Jessica.)*

Anyway, back to my friend with cancer. She is lovely. She's funny. She's always been healthy. She's a lot like everyone else is who is lovely, funny, and healthy—she just also has cancer right now.

"I can't eat broccoli anymore," she tells me. "I used to eat a ton of it specifically for its super cancer-fighting agents that make it famous. But I can't touch it now. It betrayed me. In the end, all that broccoli didn't matter."

And it's just broccoli, but it's not just broccoli, too. After surviving loss, there is a pervasive feeling that nothing matters. All the checkups, the prenatal vitamins, the exercise, the fact that I wasn't a high-risk pregnancy and my baby passed every test with flying colors—all that didn't matter, not really.

The natural next step is to wonder what else doesn't matter. What else will go terribly wrong, no matter what. It's a mental battle, and sometimes I wonder how everyone can just calmly do life as if the shield between ourselves and disaster isn't actually make-believe. As if the Great Wizard of Oz isn't just a little man who likes the color green.

But what about God and his kindness? Maybe our shields aren't real, but He is. And what about the fact that I now know what can go wrong when you make a baby, when you make a marriage, when you love someone—I've got the PTSD to prove it—but I still want all of it anyway? The shields and the broccoli might be placebos, but when you're choosing over and over again to open your heart, to love anyway—that's real. That's brave. That kind of showing up rewards us with a full, lived-in heart.

You've been hurt? Trust someone anyway. You've lost someone? Connect anyway. Life is hard? Yes. It's also beautiful. Don't feel like doing this anymore? I know; I didn't feel like doing all of this yesterday, either. Do it anyway. You're worth it, I'm worth it, this glorious life is worth it. It's not fair? You're right. None of it is. Not the very terrible things that happen to us and not the wonderful, thank-God-I-am-here-for-this kind of things that happen, too. It's not fair. It just is. Dig into what is. It's worth it (I think, I hope, I trust).

★ ★ ★

It's just four months after Luca died, and I hesitate to say it's been a good day, probably because I'm fiercely protective of this sacred grief that I carry. It's here because Luca is loved, and it's here because Luca is not. This brokenness is so much more complicated than a fractured foot that is cast then healed. Also,

I'm not quite ready for people to be like, *Yay! You're better! Now you can host my baby shower!*

But today was a better day.

It's nighttime, and TJ is telling me about something he read in the Gospel of Matthew.

"Open it up to chapter five," he says. "Let's read it together." Right away, my eyes fall here: "You're blessed when you feel you've lost what is most dear to you. Only then can you be embraced by the One most dear to you."

I read it aloud, pause, then read it again. "This means we're blessed, TJ," I say slowly, trying the words on my tongue the way I would say the new-to-me Spanish words I practiced in high school. He nods, "I know we are, Jess." That's the thing about TJ. He's so confident in God's goodness—in our steady, unfolding purpose as a family. He sees winter for what it is: the only thing that can call forth spring. He sees purpose in the barren trees. They need to store up energy to grow and bud and blossom, come spring. It's not just death. It's life, too.

"I think—" I continue, "I think we need to embrace this brokenness. It's horrible, but it's what we have, so we probably need to embrace it and look for the reasons the Bible keeps mentioning it." Whatever newfound intimacy comes of being broken is something that could never happen on its own. There are true, beautiful friendships I made in the midst of my divorce that wouldn't have found their way to my heart had I not first been broken.

In all my years spent dancing around the world, rehearsals were never evenly distributed. Whoever needed more got more. If you were fine, you were mostly left alone. I'd almost feel jealous of my cast mates who got to spend more time with the director and choreographer because they needed the help, because they needed the attention. And now it's my turn. Now I need the help. I get to spend more time with my Maker because of it, and if it's one more gift from Luca, then I'll take it. I will still cry and hurt as I do, but I'll take it.

"Is that the line you were talking about, TJ?" I finally ask, remembering the reason I'd opened the Bible at all.

"Nope," he answers, smiling, "But this is way better."

Chapter 62

A Shell
(a year after)

I don't doubt that God loves me. If you read the Gospel, you see hard things happening, yes. But you need to keep reading the story, because the hard things are never the end. If you keep turning the pages, you see a redemption that floods you with gratitude for the hard things. You see a redemption that arrives only after the hard things come first. Could I do without the really hard things, trade the redemption for my son? Yes. With my apologies to "Purpose," and "But you'll bring so much healing to others!"—still, yes. But this isn't my choice.

Hard things don't mean God doesn't love us. They mean we're here. They mean we're vulnerable, with big soft hearts, in a world that is neither safe nor fair. They also mean that redemption is coming. Does this mean we like the hard things? Maybe the best among us learn to appreciate them as they come, but if you're like me, you hate them. You hate that your son is gone. You hate the tone-deaf things people say to you. At the same time, you hate their silence. You hate the grief that is a hair shirt; no matter how many garments you wear over it, it's still there, scratching your skin raw, always too tight against your heart. You hate it all.

I think we are each living a different part of the story. Some of us are right in the middle of the hard things. We can't see the redemption coming, and that's okay. The hard things are too big; there is no room in our vision for anything else.

A Shell

There was a girl who messaged me on a social media app. We'd met briefly, but now she'd lost her daughter who was stillborn. She asked if we could talk, so I called her one evening. She was quiet, almost reserved. There are some spiders who, after making a small hole in their prey, vomit a digestive fluid into the prey's body. Then they drain out the insides, leaving the insect a literal shell of what it was.

Grief can feel like this, drain you fully.

And when the woman at the rental car counter is staring at you, her smile as wide as the ocean of pain your own smile is hiding, expecting you to be fine with the problem she's presenting; expecting you to be resilient and mature—after all, there are people dying, suffering real tragedies, you know, and this is just a car—and you stand there, unable to articulate why you simply can't deal with this. Maybe you could have a week ago, but that was a lifetime ago. That was before, the first half of your life that will forever be marked: *Before You Really Suffered*. And this is not even after yet, this is *While You Are Suffering*, and you haven't figured out how to suffer and deal with annoying strangers without completely falling apart or wanting to say a curse word or just opening up your journal and letting them see how sad you are. But you know you can't do any of that—you are too aware of social mores to do any of that—so you just stare back and your eyes get misty. You could really use a disclaimer. You could pass out a card, explaining the spider draining its prey and how this is what grief does and you are just a shell. Nobody expects a shell to be resilient and mature and game for life's curve balls. Nobody expects a shell to be fine with the plan going suddenly wrong and having to be creative in a moment when all your energy is spent simply *not* sobbing.

This girl I was talking to on the phone was in raw grief, and a lot of words had left with her daughter. "I think I can do this right now—I mean, I have to," she said, while I pressed the phone harder against my ear to be careful to catch her words. (Nothing is worse than saying "WHAT?" after a grieving mother bears her soul, making her repeat her precious words all over again.) "But—forever?" she asked. "How do I do this forever?"

"You don't," I said. "You don't do this, exactly, forever. You do it today, and today, and today—for as long as it's today—and then one day it changes. You find that you can laugh again, and it doesn't come with as heavy a cost and it isn't just gallows humor. It's actual joy. It comes again, I promise. What you're doing now, nurturing newly-born grief, isn't your task forever. You will love your daughter forever; you will grieve her forever—but the grief changes. It changes with you. It doesn't mean one day she matters less, but I promise you, this intense job of grieving is not your forever. I can't tell you when—your timeline is yours alone—but it will change. Try not to worry about doing this forever; try to sit with it as it's here, letting it lead you and teach you, but our grief is not stone. It is a living thing, and all living things are subject to seasons. All living things change."

We need others, we need their stories of redemption, we need to know all is (finally) well with their soul. We need them to be honest about how hard it was, to know that we are not alone in this darkness that invites us to stay forever. And we need them to talk about the redemption. To be like Andy in *The Shawshank Redemption* when he finally crawls out of the sewer, the prison, the life sentence he doesn't deserve. The rain washes him clean, teaches him the true meaning of freedom for maybe the first time in his life. You can see it on his face. We are starving, and these stories are bread. I am starving, staying up late, googling baby-lost mamas, finding bread in the joy their brave faces show now. I follow their precious stories, rejoicing in and devouring their joy, for I taste and know their bitter sorrow, too.

Chapter 63

Thanks for Asking
(three months after)

I first notice Chris at a mandatory warm-up before an eight-hour rehearsal for the 1st National Broadway tour of *A Chorus Line*. We're doing leg lifts. Well, most of us are. Chris has strategically positioned himself so that only his face reflects in the mirror, with his body out of view. This way our choreographer sees his exaggerated breathing—his Lamaze-like HOO HAW, inhale exhale—convincing her he's working hard. But I see the truth. His body is totally relaxed—not a single leg lifted—while his face looks like a pretty convincing impersonation of a woman in labor. Our eyes meet and he winks. *Who is he, and how do I get him to be my friend?* I wonder.

When you lose someone, you wonder what's left. Your perspective changes; all you see is what's not here. It's so consuming that you start to blend in with the emptiness. It's late, and your family has gone home. It's weeks later, and you don't know what's next, because you've never been here before. It's two months later, and people don't ask how you're doing as often. You are tired, and the line between that persistent emptiness and yourself blurs.

But then there are the people who know and love you. It's important to spend time with these people—always, yes— but especially when grief has caused you to think you've lost yourself, that you've disappeared into the profound sadness.

When you're unrecognizable to yourself, those who know us become a mirror. Your pop says, "You're still you, Jess," ten minutes after walking through your door and one week after your son dies. You still make your husband laugh, even when you're both grieving. Your brothers, your sister, your mom fill a room with so much conversation, with tears and laughter at once, holding your still, too-quiet, perfect baby in awe, because if you're still a mom of two, they're also still uncles, an aunt, a grammy of those two. And your friends touch you gently with their words and with the conversations you finally start to have with them again, and you see yourself. Like today, with Chris, my friend I met in *A Chorus Line*.

I take a ferry from Boston to Provincetown to see him. I am so seasick on the way there. But I am in good company, because everyone is. Turns out seasickness is another one of the great equalizers of humanity. I watch a super cool guy in a tight leather jacket barf into a bag, and it doesn't matter how cool any of us look anymore. Now we're all just sick more than we're anything else. I finally make it to land, and Chris is waiting for me. We talk about vulnerability, connection, what we've done and what we'll do. I talk to him about Luca and he cries; we both do. It's good to talk about Luca again. It's the end of summer, and Luca died at the end of spring. He was supposed to be my summer baby, but he never did see summer, not even in my belly. It's past the time that many people ask about Luca. If someone finds out that he died, they usually just say "I am so sorry" and quickly move on to a less terrible conversation than the one about my dead son. It's not news anymore. I get it. But man, it's good to talk about my boy, and it's kind of Chris to ask about him, to listen to me.

"I love his name," Chris tells me over burgers. "What made you guys name him Luca?"

"Thank you," I say, quietly. "Nobody ever says that. They don't tell me they love his name, and they don't want to know the story behind it. It means so much that you do." And it's true. People know the headline: my baby died. They usually don't need to know any more. It's too much, or maybe they are afraid it's too much for me to talk about—but whatever the reason, they aren't interested in much besides the news of his death.

"I like shorter names," I say. "Especially since *Taormina* is a mouthful. Also, it had to sound good with Charlee. And the meaning—that's what sealed it. 'Bringer of light'—how beautiful is that? It just felt perfect."

"And he is bringing light, Jess—through you continuing to share his story as you write. That's some beautiful light. It's an honor to see it." I don't know if I love Chris more for the tears streaming from his eyes, what he's saying, or the fact that he never did one leg lift in the entire month of warm-ups we had to do with a choreographer who is wild about leg lifts. I guess it's all of it. We talk about Charlee and we laugh, too—it's seamless, actually, talking about my kids, laughing and crying, respectively.

"I'm talking too much," I realize aloud, seeing Chris's empty plate and mine with half a burger still on it. "I once read that you know you're talking too much on a date if you have lots of food and your date has already finished theirs."

"I just love this burger, Jess," Chris says, "I ate it really fast. Plus, I love being here with you. Talk as much as you want." I'm not sure that my life is enviable, exactly, but I'm sure that doesn't matter, because it's mine. Remarkably, I'm still me. And I can't shake the feeling that I'm blessed. We say goodbye, and I board the ferry with a full heart. Yes, full. Not empty. Not today, anyway.

Chapter 64

Some Things Help
(six weeks after)

Right now, people often preface their words to me with, "I know nothing helps, but..."

Nothing helps? That's a grim prospect. Imagine showing up at the hospital in terrible pain and the doctor saying, "I know nothing helps." It's not a perfect analogy because not everyone who speaks with us is the equivalent of a doctor—but my point remains: we both need and get help and, at the risk of sounding redundant, the belief that nothing helps is both not true and not helpful.

Dear friends, I promise you, some things help. I promise you, we are never beyond being helped. Even the worst things—the death of your child—even then, there is help. There has to be. Otherwise, what does someone like me do? The word "comfort" exists because grief and suffering exist. They don't all cancel each other out; rather, comfort comes along with grief.

I'm washing my face tonight, and there is a steady parade of *Things I've Found Comforting* moving through my mind.

When my brother flies to see me while I'm in the hospital having Luca, he sits next to a stranger who asks him why he's going to Boston. Jase tells him about Luca dying, and the stranger gets quiet.

"Does your sister have faith?" he finally asks.

"Yeah, she does," my brother replies.

"Then she's gonna be okay," this man says.

I still sometimes think about that man on the plane, tuck myself into my heart, and believe him really really hard. I'll be okay.

Two months later, TJ and I walk by a gorgeous, visibly pregnant woman. She's wearing a stretchy cotton sheath dress, the kind I wore two months ago, too. I stare at her belly, round with precious life, and then will myself to look away. I don't say a word. This is life now; no time like the present to get used to it. TJ leans into me and whispers, "Do you want me to kick her?" It's perfect. I'm not so good at feeling sorry for myself when I'm laughing so hard. When we're both laughing. Life can't be so bad when it's also funny, when I'm so loved. So it's a good kind of cognitive dissonance that has me rethinking how terrible it is to be here, after all. (DISCLAIMER: No pregnant women were kicked or harmed in any way in the making of this book.)

My pop is here with us now in Boston. He, like all of us, doesn't have any answers, but he is good at listening. He's a pastor, but he doesn't jump in with a lot of the sterile answers you find in the kinds of sympathy cards filed under the religious section at Hallmark. He believes in the kindness of God, and I like to be around this kind of faith. He also understands that sometimes all you can do is listen and lend your own stories to the weight of the moment.

He tells me again about his mom dying when he was only four. I can't write the words without tearing up, because once you have a kid, every kid that ever loses anything good becomes, "God, what if that were Charlee?" She needs me so much at two; that won't stop at four. "I remember how, afterward, my dad moved out of the bedroom he and my mother had shared and into the guest room," my pop says over lunch today. "One night a strange sound woke me, so I followed it into the guest bedroom. I'll never forget my strong, reserved farmer dad wailing uncontrollably. I'll never forget how afraid I felt seeing him that way."

There is a gift grief gives. A kind of unique closeness you share with others who've been here, too. It's an empathy that enables you to see each other. Like, really see them—not just their struggles, but the way they're so valiantly struggling to stand and walk and breathe and answer the questions that hurt and look past the indifference that hurts even more. You see them fighting for their life, fighting to return to themselves like some kind of boomerang. Everyone tries to tell you: Just sit down, you just can't fly through grief. You can't boomerang back that quickly. But maybe you'll be the first. It's a quiet, whispery thought, but it's enough to make Monday bearable; and maybe by Tuesday it'll be a sentence you say out loud, and that will be enough to make you brave. Or at least less afraid of your neighbors and their curiosity that's got you avoiding the elevator and taking back doors.

Chapter 65

Faith and Despair; This Is Hard
(three months after)

"Can I ask you a personal question?" a friend asks, and I nod. "How do you still have faith in God after your baby died?"

I wonder if I'd feel like I needed faith at all if my life was just fine. Isn't this kind of brokenness exactly what the gospel is for? It is much more for right now than for innocuous Sunday mornings and soulless songs on the Christian radio station. It is exactly for when the despair stands waiting to swallow us whole, all its waters an open mouth. It is for when every self-help book falls flat because your *self* is the problem. Your thoughts are too dark, your feelings a promise of death. So, there must be something better, something outside yourself that can help. Otherwise, life is too bleak. At least, from here.

When I traveled to Kenya, I saw animals you cannot find in the Pennsylvania woods that raised me. I spoke in a rustic church with people crowded out the door. I ate food prepared by a village who saved their best, richest meat for us while they ate rice and beans. But do you know what stands out the most? A family who leads me to their very sick baby.

"Please pray," they say, those two words landing where desperation and faith meet. I pray and pray and do not see a change. Maybe God healed that baby, I don't know. I hope so. What I see in that moment, though, is a need for the gospel. For good news. We've all seen the signs in kitchens and entryways across America—something about living, loving, and laughing—and surely this doesn't cut it. And by the way, surely nobody who has ever actually grieved thinks that sign is encouraging, right? When we are laughing and happy, we really don't need to be reminded of it. It's like telling the sun to do its thing at 1 PM in the afternoon. *Yeah, got it,* the sun thinks, rolling its eyes. And when you are NOT laughing—when grief has stolen it right from your belly—being told by a sign to keep laughing, etc., is actually offensive. *You don't know me,* you think as you walk by where it stands, utterly tone deaf on the wall. All this to say: please don't remind someone to keep living, loving, and laughing—especially when they're grieving. And when someone is generally okay, they probably don't need that kind of vague admonition either. Maybe just pick another quote. Maybe try radical bleeding-heart wallpaper—subtly letting the broken know they belong as soon as they see it in your foyer (I mean, I don't have a foyer, but since this is hypothetical, I'm handing each of you a foyer, you're welcome) and avoid the signage altogether.

Also, try to skip the pretty words about staying strong. I know now that there are moments where the pain steals the very marrow from your bones and it is not strength that keeps you standing, it is only the simple fact that you are still here. Call it mercy or call it punishment, but you did not die, too. ("But, Jess! If we have to throw away our "LIVING, LOVING, LAUGHING, ALL THE L'S" signs and steer clear of ones that force everyone to be strong all the time—what signs CAN we have?" Dear Reader, I realize this is a tough one. God forbid we all have naked entryways and kitchens devoid of mandates on the walls.

Growing up, my parents had signs that said things like, "A Messy Kitchen is a Sign of Character. Wait till you meet the character who lives here!" Also, "On This Site in 1827, Nothing Happened."—things like that. And I think that kind of eye-rolling, dad-joke humor would do well to serve both the grieving and non-grieving alike in kitchens everywhere. If that doesn't work, how about just an abstract painting of the Brooklyn Bridge you bought on the streets of Manhattan from a local artist? That does the trick for us, anyway.)

The gospel—and faith in general—is for every one of us who looks around and says, *No, this is not okay.* This despair, this death, this pain and suffering—none of this is okay. There must be something better in store for our precious hearts. And that is where the gospel shows us something better. It is for the hopeless, the broken, the striving, the sick, the marginalized, those who hold our dying babies, and those who never got to have a baby at all. It is a home for the wanderers and makes the unloved lovely as they—we!—discover how dearly loved we are.

And it is for me.

More than ever before, it is for me. Now, in my grief, I need therapy. I need my family. I need my friends. I need lots and lots of help. But God, I need the hope of heaven. Whatever enabled Israel's great King David to confidently say after the death of his own baby boy, "He shall not return to me, but someday I shall go to him"—I need that.

Chapter 66

There Are Gifts Here
(one year after)

I walk into the main campus building of Simmons College. My friend is a professor here and has asked me to speak to her class of seniors.

"About what?" I ask through text.

"Your career."

I am confused, because now more than ever, I'm not fattening up my resume. I'm spending lots of time with my daughter and TJ, yes, and that's important—but it's not a career. When Luca died, I just stopped. I stopped being social. I stopped working at the popular spin studio downtown. I teach one class a week at a local Pilates studio. My career isn't exactly booming.

"I'm really flattered that you'd want me to speak to your students about anything at all—but I am honestly not doing much that looks very impressive right now. At least in terms of my career."

"Well, you're writing, right?"

"Yes. But nobody is paying me to write."

"You have a career, Jess," my friend counters. "*Have*. Right now—and I actually want you to talk about the way closed doors and life seasons have guided your career in ways that you couldn't anticipate. You have an interesting and encouraging story. I want my students to hear it—if you're comfortable sharing it." So I tell her I'll do it, and then promptly put it out of my mind, because it's a month away and a lot can happen in a month anyway.

But here I am, sitting in her classroom, listening to her talk shop before she introduces me and invites me to the front of the class. I take a deep breath and tell them I'm honored to be here. And then I just tell my story. I talk about growing up studying ballet, going away to conservatories in the summer, and then realizing at 18 years old that ballet doesn't fit me. That I have a voice I want to use, and I am not sure how to use it, really, but modern dance feels like a better fit without being a total departure from what I've been studying all my life. I cut my hair short and become a modern dance major at Philadelphia's University of the Arts. After four years, I am torn between dance and music, but I know I love an audience. My professor suggests musical theater, and I throw myself into the New York City audition scene. I get gigs, I start touring. I get a Broadway contract with the touring company of *A Chorus Line*, and it's a big deal. I come home to my first husband having an affair, and this is an even bigger deal.

I move back to my parents' basement; I share a floor with the three Giant Malamutes (this is not hyperbole; technically, they are Giant Malamutes and they very much live up to their title) who crap outside my basement door. I am in my late twenties, and my life feels over. To me, it is a life sentence to have so much time left on earth with so much pain to endure while looking at a life that is vastly different from the one I'd planned. But this isn't the end of the story. I discover this while I spend my time writing down how I feel and what has happened. I make it into prose and lyrics, sometimes singing about it and sometimes blogging. I write a book about my first husband's affair and my divorce knowing it will probably never be published, but I have to put it somewhere. I am in therapy, and I am going to be okay. I fall in love with a kind person. We write music together and play shows together. That love doesn't last—not in that form, anyway—but it's astonishing to find that I have not died with my marriage, after all. That I am doing things that living people do—all day long, I do these things.

Every day I go to the woods and walk and walk and walk until I am something. Maybe better, I guess. Just not where I was, and since I hate where life has landed me, I am glad that in this small way I can exercise autonomy. I tell the students about the butterfly I spot on one of these walks—startling blue, perched on a pile of—well, of all things—perched on crap. That butterfly is a revelation to me. That I can still be me, despite how my life feels entirely other and ugly. Despite how my life feels like crap. They laugh about the crap. That's probably a lesson, too, now that I think about it. I go home from that walk different, definitely better. We are not what has happened to us.

The students soberly listen. I keep sharing my story. I tell them how a friend calls to give me his apartment in New York City for three months, free of charge. "You've got too much to show the world to hide in your parents' basement in rural Pennsylvania," he says to me. I tell these college seniors that this wasn't the plan. I wasn't supposed to move to New York alone. I was supposed to move there with my husband. I didn't want to do it by myself, but then I do it, anyway, and I find it gradually empowering. I am taking care of myself, and I am taking just about every exercise class the YMCA has to offer—since they're the only classes I can afford in the city. I wake up one day and realize that it doesn't hurt so much to be me. I like being here in this busy city where people follow their dreams, get stuck on the subway, and hear many languages spoken in the time it takes to get from one city block to the next. I even like being here alone. I am playing music all the time, on whatever stage I can—from the world-famous *Blue Note Jazz Club* to being the hired entertainment for someone's birthday party in Queens.

Then I meet some buskers (musicians who play for donations) on the subway, and they ask me to play my ukulele. I do, they play along, and someone records it on their phone and puts in on YouTube. Within a week there are a million hits, and it's viral. This is when NYC radio personality TJ reaches out to me from the biggest morning radio show stage in America, asking to interview me for his podcast. We begin to date. We fall in love. He sends me to take a class at a small-at-the-time boutique fitness company called Flywheel. The instructor asks me to audition, and I get a job in fitness. TJ is offered his own morning radio show in Boston, and we move. I am part of the launch team for a popular national fitness brand in Boston, I play some music gigs, we get married. I am happy and in love, and we bring our firstborn daughter Charlee Jane into the world. Then I am very busy. I am teaching lots of fitness classes and mothering a small human.

I tell the students about becoming pregnant with Luca, our second child and first son. I watch their faces change as I talk about his death and how everything in my life stops. I talk about grief and how it brings what's inside into sharp focus. "It's one of Luca's gifts," I say, referring to how Luca's short life with us makes me realize that I have to prioritize meaningful work. Even if it's just taking time to write every single day. Even if it's crafting my second book, one slow, tired evening at a time.

I tell these students that I decide to shift my focus. "I realize that I need to embrace who I am: an artist, a communicator, a storyteller." I explain that fitness is important and I love it, but being up at 4 AM to teach classes and then home to mother a toddler with nothing left inside to create by the end of the day just doesn't work for me anymore. "I'm writing a book," I tell them. "It makes me feel alive when so few things do after Luca died. Even grief—even being told no, you won't be raising your son—has a hidden gift.

There will be many times that life tells you no, and this hurts a lot. And you absolutely grieve, you feel what you need to feel. But then you realize that the no isn't the end of the story. I've had some major no's in my life—but always, always, always, they have revealed a yes later that I couldn't have seen, had it not been for the no coming first.

"I want you to know that it's okay to be disappointed, and it's okay to not know what's next. But there is a path for you. And even when the answer is no at some point, the answer will eventually be yes—somewhere. And that yes will be worth wading through all the no's. We will all have trials. But there is something that happens to our hearts, something good and weighty, something that cultivates empathy and gratitude when we go through hard times that just doesn't happen in happiness or when life is easy and smooth and predictable. These trials that create deep, strong places in our heart cannot be bought and cannot be simply read about. They have to be walked through— experienced—before those gifts are yours."

I ask the students if they have had any no's that, in the long run, turned out to be for their own good. Hesitantly, they raise their hands and share their stories of disappointment and curves along the path that have brought them somewhere both unexpected and good. There is a girl who was denied entrance into the graduate school she always wanted to attend—but is now part of an internship she loves that she never would have done had she been accepted into her first choice. There is another girl whose relationship ended, which freed her up to say yes to a program in another state—something she loves and now realizes she wouldn't have had the courage to have done had she still been somebody's girlfriend. I love hearing their stories. I love encouraging them that they will be okay—although there will be hard times, maybe (probably) very hard times. I love to tell them that there is life after loss, an unforeseen yes after a terribly painful no.

I walk out of that college class realizing that I am content. No, not done. Not even close. But I am content and grateful for own my story. I am not a ballerina, but what I am drew me to the stage and an audience in the first place: an artist, a storyteller. I am not married to my first husband anymore, but I am married to my soul mate—the one with whom I am grateful beyond words to share this precious life. I am Charlee and Luca's mama. One, I get the joyous and hard work of raising every moment of every day; one, I got to carry with me for nine months, birth his perfect body, and then bury in a ceremony that took my breath away. And now his cells mix with my own forever. Now, we have a co-destiny. I have another baby on the way, and I hold hope that we get to raise this one.

But what if we don't?

Yes, that thought that is never too far.

Then we will cross that terrible bridge if we come to it, I suppose. My faith simply cannot rest on a life that is free of trouble. A life that we insist is free of trouble in order to be okay is a house of cards. It's precarious and will eventually topple. This might sound overly simple, and that's alright. Sometimes I need simple. I need to trust that God is here with me. Especially in the brokenness. And that healing is not something that only comes once. Already, it has come for me twice. If it has come twice, then it will come again. I bet everything on this.

Chapter 67

I Will Say with Them, Baruch Haba
(nine months after)

I am five and a half months along when we finally make the announcement. We announce my pregnancy on air, on TJ's morning radio show, and online—the places one makes these kinds of announcements in the twenty-first century. We decided to make a big, over-the-top video with music and everything (Okay, I think I sing one line), because the only options that feel right are either never telling anyone that I'm pregnant ever, or telling everyone in a big, produced way. Plus, TJ and I are performers, so we do lots of things in big, produced ways. We post the video, and I write this caption:

"Hi! Why make a subtle announcement about something that is both too private for words and also scares the crap out of you, right?" (Language, Jess—this is a pregnancy announcement, for goodness' sake! I know, guys, I *know*. But dear reader, this is a different pregnancy, so perhaps you can understand how it warrants different language).

When I was starting to labor with Luca, my former midwife from Charlee's pregnancy heard what happened and immediately came to our room. She held my hand and cried with me, so you can see why I love her.

"Will I be able to have another baby?" I asked, not caring that it was probably too soon to ask this.

"Yes," she said right away, "But it will be a different kind of pregnancy than Charlee's and Luca's—emotionally, I mean."

And she was right. I am so grateful. I am also confused when the few people we have told say "Congratulations!" ...like being pregnant means you get to have a baby. Don't they realize I don't know what will happen? And then I remember that it usually does. That there are many ways to add to your family, but pregnancy is definitely one of them. So I smile back and say thank you, I'm so grateful, I hope everything is okay—all the words that mean *I hope this baby lives.*

I'm five and a half months pregnant, and it's getting really hard to hide it. I don't always feel like wearing a minimum of three layers and keeping my coat on. This daughter of two charismatic ministers would like to go to church and raise her arms without being nervous that people will know. At this point, I think it's easier if people just know and I can take my jacket off when I'm hot.

"I feel really big," I recently told my doctor. "This is the biggest I've ever been in this stage of pregnancy."

"Yes."

"Yes?"

"Third baby in three years, Jessica. Your body knows what to do, and you're doing great."

So let's keep feeling whatever feelings we're having—huge, scared, tired, grateful, hopeful—all of it. And let's keep trusting that better things are coming, are probably already here. That God has a good plan and that we're doing great. Look, the doctor said so.

The responses are so kind. Well, this one strikes me as a little odd: "I hope this one lives ..."

Oh, yep. Me too! And this one: "Unfortunately, for most places in the world, this is just how it is. Mothers lose their babies; so, you're really more the norm." *Okay. Thanks, I guess? I'm, uh, really hoping to beat the odds with this one, if that's okay.* The Internet is weird. There are many more comments that move me to tears, because they are so lovely and generous and caring. I am crying all morning and exhausted from the emotion of it.

I am so emotional, all-over-the-place emotional. I am grateful. And I am sometimes very scared. When the baby doesn't move for a while, I start to feel a sinking panic. I guess it's not unlike PTSD. Maybe it is PTSD. I think about all those soldiers coming home in peacetime, being told that the danger is over, and yet they see enemies everywhere, dressed like war itself.

They see them in the mall, on the train, and in every other square on Instagram. And no matter how many times they're told they're safe, they can't help but be brought back to the immense trauma and heat of battle at the sight of whatever innocuous thing inevitably triggers them. Trauma is real. I see pregnancy announcements, expectant mamas' bellies, babies in strollers—and Luca is dead all over again.

"Hi Jess! How do you get through being pregnant again after having lost a baby? How are you not terrified?" So many people on the Internet ask me this question.

First of all, who says I'm not terrified? Second of all—I don't exactly know the answer to that question. (I am sorry if the search for that answer is the reason you're reading this book!) Here is what I think. You take it a day at a time. You wake up grateful for this pregnancy. You are so sad Luca isn't here. You get scared. You talk to your therapist, your pastor, your parents, your friends, your partner. All the time, you monitor this baby moving. You hope and pray. You keep your thoughts on a short leash. You forbid your mind to live in the space of "what if." You realize this risk is worth it. It's hard, but a lot (all?) of life's meaningful things come with a hefty price. All this to say, no matter how I feel while I am doing this, the headline is that I *am* doing this—and that is brave—and I am terrified at times (and this is still brave).

★ ★ ★

Every professional tells me everything looks good. We're in the coveted second trimester. But it was the same with Luca, and he never came home. I am grateful and cautious and continually asking God to let me keep this one. I am writing names down quietly, pairing them with *Taormina*—that beautiful word that is both a place in Italy and our last name—and also, I am hesitant when asked what number baby this is.

It's my third.

You have two at home?

Well, no; isn't that just the darnedest thing? Not every math equation adds up, and some are terribly personal, leaving you crying at the most random times.

But it's kind of nice to not be hiding this baby in my belly anymore. For one, as the baby grows, it's just plain getting super hard to do. My body was demanding maternity jeans the moment I saw the two pink lines on that stick. And also, I'm pregnant. It's freeing to just say it. Because I am. Just as pregnant as the other mamas who are currently pregnant—even if they didn't lose a child. Part of me wants to jump to the end of this book and read a happy ending, see the photos of the new healthy baby TJ and I get to take home. (I rather envy you, dear reader, because you can!) But my job is to write this book, and that part of the story hasn't happened yet. I am hoping so hard that the end of the story is just that, but I don't know. Past experience reminds me of this every single day. I don't know.

"Will you be registering for gifts for this baby?" a friend asks.

"No," I say without hesitation. I've bought one thing for this babe so far. And that is a teething sheep that Charlee picked out for her little sibling as a gift. She really wanted it, and far be it from me to not encourage the love between Charlee and her sister. So we bought it at Barnes and Noble—along with a gift for TJ and, of course, for Charlee herself.

A friend writes me after seeing the news. "In Judaism, we say, *baruch haba* instead of *mazel tov* to pregnant women. It means 'blessed be the coming,' literally. We say it so as not to jinx anything. *Baruch haba*, Jess."

This resonates. This, I can get behind. *Baruch haba,* indeed. Please let this little one come and stay and be healthy, dear God. And thank you that, as of today, she is still coming. Blessed be the coming. I feel our daughter moving a lot these days. It is good—far better than not feeling her move at 22 weeks. But it makes me more anxious because her moving is a sharp reminder that she could suddenly stop moving at any time.

"Like Luca did," my midwife says, empathizing.

"Yes."

"But Charlee never stopped moving," I continue, "so chances are this one won't either."

"I'm hoping that right alongside you, Jess." And she is. We have so many who are—people we know and those we've never met. It is incredible to be cared for so well.

Chapter 68

Looking Forward
(ten weeks after)

Today we booked a weekend away—just TJ and me—and I'm looking forward to it. This might not sound worthy of mentioning, but it's significant because grief frames a story in which you'll never look forward to anything again. It is important to listen to grief (just as it is important to acknowledge other people's grief); but grief doesn't know your future and therefore cannot predict it. Now Charlee is sleeping, and TJ is showering, and I am sitting on my couch, looking forward to life. This is encouraging.

So that is happening, but so is this. Someone tells me about their friend who had a very long labor. She was in lots of pain, they say. She didn't want an epidural, but it was going so long that she finally capitulated.

"Isn't that sad and hard?" she asks me.

"Your friend's baby—they're okay?" I ask, not bothering to ask the baby's sex.

"Yes."

"And your friend is, too?"

"Yes."

"So there could be worse things than a long labor and forfeiting the bragging rights of her 'natural childbirth' because she got an epidural she didn't want. The baby could be dead."

My friend stares and apologizes. "I'm so sorry, Jess. I forget who I am talking to..."

"I'm just not the person to sympathize over a long labor," I explain.

I suppose this is where I warn the world that grief has a way of giving one permission to be terribly blunt. To be more honest and less polite. To simply be. Without all the small alarms that usually go off in our minds when we are too transparent or too sad or too nakedly honest without even a few threads to dress it up and make it a more palatable thing for others. Grief silences those alarms. We walk into a china shop like the bulls we are, and we make a scene. And we might not even care when their fine and fancy dishes are broken on the ground because our son is dead and we have stopped caring about almost anything at all.

So anyway. I'm looking forward to life (wild applause!), but I'm still different from the girl I was on May 16, before my baby died (silence). While touring South Korea performing in a musical, the girls in the cast hang out for the first time. So, as a dumb icebreaker, I call out, "What's everyone's worst injury they've ever had?"

Someone says, "A broken foot!" Someone else: "A sprained wrist!" It goes on like this for a while. One by one, we list the typical injuries one gets that are a bummer, but really fine when all's said and done. Then one girl's turn comes, and she blurts out, "Yeah, I was raped."

We are all shocked and scrambling for words to acknowledge the terrible thing that happened to her. It was awkward and out of place, it was vulnerable and real. And I didn't see it at the time. I just felt how she'd dropped a bomb and stopped our conversation with the truth. I didn't know her grief gave her permission to be terribly honest. And now every time I mention how my baby died, I feel like that girl; like just about every single audience feels wrong. Like every place is the fine china shop and I am the bull that opens her mouth and all the dishes are broken on the floor. I didn't mean to break dishes. I just meant to be honest for once, because it's really pretty exhausting to pretend and smile and think up all the words that help others feel fine, and then feed them, one by one, to a crowd, to a stranger, to my friend, to my family—starving while I do it. I am not your emotions pharmacist; I don't know what to give you to make you feel better about this. If I did, I'd also give it to myself.

* * *

"You're an amazing helper, Charlee." We're at the grocery store and Charlee is unloading as much as she can from our cart onto the conveyor belt. She makes it a game, her small hands working to beat an invisible clock, and I think, *Yes, Charlee, you're right. Life is always better when we make it fun.*

"Happy helpers are here to help!" she replies in a sing song voice, repeating it like a mantra as we leave the store and I buckle her into her seat. I laugh out loud, and then my mind wanders as I drive. *Happy helpers are here to help.* I think about this year, about the miracle that didn't happen. Hearing: "There's no heartbeat." TJ asking for privacy and—once the doctor and tech leave us alone with the still ultrasound—together, asking God for a miracle. We didn't get that miracle; that part of the story is obvious. But the miracles, the help I didn't know to ask for— they came, startling me the way peace does to a people ravaged by years of war.

Dr. Tony Evans, a pastor, talks about comfort being like a blanket. It doesn't change the temperature of the room, but suddenly you find yourself warm, despite the temperature of the room. God has given me a blanket over and over again. It doesn't lessen the tragedy of Luca dying, but here I am, full of "moments of strange praise" (as written by Nessa Rapoport in *A Woman's Book of Grieving*) that don't seem to lessen despite what's happened. In fact, the startling contrast makes it even easier to recognize them.

I am grateful. It's a complex thing to be grieving and grateful at once, to see a story I'd never have written and a narrative that is still rich and full of wonder and awe anyway. Life is asking me to hold its vast duality in the one single space of my heart. It doesn't fit; I don't reach that far. But here I am, grieving and grateful, so what do I know.

Nobody asks me about delivering Luca, but his birth is sacred and holy. Sad, yes, but no less of an experience than birthing our Charlee—both are an act that, having walked through them with TJ, I could not imagine a day when we are both on this earth and not together. We birthed two children and buried one; we are together the way a tree is with its roots. I don't know which I am, but I love the tree and I love the roots, and I cannot fathom either the depth it reaches or the height it stands.

* * *

Luca's permanent gravestone finally arrives at my parents' land in Pennsylvania, and my mom emails us, asking if we'd like to place it or if she and Pop should. What I mean to say is that life is harder than I ever imagined it to be.

But I look at a photo TJ took. It's of Charlee, so very happy on her third birthday. We took her to her first chocolate fondue experience—just me, TJ, and the birthday girl—and Charlee is bursting with joy. It's one of the best things I've ever seen and, looking at it now, I feel that joy, too. What I mean to say is that life is richer than I ever imagined it to be.

There is a very old story that involves an elephant (some of the best stories do, I think). Three blind people feel the elephant and describe it. You know what happens.

"An elephant is long, thin, and strong," says one, after touching the trunk.

"No, that's not true at all. It's tiny, thin, and weak," another insists, feeling the tail.

"But it's neither," says the third, trying in vain to touch the top of its spine and the bottom of its belly at once, "It's a huge animal! It is powerful and weighs at least a ton!"

An elephant is all of these things together and none of these things alone. Just like life is the accumulation of so many rich, hard, glorious, and terrible things. Just like my Charlee is not only the sunshine; she is the weather. She is tantruming and angry, the storm thrown violently from the ocean to the shore, and she is saying things like, "I adore you, mama!"—she is all the grace that stills the earth after the rain has satisfied it.

Sometimes I wonder which of the blind men should answer when someone asks how I'm doing. (I realize I just compared myself to an elephant, and I'm okay with this.) I'm well. There is peace here. I wonder why, and I'm not in a hurry to answer this question. I am cold sometimes, but that makes sense to me—I was dropped off in a cold place this past spring. What I didn't understand was that faith is a blanket. I didn't know that warming a soul in the season of winter is a sacred rite for those who experience it. I didn't know God could meet me here; that I could say in this place, "It is well with my soul." Not because this was my plan. I don't know the plan, really, but I cannot see the miracles of pain and wellness, brokenness and wholeness, mourning, and deep abiding joy without recognizing both that God is here and that life—all of it—is for living.

Chapter 69

Mary's Son Died, Too
(six months after)

It's nighttime, and I'm feeling down. A thought appears that doesn't sound like my voice; I'm not thinking about Christmas or even necessarily Jesus. But here it is, anyway: *Mary lost her son, too.*

The thought is gentle and kind; someone doesn't want me to feel alone. I blink. I cry. I do what you do when someone tells you what you need to hear. I do what very thirsty people do when they're offered water: I drink. Mary, mother of God, lost her son, too.

Not as soon as I lost mine, true; but she had a son and he died. He's alive now (not to compare Luca to Jesus, exactly, but so is mine). But that death changed their relationship. He wasn't at Sabbath dinner any longer, and I'm not sure what she did on his birthday, but he wasn't there eating her cake. It's easy to feel like grief carries a stigma. To suddenly be right back in grade school, where it was *really important* to be like every other person. But when your kid dies, that illusion shatters. Now I'm often the only one in the room who carries this kind of grief.

But Mary, who is blessed among women, lost her son too.

When Jesus died, God didn't strip her of that title. She will always be blessed among women. More and more, I realize that grief is no respecter of persons; that it is less a stigma and more evidence that you loved someone (and still do) deeply. The fact that they are no longer here matters less than the fact that the love is.

I think about Mary, and I feel the way I do every winter when I look up and see Orion, my favorite constellation, back in the sky: I'm in good company, and it will be okay.

Also, for those of you who'd like to read something lighter, TJ made me dinner tonight. He baked two huge sweet potatoes for an hour, and that was that. Yes, I had one plain sweet potato for dinner. The funniest part about it was that neither TJ nor I even commented that this might be an odd thing for people who are as far removed from the Irish Potato Famine as we are here in twenty-first century Boston. Also, we're clearly not staying away from carbs. What we're staying away from is *actual* dinners, I guess.

* * *

I feel confident that this baby is coming. And sometimes I feel terrified that she won't. "I was going to surprise you, Jess— but I'm booking your favorite photographer to be at the hospital and take photos right after we meet this little girl," TJ tells me over dinner last night. I look at him, thinking about what this means. I am grateful that this means he must think she's really coming, that we get to take her home. *But what if we don't?* I think. *What if this is one more thing we have to cancel?* It's a familiar thought. But I am pregnant. It's okay to plan on her coming. It's okay to hope and to join all the other parents who buy baby things in anticipation of a baby coming. The one that I feel every day now, kicking and flipping around inside of me. The one that I pray God lets me keep.

When I was only about six weeks pregnant, and still a very long way off from telling a soul other than TJ, we were at church. Our Pastor Matt was on the stage and, out of the blue, he prayed a very specific prayer. "I don't usually do this, but I feel led to pray against premature death this morning," he begins, following it with just that. TJ and I stand frozen in place, hands clasped together, finally daring to look at each other once Pastor Matt is finished his prayer. TJ smiles at me with such peace that I can't help but feel it, too. *Just because something terrible happened once does not mean it will happen again,* I think. God is letting me know that this one is going to be different.

But what if I'm wrong?

Then I will cross that terrible bridge when I come to it. Just like I did when Luca died. And just like I did when my first husband left. There will be grace in the moment—if the moment comes. There is no grace in the what ifs and the anxious thoughts and the fear driven scenarios. So I try to stay here, in the moment. I forget to do this a lot, but I try.

Chapter 70

This Is Fine (and Awful and Full of Grace)
(eight months after)

I move back home in my late twenties, having just found out that my husband at the time is in love with someone close to me. They're having an affair, and I don't know what to do. I didn't sign up for marriage in order to be divorced. That was never the plan. So what now? My mom asks me if I'd like to meet with a counselor—someone she and my pop work with from time to time, someone they trust.

I am numb, but I figure it can't hurt. There is nothing lower than here. Somewhere else might be better—even if it's just crying on a couch across from a counselor instead of crying in my parents' basement.

My mom and I walk up the familiar lane that leads to church. It's the church I grew up in. It feels like a good, safe space, filled with good, kind people. But none of that matters today. Now that my heart is broken, the familiarity almost hurts; it mocks me with what should have been. My mom takes me to a side room where the counselor, Tim, is waiting for me. He is quiet and appropriately somber as he introduces himself. I sit across from him, and my mom excuses herself, shutting the door behind her. I take a deep breath and tell him everything. I tell him details that are not for this book. (Maybe another one someday, but this is Luca's book.) Tim listens, occasionally taking notes, but as I go on and on, he finally puts down his pen and simply lets me talk about the Terrible Thing that has broken my heart. A long time later, I finally stop and take another deep breath.

"I think you needed to tell someone this story," he acknowledges. "I felt like I should just listen, rather than interrupt with questions." (It's important to note that just listening is a powerful act. Sometimes it's the best way to support another.)

"But," I reply, "Are we gonna be okay? Will my husband and I be okay?"

"Yes," he says, simply. My heart grasps at this. Finally, here is someone who thinks I can still have my life. I can still have my husband and my marriage and the backdrop that so comfortably frames me.

"So you think we can make this work," I confirm, relieved.

"Oh," he says. "You asked me if you and your husband will be okay. This is a different question than if your marriage will be okay." There is compassion in his voice as I look at him, waiting for him to explain.

"They are not the same thing. Honestly, Jessica, it is not looking good for your marriage. The things that he has done… well, he's already broken his vows. He divorced you in every way but signing the actual legal papers—which is the least significant part, really."

My heart sinks as I continue to listen.

"But you asked me if you and he will be okay. I know that with God's healing, you will be. I can say this confidently to you today, not knowing whether or not you will stay married—and, after hearing your story, I'll be surprised if you do. You and your husband might part ways permanently, but God will see to it that your heart will eventually be okay."

This is not what I want him to tell me. But I nod. And for the first time, I contemplate the great mystery of both irreparable damage and building something else entirely. Looking back, I realize that my counselor was not saying that the house I loved could be fixed, sagging floors made to stand and torn-off roof brought back. What he meant is that God could and would build me a new house. At that point, I didn't want a new house. I wanted the one I knew, the one I loved. It was so profoundly painful to lose that house. It had cost my whole heart to build it. I didn't know yet that God's redemption could go deeper than my pain and loss. I didn't know that I would one day love my new house so entirely, so wholeheartedly. But I couldn't at that point. I had to grieve. I had to walk through the pain of loss. I had to walk that broken road for reasons I may never fully understand—but it's undeniably connected to TJ and Charlee and Luca and my full life now. And because I will always love where it led me, I will always bless the broken road.

And if I were to lose this baby, too, then once again, I hope I would choose to say God bless the broken road. Eventually. For the places it leads me cannot be denied—they are beautiful. Eventually, again. They take my breath away. And, like that counselor told me, God will see to it that my heart will be okay. That is an easier thing to write down than to really believe. I hope you know I realize this. And of course, this will take time. Maybe all of the time I have here on earth, I don't know. I pray every single day to keep this babe. The darkness of any other road than the one that allows me to bring her home is unfathomable. Losing one baby does not make the thought of losing another baby easier. In fact, even when Charlee has just a slight fever, I now have fears that I never used to grapple with.

We are broken and changed; we are healed and changed. We are fluid, a changeling, like every wild and blessedly living thing is. And through all this growing and breaking and healing and rearranging of my breath inside my body because so much takes it away—I think I see what the psalmist means when he wrote: "...Even the darkness will not be dark to you; the night will shine like the day, for darkness is as light to you" (Psalm 139:12 NIV).

On the dark roads and on the roads full of light, there is a constant that brings me back to hope and staying firmly and bravely inside my own skin to discover what life offers. God lives everywhere, see—just as much in the dark as in the light. But I wonder if I can see Him even a little bit better in the dark. I wonder if I search for Him more there. If my desperation is a magnet that draws Him closer. When night descends, He is here with me. And I didn't know this, really, until I felt it for myself while I was standing (crawling? huddled?) in the dark. Being in the dark is the only place to learn about what happens there.

I remember as a small girl, trying to sleep in my bed, but feeling scared of the dark. I'd see the glow from the TV in the living room illuminate my own doorway, and I'd exhale. That light told me what I needed to know. My pop was here with me—downstairs, too. It made all the difference I needed to let my fears, along with the tension in my body, go and fall asleep in peace. Day or night, light or dark, good or what feels terrible—it is not simply all the same to God because He doesn't care how we feel or whether or not we're crushed. It is all the same to God because He has no off hours; night and day, He is here. All the time, present tense, He is here, caring for our hearts.

★ ★ ★

Grief is still present. I'm not sure when it becomes something else. I am not even sure that it does entirely become something else. But maybe I carry it differently; I mean, I already do.

It's the first night in the hospital after we find out Luca has died. I put those little tablets in my mouth that begin the induction process. They don't feel real, though—they dissolve like some kind of chalky candy, like a placebo. This is all just make-believe, right? Surely I am not about to labor and birth my dead child. Surely these things in my mouth can't mean all that. You don't even swallow them; they just simply disintegrate. Surely something that innocuously fades into nothing isn't priming my body to do what cannot be done, what should not be done.

Sometimes I am calm—surprisingly so, even for me. The nurses come in and they are as somber as you'd expect, but I ask about their lives, because I want to know. TJ and I talk about our faith. I need to do this. I need them to know that all is not lost. I need them to know that the storm is great, and even though I am drowning right now, there is life after death. I've seen it before. "Jess has already been through a lot," TJ tells our nurse, Jenn.

"My first husband had an affair. It was terribly painful and messy, and yet we all healed." I talk about forgiveness and how it's the bridge that most people said could never be built. I talk about the other woman. And yet she isn't anymore; she is kind and hurting and healing. She is a lot like me. She is dear to me. Jenn looks at me with compassion. "It's too much," she murmurs, "that and now this—it's too much for one girl." And I agree; it is too much.

But that is why I need to talk about what God does with all of the too much in our lives. How he takes it all—not necessarily from us. I don't know a soul who is exempt from heartbreak and pain—not even Jesus himself—but God takes the heartbreak and everything that feels so ugly and impossible and He weighs down our heart with it. Makes it so incredibly valuable; makes the view behind our eyes valuable, too. It's like when my oldest brother fell off a building. He not only survived, but was still walking. Stunned, shaken to his core, he asked, "How do you live through something like that and just go on eating chips on the couch in front of the television? How do you not make life count?" How indeed.

I don't know if you read the Bible, but it's a very old book, and I've learned there is wisdom to be gained from things and people older than myself. In a culture that romanticizes youth, it becomes dangerous when we don't see age for the glory and help that it is—but that's a whole other book, I think.

Grief has a way of sifting through our perspective and our actions and leaving only what is valuable, while tossing what never has been all along. I read these words: "But what happens when we live God's way? He brings gifts into our lives, much the same way that fruit appears in an orchard—things like affection for others, exuberance about life, serenity. We develop a willingness to stick with things, a sense of compassion in the heart, and a conviction that a basic holiness permeates things and people. We find ourselves involved in loyal commitments, not needing to force our way in life, able to marshal and direct our energies wisely ... Everything connected with getting our own way and mindlessly responding to what everyone else calls necessities is killed off for good" (Galatians 5:22-23 MSG).

When we let grief do its good (also painful, also eviscerating) work in our hearts—when we don't hide it or pretend it away. When we let all the accompanying feelings dig deep ravines into our being. (Ravines that eventually allow greater love to sit there; just like the way the waves crash into rocks again and again, eventually causing depressions that create pools after the tide goes out. There is now water where there wasn't—solely because the waves relentlessly crashed on the rocks.) When we forgive those who wrong us and finally dare to look around at what is here, what is left, what is ours. Then, we see the "gifts He brings into our lives." How can I miss it? The compassion that I never would have had, had my own heart not been broken twice. This understanding that there is a plan and no, I don't need to "force my way in life." I can trust that the right doors will open—that some doors that aren't right are closed for a reason. That I can trust a closed door to be right and good, and I can walk away with grace. And the "ability to marshal and direct our energies wisely"—dear ones. Is there much better than this?

My husband says the most precious commodity we have is not money (for you can always make more), but time. We have a set amount of time, and one cannot make more on this earth. So to understand that we don't need to spend our precious time on projects that are not for us is an incredible gift. To be able to say no without guilt or attachment to anything other than what a cat might feel watching a Labrador swim in the water: that is something, but that is not for me. This is why, once Luca died, I stopped running myself ragged with busyness. I started getting a healthy amount of sleep at night. I stopped wasting my energy on things that, it turns out, do not ultimately matter to me (memorizing intense training manuals to teach fitness classes, to name one). I became more focused on writing. On creating. On mothering and grieving and wife-ing. (I realize that's not a word, but "mothering" is, so why can't wife-ing be a word, too? It is! It's one of the greatest descriptors of my life, being TJ's wife.)

Grief has allowed me to see this plainly. Gifts from Luca; gifts from God—these are part of grief. And I cannot have the gifts that come as a result of grief without having the grief, too. It is the common denominator.

Chapter 71

Birthing Luca; Birthing Grief
(during, and minutes and hours and days after)

Sometimes I am calm, and then there are the other times when I don't know what to do with myself because it hurts so badly inside. I remember when I am in a small, single hospital bed—my almost 36-weeks-pregnant belly making that even a little crowded—but I ask TJ to come into bed with me anyway. He crawls in beside me and presses me hard against him. It is so good to feel that pressure. It's different from the pressure inside; the heat and pain and loss that are telling me that life is this. Forever. My son gone. Forever. Me a shell without him. Forever. A baby-lost mama. Forever. I cannot cry the tears fast enough, and they come out in gulping sounds; I can hardly catch my breath between sobs, they are so violent. I am drowning and gasping—not for air—but for something I cannot have, my first son, my second child. I feel more pressure on my huge body as TJ presses his hand into the small of my back, my body curled sideways on the stiff cot. *But I have TJ*, I think. *God, I have him.*

He is as close as my large belly allows. TJ is quietly telling me that he's here, and I know he's here. It's good to be less alone now. It's good that there are two of us who made Luca, that there are two of us who won't bring him home. It's terrible, yes, but it's comforting, because that means I am not actually alone.

TJ tells me about God's plans, and he is so calmly confident that I am able to rest here. His words are a place to lay down. I run out of tears, and we are quiet together. There is a rhythm to our breath and the shuddering that a body does once it has spent itself on tears. "Can I play something for you, Jess?" he asks, both of us quiet now for a while—a space that will go on maybe forever. Maybe we'll never speak again. I nod. TJ plays a sermon from a pastor. I don't remember much of it, but I remember feeling some comfort. I remember that it involved Mary—and I know that Mary also lost a son. There is one part in the message that stands out still, something about loss and shattering and everything feeling wrong. Something about being in a strange and unfamiliar place—that is the context I remember, anyway, because it resonates.

"This is when God wants to blow your mind," the preacher promises. TJ looks at me and quietly says, "I think God is doing things we cannot understand from here. I think someday we will see that God is here with us, that God has our Luca and that we will see him again, and that it was after this point that God really began to blow our minds." I nod. What else can I do? I don't have enough energy to tell him I am not ready for this. Not Luca being gone, not my mind being blown. I want the miracle I was expecting, the "normal" miracle of birth and raising your baby. That's all I want. I don't want the miracle of my heart breaking in half, of my arms empty, of the slow work of healing, the arduous work of waking up in pain again and again and again and living.

"But I wish it were any other way," I manage to say.

"I know. I do too, Jess."

* * *

The grief I feel that night—and for many nights and weeks and months to follow—is a violent, creative thing that cannot sit still. It demands everything. It rearranges, gets to work, builds a tower inside of me. But grief comes without a sander, so the wood is ragged and its edges as constant as my heartbeat. I cannot even take a single, necessary breath without the tower making itself known. Nobody asked me if it was okay. Nobody asked if the wood could be crude, if the size could take up everything. Life simply took Luca and built this tower and I must be careful because if I talk too much, if I really let myself go, I will say something that reveals the tower. So I mostly stay home. I mostly stay where people know about the tower and they are careful not to jostle me or expect a lot because they know it is very hard to do even simple life tasks with an entire tower made of splintered wood inside of you.

And now, not even a year later, the tower is still here, but I do not hate it anymore. It still has splinters, but that is this tower. I used to sneak down to my brother Jason's room when I was little and he was at school and admire his cactus trees. (I could have just written 'cacti,' but I feel like you need a degree in horticulture to employ a word like 'cacti' in your book. You, the reader, would read it and think, *Wait a second, didn't this writer go to art school? How does she get off writing something like 'cacti?' Just who does she think she is anyway?* And your outrage would have been warranted. So I spared you from entertaining, (understandably) judgmental thoughts and decided to stick with 'cactus trees.' I think we can all agree I made the right choice.)

My parents warned me about the cactus trees in my brother's room. So I'd cautiously approach them, and then gingerly touch the sharpest spikes (oh my gosh, spikes? Is that the word? Thorns? I know every rose has its thorn, of course, but what does every cactus tree have? A catchy '80s rock ballad about this would be really helpful right about now. Also, this further proves my point that I do not know enough about the subject of plants to use words like "cacti."). And it is an entirely different thing to accidentally be stuck by a cactus rather than slowly, with reverence for its danger, touch it on purpose. I hope it makes sense to say that I can do this with my tower now. I can touch it, knowing how dangerous it is, but I don't stick myself with its splinters nearly as much now.

Most nights I don't cry myself to sleep. There is a lot of peace here. There is hope, and there is joy. Can you, imagine that—joy. Stark and bright, like dawn lighting up the dark sky. Like the prophet Elisha telling the widow with just a little oil to borrow every jar she could find. To take that little bit of oil and pour it into the empty jars. The surprise she must have felt pouring and pouring and pouring, finding the oil had multiplied. Finding she had more than enough. Finding life was the exact opposite of what it appeared. Finding that she could live. Oil and joy in abundance, we can live.

And then there are the moments stolen away when I spend time with my thoughts that acknowledge the boy who is not here. It is a tower, and it is a storm. But today, this storm is a little more connected to the rain that makes the flowers grow, I think.

One day, I couldn't believe it when I saw my ribcage and blood vessels and sinews and muscles so close to the tower. In some places, they were even connected. Like the tower is no more foreign to myself as the space that is soft and hollow between my neck and collarbone. And then another day I noticed that everything I am—my spirit and mind and heart and soul and personality and likes and dislikes and aching and joys and shoulders and knees and everything else that houses my soul—well, I saw all that, and I was surprised to see the tower right alongside it. Casual. Every morning roll call involves this tower. And it's okay. It's me. It's also my love for Luca. So you must see why this is okay.

God, I miss Luca, and I wonder who he is. I wonder what it would be like to watch Charlee and him be siblings on earth. I allow myself all of it. To wonder these things, to cry, and to be present with Charlee and make plans with TJ. To thank God for this small girl kicking inside of me, as if to say, "You've got me too, Mama." And to one day show her the tower. Because she's a part of it, too. She is here because of the tower. It's strange to say, but no less true.

Chapter 72

How Many More Ways Can I Say Grief
(ten months after)

Every year I go out and visit my family in Los Angeles. After Charlee was born, I didn't change this lovely rhythm. I just made sure to book the trip during Boston's winter; the sun and warmth, a promise of what will come to the Northeast again. TJ and I have been talking about this like it's going to happen, but we are waiting to confirm whether or not TJ is going to sign another contract for his job, as he is nearing the end of his previous one. He signs the contract, so I start looking for flights. The sweet spot for taking such a long flight is the second trimester, so I need to make it happen in the next four weeks. Now that it looks like it's happening, TJ texts me: "Let's talk about if the risk of flying is worth it. Have been googling it, and it looks like there is a risk—which is something we want to avoid."

Now, yes, absolutely—we avoid risk, especially when it comes to this baby in my belly. Especially on the heels of losing Luca. But I'd never thought that this trip might not happen. And now that I am facing not going, I am considering how unfair everything is. Other than the obvious, I mean. Of course, it's unfair that our baby died—unfair is putting it ridiculously lightly—but now we are handling life with kid gloves, and that approach doesn't always feel right.

I feel like life is meant to stain your knees and show up under your nails from the digging and kneeling in dirt and messy work of experiencing it all. Does this mean that I go out and devour unpasteurized cheese throughout my pregnancy with a devil-may-care attitude? Nope. But does it mean that I stay home doing nothing for fear that doing something could be a risk? That's what TJ and I talk about. I am more devastated by TJ's sudden reticence for me to take this trip than I care to admit to you. I grew up having silent, still-there-though tantrums. The kind that are wordless, that make you withdraw from the world. (My parents call it sulking. In fact, one time my pop spanked me for sulking—which, of course, made me sulk even more.) I do the grown-up version of this for a while once TJ and I get together later in the day. I stare out the window while he drives, and the silence between us is telling. I don't like it, but I don't know how to change it.

"Can we talk about this?" TJ asks.

"I am just so sad."

"Okay, but we haven't made a decision yet, Jess. I just think we should talk about the fact that if there is any risk involved with you flying across the country—even a low one—then maybe now is not the time."

"But pregnant women fly all the time," I say.

"But those women didn't lose a baby."

"But why is the rest of my life punished because something terrible happened? Why deprive me and Charlee of a trip that will probably be wonderful? It's like I'm getting punished for going through trauma, and it's not fair."

"I'm more focused on what's safe than what's fair," TJ says quietly.

TJ is probably the most cautious person I know. Recently, he was watching me struggle into yoga pants. By definition, yoga pants are very tight. That's how they stay up. Now, they are definitely tighter at 25 weeks pregnant with this rainbow baby, but these tight pants also stretch. This is why we all wear them; they don't hurt us when we sit down. It's really nice. "Jess, please don't wear such tight pants—you're hurting the baby."

He says this definitively. He says it like he's googled "tight pants and pregnancy" and come up with alarming evidence to defend his stance. "TJ," I say laughing, "The baby is sitting low—and there is so much between this baby and these pants—she doesn't even feel them, I promise."

He gets up, because he doesn't believe me and feels my stomach for himself. I guide his hand much lower, to where the top of my pants are resting. "See? I say, "This is where she is—down here. I promise you, she's fine with me wearing these pants."

He shakes his head. He doesn't much like it, but there's nothing he can do. I mean, I am teaching a Pilates class. I am supposed to look like I have done a round of hundreds at least once or twice in my life, pregnant or not.

"Can we consult our midwife—and our doctor?" TJ asks, "If flying is any risk at all—wouldn't you want to be aware of it?"

Of course I would, so I nod. And we talk more. And my sulking tantrum dwindles away in the conversation of the day. Not going to California is not the worst thing that has happened to me, I know. But all the fallout from the worst thing that has happened to me can just feel like too much sometimes.

Our midwife gets back to us, saying there is no risk. That I need to get up and walk every two hours to keep the blood circulating and drink lots of water, "but we would tell that to any person, pregnant or not," she says. "There is no extra risk to the baby," she assures us.

"I want to have a conversation with Dr. Ridley, though, too," TJ says, referring to our high-risk doctor, so I call her the following day.

In God's good way, Dr. Ridley ends up calling TJ back instead of me. She is as straight a shooter as they come. She was the one who gave us Luca's autopsy results. She opened it with, "I have the best news I can give you, under the circumstances. It was a cord accident—tragic and random—and I have zero concerns about a subsequent pregnancy for you." When I mentioned to my therapist that I was afraid maybe Dr. Ridley was just being nice, she looked aghast. "Do you know how many women I have to comfort because Dr. Ridley is more concerned with relaying the facts than being nice? She didn't become the head of obstetrics at MGH and a world-renowned high-risk maternal fetal medicine doctor because she's nice, Jess. She's wonderful, but nice is not one of the words I'd use to describe her. If she has a concern, she tells you. She doesn't hold back—it's her job to not hold back."

TJ asks her for the facts, asks if she thinks I should fly at this stage in my pregnancy. She tells him what our midwife said. TJ feels more peace because of it, and suddenly I do too.

"So, I can go, then?" I ask him.

"Do you promise me to walk around the plane every thirty minutes? This means roughly twelve times between takeoff and landing?" I think about how every two hours is the professional recommendation. But it's TJ, so I compromise. Actually, considering all of the books on negotiation he's read, I feel like he's shooting ridiculously high on purpose so that I will meet him somewhere in the middle (which still happens to be above and beyond what the actual doctors—whose job it is to protect both mothers and babies—recommend, I may add).

"How about every hour?" I suggest.

"So, six times, then?"

"Yes."

"And you will drink lots of water—even though it means you will have to constantly go to the bathroom?"

"Well, I guess that will get me up and walking more, then, huh?" I say, smiling now.

He's smiling too.

"I just want our family to be safe, Jess."

I want the exact same thing. And I also think we can live a life that is full, rather than staying in the shadow of the terrible thing that happened. Terrible things happen. They happen whether you travel or stay home. Use wisdom, consult your doctors, and also live your life. If possible, let your daughter see the Pacific Ocean and palm trees. Make sure she knows her family, even though you live in Boston and they live in Los Angeles. It's okay to feel afraid, but don't let fear be the one making the decisions. If so, I promise you it won't turn out to be your best life (as annoying as that phrase is). It'll hardly be a life at all.

* * *

I'm at a routine appointment for this baby. Having seen the nurse, Charlee and I are waiting for my doctor to walk in when a researcher shows up instead, introducing herself. She says I qualify for a study they're conducting on the placenta—developing more ways to test its health while the baby is still in utero. "Would you be willing to take part in this study?" she asks. I tell her I need to talk to my husband first, and she leaves.

When I see Dr. Ridley, I ask her the one thing I've been thinking since the researcher left.

"The scientist who was in here," I begin, "said I qualify for this study—is this because Luca died?"

She looks at me with a kind smile. She smiles easily, and I like this about her. She actually smiled while giving us Luca's autopsy report, specifically, about the good news about me having another baby; I guess she doesn't always get the opportunity to tell people who have been rocked by death that there's any good news left.

"Jessica," she tells me today, "You qualify for this study because, believe it or not, we consider your pregnancy normal. That scientist doesn't know about Luca. The high risks that would preclude someone from participating aren't yours to deal with, which is good news."

I smile, too. I am not normal, but it's nice to be included with all the women who enter this office and have baby showers and buy baby clothes and, when the time comes, expect to be kept up at night by their baby crying, rather than a grief that knocks around the walls of their heart like an echo that won't find silence.

"We consider this pregnancy normal." They consider it to be just like all of the other pregnancies that result in a baby who comes home. I tell myself this a lot. Women have babies all the time. This is a fact that doesn't have to hurt me; it gives me hope. Just because something very bad happened once, it doesn't mean that the rest of life—my anxiety, the normal moments when I don't feel this babe moving—is foreshadowing another disaster. Perhaps it's the moments of peace that tell the real story that is unfolding.

Chapter 73

Wonder, Too

(still ten months after)

It's 4 AM and I'm suddenly awake. It's not anxiety that's done this, though. At seven months pregnant, it's a full bladder. (Hi. I'm Jess, and I'm brutally honest. If you ever suspected that my bladder sometimes gets full, now you know for sure! This is nothing if not a tell-all book!) Now I get to lay in bed and feel this baby move. I get to feel my baby move. I can't help but remember the blurry days after I deliver Luca. The mornings come with a cruelty, a quick return to reality. I leave the hospital so profoundly sad, that TJ asks for medicine for me.

"Is there anything Jess can take that will help her sleep in peace?" he says to the doctors, the nurses, the midwives—all the people who are, as gently as possible, introducing me to the rest of my life without my baby. There is a prescription and then a little white pill that TJ makes sure I take every evening. I am grateful he thought of this—I think of nothing outside of how dark life has become and how desperate I am to find a light for Charlee, for him, for myself. Anything to say that look, God is still here; look, this is still the family—the life—that grace built. Every night, I drift into a dreamless sleep that I spend the day looking forward to. It is a break. It is some care and some comfort. It is another way TJ is loving me. In the early days, my body would stir before consciousness, and I'd think Luca was still inside of me. Then the daylight and the truth of my soft, empty belly would rush in with a power that carried me away in despair. But now I am here.

I stopped needing that pill a long time ago. I gradually started to sleep on my own. Now I am here, and I get to live life with another baby inside of me. Sometimes I ask God to reassure me, and then I feel a motion that is both inside me and yet not from me. It is strange and wonderful. It is more wonderful than I ever knew, I think. I spend a lot of my time appreciating this. Just like I appreciate the pain, the missing, the hope of Heaven— all the ways a mama loves her boy who isn't here—I also get to appreciate this baby who is here: the rainbow that comes with the storm.

★ ★ ★

This morning I get two texts, sent a few minutes apart.

"I woke up at 4 AM with you on my heart; I've been praying for you this morning." And also: "I had a dream about you last night; I've been thinking about you all morning." My first thought is, *Oh no, what's about to go wrong now?* I don't mean this to be funny. I'm actually terrified. But then I think maybe this particular brain pathway, blazed by trauma and loss, is neither the truth nor the only option. There are better and worse thoughts to allow in: I can choose better. Maybe these dreams and prayers simply mean I am cared for. And that's actually good news.

I think about the word salvation, and how Christians have attached it to some eventual escape from Hell. But it is more than this; much less about escaping and much more about fully living. The word 'salvation' means wholeness. To live fully, wholeheartedly. To have every part of our complex selves alive and working together, symbiotically with our Creator, to cultivate this one precious life. To break, as all living—and therefore vulnerable—things do, but not stay broken (at least not in the way you'd mean when you scream, *MOMMMM! THE TV IS BROKEN!* super loud and up a whole flight of stairs, because God forbid you move off the couch and talk to her in a way that isn't reserved for the final rally of your high school spirit week. We get to move forward; we get to move).

Maybe we stay broken as in soft and vulnerable, translucent in parts to let our bright spirits shine through bodies that have been through this journey of birth and the exhausting experience of becoming, every single day since. We are in awe of the way our broken, needing-to-be-mended parts come together and create a whole that is actually more vibrant than whatever we once were. Our minds, bodies, and spirits singing in harmony with the song that birthed creation.

We discover that if darkness and light are the same to our Creator, perhaps we, too, keep bravely bearing our soul on each patch of life we stand on, making it a little more similar to the next patch and the next; making the darkness and the light not so different, after all. For in all of it, we live fully.

We realize there is purpose in the mundane. In the seemingly insignificant moments that are strung between the milestones we hang our hopes on. Because these moments are where we cultivate gratitude. And where gratitude lives, there is joy. Gratitude and joy are Pollux and Castor, the twin sister stars shining extraordinarily bright in the dark night sky.

Yes! Gratitude and joy. I'll say it. My son is in Heaven, and there is still joy to be found right here, right now. I hope you have dirty nails, too, from all that ridiculous and exuberant digging for joy that you are doing. I hope you dig for it with others, and if you ever walk that precious rite of passage that comes to those of us who've been left on Earth—grief—I hope you learn this: we can dig for joy, still. Not right away, but some day.

Wholeness, salvation, is something that God gives and brings. His gift is discovered in struggle right here on Earth, while wrapped in our own fragile skin. You don't have to wait for your funeral to feel it. It comes now for the brains broken by trauma and the hearts afraid to love. It woos us, our hearts, our bodies until we're working and blooming and making the world wonder how it is we do all this still.

We are reminiscent of a kind of resurrection that we see in nature. Spring blooms and summer bears fruit and all of this burgeoning life leads to the shedding of fall, the death of winter. Death then resurrection is the theme of the Gospel; now I don't simply believe it, I rely on it. I need death to lead to life or else what do I have left?

My Charlee reminds me of life all the time. That this is an option. She pulls me back into the present, into the here and now she demands for me, her mama, to occupy and fill with song and laughter and laying side by side while I marvel at the weight of her against a body that so recently held and delivered and relinquished a son. Salvation. Wholeness. Gratitude and joy. It's all for me—along with grief. It's not one or the other, after all. And it is for me now more than ever.

Similar to how food is truly for the hungry. Of course food is for everyone, but the hungry are driven and single minded when it comes to making sure they get food. There is nothing like brokenness to drive us to become whole. And there is nobody I've found who does this so gently with such personal care and grace and creativity as God. Nobody else is able to.

And here is the thing: none of us are special. Or maybe it's that all of us are special. But what I mean is that we are all unique, and none of us are less than. We are all precious, vulnerable souls knit together under bones, and if wholeness is for me, then it's most certainly for you.

Chapter 74

Manna

(ten+ months after)

I watch Charlee in awe as we board our flight to Los Angeles. She is so excited, so happy to be going. It isn't complex; there seems to be no weighing of decisions going on in her beautiful head. She just bounces onto the plane with a backpack trailing behind her that is bigger than her torso. And then there is me, painfully aware of what could happen. I hate living in this shadowy place. I don't think I let it determine my steps—after all, I still go to L.A.—but in the back of my mind, I have this nagging thought: *What if the plane goes down and TJ loses his whole family?* I don't let that thought grow. That's what you have to do—although the thoughts are seeds, don't plant them, right? Statistically, I counter in my own mind, there isn't much chance of a plane crash actually happening. I realize that. I dwell on it. I keep boarding the plane.

Less than 1% of pregnancies result in stillbirth. That's a statistic, too, but it didn't help my son. And what about those fateful 9/11 flights? They were also leaving from Logan in Boston, flying out to LAX. *Okay,* I think, *This is enough.* I love how Charlee knows nothing of this land of What Could Happen. She's never been here. She gets on a plane because that's how you get to Los Angeles. The worst thing that could happen on the flight is boredom. It's lovely. It's so good and pure. I am grateful to be around it. It's much better than this panic that keeps tapping my shoulder, reminding me of disaster's proximity. So what do I do with all of these thoughts that have been given a voice by trauma? I acknowledge them. I understand that bad things happen. I also realize that something bad is not, in fact, happening right now. This is important. I look around and see Charlee's peace and joy. I take note of the colors around me. The seats with seatbelts, the rows of everything stretching in front and behind. This is what's real, I think, as I take in my surroundings. The apathetic looks on faces around me are also reassuring: nothing terrible is happening.

I text TJ: "We're both okay." I also see a gift, and it's this: I feel immense gratitude for what The Land of What Could Happen brings me. For a daughter who is alive and well by my side—albeit whining and grumpy and asking when we're going to land and, oh man, this is a 6-hour flight and it's only been 45 minutes. (Actually, in her defense, she did amazingly well on our flight. A toddler traveling champ. God bless JetBlue for providing her with her own little screen right in front of her own little face. God bless screens.)

There is a story in the Bible that involves Moses leading the people of Israel out of Egypt, where they'd been slaves, into the promised land. God thought of everything, even their food. At some point during their wandering for forty years in the wilderness—by the way, that's a wild story arc to mention casually. I mean, I have a hard time with six-hour flights. *Forty years of wandering in the wilderness* seems pretty unfathomable as I write this from the comfort of my couch in Boston. And I'm sure the whole nation of Israel involved some toddlers. Toddlers and zero screens. *Whew*—but my point is the food God provided and the lesson that brought; so back to that.

I am not much of a camper. Okay, I went once, with my dear friend Ireland, when we were about ten years old. We camped at the bottom of the hill on my parents' property, by our stream. Our plan was to stay down there as long as we could. We'd live like pioneers. To make bread, we'd grind the wheat we were pretty sure was growing in an adjacent field. That was our actual plan. Looking back, I don't think that was wheat. And we had no idea how to grind it if it was. We still don't, to be perfectly honest. So there was no bread on that camping trip. Luckily, Ireland had brought a cooler full of Slim Jims. Once we'd polished those off, we snuck into my house at the top of the hill and raided the kitchen.

As we did, we pretended not to know any of the occupants—albeit, all of them were related to me—before sneaking back down to our tent at the bottom of the hill. We lasted two nights by the stream. By the third day, Ireland's foot had mysteriously swollen to twice its size, and I was rocking a pretty high fever. We crawled back up that hill to the comfort of air conditioning and blankets that didn't smell like the moldy sleeping bags we'd been using. We gave up. If we'd had a white flag, we would have waved it. Once home and in need of medical attention, we no longer bothered pretending to be strangers. I was like, MOM! We need HELP. My parents never said anything about our demise as pioneers, but they also never encouraged me to try camping again.

To recap:
CAMPING: 1
PRETEEN GIRLS: 0
SLIM JIMS: 0 (This reflects the actual number of Slim Jims I've eaten since that ill-fated trip.)

I'm pretty sure TJ and I will never camp. In order to go camping, I feel like you need to have at least one person in the party who is confident about putting a tent together, who feels pretty cool and collected when a bear wanders by. Neither TJ nor myself is that person. Also, TJ thanks me for not even trying to camp. I am pretty sure that his never-presented-itself-once-in-his-life itch to camp is scratched enough on our short walks down to the stream when we visit my parents' house. (Also, I never thought the words "scratched enough" strung together like that would be in this book, but here we are. At least it's not the title, I guess. But it will be the title when I finally get around to writing my full anthology on rashes.)

Okay, enough diversion. Let me try once again to tell you a very spiritual story about God's provision. I think you can pack food for even a week's worth of camping, but nobody can pack anything for forty years. So let's talk about the Israelites. (I'm referring to the Old Testament here. I love how the Bible really simplifies categorizing the text. I can imagine a bunch of scholars of antiquity in a room, musing together over questions, like, "What do we do with the old stories and what do we do with the new stories?" There's a pause. A mulling over strategy and presentation. Finally, the new guy speaks up. "Uh, guys? What if we just, like, put all the old stories—like, the ones before Jesus came—into one big group and call it, like, the Old Testament?"

Everyone starts nodding slowly. This could work. "But then what about the stories that involve Jesus, His new agreement with God, and the brand-new church? And all those letters?" a concerned voice chimes in. More silence and hemming and hawing. They're stumped. Then the new guy speaks up again.

"Well, I mean, if the old stories are the Old Testament... maybe we call the new stories the, um, like, the *New* Testament?"

Silence. Then one of them starts laughing and they all join in. "And that's why they pay us the big bucks!" they proclaim, nodding and clinking their chalices together while mumbling "So clear!" and "Would be impossible to confuse which stories go where!" and "Best new hire, right here!" indicating the new guy who had the guts to speak the obvious. PS, this probably did not happen, and I am not a Bible scholar.)

Anyway, when the Israelites (God's people who we find in the Old Testament—a term that some new guy may or may not have suggested we call it) wandered in the desert (I often confuse the spelling of desert with dessert and the thought of wandering for forty years in donuts and ice cream and eclairs and petit fours doesn't sound quite so awful, really) for years and years, they very quickly ran out of food and became understandably scared they would starve. I probably would have done the same once we realized the Slim Jims were gone during my own ill-fated stay in the wilderness (okay, so it was the bottom of our hill, but it was very wild when my pop didn't mow it), had there not been my family's fully stocked kitchen literally a hill-climb away.

God provided us with my mom's groceries, which is awesome, but what God did for the Israelites is probably even more impressive, if you're into, like, miracles. The story goes that He rained something like bread down every single day. He made only one rule—don't try to take any of this manna to save for later. Take what you need today. The crazy thing is, look what the Bible says here: "The people of Israel went to work and started gathering, some more, some less, but when they measured out what they had gathered, those who gathered more had no extra and those who gathered less weren't short—each person had gathered as much as was needed" (Exodus 16: 17-18 MSG).

This tells me that God provides what we need right now. We have everything we need right now. Don't try to figure out how you're going to work out scenarios that aren't even real—we don't see the provision for the future, because we're not there yet. It's like trying to see a mountaintop view from the bottom of the mountain. Just because you cannot see it from where you are doesn't mean it doesn't exist. It's enough to know that God is there and that when you get there, He'll meet you. That we all need to do our part in terms of gathering and working, but at the end of the day, we won't be short.

I love that God refers to Himself in the Old Testament as *I Am*. Not *I Used to Be*, or *When You're Feeling Better, I Will Be*—nope, *I Am*. No matter how you're doing, where you are—God is present and active and here. In this moment, right now, always. And He is providing for us. Not He'll give us what we need when we're good enough or more grateful or feel less terrible or finally fold all our laundry. He gives us what we need right now, present tense. Because He is *I Am*, present tense.

When I was fresh out of college with a BFA in dance performance and frustrated with how hard it was to get a job, I got cut from an audition and dejectedly walked out of the theater, asking God what He was up to. I prayed for some encouragement, and in that exact moment, a nearby houseless man shouted across the street in my direction, "Hey girl! You a dancer? Cause you sure look like one!"

Pretty random, but I felt God's answer. *Thanks for affirming all the hard work I've put into dancing, with that shout-out, God,* I thought, *But I was meaning, like, could I get a J-O-B? THANKS.* (Shortly after, I did land a job. And another and another! But that man calling me out as a dancer in that moment was the fuel—the little bit of encouragement that I'm on the right path, despite feeling discouraged—I needed to keep showing up at auditions with hope in my heart.)

Another time, more recently, I was really missing Luca (okay I do this all the time; I will try to be more specific). In this moment, my grief was especially raw, and I was feeling like it was very unfair that we are a tiny family when we are supposed to be bigger. One whole person bigger. TJ, Charlee, and I were walking out of the grocery store when a man called out to us, "Wow. What a beautiful family you are! I just had to say something because you're such a beautiful family." And I just knew: it was encouragement from God, exactly what I needed. My heart felt lifted, and I thought, *Who am I to think we are anything less than we are. Luca might not be visible to everyone, but he is here with us. My family is not small. We are here, and we are beautiful.* I smiled and thanked the man and realized again, my heart is being taken care of.

Now back to the Israelites being cared for so well. Despite God specifically saying to use all the bread that day and trust there will be more bread from Heaven tomorrow, some of them tried to save the bread anyway. I can't blame them. The bread-savers were simply gunning for a little more control. A little more peace when they lay down at night with that extra bread tucked away, thinking, *Well at least I know I have bread for my family tomorrow, too—just in case.* It's really hard to trust that someone else knows how to take care of yourself, your kids, your deeply loved ones better than you do. It's especially hard to believe this when our deeply loved ones die.

I don't have all the answers. I have seen God do incredible things with a broken heart. I have seen God step into the aftermath of worst-case scenarios in my own life (My husband *is* having an affair. He *did* leave. My baby *did* die. I am forever a mama of a child who isn't here—all the thoughts that we safeguard our mind from thinking that somehow then become the thoughts that reflect reality—how do we deal with that? What happens next?).

Despite these tragedies, God enables my heart to stay soft and my life to be full. He takes my losses and gives me a hope that tells me there is a difference between my baby being gone forever and my baby being gone from here. He allows me to wake up in the morning with a powerful thought that there is love in the universe, and it is shaping lives into purpose and flowers into blooms and oceans into deep blue basins of life and my own heart into a place that doesn't hurt. That somehow love is a force that will win, and so I place my bets on it. Sometimes exhausted, sometimes hesitantly. But what else can I do.

When the Israelites checked on the hidden bread they'd saved the next morning, they saw that it had become moldy and worm-eaten overnight. Their plans to protect themselves didn't work. Ours generally don't either. They learned they had to simply have one plan—to be present and rely on God's provision for today. To see what *I Am* does now. When I am afraid of what could happen, that's my own version of trying to gather more than what I have—and need—right now. All the contingency plans I make in my mind—the way I will safeguard my heart in case terrible things happen, the way I will make sure they do not happen, the anxiety I feed on, awfulizing this life that I have, dwelling on what bad things could happen—and what I would do in response. All this is me taking some extra bread and tucking it under the bed, trying to make sure that tomorrow I am safe, that we are always safe.

But the truth is we aren't safe. At least not in the way we think we want to be, and certainly not here. We aren't safe from heartbreak—not if we have living, open, vulnerable hearts. We aren't safe from bad things happening. And yet we are alive, gloriously experiencing what that means today. And all the todays to follow.

We are hurting and healing and constantly running back to the present, where *I Am* lives, where our needs are met. We are safest here, I think. Where *I Am* holds our hearts and draws pictures with our faith and we glimpse an eternity that does not disappoint us (finally). Where *I Am* sees our grief as the sacred and precious thing it is, the shape of our heart revealed in tears on our faces and the silent steady withdrawal from the life we knew. *I Am* sees a heart on fire and says, *I am here with you.*

And none of us who currently grieve are ready to hear about the worth of lessons learned, maybe ever. There is no trade off we would accept for the loss of a person we love. And yet, grief allows us to be reborn. It's like we die with our person, and then find ourselves shockingly still here. We find that, in time, there is still an invitation to live. We leave our own hearts for dead, too—our own spirits dreamless and still—and there comes a moment in time when we see something. A shift, a breath, a steady rhythm of life that is undeniable. We catch a dream that flourishes in conditions we hadn't known were fertile. We are shocked to find all of this within. Steady heartbeats, again and again. A cadence, a tap, tap, tap—the sound of life in Morse code that we finally recognize as our own. We find that God cares for our hearts and the details of *I Am's* care become tangible in the days when we are reduced to one great desperate, breathless need.

I take a deep breath.

Grief doesn't always feel the same. It ebbs and flows. One day we wake without hurting quite so much, and we are in awe of the lack of pain that has snuck in. A pain that had introduced itself in such a permanent manner that we'd mistaken it for a limb or even an organ and are shocked that it's suddenly different. Not gone, but different.

The lessons grief gives—well, I have learned to look around me. This is my manna. This is what I have today. It is enough, perhaps even more than enough. *I Am* is here. It is enough. Today I am pregnant. This is manna. I will live here and be grateful. I can't try to react to tomorrow, because it's not here, and grace is for now. I can't make a contingency plan for how I'd handle this baby dying, too, because that isn't what's happening. I have no grace for what isn't real, for the stories anxiety tells me.

Right now, as I write this, my baby is kicking me, blessedly assuring me of her precious life. So I will eat this manna—just today's portion—and trust that tomorrow I will have what I need, too. Hesitantly, tremblingly so.

We exit the plane. We make it safely to Los Angeles.

Chapter 75

"Awful, Thanks"
(eleven months after)

When you're not doing strictly okay, the question, "How are you?" can feel terribly personal. I'm not suggesting we change our approach. It's good that we care about how each other is doing—or at least, that we ask. But when I carry feelings that don't elicit a one-word answer—(Fine! Good! Okay!)—and when everyone knows you're going through something terrible but nobody expects you to talk about it, and certainly not *now*—the simple question, "How are you?" can feel like surgery. And now there's this: "How's the baby?"

Unless I'm mid-ultrasound, I generally don't know for sure.

"If the baby is moving, it's, like, alive, right?" I've asked this to various professionals and received unanimous assent in return. (Boston is just as smart as you think.) But when you've had a baby inside of you who was fine for just about nine months and then suddenly died with no warning—and you spent whole hours walking around having no idea this had even happened—well, that makes things more complicated. Perhaps I should sign up for a non-stop forty-week ultrasound so I can accurately answer the question of how my baby is doing. Or I could do this:

Well-meaning person: "How's the baby?"

Me: "I don't know, but it moved 33 minutes and 5 seconds ago, so I doubt it died in the space between then and now. Here's hoping. Also, I like your shoes."

Or: Well-meaning person: "How's the baby?"

Me: "I don't know. How's your prostate?"

(I guess we've established that the well-meaning person is male.)

Well-meaning person: "Um … I don't know."

Me: "Crazy how super important things can be inside of us, like a baby or a prostate, and we can't totally know how things are going because we can't see it or touch it. Nice shoes, though."

Or: Well-meaning person: "How's the baby?"

Me: "I'm heading to an ultrasound now—would you like to come and see for yourself? Man, I really like your shoes."

Disclaimer: I sincerely appreciate the people who ask me how I am and how the baby is. I see your care, and it's kind. These are simply thoughts resulting from this doozy of a year, of hard loss and the decision to again walk down this wonderful, terrifying road of pregnancy after loss.

Chapter 76

We Are Breathing, Changing, Healing Creatures
(one year after)

We are back at the doctor for another ultrasound. TJ and Charlee come with me. In the waiting room, I can feel the baby move, so at least I know she's alive. We step into the dark room, and everything the ultrasound tech does is so routine and normal that it almost fools me into believing it is. But after Luca's death, nothing having to do with pregnancy feels routine and normal.

The ultrasound tech squirts the jelly onto my large belly and grabs the wand before placing it on the babe, with just my skin separating them. "Here's the brain," she says. *The brain? I think. Doesn't she want to make sure the heart is beating? I mean— first things first, right?* She shows me the steady, strong heartbeat a minute or two later. There's no fanfare from her, because she expects it to be beating.

She expects it to be beating.

I think about my own expectations. About the pathways in my brain forged by trauma, making me react to a terrible thing that happened once whether or not the terrible thing is happening now or will ever happen again. I also think about the time recently when Charlee and I went on a play-date with another little girl and her mom. The little girl started the very beginning of a tantrum, and I watched as the mom pulled her close and calmly reminded her to rule her spirit. This is also a choice. I can forever react to the trauma of losing Luca, or I can rule my spirit and look at this screen now and let the truth wash over me. There's my baby girl. She's just fine. "I couldn't read a better ultrasound than this," the no-nonsense ultrasound tech tells me. This is the truth.

She waves the wand over my baby's face, and we watch in astonishment as she blinks at us. We see her nose and eyes and mouth; we see her blessedly alive. I take it in. The truth. I remind myself that the truth does not always hurt me. And if Charlee's young friend can rule her spirit, so can I.

I think about how each time I choose to focus on my present truth rather than the terrible thing that happened once, new pathways are forged in my brain. None of us are done evolving. The very word "neuroplasticity" tells us the brain has the ability to change—again and again—over the course of our lifetime. It's not called a *neurostone*. The word "plasticity" signals flexibility and movement. It lets us know the broken places left in trauma's wake don't have to stay broken. This isn't just good news, this is a way forward for all of us who experience trauma.

Later, when we're home, Charlee watches me put lotion on and asks why I do it. "Because if I don't put lotion on my skin, it's itchy and uncomfortable," I explain. She watches me in silence for a few more minutes before saying, "I think this means the baby is coming soon, Mama."

A year ago, when we were in a different room and my belly was swollen with a different child, Charlee adamantly told me, "The baby is *not* coming, Mama." I didn't believe her, of course. She didn't know; she was two and struggling with the fact that she was no longer going to be an only child. But she was right. I mean, now I know she was right. Was she intuiting something? I don't know; I don't think I will know this side of heaven. And I don't know if I will need to know once I am there. But I am grateful for this now. I am grateful to hear Charlee tell me the baby is coming soon.

Chapter 77

Kairos

(nine months after)

TJ and I are in church. There is loud music, and there are people moving exuberantly, and then there is me. I am sitting with my eyes closed and my heart open. I am blocking out the rest of the world, trying my best to commune with God. This seems like such a high thing, like I shouldn't be able to do this in boyfriend-cut maternity jeans and a Free People jacket. I am casual and tired and ragged from small talk that feels like it takes more than it gives. But I have a suspicion I cannot shake that God has etched meaning into this life. That despite the world telling us that television has better stories than our own and that we should ignore one and pay attention to the other, we can close our eyes and see how love shows up like the final piece of the game of Clue. And instead of Colonel Mustard in the kitchen with a candlestick, it is Jesus with his own life's blood, and it speaks to me a lot now that Luca has died.

I am sad and unsettled and telling TJ afterward that church made me cry. He asks why, and now I am pouring out words about Luca and how I kept imagining him in heaven with God, and if that's not an act of worship, I don't know what is. I am also pouring out tea from the kettle into my porcelain cup, because now we are in a quiet restaurant by a window with a wintry mix knocking on the glass. This sleet seems to make everyone else mad, but the weather is just weather. I have learned that as long as we are safe, everything else is probably fine. I mean, put on a coat, use an umbrella, it's fine.

At church, the teacher tells us there are two words for time in the ancient Greek language. One is what you'd expect: *chronos*—chronological time. But the other is *kairos*, meaning "the right or opportune time." I think about how worship this morning looked like pictures in my mind of our son and how he is well and carried by God somewhere that is good, though not here. I haven't seen this with my eyes, but I see it with my heart, and maybe that weighs more. It's wrong that Luca's not here—I feel like the *chronos* is off in that regard, because he left too soon. But when I quiet myself and see him well and see God as kind—this is right, this is *kairos*, the opportune moment for me to lift my eyes.

Chapter 78

#not*ts

(eleven months after)

When I toured with Broadway shows, my body was a machine—so strong and muscled, hardly any fat on it. One time a massage therapist told me she'd never worked on a body so lean before. I never know how to respond to comments like these. "Thanks for saying I have less fat than a lot of other people you touch, I guess?" But saying thanks feels like I am saying it is a better way to be in a body, and it is not a better way. It was simply part of what happened to my body, probably because of the extreme amount of dancing I did, so it was my way of being a body.

One time, I went to Disney World with my mom, sister, and young nephew. I was either an old teenager or a young adult, depending how you look at it, so, you know, cool enough to head out to Pleasure Island alone one night. On the way, a stranger—a guy around my age—sat next to me on the bus. He asked me tons of questions, and, at the time, I didn't understand that I don't owe answers to anyone—let alone a stranger on a bus headed to Pleasure Island. One of the questions was whether or not I had a boyfriend at home, and I said nope. Anyway, by the time we got off the bus, it was clear that there had been some kind of misunderstanding, because he stood up next to me and, noticing I was a little bit taller than him, said, "Wow! I've never dated a girl this tall before." I wanted to tell him that he was still not dating a girl this tall, but, if you can believe it, my homeschooled self was too shy to tell a stranger I'd just met that we weren't dating (God forbid it would make him feel uncomfortable. No problem, I'll just be the uncomfortable one).

Anyway, my point is the commentary on my body. That "wow!" over my height (in case you're wondering what kind of height elicits a WOW! from a guy you meet on the way to Pleasure Island, I am 5'8"). It's not okay. Nobody needs to comment on another person's body. We can say objectively complimentary things like, "You are beautiful!" or, "That color is so fabulous on you!" or, "You look like the kind of person who brings a lot of joy into a room!" etc. I'd say the rule of thumb is that if a statement obviously elicits a thank you from the person to whom it's given, say it loud and proud. But if it's just like, "You're tall!" and the person says, "Well, it depends on who I am standing next to—I bet an elephant would not agree," then, skip it. Also, if we're listing rules of thumb, another good one is don't assume someone is dating you because they innocently answer the questions you deluge them with—one of them being relationship status—on a bus to Pleasure Island.

Another time when I was touring with *A Chorus Line*, my knee started to bother me, so I saw the resident physical therapist. He did a thorough examination and then asked me one thing, "Is there a guy who can take you out to dinner?" I wasn't quite sure what this had to do with my knee, but I nodded anyway. I have so many dear friends from that show, many of them are guys. We all eat dinner. "Great," he replied. "After the show tonight, have that guy take you out—order the burger and eat the whole thing. You need a little more fat on your body to cushion your joints. That should make you feel better."

My cast thought this "diagnosis" was hilarious. I think the only real way a burger could have helped my knee at the time was a frozen patty placed directly on it after the show to help with the inflammation—but still, dinner was delicious that night. And yes, it's ridiculously sexist to give this advice to a girl who could certainly take herself out for a burger—a girl who lived in

New York City alone—and was capable of many things (eating burgers was only a small percentage of those things). And I hope I do not need to write the very obvious additional option, right? (A woman could also take me out for a burger; I don't think either case would actually make my knee feel better, but it needs to be said.) My point is that I was this sinewy, muscular, long-legged girl for a very long time. (And that PT gave bad advice. The only really good part was that I got a burger out of it.)

When I met TJ, a video of me performing on the NYC subway on YouTube had just gone viral. I was getting all sorts of comments from the World Wide Web on my performance, my voice, my body, myself. It was awesome and it was totally weird. People were so kind, but there were also the mean ones. And those always seem to stick more than the others, don't they? In a long list of comments under one of my videos, there was one that was short and to the point: "no tits"

That's all it said, not even any punctuation. I remember thinking this would make a funny hashtag—#notits—and maybe I should start using it as a tagline. I recently told TJ this story, and I started laughing so hard before I even got to #notits that I could barely spit out the words.

Speaking of a #notits moment, I have another memory that has managed to stay with me through the years (Like mean comments on the Internet, #notits memories tend to hold on). I was maybe twelve, and when you're twelve, homeschooled, and a pastor's kid, Youth Group is The Event. It's on Friday nights, because it's cool. I used to take considerable care with my outfit every week. This particular week, I am dressed in one of those V-neck sweaters that have such a loose knit, it is potentially see-through when you stand in front of a light. But I am a ballerina, and who says leotards are only for the studio? I wear my long-sleeved black V-neck leotard underneath the sweater—problem solved!—throw on a pair of jeans, and I am ready for my pop to drive me to my Social Event of the Week.

Right before leaving, my pop pulls me aside and we exchange a conversation that is forever seared into my consciousness. And by conversation, I really mean I listen and then mumble something incoherent while quietly dying at the same time. "Hey Jess," my pop says, "I noticed what you're wearing for Youth Group tonight … and it's very … low cut." Abstract horror fills my being at just the words "low cut" uttered from my pop in reference to me. I am too shocked to say a word, so he continues.

"Now, I realize that you don't have breasts yet …" *No, no, no, no, no, no, no, nope, nope. Dear God, make me a bird so I can fly far, far away from here,* I think, as he goes on. "But someday you will …" *Dear God, this can't be happening. Surely, my pop isn't talking to me about not having breasts (don't ever say this to me again!), and also, someday having breasts… (also, don't ever say this to me again, either!).* "But no matter what your body looks like, it's important to know that your body is sacred and not to be shared with the world—it's so special, like a secret, you know? And that sweater isn't really keeping a secret." Okay. Secrets are a better topic than breasts, but we are still on very dangerous, shaky ground … I'd still like to be a bird and fly far away. But not a chicken. Everyone talks too much about chicken breasts. I want nothing to do with anything that has breasts. Or doesn't have breasts—like, well, me, for that matter.

"So even though you don't have any cleavage to show right now, someday you will, and I don't think it's appropriate to wear revealing clothes to Youth Group."

I die all over again at cleavage and mutter something that sounds like an assent and run to my room as fast as I can with hot tears in my eyes. Words like *cleavage* and *breasts* and *body* coming from my pop are too much. I throw off my condemned sweater and find a turtleneck instead. My pop and I never mention the conversation again—not even to this day, actually. And to be fair, it is a much gentler and kinder #notits moment—brought about because he honestly loves me—than the one I'd face on the Internet years later.

Then I had Charlee, and I was amazed at my body. It got so soft and matronly with her birth. Not even the meanest internet troll could have looked at me and commented #notits. For the first time in my life, I had breasts. Milky, soft, round breasts. The kind I used to wait and wait for as a teenager, minus the milk. The kind that never did come—not until a baby came, too. But that wasn't all I had. I also had thighs! I couldn't pull my tiny jeans up past my knees; they were no match for my new-found thighs. I remember looking at my non-maternity clothes and wondering what tiny woman used to live in my apartment. Then five months happened, and my body went back to its little self. I look at photos now of me holding a chubby, five-month-old baby Charlee, and I'm so small. The girl who fits into tiny clothes had come to stay in my apartment once again.

When I got pregnant with Luca, it is what you'd call a #fitpregnancy (I know, I find that hashtag mildly annoying, too). But I was deep in the world of fitness and working out all the time; I was just growing a bump, while the rest of me was muscular and hard. Then Luca died at 35 weeks gestation, and I had a postpartum body and no baby. My breasts engorged with milk and my belly was soft and loose. My thighs were round again, and I had love handles. All of these things weren't new to me, since I'd gone through it with Charlee, but it makes quite a difference to have that body without a baby along with it. I worked out, though. Not as hard as I had after Charlee's birth, I think. Grief takes a toll on you in every way. It demands what you don't know you can give, both physically and emotionally. So, some days my workout would look like a long walk with Charlee in the stroller and then carrying her in the pool all afternoon. Not exactly #fitmom status, but I had stopped hashtagging stuff, anyway. All I was doing was writing about grief, and it felt too cheap to hashtag Luca or grief or stillbirth or any of the ways we try to reduce our lives into categories the way we file bills and important papers.

It was a hot summer, so I was mostly wearing loose dresses anyway. I don't think I got back to my pre-Luca body before I got pregnant in September. Then I miscarried and got pregnant again, two weeks or so later. For the past four years, I have either been pregnant, nursing, or both. Over the past twelve months, I've been pregnant three different times and given birth once. I stopped caring about #notits, but the truth is, all my babies—both here or not—have given me tits. And this little girl I'm carrying now has given me thighs and a butt and love handles and armpits that have lots more skin than I ever remember armpits having.

Sometimes I wonder what my body will be like after this baby. But it doesn't really matter—my body will be mine. I am so grateful I get to give birth to another child that there just isn't room to be too concerned about #notits or #tits. TJ tells me all the time that my body is sexy. He doesn't even mention the superfluous armpit skin. (I don't either, in hopes that he still hasn't noticed.) But this body was made by the love TJ and I have and the humans our love has brought into this world. This body of mine is powerful and changes depending on the season. When I was dancing in three-inch heels and performing eight shows a week, my body was doing its job. Now that I am growing another baby, my body is doing its job. Once I birth this baby, my body will lose this weight (I think, anyway), and will do its job to be strong so I can chase and lift my girls.

It's strange to be in the same body you've had since you were small, since you started to identify as a self at all—separate from your parents and your siblings, which is a revelation in itself; that you are altogether your own, connected but not the same as those who brought you here—and notice so many changes over time. Pregnancy is beautiful and strange, and I know I am incredibly lucky to get to be pregnant so many times. Pregnancy, birth, breast-feeding—it's taught me that the human spirit is not the only resilient part of us. Our bodies are wildly resilient, too. There are lessons in the way we expand and decrease. Like how we trace the stars in the sky and they tell stories, we can trace our scars, and the pictures they make tell stories of bravery and love and a life that is wholeheartedly lived. I'm trying to pay attention.

Chapter 79

Spring
(eleven months after)

The winter is melting, becoming spring outside my window and under my feet. I've stopped reading books about grief. I've switched to novels, because I need windows more than I need mirrors right now. Each night now I read about what it's like to be an African woman living in America; she doesn't quite fit here, so she moves back to Africa, only to find that she no longer fits there either. There's longing in this story—a glimpse of a life that isn't what you dreamt, but still rich, still beautiful, still worth your entire heart. I get that. There are also no dead babies in this story, so reading this book is like getting out of your house and going for a walk. The fresh air is really nice; you didn't know you needed it until you're breathing it in, until your thoughts are less inward and the sky is a reminder that you're small, and surely your problems can't be quite as big as you think.

Charlee asks for stories all day long. It's her currency. I like to give them out for free, but I get tired; sometimes I use them in bedtime negotiations. "Mama, tell me the story about when you played with the plant after Pop said you shouldn't and you got spanked." She asks for stories with cause and effect. About choices and consequences. Her mind is categorizing everything, especially all of the what-happens-nexts in life. Someday I will explain to her that, yes, consequences are real. That we don't pray and hope for peas but plant strawberries and then get mad when we have strawberries next summer (terrible example, because who would ever get mad because they have strawberries?). But

I will also tell her that our path is grand and worth walking and also treacherous and unfair. I've learned there is all of it or there is nothing, so I choose all of it.

We pray for things like strength and resilience and courage and patience, and they can come in awful ways. It hurts to climb the mountain, and we think it actually might kill us during all the days of nothing changing—of uphill hikes and the conviction that nothing comes easy. But then, you're there, you've climbed it. And that's not all—you're kinder, more patient now, too. This has way more to do with how you got there than actually being there, I think. And I've found that where you are is not nearly as important as *how* you are. So this kind of being there—the more patient and kinder way of being there—is important. When you get to the next mountain, you'll bring along with you the confidence gained from the last one you climbed. And that confidence is a real hero.

My grief is not so terrifying anymore. It does not feel so bad or wrong or unfair; it is simply here, too. It seems to be less demanding now—like, along with the rest of us, it, too, has learned some restraint with the aid of time. Is it weird to think that my grief has grown and matured with me? Maybe. But it's weird to be grieving at all when you used to be a kid who looked at life like it was friendly and even—if not easy—something to anticipate and jump into.

It used to be that I'd enter a room only after my grief had already gotten there first. I'd creep in with the long shadow it cast, careful to stay hidden there. My grief would fill the room, and I'd find that it never really mattered which room it was— from church to our favorite restaurant to our bedroom with TJ sleeping peacefully next to me—grief would take over, announce itself, and basically obscure my identity so that I stopped trying to compete. I felt it was all I could see; all anyone could see.

Maybe this is why leaving home after Luca died scared me so much. I couldn't control my grief and how large it was. I couldn't control that my grief was, and is, so intimately connected to my son, and how incredibly personal and raw this makes it. I wasn't ready for casual people to notice my grief. I can remember vividly how much it hurt, though, when people completely ignored it and brightly asked me, "How's life, Jess—good?" It wasn't that they asked—it was the way they quickly answered their own question with "good," casually taking the liberty to fill in a blank that had wrecked me. *My son died. Please don't call this good*, I'd think.

I remember being at a large church function just two weeks after Luca died. Out of all the people we knew, our pastor was one of the only ones who acknowledged what we were going through. I am sure he has no idea what a lifeline that was. Everyone else glossed over it, and I was surprised by it all. How strange it was to be grieving in a non-grieving world. How hurtful it was that most people ignored the thing that had swallowed me whole. I'm not sure what else they saw, because I was convinced nothing but my grief was left. It's like someone sees Jonah inside the whale, and instead of even mentioning that he's now living in the belly of a large fish, they simply smile and nod and say "Looking good, Jone! How ya doing—good?"

At this function, I met a stranger. A woman in her twenties who listens to TJ's radio show introduced herself, said that she's a fan, and then simply said, "I know what you're going through, and I cannot imagine how you feel. I saw you guys standing here and my heart broke for you. I am so sorry you lost your baby boy." Tears filled my eyes—but these were different. Maybe even healing. I blinked. I thanked her profusely. "You have no idea how it feels to hear you talk about him. To hear you care. To hear you acknowledge this. Thank you so much; it matters more than you possibly know." And it did. It's like that Maya Angelou quote that has been made into a meme no less than a thousand times, with varying sunsets and mountainscapes behind it: "I've learned that people will forget what you said, people will forget what you did, but people will never forget how you made them feel."

I can't even remember this girl's face, but I will never forget how she made me feel that night. Seen and counted. And like Luca was seen and counted, too. Words, my friends—they matter. They are seeds—all of them—and it is our responsibility to be mindful of what kind of garden we are growing with the words we throw out to our family, our friends, our co-workers, and the broken strangers we come across for five minutes out of a lifetime. What an honor it is to add something rich and fruitful to their story—to make those five minutes grow into something good.

Chapter 80

What the World Needs
(twelve months after)

TJ and I are sitting down at a cafe when the waitress walks up. We get the drink order out of the way, and she centers the small talk on my belly.

"Do you know what you're having?"

"No," I say, not wanting to get into anything more than that.

"Well, let's hope it's a girl!" she says bluntly, like it's an obvious thing to hope for. I stare, shocked she'd make this kind of statement, and finally ask, "Oh. Why?" She smiles cutely, "The last thing this world needs is another man—have you seen the news?"

"I'm just grateful it's a human," I answer.

TJ raises his hand with an exaggerated, "HELLO."

"Well, no offense to you," she responds.

"Of course not," TJ says dryly, smiling too. Because I know him well, I can read his sarcasm. Because I know him well, I can agree with his sarcasm.

"I think Jess here can attest," TJ continues while gesturing to me, "that I'm not altogether terrible."

"He's actually wonderful," I'm gesturing back now; it's a regular ping-pong volley of gesturing between us. "He's exactly what this world needs." And then we order salads.

This waitress cannot know, I realize, that she is talking to two people who recently buried their baby boy. That we'd give anything for the privilege to raise him into a man. We run into a friend afterward and convey this conversation to him.

"Did you tip her?" he asks. We did, because withholding eight dollars won't help this kind of ignorance. But maybe talking about it will. I'm grateful to have been raised by parents who model an egalitarian marriage, who only act on major decisions after they agree. I'm grateful to have parents who taught me that equality is not gained by stripping honor from or lessening the value of men, but from standing right next to men, by creating a culture where men and women honor each other. By leading and following, respectively—depending solely on our gifts and roles in that season, regardless of our gender.

The future is not female, and it is not male; it is all of us together. I am deeply grateful for a baby whose heartbeat I got to hear today, no matter what the sex. And every day, I miss the boy who would've become a man. Our Luca, bringer of light, was—even in the too-short time he spent with us—exactly what this world needs.

Chapter 81

Luca's Song

(one year after)

It is May, ten days before Luca's birthday. Or is it his death day? I can't figure out what it is, really—but it's his day, May 17th. I decided that we need to come up with a plan, but I am not quite sure what that plan is. I wish it was a weekend, but it's just a Thursday. TJ will be working and Charlee and I will be together. I wonder what the day should look like.

I wrote a song about Luca. I want to record and film the song and release it on his day. I envision a piano and a white room with lots of light—and I think it's going to happen. (Please, if you marry, marry someone who makes things happen. Good things, I should specify. My first husband made lots of things happen, but they were awful things. So be very specific about what kinds of things you want your spouse to make happen.)

That is the plan I have for Luca's birthday. I feel alive when I create, and his death has reminded me that my time and energy need to be focused on what makes me feel alive. Of course, I don't stop brushing my teeth and cleaning the apartment, abandoning all for a creative frenzy, because the muse doesn't always hit me that way. But I recognize that the gift of creativity is mine for whatever reason. My job is not to question if it's good enough. My job is simply to create, to do it until I run dry, convinced that I have nothing left to give. And then do it again when I wake up, amazed by the ideas that draw me back to the blank page, the still keys of the piano, the notes that string together a melody. I am amazed that creating keeps happening at all. I don't take it lightly. Through so much loss in my life, creativity has kept me here and present, useful and hopeful. After all, creativity is a form of problem solving. And right now, I am faced with the problem of grief. So I get to work. You can say that phrase two different ways: "I get to work"—like it's a command life demands of you. Or, "I *get* to work—like it's a privilege afforded to the living. Luca has reminded me of this. I get to solve problems, add beauty and value to life—even with my grief. I must obey; it is part of honoring him that I do it. And this video is part of that. It just makes sense to release it on his birthday.

It is last summer on a very hot day in Pennsylvania. We are visiting my home in order to bury our son on the land where I grew up. TJ had discovered that a trained-in-Italy chef lives near my parents'—attends their church—and in typical direct, go-get-'em TJ fashion, asks her if she'd consider letting us pay her to cook us dinner. She comes up with a price, and it's settled. They live on a farm with chickens and rabbits and bees and so many gardens. It is lovely, the kind of place that city people need to be reminded exists in America. Sarah, the chef, and her spouse give us a tour of their beautiful land, and I notice TJ stepping very gingerly through the tall grass. As much as he loves the country, he hates ticks, and so I know the battle that is raging within as he braves the tick habitat we are currently traversing. I will tease him about this later as he checks himself for ticks for the tenth time today. Chef Sarah settles TJ, my pop, a friend, and me onto her covered porch. It is a pleasant respite from the summer rain that is falling now, lifting the oppressive humidity, if not my own profound sadness.

Sarah presents each dish, telling us the theme and why she chose it. It is like poetry, hearing her describe it—each dish complementing the last, not only in taste but in symbolism. "While choosing this meal, I thought about the soil," she tells us,

"About how it is not beautiful or particularly inspiring by itself. It's under us, we walk on it—it's not even very noticeable. But then, it's the only place for the vegetables, the flowers, the trees— so much of what we rely on for beauty and sustenance—to grow. Without the dirt, none of it would exist." I listen and try not to hate the dirt that has enveloped my life. *It's all mud and crap,* I think reflexively. No, no—actually it's not. There are already blooms that I cannot disregard—even being here at this dinner in a farmhouse in Pennsylvania with my wonderful husband, my father, and a dear friend—that is a bloom. It is still beautiful. There are just blooms and dirt and blooms and dirt, and right now the dirt is overpowering, but it won't always be this way. I cannot see the things that will grow from this dirt now. I cannot fathom it, actually. How can this dirt grow anything at all?

I hate this dirt.

But it is still dirt, and this is what dirt does. Grows things, good things. I promise those things are coming. I hear this from somewhere, certainly not me. It is the same voice that reminds me about the moments before, when the darkness felt final. When my first husband left, and my life and heart felt irreconcilably broken. But now I see all that terrible dirt was the beginning of the most beautiful garden. My marriage with TJ grew from that ground—so did our daughter Charlee and our precious life in Boston. Was that dirt special dirt? No, it was just regular dirt, but it grew beautiful things.

"There is a piano in our barn," Sarah tells us, after we have savored the last dish and the rain has stopped, as if on cue—like an invitation to get up and explore the land, the barn, this life right now before me.

TJ and I walk into the barn and the piano sits there like therapy waiting to happen. I haven't been able to sing a word about Luca—not yet, anyway. But I sit down, play some chords, and finally, the words and melody come. I don't know this yet, but it is the beginning of Luca's song, and it feels good to create it. I didn't know if I could—if I'd finally found the thing that can't be circled in rhyme and song. But actually, I don't think that thing exists. We are just either ready or not, and I wasn't ready until now.

TJ knows to let me go as long as I need. The air is stale in the barn and the piano is out of tune, but none of that matters. I am on fire with the task of planting seeds in this dirt; my hands are dirty from it. The terrible sadness of it gives way to the power of creation. It is not altogether unlike what called Luca here to be ours in the first place. The love that TJ and I have, mixing together, creating something out of nothing—a whole person where there was once a void. In a way, I am doing that still with Luca, creating something where there was nothing—again, for love—but now the love is more specific. Now this is for the love of Luca, a sacred, beautiful thing. My person who is both here and not here. All the dirt in the world cannot hide it or dull it forever.

The first, tiniest buds are showing in this barn. Today I sit down and write out the lyrics to Luca's song, to the song I already know by heart. I fill in the notes, compose a harmony in my mind. As the early morning light streams in the window, my tears blur the ink on the page. Notes, lyrics, love, tears all mingle here.

I am still not ready to call it spring—but perhaps it is a promise of spring. It is the thought that spring will come again, a thought that helps.

Chapter 82

His Stone
(nine months after)

My brother tells me about his recent trip to our family home in Pennsylvania. He's lived in L.A. with his family for a long time now, but growing up in the woods and hills of green Pennsylvania has a way of bringing you back no matter how far you go.

Those acres in Pennsylvania aren't just land, they raised me. After I got to travel the world—seeing it from various stages, planes, buses, hotel rooms, and conversations that revealed a different kind of world: lovely people who think, feel, and see differently from me—after all that, I ended up home again. But this time it was after my divorce. This time home healed me.

There was something stabilizing about waking up to the same trees and sky through my window all those years later. Something comforting knowing that, though my (first) husband had left—leaving me feeling devastatingly changed—there remains the sky and trees: unchanged. It helped. I'm always grateful for help.

"I wander down the big hill—the one with the hollow tree at the bottom, where Mom hid our Easter baskets one year," my brother is saying. I nod; I know the place. He continues, "I'm following the trail to the Old Fishing Hole—where we all got scared by the snake that one time."

When you grow up in the country, this kind of thing is bound to happen. We were scared by snakes a few times, actually. "I checked on Luca's grave, Jessica. Have you seen it since Pop laid the stone?"

"No," I say simply. We haven't been back since Christmas. It was freezing then, which is the excuse I will give you, but as I've already written to you, dear reader, enough was simply enough. I didn't have the guts. And TJ gave me permission to do it later, to not do the hard thing at that time.

"I know it's a grave, and it's sad," my brother is saying. "But it looks beautiful, and I like what you had written on it." I don't answer because I can't. My sister is with us, and I feel her hand on my shoulder. The silence between us all says what I can't.

I'm grateful to discover this: the heart has no bounds. Grief and joy, loss and gratitude—all coexisting. All born of love. All here. God, this life is an extraordinary thing to witness. And it probably goes without saying that I really wish my brother didn't have to tell me about how he liked what I wrote on my baby's grave. That my life didn't give him reason to. But there is love here, still—even in this terrible, kind, gentle conversation—and this is the thing that I continue to find astounding.

Chapter 83

For Better, For Worse
(twelve months after)

I'm at the hospital, talking to my nurse Margie. Charlee gives her a Fig Newton and a rock, and Joseph and Mary could not have acted any more appreciative for the gold from the actual Magi than Margie does when Charlee hands her a rock and her snack. Nurses do so much more than physical work.

Margie commutes from New Hampshire to Boston. She tells me a story from that morning. She's driving early—right as the sun starts to light up the sky—when, ambling across the road in front of her, is a moose. I've never seen a real moose. Growing up, a friend gave me a book about a moose named Jessica. I wasn't sure how I felt about a moose having my name; I'm still not. But maybe the moose is just as unsure about a human having her name, now that I think about it. Anyway, that book was my closest association to a moose.

"I'm awestruck," Margie tells me, "You sort of know that a moose is tall, but they're so much taller even than you would think when you see one right in front of you. The moose crosses the street to the river, and seeing it is just spectacular." I'm nodding. I'm also wondering what the plural for moose is. Meece? Mooses? (Focus, Jess.) "There's a man walking his dog," Margie continues, "So I slow down and roll down the window. I ask him if he saw that moose. It's too awesome not to tell someone about it. I don't even care that he's a stranger. He saw it too, and we are just both laughing and yelling about how huge it was!"

I think this is profound. I'm not suggesting you go find a moose right now. (But I won't stop you. Although I really don't know that mooses/meece aren't dangerous, so be careful.) I am saying let's tell each other about what is truly wonderful. If you witness something awesome, say something. Brighten the world by talking about what brightens your heart. Slow down, roll down the window, and let's tell each other something good.

This is why I can't stop writing about TJ. About the love, the kindness, the good, the opportunities for growth this marriage gives me. Before I met TJ, I was just driving, focusing on getting somewhere else, rather than seeing the beauty that is right here. Now there's a moose crossing the street. And there's a river. These things I notice are wonderful. There's a stranger who I can't help telling why life is rich this morning, this afternoon, tonight, tomorrow, ten years from now, forever. I'm not saying everything is perfect. I'm also not calling TJ a moose. What I'm saying is that life is beautiful. And I've always known this, but I'm better at noticing it with TJ.

* * *

"Let's talk about a plan, Jess," TJ says to me seriously.

"For what?"

"For if you're not local and go into labor," he answers.

"I'm always local, though—"

"You're not. You were at a park with Charlee today," he disagrees.

414

"That's not even a half mile from home, though," I disagree right back.

"It's not home."

"Well. Okay," I acquiesce, because the truth is, we don't live in a public park with a sandbox. It is, in fact, not home, even if Charlee wishes it was.

"So, let's say you're at the park," TJ continues, "and you go into labor. What do you do?"

"I call you," I say, stating the obvious.

"Wrong."

"That's not the wrong answer."

"You call an ambulance," TJ says.

"Are you serious?"

"I'm serious, Jess. You call an ambulance. They'll get you and Charlee to the hospital quickly—faster than I could. You call me on the way. I'll meet you guys there."

"TJ. I'm not calling an ambulance when I go into labor."

"What do you suggest?"

"That I call *you*. That maybe I walk to the hospital?"

He sits up straight, eyes wide. "I *hope* you're kidding about *walking to the hospital!*"

I wasn't kidding, actually, but I decide this is not a hill I'm willing to die on. But I double down on calling him. "Why can't I just call you, though? Going to the hospital in an ambulance because I've maybe had one contraction or my water broke is so embarrassing! And what if I'm home with you? You'll just take me then, right?"

"If we're home together, I'll still call an ambulance. I'll follow you guys," he states.

I give up and ask him if he'd like a burger for dinner tonight, because I really want one. If I were to do the age-old flower test—"he loves me, he loves me not..."—I would definitely land on the "he loves me" petal. Also, apparently if I go into labor anywhere other than the actual lobby of the hospital, TJ is bound and determined to make sure my ride there is none other than in an ambulance (because Air Force One is unavailable). Which sounds like just the thing for someone who dislikes the kind of attention ambulances bring. Wish me luck.

★ ★ ★

"So if there's a strong heartbeat, then this baby is probably still alive, right?" I ask the nurse who's holding a Doppler on my belly. "Definitely alive, hon," she answers gently. I'm at the hospital, having walked in with the terrifying and overwhelming thought that we lost this baby, too. This kind of anxiety hadn't happened yet—afterward, everyone is proud of me that it "took this long"—but the time it took to get from I'M FINE AND LIFE IS NORMAL to PLEASE GOD NO THIS BABY DIED, TOO is startlingly short. I thought I was beyond this. (Actually, Jess, everyone needs assurance.)

Usually, I feel this babe moving all throughout the day, but when I stop to think about it that afternoon, I realize it's been a little while. So, then I push and poke at her and feel ... nothing.

Just like Luca. I have to go to the hospital anyway for therapy, so I get in the car and drive. I can't feel any definitive movement on the way there, so by the time I walk into Labor and Delivery, fear has turned my insides to water. I am wondering how to tell everyone that this baby has left too. I don't want to plan another funeral. God, no. *God, I trust you*, I also pray. My therapist Nancy calls me back and, right away, I tell her that I am feeling scared because I haven't felt my baby move for a little while. She is calm and professional.

"Okay," she says, "Let's get you with a nurse in triage—sit right here in my office, and I will be back as soon as I secure everything." I sit and pray and am scared. God, am I scared. Nancy reappears and ushers me into the same room where they listened for Luca's heartbeat almost exactly one year ago and could not find it.

"Do you want me to stay or leave?" Nancy asks as I heave myself onto the reclining chair and the nurse gets the gel ready.

It really doesn't matter to me, and I tell her so. Nothing matters except that this baby is okay.

The nurse mentions my shoes, calls them quite a fashion statement as she squirts gel on my belly. I nod politely and thank her. I don't know if calling something a fashion statement is actually a compliment. (The first time I rapped for an audience, someone from the crowd approached me afterward and told me I was brave. I didn't know if that was a compliment, either.) I also don't care. The truth is, I wear these bright red sneakers all the time because they slip on—meaning I don't have to attempt the impossible task of bending over and tying my laces. I also don't understand a world where we can talk about shoes while waiting to see if your baby is alive.

I hear the heartbeat right away. *Thank God, thank God, thank God*. The relief brings me back to myself. I feel like crying, but I don't. I do later, but not now. Nancy hugs me. We have our therapy session, and I marvel that this is not my Luca's story. I am shaken. I walk slowly out of the hospital and get a salad. These are the normal things we do, despite everything. With our salads and polite smiles we blend in with a world that, to my endless surprise, doesn't seem to be panicking about which is worse: being afraid of the dark or being terribly familiar with it.

This week is a doozy. Gripping anxiety, Mother's Day (which is lovely, thanks to Charlee and TJ, but also complex), and Luca's upcoming birthday—all in a span of seven days. It's a lot, and I am tired. I'm also so deeply grateful—for Charlee, Luca, and this babe in my belly now. For TJ who gave me these gifts, which is a powerful thing to give to another. Parenthood. Hearts that bleed and the ability to still have moments of fear, but because you're suddenly the parent, you get to be the one who looks into the darkness and tells your child it's not as scary as it seems. That we're all going be okay and to keep walking forward, because God is there in the midst of the darkness. You've seen Him there; it's perhaps the greatest revelation of your life. The dark doesn't last. We out-walk it; our hearts out-love it; God outshines it.

Tonight, I am going to sleep grateful that this story is different. That we heard the heartbeat. That I am not planning a funeral. Tonight, this is enough, and my heart is full. In my bed, I cry, but this time the tears are thankful.

Chapter 84

Luca's Parents
(before and after)

It's only the second time TJ and I hang out after we first meet, and we talk about having kids. Don't worry, it's not weird. I'm not like, "Hey lemme know if you want me to have your babies or nah, and then maybe I'll tell you my middle name." It's more like, "Is this something you see for your life? Yeah? Me too." And also, telepathic message: I'll say yes if you ask me to dinner. Or coffee. Or to cross the street because we're both headed uptown and the walk sign is on. Anything romantic like that is fine; I'm low maintenance. And also, I won't admit it to anyone yet, but I like you.

He asks me out to lots more dinners, and then we finally have the biggest dinner of all in a tent with one hundred people we love, and I'm wearing a white dress. He starts talking about those babies we both want, only this time it's for real. And we don't quite realize just what kind of fragile miracle it is at the time—we learn about that when the miracle comes and goes way too soon a few years later—but we get to hold our daughter; I get to fall in love with TJ all over again as Charlee's dada.

It's incredible. It's better than I could have imagined, being her parents; it's harder than I could have imagined, being her parents. It's the first bit of tension we've seen so far—and the resolution comes again and again with a weight that anchors me to TJ even more. I didn't know that even more between us was possible until we had Charlee, until we had Luca, until I'm carrying this baby now and he's praying and having faith while

I'm praying and taking extra trips to the hospital just to make sure this one's still alive.

* * *

There are fresh strawberries in our kitchen, and it's hard to feel poor when this is the case. Speaking of poor, my name means "wealthy one." Growing up, this embarrassed me. In my church community, everyone else seemed to have names that were some kind of derivative of "beloved of God," and then there was little homeschooled me—two pastors for parents, but a name that essentially means: *show me the money*. You know— *cringe*—shallow. Whenever asked, I said, "My name means 'wealthy one'—but spiritually. I'm wealthy, *spiritually*," I'd amend. Everyone just nodded without questioning it, moving on to ask Elisha, another girl in my Sunday school, what her name means. And that lucky duck got to say, "salvation of God." No need to add any depth-giving explanation to a name like *that*. Mic-drop, move on. We're not worthy, Elisha.

"Luca isn't with you the way Charlee is, but he is with you," my therapist tells me. "And someday, the kind of with you that he is won't feel as terrible as it does now." I glimpse this sometimes. Like when Charlee takes a long time to go to sleep—this time last year, it was a problem. And I felt frustrated and impatient, like I don't have this much time to give to bedtime. Something inside of me was whiny about it. But Luca, he shuts up that whine. Impatience has lost a lot of its voice since he died. Now when Charlee is up too early or too late, I feel grateful that she's this kind of with me. The kind that wakes me up sometimes; the kind that means she's here in every way a human can be. This calm inside—it's a gift. It comes only after hard work and sacrifice, and that makes it all the sweeter. It's a kind of wealth, maybe. And it makes me not mind the meaning of my name so much after all.

* * *

I'm in Lord & Taylor, remarking on a pair of underwear I'm holding. To find something softer, I think you'd have to hold an actual cloud. "That's because it's the very best—from Switzerland," a saleslady explains. I think about my two dear Swiss friends I've met here in Boston, and I'm oddly proud of them and their nation's fine underwear. "Is this your first?" the lady asks, looking at my belly. They always ask this.

"Third," I say. I have to. Though it'd be nice to skip the questions that follow, I can't pretend Luca doesn't exist. I have to honor him, even in banal small talk.

"What do you have at home?" the woman continues, wrapping up the Rolls Royce of underwear in tissue paper. How do you say you have the best little girl and also grief while buying underwear from a stranger? I say it anyway: "A daughter. My son died." The woman's horror stops her questions. She says she's sorry and can't give me my card back fast enough. I decline a bag, blinking back tears as I leave holding a pair of fine underwear in my hand.

It was similar with the lady who waxed my brows today, too.

"First baby?"

"Third."

"Who's at home?"

"One."

I know the math doesn't add up, so I explain: *My son died.* She can't kick me out with hot wax on my face, though, so instead tells me about another client. "He's here all the way from the United Arab Emirates with his wife while she's pregnant and delivers. So you see, everyone comes to Boston to have their baby, because it's the best in the world. This child is normal?"

I cringe at the word. We don't use it for people; the implications are divisive and hurtful. I don't even use it for feelings anymore. We just are and we just feel, period. It's a blessing to get to be both. Luca was "normal," but he's dead, and that is not normal. Except we all die, which is normal. Now he's normal but not here—and that's not normal. Heaven is a lot better than normal. It's all a lot.

"The baby is healthy as far as I know," I say. She smiles, "Of course. This baby will be fine. How much longer do you have? You said about eight more weeks?" I nod. "Come back once more before then, so you can have nice clean eyebrows when you deliver." I almost laugh out loud; my eyebrows are the least of my concern when it comes to birthing this baby. But still. She is kind and encouraging and knows what to do with wax, so I will probably come back.

* * *

I keep marveling over this: I get to be pregnant again. People ask how I'm doing, and the answer is too much to explain. I'm grateful. I marvel at God's kindness. I'm scared. What if this baby dies, too? I don't think you're supposed to say that. I also have peace. In my life, The Worst Thing happened a couple times, and I can't deny what I've seen. That life is rich, still. That grace outlasts pain. That maybe the grief has helped me see the richness and depth and weighty-beyond-belief value that lies in all the moments I may never have noticed otherwise.

The day my first husband left, I found out about his affair after he slammed the door. It was the noise that introduced me to another chapter. Divorce and loss and betrayal and this misplaced sense of identity that had me combing the woods of Pennsylvania for a long time afterward, hoping that one more hike would bring me back to myself.

After the door slammed and I heard his Jeep rumble to life, I called him over and over again. When he finally answered, he simply said, "Everything's true. I'm having an affair and I love her and you'll never see me again." He hung up then and I called back because life is not like the movies. You can't just declare something and not worry about a mortgage you share, the cats you have, the life you so easily and innocently entwined that now must be painstakingly pulled apart, one thread at a time. "You have to come back," I said when he answered again, "We own a house. You have to come back." It was a strange thing to fixate on, but the emotional mess was too overwhelming; I didn't know where to start. The practical mess could start with phone calls and paperwork and advice from friends who know something about the law. It could start with, *You have to come back. You might love her, sure, but you still have to come back because we own a house.*

My brother Jason took a red eye from Los Angeles, and I went with my parents and sister to pick him up at the Philly airport. I kept crying silently and blinking and wondering why my brother can come so quickly from so far away while my husband left from right next to me in our bed not 24 hours ago. Jase hugged me quickly, and we all exhaled when he arrived. "Do you have a bag?" asked my pop. Jase gestured to a tiny laptop bag over his shoulder, "Just this." He paused and then smiled sheepishly before saying, "But I forgot underwear. Can we stop for some?" We all laughed. Like, really laughed. I found it hilarious, actually, that in this time of crisis, my family will stop at the nearby Target for underwear for my grown brother. This is life. We are devastated, introduced to grief with the sudden slam of a door. We lose ourselves, but, as we laugh with our family over the mundane life necessities like underwear, we are relieved. We discover we are still here. That we still need underwear. We discover that life is not ever only one thing, even in the seasons that join us to suffering in a way that feels permanent.

My husband will always have done this—so then how could I not always suffer? But we glimpse a way forward in the kindness of those who love us. The drop-everything-and-fly-to-your-side actions that tell us we are worthy of love and care. And we glimpse a way forward in the inane details—buying cheap underwear as a family of fully grown adults—and we laugh at it. I thought laughter wouldn't be able to find me in all this suffering. Surely I'm completely obscured by it; surely joy and mirth fly right on overhead. But that night, I saw that real laughter could still see me, still land on my shoulder, press itself against my chest, help me breathe in a way that hurts less, even for a moment. I saw that life is nuanced, that no season ends us because no season is ever just one thing.

And even now, lying each night next to TJ—the man who came after all that loss and suffering—getting to watch his chest move up and down with the miracle of breath. Knowing that under all that glorious skin and bones and muscle is a heart that loves me well. Hearing Charlee say "Mama" and getting to be the one who answers to that name. Well, I don't know what will happen, but I never do. I do know this: there is so much good here. More than I deserve or fully understand. I try to focus on that. This is where God's peace lies, I think, so I try to stay right here. Breathing in and breathing out.

Chapter 85

Diaspora
(six months after)

I wonder if you know the word *diaspora*. If you don't—if you've never needed that word to describe how you feel—well, that's not a bad thing. I didn't learn its meaning until my late twenties. I was fresh off a Broadway tour, reeling from the news that my husband was in love with someone else. Oh, hi. Did you expect that, if I'm going to veer away from the topic of death, I could maybe land on a lighter subject? Because I could talk about my recent attempt at making croissants. I could write about this all day, but all you really need to know is they take FOURTEEN HOURS to make, so you should probably just either quit your job or plan to take ALL of your vacation days before trying it yourself. Or just go buy one at the corner coffee shop for three dollars and enjoy the next thirteen-and-a-half hours of free time. But, man, fresh-out-of-the-oven croissants are delicious, and I am already planning my next black hole of time I can give to this project just to have another homemade croissant. So now that we've talked about croissant-making, I think we're ready for something deeper. Like my first husband's affair.

After being away for work (touring with a Broadway show), I get home to my husband and discover a shocking narrative in which I am the woman betrayed. (I know, I *know*. You're all like, uh, that's the story I want to hear. Sorry, reader, I'm talking diaspora here, not nearly as scandalous as an affair. My apologies.) I move back into my parents' house. I lose my marriage, my home, and my job all in the space of one weekend. (So, you can imagine the fun I have answering that bland Monday question around town:

And how was your weekend?) Nothing is familiar, except when I come across the word diaspora: the dispersion of any people from their original homeland.

I remember seeing that word and thinking, *If somebody else created a word that defines this way I feel suddenly expelled from my own life, then I'm not the only one who's felt this.* It's isolating to be a victim. The story changes, however, when you discover you're not alone—that others have been here and moved on and healed and even thrived—this discovery is a bridge from the cruel place someone has put you to the empowered and whole place you belong. I read about being forced from your own homeland, and it feels familiar to me. Different in many obvious ways, of course (I am, after all, an American living in America), but longing for a home that I can no longer go back to—that I didn't choose to leave—is resonant.

I can tell you about the long walk I take in the freezing winter night air that belongs to the American Northeast in November. About how I purposely don't take my jacket or ID or phone. How there is something passively self-harming in that choice. Maybe the cold will numb me. Feeling hurts too much. Maybe something bad will happen, and I won't have a phone to call for help. For the first time in my life, not being alive—not being here—feels like a comparatively nice option.

My pop's cousin had never written me a letter before. But soon after my first husband leaves, I hold her letter in my hands. My eyes are blurring with tears as I read the phrase, "You are your grandmother's granddaughter." I read the sentence over again. I've been wondering who is left now that my husband is gone, my marriage over. In my pain, I have a vivid recurring dream. I see myself peeling off my skin the way you would wet clothes; I tenderly fold it all up and lay it in my dresser drawer, the way my mom taught me to do. I'm cold as I walk outside and hear whispering. "Of course he doesn't love her," everyone says as I walk by, "She is only bones, after all."

But now my cousin writes this to me. She has seen me perform. She has watched from the audience, seated next to her own mother—the dear sister of my own grandmother, who died before I ever got to meet her.

"We drew our breath in sharply, Jess," my cousin writes. "You were a revelation. You were proof that your grandmother Helen is not gone, after all—had never really left—not while you're here." The words give me a sense of belonging, of home. I am no longer the Girl Left For Another; I am my grandmother's granddaughter.

Because she was, I am.

There is the twenty-something woman I know a little from church. She reaches out when she hears of my divorce. "You may not want this," she writes, "but I'd like to meet you for dinner. I went through a divorce too. I'd love to be there for you now. Let me know." We meet once a month at the Cheesecake Factory. She is my only divorced friend; in so many ways, she's raising her hand and saying, *Me too*. To see her thriving shows me that there is another option. Maybe I won't always feel this way—maybe this exile leads to a homecoming worth the wait. Maybe it's okay if home is different from the one I was forced to leave. At the time, I don't know if this means marriage again, but these dinners with a stranger-turned-friend give me a glimpse of wholeness and joy on the other side. I wonder if the same awaits me, too, and before I realize it, hope has snuck in with the thought.

My mom says we are hurt by people, but also healed by people. I'm not sure why I am able to read my cousin's letter and believe it so hard that it actually anchors me. Or why I can open my heart to a near stranger over cheesecake, let her look inside, and believe her when she tells me it'll be okay. All I know is that these are some of the interactions that call me home. That create a new home. That show me home is still possible. That in the wake of great hurt, healing comes from angles I never could have anticipated.

Our broken heart is the perfect sieve to let the good in. And in those hard months, and again with Luca, I learn this is always an option: to let the good in along with the hurt. To let them mingle until the hurt is swallowed whole by some good you never knew was waiting for you in the Cheesecake Factory or a letter that shows up in your mailbox. It's an option to recognize that, though you're not home now, maybe you're also not home yet. It's an option to go out. Just go (I mean, sometimes we don't have the choice). And maybe, along with the Israelites long ago, we discover there is bread in the wilderness. That a promised land awaits; perhaps there are other ways to get there, but through the wilderness is definitely one. And along the way, when we open our heart to those who reach out, they may very well be the ones to lead us home.

And now, though grief tries to call me away from my home, there is Charlee. She is cupping my face with her toddler hands, telling me to smile, to be happy, Mama. "You make me happier than you know, Charlee," I tell her. And it's the truth. There is TJ, walking along the Charles River with me every day. Listening to my grief poured out in sentences I don't need to filter. Do you know how amazing it is to be able to say exactly what you mean to another human? To do this when you are low and there is no need to try to make it seem better or lighter or anything other than what it is? This is home. A promised land of sorts. And it's okay that grief and memory live here, too. Home is where the heart is, as the saying goes—and if we are lucky enough to love deeply for long enough on this earth, then grief is also where the heart is. I am not sure if my heart is full or heavy. But it is valuable and not going anywhere, I know this.

This time, though my heart is grieving, I am not exiled to the wilderness. I know where I belong. I am still TJ's wife, Charlee's mama.

Luca's mama, too.

Chapter 86

All Thy Waves and Thy Billows
(his birth)

I keep thinking about the time between discovering Luca is dead and the start of Pitocin, of labor, of doing the unthinkable. "It doesn't have to be right away," the doctor tells me. "You could go home, sleep; we could induce you tomorrow."

I have never been one to procrastinate. The anxiety and dread have never been worth it. I'd almost always rather get something over with, and I am not so good at compartmentalizing. As a young homeschooler, I would ask my mom to assign all the week's math lessons on Monday. Math was my least favorite subject, and I liked the idea of getting it out of the way first, so I would try to do as much of it as I could on Monday. Also, I couldn't fathom going home to my building, running into neighbors—even strangers who ask so many questions of pregnant women because everyone does, everyone—and fielding their conversations. It felt like picking through a minefield, and I could hardly even stand upright under the weight of grief. I couldn't spend any time pretending—not even the short length of time it took for the elevator to take me to my apartment on the seventh floor.

"I'd like to do it right away, if that's okay," I say.

We walk from the building where they take care of you when you're pregnant to the adjacent building where they take care of you in labor. We step outside into the sunlight and even that feels false. I put on a brave face because Charlee. She's with us. She is happy and has no idea how vastly our family has changed. I walk, one step in front of the other, my pregnant belly leading the way. Charlee's hand is in mine, and this is grace. She is two, her hand is tiny. She is two, her hand is powerful. I find more courage in her grip than I do in all the words the doctors have been telling us since the first one said, "I'm sorry, there's no heartbeat." I love her for the skip in her step. She is the sun that is still shining somewhere in the universe when you've been plunged into darkness in your corner of the world; you watched the sun slip under the horizon right as they told you, "I'm sorry, there's no heartbeat," but here is your child reminding you that the sun doesn't stop shining just because you can no longer see it. How lucky are you to have watched the sunset and yet, still hold the hand of the sun. These are the kinds of things you hear about—stillbirth, I mean. You don't even read about it, because who would do so on purpose? It's too terrible. It is oxymoronic—a meeting place for birth and death; such places should not be.

We get to our room in labor and delivery, and I go to change into my hospital gown. TJ talks to Charlee about her brother Luca. He tells her he's not coming home with us, like we thought. That he's going straight to heaven and that we're sad about this, because we were all so excited to meet him and be with him—but baby Luca is not sad or scared or hurt and we'll see him some day. Charlee nods and remains unfazed, as only a two-year-old can. My sister comes to get her, showing up with tears on her face. "Jess," she says, despondent. "I know," is all I say, tears coming down my face, too. But Charlee runs into her aunt's arms, and everyone cheers up in the face of such joy. They talk about mac n cheese for dinner and watching whatever show Charlee wants. She isn't sad as she leaves. I watch the second sunset that day as she walks out of the room holding my sister's hand, and I am left without a person to be brave for.

The nurse gives me Pitocin to induce labor; it feels like a failed placebo dissolving in my mouth. I don't know how to tell you to ready yourself for the unfathomable. We aren't ready, sometimes we just do it because we have to. My belly is so large; Luca is here but not here, and my brain keeps trying to understand this while my face responds with tears and a voice that cannot hold steady. I am profoundly sad. It feels infinite.

My parents pastor a small church that, growing up, was the center of my community. I loved one particular worship song, even as a child. I don't even know why—it's not a typical kid's bop. I'd sit in the horse-barn-turned-church (yes, the church was originally our horse barn. I've always been rather proud of this. The church is still called The Barn to this day.) that we met in every Sunday, and something deep inside would resonate with my favorite lyric, "All thy waves and thy billows have gone over me...laid me low..." I think about it now because I appreciate the veracity of those words. I think about the time I tried to ride the waves into shore at the beach. My pop and my brothers were with me and I was told that if I get wiped out by a big wave, to just let it take me. *Don't fight it, and eventually, you'll be able to tell which way is up again. That's when you can sit up, stand up, breathe. It'll happen, but don't fight the wave as it knocks you under. Don't tire yourself out,* they said. Eventually, I wiped out, and I was rolling around under the water for what felt like a long time. I remember the noise as the water roared over me and I kept flipping, turning compulsory somersaults underwater, unsure which way was up. But, like they said, the ocean calmed again, allowing me to stop turning. To sit up and breathe. I was okay, tired and appropriately scared of the power of the sea, but okay.

As my body readies to give birth to my baby who will never come home, I don't fight anything. I let grief wash over me. I listen to it roar past me. *All thy waves and thy billows have gone over me, laid me low.* I can't tell which way is up, but sometimes there is calm. Sometimes the nurse comes in and holds my hand and we quietly talk, all three of us—TJ, too. I tell her about what God has already done. *Surely, he will do this again* is the thought that keeps persisting in the gaps, in the pauses I take for breath and tears, while telling her about my first marriage, showing her the scars on my heart, the tattoo on my wrist that says: *peace.*

TJ is on a cot, and I know I've mentioned this already, but it is so important because I ask him to please hold me. My hospital bed is built for one person and I am currently big enough for two, but he crawls into bed with me anyway. He joins me and I pray that all who are grieving can write that sentence about somebody: he joins me. In that narrow bed, I press my body into his, and I cry with a voice I did not know I had. It is universal, bigger than me. It is the voice I remember when I see the image of the orca known as Tahlequah, carrying her dead calf for 17 days before releasing her baby to the sea. It is grief in the shape of my body about to give birth to my son, trembling and moaning. It is the shape of my soul, already giving birth to grief, already making way for a new kind of mother, a grieving one.

Like everything in life, this goes in cycles, lasting through the night. Deep moaning, quiet talking that feels hopeful somehow, sleep sometimes, and then early in the morning, it's time. I feel my baby's body start to leave my own. It's different than Charlee, as Luca isn't alive to assist in the act of being birthed. I feel him start to exit—a foot, a hand, I am not sure what part of his precious body I can feel pressing against me, finally meeting the outside air for the first time—but I suddenly need to push, so I ask TJ to get a nurse. The nurse checks and tells me what I know, "Please don't push until I come back with the doctor," she says. When they're ready, I push and it's easy. He's small, not quite 36 weeks—five little perfect pounds, even—so he slides out of me in two pushes.

It is silent, the air is still, and I have the clarity that comes from doing something intensely focused and physical. The nurse puts him in a blanket and a hat and hands him to me. I am not nearly as scared as I thought I'd be. I am not scared at all. He is beautiful; God, he is perfect. The fact that he is dead matters far less than the fact that he is mine. Holding him is the moment when it is calmest. The ocean stops churning, and I sit up, I breathe. I don't get a lifetime to hold my baby. I don't even get seventeen days to hold my baby, I get some hours. I watch his face again and again, willing myself to still see it when I close my eyes. To be able to do this tonight, after they take him away, tomorrow, forever. We take photos of him and believe me when I tell you it is far less strange than you think. You thank God for the photos, you hold onto anything you can, because your baby left before you got to see his face alive. Because all thy waves and thy billows have gone over me, laid me low. Because the next time the ocean calms and you sit up and breathe, you need to remember his face.

Chapter 87

Fire Ephemeral
(thirteen months after)

There are moments of peace.

I am not guaranteed that I will bring this "rainbow" baby home. I actually think I will—most of the time. But the bubble has broken; bad things happen to anyone. To me, actually. Bad things happen to me. Not all the time, but sometimes. I know this now, and I can't go back. All of the women who walk around blissfully planning their baby's arrival have no more assurance of bringing home a baby than I do. But I know what can happen. I am learning to live in the shared space of This Terrible Thing That Has Happened and also right now. Right now, this space is calm. I remind myself that fearing terrible things would have prevented me from experiencing my greatest, deepest joys in life (my marriage to TJ, after a shocking divorce, for one). I am not willing to give this up. So I have to trust that if another terrible thing happens, the same Source of peace, grace, comfort, and healing will still be present and taking care of me. I have to trust that I will be okay. And in that trust, there is peace (most of the time).

It is June now, and I am so visibly pregnant that strangers remark on my round belly. It's my birthday, and I marvel over the difference between this one and the last. Last birthday I was only two weeks past Luca's death, his birth, his coming-and-going-way-too-fast. I had just started therapy with Nancy, and she met with me every week. Not just physically—she met me where I was, emotionally. Allowed me to live in the space of grief, sorrow, deep pain, and also hope. She never thought I was strange for holding all of this in my heart, for taking care of all of these feelings and giving voice to them in her office, in my writing, to my husband—to those who would listen.

While going through my divorce from my first husband, a friend gives me a bouquet of wildflowers. "Mostly, wildflowers aren't planted or even cultivated," she writes in a note. "They grow in wild, overgrown places and show up unexpectedly. They can survive on natural rains and don't require chemical fertilizers. Basically, they're tough. And despite harsh conditions, they grow anyway. They're also beautiful—even more so because they grow in places where other blooms would fail. The wildflowers make me think of you. Don't let anyone tell you that you can't grow here. You're a wildflower; you will continue to bloom, anyway."

I am a wildflower. I wanted to be planted in a garden that I manicured. It didn't happen. But I have learned that growth happens in the most unexpected places. From dirt and mud and messiness, in the deep shadows of the valley. Not to bore you to death by turning this into a horticultural essay, but I need to mention the fire ephemeral. It's another flower that another friend compares me to. (Takeaway from this chapter: when a friend is grieving, compare her to a flower. One more takeaway: make friends who compare you to flowers.) While sitting in her cabin, she asks if I know about the fire ephemerals. I shake my head, so she continues. "These seeds only burst open in the hottest flames. Only the most devastating fires that tear through a forest result in the most vibrant blooms nature has to offer. The fire ephemeral. I'm encouraged by them—and you remind me of them."

I don't ever want the devastating fire. None of us do. I'm not used to grieving—and certainly don't want more tragedy in my life. But also: Look at these blooms. There are fire ephemerals where there was once just dirt. I find these beautiful blooms in motherhood, in my marriage to TJ, in the way my heart has decided upon gratitude. None of this came from me. All of it is God's grace, and all of it is inextricably connected to the devastating fire. Where those flames raged, a rainbow of blooms—red, yellow, purple, orange—now blaze against a backdrop of ash. I cannot tell you that I understand why Luca died. I can tell you there is mystery and tragedy in this life. There is also grace and love and faith. All of these things often intersect. And what buoys my heart is that my son is not gone forever. He is gone from here, but one day I will go be with him. I don't know what that will look like. Heaven is a mystery to us on Earth. But I can only imagine the reunion it will be.

When we walk into the lobby of our apartment building, Charlee runs ahead, rounding the corner before anyone else, because she cannot wait to press the elevator button. For a moment, we don't see her; but by the time she turns around, we're there, too. I have a picture in my mind of a boy arriving in Heaven. He has the kind of complexion of those whose face regularly gets sun and whose heart regularly gets joy. Like most kids, he cannot wait, so he runs ahead of the rest of us. He's there first. He's right around the corner—right where his parents can't quite see him anymore. But by the time he turns around, we're there, too. Maybe he'll call us slowpokes. But I know he's not afraid we're not coming; I know he's not afraid at all. Can you imagine that? Can you imagine not being afraid at all?

I wish my boy were here.

This kind of longing fills a whole heart, could be the full story, it is so deep and wide and present. And I am so grateful that he is somewhere wonderful; that he himself is wonderful while there. And that he is living in a place where it is possible to be completely unafraid. I think about how, when Charlee rounds the corner first, she isn't afraid because she can't see us. She knows we're close, knows we'll be there soon. I like to think Luca feels similarly right now. He's rounded the corner first, but the rest of us are close behind him. And we'll all meet up at the elevator.

⋆ ⋆ ⋆

Once a week now I go to the hospital for something called a "non-stress test." I'm not sure why it's called this—it's stressful. I lay on a cot and someone—usually a technician named Betty—straps a Doppler onto my belly to monitor the baby's heartbeat and movement. Hearing the heartbeat right away is always a great relief. I cannot quite explain the magnitude of it, but let me try. When I was pregnant with Charlee, I did yoga on the beach. It sounds really dreamy, but actually, it was awkward. I couldn't bend like I was used to, there was sand everywhere, and by the time we were all laying down in savasana, I felt like the sun had something personally against me, it was bearing down so hard. I was boiling. As soon as I could, I went right into the cool ocean water, and I was so hot that I wouldn't have been surprised if you could hear a sizzle as I did. That kind of relief can give you a sense of a fraction of how I feel when I hear the sound of my baby's heartbeat.

Betty straps another belt over me, "to see if you're having any contractions." One more belt and I'm pretty sure I'm good to jump out of a plane. Finally, she hands me a clicker. "Press this button whenever you feel the baby move," she instructs me. "The monitor tells us, but we like to know if you can tell, too." I'm not sure if they're testing my intelligence or my baby's ability to move—or both. I can't get past the clicker. Suddenly my baby and I are two unlikely and unwilling contestants on a game show. Let it be known that if I were actually on a game show, I probably wouldn't pick someone who's only been alive for 34 weeks as my partner. Babies are invaluable. We know this; this book wouldn't exist if they weren't. But when people can "phone a friend," they don't call a baby.

I'm tense as I wait to feel movement. I realize that I have a death grip on the clicker, and my neck and shoulders are drawn tight in anticipation. I relax and let my head fall back on the pillow and pretend to rest. I'm not resting. I'm waiting to click. It feels too long—like I'm failing this test. And then, suddenly: BAM! A reason to click. I click so fast, it's like I'm racing the clock, like I'm trying to win the million-dollar question.

There are more movements and more clicks, and *OH MY GOSH THIS GAME IS NOT AS HARD AS I THOUGHT! WE'RE GOOD AT IT!* I'm oddly proud about something I have no control over. I'm also unfathomably relieved.

"The baby is great," Betty says, soundlessly entering my room. "You'll be out of here soon." She stops the machine and for the first time in twenty minutes, I relax my grip on the clicker. We passed, my baby and I. Today we passed. Today I am pregnant. Thank you, God, for this. I've been saying it daily for almost nine months; I can't speak for tomorrow, but today I am pregnant, and for now, that is enough. It has to be; it's what I have.

* * *

"I'm excited to spend concentrated, one-on-one time with you while you're in labor," TJ tells me. He's not joking. I take a breath; I soak in his words. I see how much he loves me. *This is what my parents prayed for*, I think. People ask if I'm ready to have this baby. I guess they ask because what else do you say to a woman who looks large enough to go into labor before she can even answer the question. It's small talk that evokes big feelings. I feel peaceful, mostly. It's also hard to imagine bringing home a baby after leaving Luca at the hospital. It all feels surreal. The anniversary of Luca's due date was two days ago. I think about last year. How I prayed that I'd get to meet Luca's first birthday, his due date—all of the firsts—with his younger sibling in my belly. I prayed and look what God has done.

I also hesitate to write that because this isn't the first time I've prayed. I also prayed, and Luca stayed dead. I continue to pray, but I have learned prayer is not a way to manipulate my life to get what I want. It is a way to surrender to God, to join my spirit to the Holy Spirit, and to allow peace to fill me despite circumstances that are not peaceful. To change my perspective. To close my eyes and open my heart and see what I find. To say aloud what I am grateful for, to allow gratitude to light up a path forward, to shine light on where I've been and enable me to see it with more clarity. And, yes, I can ask for what I want. But I understand that sometimes I don't get what I want. And this isn't a reason to stop praying; rather, this is a reason to continue to join my heart to God's and allow the Spirit to usher me through and into life. Real life, with moments that involve every feeling—especially painful ones. To allow the Spirit to be close to the brokenhearted, to be close to me. To etch out meaning from what the world is quick to call wasted days of suffering. Because if you're not happy, then what are you doing with your life?

But history teaches otherwise. Think about Winston Churchill, leading Britain through very dark days in World War 2—battling his own depression as he takes his country from an almost sure defeat to victory. History tells us he wasn't exactly happy when he did this, but he was purposeful and walking according to his values. Think about Joan of Arc—a girl, really— leading France to victory, and doing this with the weight of deep conviction rather than something as flighty as happiness. Think of Christ Himself suffering on a cross, doing so without any happiness, but knowing that the love it demonstrates is a greater thing than his own happiness in that moment.

I've found that the idea, "Whatever makes you happy," is not always a map that leads us to a place of deep purpose and contentment with our choices. And I've found that, even when we are not happy, we can ascribe value to days that are hard. We can ascribe value to days that are ordinary. We can ascribe value to a life that is ordinary and sometimes hard and sometimes lovely and always ours. I've found that letting go of this moving target called happiness gives us a much richer life.

I have a pair of socks that say: BE SPIRITUAL. I'm not sure what that means, but I like the way they don't slip on hardwood floors while I walk, so I wear them a lot. I think we're always spiritual, that the parts of ourselves nobody can see weigh heavy in our lives, no matter what our socks tell us to do. I also know that crushing loss *is* spiritual. We walk around looking mostly the same, but our insides make it hard to breathe and impossible to laugh. And then comes the phoenix that rises from the place we left for dead. Beauty from ashes—it's just as spiritual as the loss, while it rebuilds joy from a deep place that slowly gets revealed like some kind of version of *Fixer Upper* starring yourself. Your heart. Where you were, where you are, who you are—it's all spiritual, and it all intersects, and suddenly Lauryn Hill's lyric, "everything is everything," makes sense. It's humbling because you can't do any of it alone—break yourself in the first place or put yourself back together. You can only live in wonder and think, look what God has done.

I'm back at the hospital. I am now 37 weeks pregnant, and there is some consolation that this baby girl is full term. Nobody can give me a guarantee, but I will take consolation. My OB-GYN asks me how I'm doing. "Okay. Really pregnant. Sometimes I get afraid when I can't feel her move. But only sometimes."

"So let's bring her out, then. I'm happy if we wait until 38 weeks. Then let's induce. How do you feel about that?" It's so casual, talking about when I will birth this baby I first carried in my tears, then my hopes, then my prayers, and now my belly. "So, like—next week?" I ask. My doctor pulls out her calendar.

"Pick a day," she says. I am 38 weeks exactly on a Saturday. TJ isn't on the air on Saturday; we can both sleep as long as Charlee allows. That feels like a good day to have a baby. We set the date for the following Saturday, and I text TJ as I leave: "WE ARE HAVING THIS BABY NEXT SATURDAY."

Chapter 88

Willa

(thirteen+ months after)

I'm tired as I write this, but there's something about a story that needs telling that gives me life. Saturday comes. While we wait for a call from the hospital, I take a shower. The bathroom door opens, and I hear TJ call, "Let Mama be alone in the shower, Charlee, okay?" Her little hand pulls back the curtain, and I see she's already undressed herself. I tell TJ to let her come in while she determinedly jumps in anyway, not waiting for permission. I've asked Charlee many times if she wants to shower with me—mostly for the convenience of getting us both clean at once. You know, crossing off something on the endless to-do list. She always says no. Until now. "Mama," Charlee asks, looking at my pregnant body, "can I wash you?"

She doesn't know what I'm about to do. Birth is messy, intense work. When it's time to push your baby out, everything ceases except this wild, must-be-obeyed urge to push. Pregnancy and the act of birth is not unique to any one woman. It makes you feel just as connected to Beyoncé looking like a pregnant goddess in a magazine as it does to the pregnant stray cat who can't seem to lay comfortably in your parents' barn. We're all the same when it comes time to push. We won't all be mothers—and not all mothers will carry their babies—but birth connects all of us. We were all born. We all enter this world naked, vulnerable, and needing more than we can give.

I'm not sure what you're supposed to do in the hours before you give birth, so I spend the morning vacuuming. I throw underwear into a bag. TJ packs both of us a book, which makes me laugh. (I am pretty sure I won't do any leisurely reading in the hospital, but a girl can dream, right?) But that moment in the shower with Charlee, well, I wouldn't have thought to do this—my firstborn washing my back and belly, my shoulders and arms. It feels important. It's an act symbolic of something I could never do alone: being a family. I can be a lot of things, but on my own, I cannot be a family. I feel her little hands on the tight skin of my belly, and there's so much peace here. I breathe and take in the wonder that is us. People have been asking if I'm ready to have this baby. I always say nobody is ready to have a baby. But here—while Charlee gracefully washes my body—I think, *Okay. Let's do this.*

I think about how Charlee told me that Luca was not coming. God gave her a kind of intuition that not everyone has. I certainly don't. But this moment is so different. She's helping to prepare the way. She knows this baby is coming, and she's helping to bring her home to us. It feels like a rite of passage, a good omen, the prayers of all of us piling so high that they change the landscape of my life. It feels like she's anointing me to bring this baby earthside. I don't rush my first baby washing my body. I don't correct her as she uses entirely too much soap. I close my eyes and let it be.

The hospital calls and says to come in at 5 PM, so TJ and I go out and grab a meal. This is a strange chunk of hours to fill. We go for a walk. We hold hands just like always. God is so good to give me someone to be just-like-always with. We go back home. I grab a toothbrush and a phone charger. We stuff the five newborn onesies our neighbor lent us into a bag. Other than the lamb toy Charlee asked to buy this baby, I haven't bought her anything. There is a bassinet another friend lent us set up by our bed. I laugh to myself, thinking if this baby is anything like Charlee, she will never sleep in her bassinet. I look over my bedroom and take a deep breath before I kiss Charlee good-bye, and TJ and I head to the car.

I walk back to Labor and Delivery with a round belly; the same round belly that Luca lived and died in. I get to be back here with another round belly, and this is not lost on me. I don't know how you're supposed to feel when you're about to deliver your rainbow baby, but I am actually not very nervous. I feel stronger by the second—still afraid, but more and more sure. Also, I am tired. It's been a long nine months. It's been a long 13 months. And then before that, it was another long nine months of being pregnant with Luca.

"You're tired, hon?" The nurse asks me.

"I am really tired. It's hard to sleep well when I am this big."

"Let me see if the doctor can give you something to sleep. We're going to start the Pitocin now, and labor should be kicking in soon." I nod gratefully. They give me something that makes me wonderfully sleepy. Right before I nod off, I see TJ grabbing his book. We smile at each other, an admission that he was right to pack it, after all.

Then proceeds the most peaceful labor and delivery I could imagine. I sleep all night. At some point the labor gets more intense, and the anesthesiologist immediately comes in and administers an epidural. It's lovely. He is attractive, not that it matters. What he does for me is really attractive—three cheers for less pain! I really appreciate living in this century. I like modern medicine a lot. Indoor plumbing, air conditioning, drugs to make everything hurt less—it's really all just so nice. I fall asleep again with the help of the epidural, and the next time I wake up, it's to a lot of pressure. My body is telling me it's time to push. I wake up TJ, who's fallen asleep on a cot next to me.

"Get the nurse, please. Tell her I need to push." I don't feel stressed out. I feel peace. A team comes in, and they judge by the monitor I'm hooked up to that I'm right. I know I'm right; it's time, with or without them or the monitor. My body and this baby are telling me: *it's time.*

Giving birth is timeless. It is collective. Every time a woman births a child, she is all of us. She is humanity preserving itself. We are inextricably connected by this primal and creative act. And all these things you do—your partner and a nurse grab each foot; you are naked from the waist down; you are breath and power and moans and prayers and pleadings. You are reaching to a place past yourself—or perhaps it is a place dormant until this moment. Perhaps it is a place that is so wholly and purely yourself, and you never understood the strength of you until now. A place where all of you is focused on the one thing that maybe all of your days until now was leading up to: giving birth.

I push and everyone tells me how strong I am. I don't know if it is strong. I have no choice. This is the only way right now. What is strong is leaving your baby's body in the hospital and going on living. What is strong is deciding to let the hard facts of life roll over you like roaring water that smooths the stones that make the riverbed. What is hard is saying God gives and God takes and blessed be the name of God when everything inside you is a blazing inferno of pain. Saying it when everything has been taken from you—everything. A whole son. Every child is everything, an entire universe. No child on Earth is just one kid. No, when the news tells us that parents lost their baby, their child—we need to understand that those parents lost everything. They will never have that everything again. And waking up, putting one foot in front of the other, deciding to live again, celebrate holidays and make plans and take risks and make commitments—that is as strong as it gets.

I push again. It's hard, but it's nothing compared to what I've already done. I have been pushing less than five minutes when the doctor tells me that one more good push will have this baby in my arms. I do it. I push with everything I have. And then she's here. She's a wild mess, still covered in the hidden parts of me. She is breathing and crying, and TJ and I stare at each other in wonder as they place her on my chest. I don't know how to describe what it's like to have your baby placed on your chest for the first time. There is nothing like it. And if this statement is true, then it is also true that I don't know how to describe what it's like having your living baby placed on your chest for the first time just 13 months after they placed your dead baby on your chest. I can tell you what it's not. It's not like, *Oh, I can finally be happy again.* Happiness isn't a word I can use for this moment. It's too cheap, too flimsy for the weight of this. It is also not devoid of grief. How can it be when this rush of joy and splendor comes from the exact same place as the grief?

She is so loud and wonderful and her body moves up and down with her breath and I marvel at how she gets to stay with me. TJ and I call her by her name.

"Willa," I say over and over again. I'm holding her; I'm holding our prayers and tears and desires for our family. The Lord gives, and the Lord takes away. Blessed be the name of the Lord.

TJ and I keep locking eyes over Willa. She is perfect. I don't mean to put pressure on her. She is human and will make mistakes, but she is also perfect and glorious and living, and all of the deep fear I've held at bay by simply turning my back to it the way tourists turn their back on Niagara Falls to stay dry, simply pretending they don't hear the roaring of the great waters over the cliffs, simply pretending they are not still soaked by the mist that covers you whether your back is turned or not—

drains away because she is here. Inside, I feel quiet. There is so much peace and joy in the room that it is palpable. We cannot help but give it a sound. We laugh. We hold her and laugh.

"Willa Fae!" It's the name I whispered to TJ months ago, late at night in our bed. "I think I found a name I love," I say quietly.

"What?"

"Willa," I say, simply.

Silence.

"What does it mean?" TJ finally asks.

"Strong protector. I want to think of her as strong inside of me. And I want to think of our God who protects her. Who can do what I cannot: keep her alive and thriving."

"I love it," TJ says. I cannot believe it is this easy. Our baby has a name. Later, we decide on her middle name, Fae. It means, "confidence, belief, trust"—all powerful words I want to be meditating on as I carry her earthside.

I lay in my hospital bed and marvel: I just had a baby; my body is in no rush. If I'm being entirely honest, I look at my belly a lot—measuring it with my eyes and feeling fully done with needing it so big and soft. But right now, it needs to be like this to have so recently grown a whole baby. I am trying to remember this. It's okay not to rush to a whole closet full of clothes that used to fit. It's okay to have hips and thighs and breasts and be full of milk and love and exhaustion and a slowly shrinking uterus and hope and compassion (for both my baby and myself as we learn each other).

(Also compassion for TJ as he recognizes the importance of bank accounts and his job and still getting produce on the weekends at Haymarket while I'm holding a newborn, thinking: *Certainly nothing matters but this. Surely, we should all stop everything—probably not do anything ever again—as we stay in our living room and hold our babies. We should probably do this forever.*) I don't want to forget what it feels like to be pregnant, to give birth. To feel weak and humbled by pain; to then suddenly be all focus. To find that the scattered parts of me have run back to this one place, this birthing bed, this urge to push, this dimness of all else. I stare at the brightness of a goal; I become the brightness of determination until my baby is here. Crying or silent, it is birth, and I am strong. I have done this.

Also, I am so weak that I cannot walk. I am bleeding enough to wonder how I can be okay. The maternity shoot was too soon for the whole truth; someone take this photo of motherhood. Me, half-dressed while my body is doing what I can't even explain— feeding a whole new human. I am so hot. Apparently, babies and lemurs need a temperature found only in the rainforest to thrive. I am not thriving, and I beg the nurse to make the room feel just a little less tropical, please. I go to the bathroom and do a thousand small tasks involving pads and balms and mesh underwear and ice and a squirt bottle. I do this just to pee.

My baby cries and I go back to her. That sentence is motherhood. My body will heal and we will find new rooms and fresh air and that sentence is still motherhood. My baby cries and I go back to her. I am so grateful to get to do this with Willa. Again and again and again, Amen.

Chapter 89

Describing the Sailboat
(one year after)

After my first husband has an affair, I decide to leave our home in Pennsylvania. I am debating between Nashville, Los Angeles, and New York City. I close my eyes and fantasize about living in a city of strangers. I crave anonymity. In the beginning, the shame of my husband leaving weighs heavier on me than the need for comfort and community among people who love and know me. I tell this to my therapist at the time.

"I'm leaving, I'm moving," I inform him at our first meeting. "I'll get a job waitressing and make it work, somehow. But I can't stay here—not where people know me."

"But here is your home," he quietly reminds me.

"It hurts a lot here. I can't take seeing people I know. I can't answer their questions about Drake and where he is and why they haven't seen him in a while. Going to church feels like walking through a minefield. Like, I never know what conversation is going to come out of nowhere and blow up my heart."

"I understand. It makes sense. But Jessica, if you run away now, you will spend the rest of your life running away from home. And it's not like you can run away and never come back. Your family is here, your church community—your lifelong friends. If you leave now, every time you come back, you'll be right back here again, right where it hurts."

I'm staring, because this isn't what I want to hear. I just want to leave and hide and never come back. I want to start over. "But how can I stay here?" I finally ask.

"You stay here and allow your community to be close. You allow the trusted, safe people who love you to get past the walls—when you're ready. The Bible talks about how important community is—not just for parties and fun times, but to grieve with each other. We are supposed to rejoice with those who rejoice, and also grieve with those who grieve. I wonder what happens if you let people grieve with you. My guess is that you'll heal here, allowing this to continue to be the home it's always been—and when you're no longer running away to hide, you'll have the freedom to leave and go as you like, without any sort of emotional toxicity attached to here."

"So—stay." I say, my tone flat, the word bitter in my mouth.

He smiles, "At least for a while. See what happens. Let people grieve with you. See if that's not part of your healing— staying here and allowing your community to see you now. At least give them the opportunity to engage with you in grief."

For the past year, writing about Luca has allowed others to see me. Writing has been the way I refused to hide; I've stayed put, right where I am devastated. And people have gone above and beyond, being present and showing up and simply sitting in grief with me. They didn't always say the right words, but every attempt, every demonstration of love, helped me be the grieving mother I am. We don't need permission from others to be ourselves, sure, but when a community both sees and validates you, it becomes a simpler thing to be a whole-hearted human. And being a whole-hearted person—whose mind and spirit and body and values are all in sync—allows us to fully enter into life. I wonder, sometimes, if it isn't grief that keeps a person from re-entering back into their lives, but rather a hurried attempt to sweep the feelings away. A nagging sense from a culture that moves with lightning speed—to both have our meals ready *now* and read content in less than thirty seconds—to become "normal" again. (After all, the loss happened a while ago now.)

But grieving at least somewhat transparently through my writing—a small space on the Internet where I have essentially hung a sign that says "GRIEVING"—has given a community a chance to see me and acknowledge this process. This has helped. I'm floored by the grace extended by others. And now, holding Willa—this brand new, earth-side baby—I am so excited to allow people to see me here. I am so excited to allow my community to rejoice with me too. A healthy community rejoices with those who rejoice and grieves with those who grieve. To get to do both here, with my people—in the span of thirteen months—well, it does something to a heart. Also, the joy isn't emotional white-out for the grief. What is astounding is that my heart proves to be big and nuanced enough to hold both. My thirteen-year-old self—with the fixed, black and white thinking mind was proven wrong. Turns out when I am feeling terrible, life is not actually altogether terrible; and when I am feeling joy, life is not only and always a thing of joy.

I don't think this is a book about resilience, because there are days when I am not resilient. Life overwhelms me. Not just the obvious things (divorce! stillbirth!), but stupid, everyday stuff. I don't get invited to the event. I wonder if I'll ever accomplish lasting work. So many more people are younger than me now—and they're not just kids and babies: they're adults doing awesome stuff. I read other authors and wonder if I should just put down my computer, because they already said it so well. Perhaps I should just eat a hot dog instead. But the simple fact of the matter is that I feel better when I write. A lot better (and

I don't really love hot dogs). So even if just for selfish reasons I have to keep doing it. And this catharsis is better than getting high or sleeping all day or eating tons of corn dogs (okay, but corn dogs are really stupidly tasty. Also why do I keep mentioning hot dogs and hot dog variants?).

This is not a book about being strong, because my child died and my bones felt like dust under my skin and things were very hard for a long time. I don't know if it's strong to do what you simply have to do. Also, that is not a kind of strong I'd ever choose. I don't think anyone really wants to be a warrior. Not the kind attached to having lost a lot, but "Look at you! Still...here!" people say with a mix of patronizing admiration and pity. Being brave means doing scary things. I don't ever wake up hoping to do scary things. I want to have done scary things bravely, sure; but I don't want to have to do scary things today.

I attended an ugly sweater Christmas party after my first husband left. I went alone and the whole thing was comprised of couples. They had matching sweaters, as if their matching rings and last names weren't enough. I had recently moved to New York City and was back in my Pennsylvania hometown for Christmas, and someone said, "I could *never* move to New York City by *myself*. You are *so* brave." I smiled and thought: *This wasn't the plan. I moved alone because he left. You have no idea how much this makes me cry.* In less than thirty minutes after arriving, I thanked the hosts and felt hot tears mixing with the cold December air as I walked to my car. Moving to New York City didn't feel brave. It wasn't a victory lap. I cried a lot. I barely had money and slept on a mattress on the floor in a room with no door. One night my roommate told me he suspected he was a psychopath because he had no feelings. What I mean is, I wouldn't have minded a door. What I mean is, it didn't feel dreamy.

I am shocked by our resiliency. Shocked. I see so many people pivoting because of the curve balls life throws at them. They are performing an about-face and making it look like a dance. They are leaving newly locked doors and finding new open doors, even building new doors, then walking through. The end is never the end. Moving to New York City alone felt hard and weird and sad. For a long time, that's all it felt like. But being in New York City alone is also where I became whole again. I started taking the Brazilian martial art called *capoeira* religiously, and this group of precious people gave me a new name—*Cisne*, they called me; a word that means *Swan*. (I was very relieved they didn't give me *giraffe*—I am tall, after all—or something like *naked mole rat*. I am not sure why they'd call me that, but it was a hard season, and no new bad news would have surprised me.) My capoeira group had no idea how much this grieving soul needed a fresh start, a new name—something to show me life hadn't ended when he walked out.

I fell head over heels in a crush with a man who called me Cisne. I am not even sure that he ever once said Jessica in reference to me, and I was fine with that. He kissed me one night, and I called my brother, wondering who I am, kissing a man in New York City who calls me a word that means 'swan' in a language that feels like an invitation to a world that might finally let me taste happiness. I think I wanted my brother's permission. I think I didn't trust myself to know it was okay. My brother told me that maybe different was good, considering how much the life I knew still made me cry. "And more importantly," he said, "Did you like kissing him?" I smiled over the phone and got quiet because I did. I had no idea any of this was waiting for me in New York. I thought maybe I'd get a job performing, throw myself into work and show the world how talented the girl my husband left really is. I didn't know I'd meet people who were so different from the church and theater circles I was thus accustomed to. That we'd gather in the Y most nights of the week, singing songs in Portuguese, learning about discipline and grace and which way to duck when the person across from you kicks. I didn't know how much I'd enjoy the feeling of being in my own skin, fall in love with seeing the city and the people who comprise it through my own dark eyes. I didn't know I'd get to, I mean.

I didn't know I'd meet TJ. Meet him in a way that allows you to eventually see a person down to their soul, where they hand you a flashlight and let you point it into their hidden corners. And you keep coming back, because it's beautiful and you don't think anywhere else—certainly not leaving to go other places—can compare, so you sit on his couch night after night, handing that flashlight back and forth, both entranced by what you see. Slowly, my time in that city blurred into something so dreamy, so joyous and good, that it made me wonder how humans can start wars—Do they love anyone? Do they love any children? Do they know who we all once were? Who we all are still? Have they not had the incredible privilege of shining a flashlight into another's soul? Because if they truly had, well, I'd think that would take war right off the table.

I didn't know about Boston, that magical city by the sea with a grid that is as confusing as the streets are charming. I didn't know how New England can get into your soul like a person who enchants you. There's a reciprocity. The same way musicians are made better by an audience that really knows how to listen, the New England coast has a way of making a person feel like they belong, like they should write all their thoughts down because this sea has been listening to some of the great thinkers for a very long time and you might not know how to sit as still in the twenty-first century as they did, but you don't mind learning and this spot seems like the kind of place where you finally can.

I didn't know about the wonder that is witnessing and loving my Charlee. How motherhood is so vastly beyond the exact bottles and strollers we should use—all the stuff that comes with babies. Rather, it is the greatest, least-filtered mirror the world has ever held up to my soul. Motherhood reveals me in a way I did not know was possible, and I am in awe of both what I can't do (be perfect!) and what I can do (love like this).

And then, of course, Luca.

Having him and losing him and wondering which it is until I see him again. The way we move forward is astounding. How endings and beginnings mingle, over and over again here on Earth, lets me know Heaven and Earth are close. I'm sorry for all the painful endings. I'm so grateful for the beginnings, the always-hope that lands deep in our bones, making us think we should probably keep getting up, keep opening our hearts and palms and eyes this morning after all.

This book is about grief and how it is a normal part of life. I am not saying that you will experience losing your child; I think you probably won't, and the statistics agree, dear reader. But if you live with a trembling open heart that connects to other people in a world where people can leave in so many ways, you will probably experience some kind of loss. Hopefully not until you're like 95 with your eyes on Heaven, but even then, I am told it hurts. I am here to highly recommend leaving your heart open and trembling, because what happens then is love. I cannot figure out one other good enough reason to go through pain, but I also cannot even begin to say that love isn't enough of a reason.

I remember sitting in my college Adult Psychology class, listening to my professor tell us that work is what you do, not who you are. That when you're meeting someone, try to go beyond asking them what they do—what they get paid to do, at least. Try to discover who they are. He said that at the end of every life, nobody is spending their last thoughts on Earth wishing they'd worked more. Every single person is thinking about their connection to others—who they love and who they are loved by. That's it. This is why Jesus says that it all boils down to love. Love God and love others—if you can't make sense of any other laws or rules, figure out these two, and you've got some compelling reasons to get out of bed every day, grieving or not. Seeing others and being seen is the thing about humanity that makes you realize this is all worth it. Make sure this is happening. Do it as often as possible. Let it take your breath away. Fleeting or not, I promise it's worth it.

This book is also about grace. My friend recently texted me: "Jess, lately you seem to know what to say when I feel like this. I keep seeing awful news stories that truly haunt me. Every kid that is hurt is my niece—I am not even a mother, but it's enough that a kid is hurting somewhere—enough to make me so scared for my niece. Enough to make me feel like vomiting and like life is really just a matter of when the monster comes out of the closet. Not even if, but when. I don't know what to do; I am just afraid of the inevitability of really bad stuff happening, I guess— and I am not so sure that I will be able to face it when it does."

I understand this completely. In life, so many bad things happen that it does feel like it's only a matter of time before they happen to me. And, again, if we are lucky enough to live for a long time, we will experience some type of loss. And when we do, it is always surprising, and it is always hard. I think about this and write her back. The truth is, nobody gets a preview of their upcoming tragedies and gets a chance to think, "Okay, yeah, I can handle that." If you'd shown me a preview of the photo of me holding my sweet Luca dead in my arms, my insides would've trembled, and there's no way I would have been able to face it. Grace doesn't come until it's needed.

When we imagine potential tragedies, we cannot imagine the miraculous grace that carries us through these times. It is impossible to see the grace from the outside. It's like being on the shore on a cloudy day and looking out on the ocean and seeing lots of fog on the horizon. From where you are, all you see is the fog. You don't see a way through it, because you're not in it. But let's say there's a sailboat. You can't see that far, but the person in the sailboat sure sees it. It's their lifeline; it's all they see. It is the reason they aren't drowning.

It is the same with grace for the person grieving. From a distance we see the broken heart, and we are terrified of the broken heart; but when we're on the outside of the tragedy, we cannot see the God who is close to the broken hearted. What that feels like in our grief. How it makes even the beauty of the sunset feel personal. How grief cuts into us so deeply that we cannot imagine still functioning, and yet we do. Somehow, someway, we do.

I encourage you to take it one moment at a time, to breathe deeply and move your body and allow endorphins to help you, too. I encourage you to try not to assume that how grief feels today is how it will always feel. I encourage you to write everything down and if you don't like to write, then talk to someone and tell them how you feel. I promise there is grace that walks you through this. And I encourage you to remember that safety is a myth. We are not born into a safe world. We have a kind God who loves us, and yet we wrestle with the tension of living in a world that is not safe. We do many things to take our minds off this. When we read horrifying headlines, we comfort ourselves with the lie that whatever happened to them could never happen to us. We try to protect ourselves, our loved ones, our way of life the best we can; we exhaust our money, energy, time and emotions this way. But grief is generally the aftermath of discovering that we are not in control. It is shocking, it is terrible—but dare I suggest it might also be freeing? Could it be a good thing to step into reality, to lift the veil, the myth that tells us if we do *insert our own behavior, * we will definitely get *insert desired result? *

I would argue it is always a good thing to be able to make decisions based on reality. For me, it has been a good thing to continue to learn to let go of what is not mine and to understand that all of this is fleeting. It has allowed me to more deeply savor the good, to see it and take it in like the nourishment it is. It has allowed me to grow in faith, trusting that, though this world is not safe, nothing can separate me from the love of God. That somehow this keeps me, holds me still, in a way the world cannot.

I am not sure even what tomorrow holds (although, I imagine it is the wonderfully mundane work of a Wednesday with little kids, some time at the gym, some work in front of the piano, the blank page, the stove, talking with TJ, the endless work of cleaning up. These are the events I hope and pray tomorrow holds for me, anyway), but I have seen God in dark places— watched Him show up in the fire, the way I first heard about in Sunday school.

As a kid, I learned about the Hebrew children—Shadrach, Meshach, and Abednego (the former two names, we used for our dogs. I suppose Abednego was just too laborious of a word to yell out the front door day after day. But you know you have two reverends for parents when your family pets are named after Old Testament almost-martyrs)—how the Babylonian King Nebuchadnezzar threw them into a fiery furnace because of their faithfulness to Yahweh as the one true God. But when he looked into the furnace, he was astounded to see not only the three Hebrews perfectly fine, walking around casually, suddenly unbound; he was shocked to see a fourth Man appear, one that he described as looking like "the son of the gods." He saw Jesus in the fire.

Jesus shows up in the fire.

Sometimes grace looks a lot like people who come to you with food and kind words and a nonjudgmental way of listening that tells you it's okay to curse or hike a thousand miles this week or paint a picture that nobody will ever see or eat cake or just be really mad because this wasn't supposed to happen. Sometimes grace looks like the exact right line of prose in a book that lets you know you're not alone. Sometimes grace looks like a doctor prescribing lorazepam so you can sleep. Sometimes grace sounds like prayer—your own, or most often others. Sometimes grace is peace when there should be none. There is not one way grace looks, but I continue to see it and I have come to rely on it and I will talk about it for the rest of my days on earth.

We cannot imagine the people who cover us with kindness and cry with us. We cannot imagine how there is a sacredness to grief and how, for a while, the world lets us off the hook. In this made-up scenario of trying to fathom grief from the outside, we cannot see the laser-sharp focus that becomes ours when we lose those we love deeply. We can see the fog—the terrible tragedy that has befallen another—but we cannot see the sailboat so well or even at all from the shore. I suppose this book is about the sailboat.

In *A Woman's Book of Grief*, Nessa Rapoport writes: "This is the teaching of suffering, if you allow it, as if in a great stroke the world you occupy divides itself. Here is what matters; the rest—no." It is a strangely freeing thing to walk around this world with the sharp and sudden realization that most of this doesn't matter. You feel wildly indestructible, a superhero whose cape is grief, with a version of X-ray vision that allows you to see every shallow thing for what it is. In this world of social media and rampant comparison while running a rat race where the prize seems to be exhaustion (for what?), the realization that spending your heart and time on what is truly lasting and valuable is both revelatory and revolutionary. It is, actually, part of the gift of grief. It comes in the sailboat. This book is about the work of grief—the sailboat we can't see because of the fog—how it takes our hand and walks us through unimaginable loss. How grief is awful and normal and also, an undeniable part of love.

Chapter 90

Our Skin
(fourteen months after)

Willa's skin is so smooth, it's almost like touching nothing at all. Or like the one time I went to Aruba and the ocean was warm, so different from our northeast waters that call forth feelings of bravery and courage and adventure as you wade in them, but certainly not warmth. In Aruba, a swim in the ocean isn't something you have to survive like it is here; you casually walk into the island water and hardly realize it is no longer air you are wading through. The only difference is it's heavier than air; and, well, it gets you soaking wet.

Willa's skin is something between air and water. My rainbow baby cries like she doesn't realize she's helped us immeasurably just by showing up. *It's okay*, I'll tell her forever. It's okay (I'll make it so forever). I wear her on my chest and marvel at the weight of her body against mine. I don't know how to take it in; I can feel my heart reaching, grasping, growing just to really feel it.

I miss the weight of Luca (this is no small thing).

I marvel at the weight of Willa (this is no small thing).

While grieving my first marriage, I kept thinking about skin. Isn't it strange? Grief has a way of finding new paths in our mind. I follow it; it's all I can do. An image from long ago returns. It's one I've already written down here. I'm at the airport, quietly ablaze with sorrow. I close my eyes. I see myself taking my skin off. People walk by and I hear them whisper to each other, "Of course he doesn't love her; she's only bones, after all."

The nurse hands Luca to me. The things we are forced to hand each other—wearing an air of normalcy as we do it—astounds me. A hand reaches out, extending divorce papers for me to sign. My dead son is placed into my arms. How do we do these things and live? I ask this, and still, I do it. I am in awe of humanity's resilience—our ebb and flow that the ocean, it seems, must have first learned from us. Luca is wrapped in the same kind of hospital blanket that my Charlee first wore. The one that's warm and a bit stiff. Blue and pink stripes on a no-nonsense fabric that swaddles hardly at all (the nurses are magicians to make that stiff blanket swaddle). He is perfect. His face like one of the tiny blooms that shows itself too soon. *God, you're beautiful,* you think. *But winter hasn't left yet. It's too soon for you here.*

His skin is breaking.

"A baby's skin is very fragile, hon," the nurse says softly, her tone kind. "It's the first part to break down."

Charlee is upset this morning. She is making the kinds of choices that rack up consequences, one after the other. I lay Willa down, and Charlee pulls on my shirt. "I need to snuggle, Mama." We crawl into bed. She crawls into my arms, and we are how we've always been. Since the first moment I met her on the outside, skin to skin. She grows and changes, and now she says things like, "*Literally, MAMA!*" And here we are, still needing to feel each other's skin. It is okay to be here, to feel what we feel. Mary Oliver writes, "You only have to let the soft animal of your skin love what it loves." Our skin is breathtaking. With it we break down, we bind up, we hold each other, we grow. We age, we die. We discover we aren't our skin at all.

* * *

What if we dressed ourselves the way we dress our babies. Soft material that bends and curves like water. Nothing too tight around the waist. What if the act of getting dressed was self-care. What if we wore short skirts and everyone thought, "How glorious that she has a body; how glorious that she is here." What if we stopped staring at parts of ourselves like outliers. Like how did YOU get here. What if we saw the softer, looser skin around our belly button—the part that still moves a little even after we've stopped chasing our daughter, her laughter in the key of our soul, our breath; more music than the songs on the radio—and instead of wondering when it's going back, we ask our skin its story.

And then we listen to how it started with connection, right here in the belly. "In the womb," Skin says, "I was tied from my belly to my mother. And then many years later, I stretched and expanded and housed that laughter that you hear right now." Then the heart interrupts, "I still stretch and expand and house that laughter. Skin, you're not the only one softer and bigger because of her."

What if we start saying things like *thank you* when people give us lovely words. When they say, *You are beautiful!*—what if we say thank you (because we are), and that's all. We don't have to tell them why we're not. How our clothes are dirty and our hair even more so and, *You can't be serious! Look at the dirt and grief under my nails! I feel so GROSS right now!* We could let our thank you be enfolding. Like batter is to drops of vanilla, then swirls, then it's everywhere. We could agree, let encouragement come inside and mingle with our skin and our heart until we can't remember what was always here and what was given to us by others.

Chapter 91

The Worthiness of Living
(fourteen months after)

I'm at the pool watching Charlee swim with my mom and sister while Willa sleeps on my chest. Last summer I also came here with a soft, changeling body—the kind a newborn makes. But I didn't have him; I didn't have my newborn.

I think about the trees that have been carved into. I'd see them a lot where I grew up in the Pennsylvania woods. Someone cut deep; they carved a heart with a knife, and the two don't seem to belong to each other. It's where love and pain meet; we all see the heart carved into the bark, but we forget that it didn't get there easily. I don't know that love ever does, really.

There's that part of the Bible that people often quote— "For God so loved the world..." is the first half, and then it immediately references pain and loss: "that He gave his only son." Again: love is not easy or cheap. Not divine love, anyway, and as far as I can tell everything else trickles down from there. There is tearing, there are scars. What was seemingly perfect—or at least as-of-yet untouched—is made imperfect. And then these carved-up trees bear a heart. I see it—the deep cut that marks love on these trees—and I think, *Yes, okay, me too.*

Last summer I'd find myself in mundane conversations with strangers around the pool. They were nannies or other mamas, and our kids and the heat brought us together. We'd talk about nothing of much substance—summer programs and bedtimes— and then I'd feel compelled to show them the place where I'd been carved into, to show them the heart the knife had left. There's no appropriate segue for this kind of revelation, but I felt like if we could all sit around and talk about nothing, then we could just as well talk about something, so I told them about Luca. These women listened; they murmured words of sympathy. Charlee kept me present and connected, playing with her. Or we'd share a lounge chair; she napped while sprawled across me, the very weight of her two-year-old body adding substance, keeping me right here, right now—the anchor I needed. My grief and the normalcy of mothering a toddler blended in around the pool until it was just one thing, actually: my life.

Today we're back, and here's Willa too. Last summer is a lifetime ago. Last summer is as close as my heart buried in my chest. It's good to be here now. I don't understand the knife, the carving, the road to here—but I can't deny their connection. And even after all those times when I was never sure I'd say it again, I can honestly say it's good to be here now.

* * *

"Tell me what writing means to you, Jessica." I'm sitting in my therapist's office. I've been doing this every week for over a year now.

I remember the email I write to her after we leave Luca at the hospital and just...come home. We come home and take care of the business of living. A lot of time it's a joy—all these tasks that mean I'm here and alive—but last summer was like trying to tend a garden on the moon.

But they don't have gardens on the moon. There's no life, no vegetation there at all.

I know. Tend your garden anyway.

But I can't.

Tend your garden anyway.

The social worker at the hospital gives me a name of a therapist, and I email her right away.

"My son just died. I don't know what to do. Are you taking patients?" She says she is so sorry and that I should come next week. We meet the day before my birthday, and when she offers me a roll of toilet paper because she can't find tissues, I know we'll get along just fine. Now it's a year later, and I'm sitting in her office with a tiny baby in my arms. I tell her about a popular app that is publishing an article of mine as part of their online content. "So that's pretty cool," I say.

"Tell me what writing means to you, Jessica."

I tell her about that place in the back of your brain that reacts to trauma. I've heard it called the reptilian brain, responsible for the fight-or-flight reaction. These options work well when you're, say, battling a wounded badger. But in most cases in modern society, when you can't use all that adrenaline because there's nobody to fight—when you might be on the moon, struggling to stay on the ground, but it's still your garden and you have no choice but to stay and tend it—this sort of adrenaline is not helpful.

So instead of fighting or running away, I write. It's my chrysalis. And maybe now is the part where I am neither a caterpillar nor a butterfly; I am the goo. I am what seems like a puddle of nothing before it becomes, during the in between. Choosing the exact words to describe what's happened and how I feel changes me from a victim to a storyteller.

And we need storytellers.

We need stories that connect grief to love. Stories that show how faith never leaves us where we started, points a flashlight in the dark, and helps us walk forward. Stories that reveal we're not the only ones struggling—that we're never the only ones doing anything at all. Stories that are an invitation for all of us to jump right into life today, right now. To open our eyes and look around and be astounded and moved and then do something about it. Maybe write it down. Maybe protest. Maybe call your grandma. Maybe pray for your kids. Maybe do it all. Maybe bag groceries and make eye contact with every customer and ask how they're doing with sincerity because you care to know. Clearly, I'm spit-balling here. You know much better than me what you should do, but my point is—live.

Meet people, discover who they are beyond the first glance, let yourself be seen, ask questions, fall in love, make babies or don't make babies, adopt animals, visit with your family, share your opinions, change your mind once you know better, truly listen, join a community where you have some accountability, be someone people can rely on, care about others deeply. We gain an acute need for true connection when life feels messy and our hearts are broken. Grief has a way of revealing how much we matter to each other, how much we need each other. Just like wine needs a glass and thirst needs contentment as it does its work of warming a person on the inside, drawing them into the present by tasting this, here, now before it's gone, storytellers need ears and hearts and softened, open faces to take in their narrative. We are tellers and listeners, and we are best when we're together, I think.

So the next step, then, is to keep doing the things that emphasize our connection. Even when grief has shifted from the burden we can hardly bear to a warm hand that walks us home each day (sometimes that shift takes just about forever), keep doing it. And then maybe, just maybe, we become more like God who, not only does love, but *is* love.

Isn't that beautiful? That the word we use to describe the person of God is love. And I cannot help but look at this earth and how things work—the connection between the moon and the tide; the connection between the trees and our need to breathe; the connection between the bees and the flowers—and wonder if maybe connection is the entire point of all of this.

I have a friend who's spent a lot of time visiting his elderly friend. One winter he knew she had no heat, so he brought her blankets. He checked on her when it got really cold. Once I went with him to bring her eyeglasses. She graciously listened to us sing songs. I went thinking we were helping her, and I left realizing I'd been helped. You can't sing for someone and watch their face soften to your song, your lyrics, your mood and not realize we've all gone somewhere together. And together—that's it, right?

There are many kinds of together. I don't know why this world sends messages about romantic love being it, but I don't think that's right. Romantic love is part of it, sure—but so is going somewhere together while you sing and she listens and she can see better with new glasses and you can see better with a softer heart. That's it, too. (And giving someone the gift of a softer heart—this beats glasses any day.)

Once I drove by a graveyard and saw an older man decorating a Christmas tree near one of the stones. Here is another way of being together, another way of taking care of each other, taking care of your own love, your own grief, learning how to be with someone who is no longer here. By the time I parked, I was blinking back tears and answering Charlee's questions about snacks (yes, you can have one). I cannot fathom decorating multiple trees in a season. I don't foresee ever being the kind of person who has different trees with different themes in different rooms in the single month of December. Oh my gosh, one is enough. But knowing this man loves someone enough to be able to say, "That's her stone—the one with the Christmas tree," makes me stop. That's it.

I got Luca an ornament for the tree this year. It's so pretty, lily of the valley on tempered glass. I am not always sure how to take care of my baby who isn't here, but I am also not always sure how to take care of my babies who are here. It felt right to get him an ornament. Sad and right, yes, but I will take that over sad and wrong. Let's keep finding ways to take care of each other, to be together. Let's love each other enough to decorate trees in places we don't want to be. Grieving or not, let's keep finding connections that lead back to each other.

I finished my session with my therapist, still trying to answer her question about what writing means to me. It's a way of valuing life—all of it. Selfishly—or maybe blessedly—it's a way of slipping away when the pain becomes too great. A way of escape when the walls around me are too constricting. As renowned choreographer Twyla Tharp says: "Art is the only way to run away without leaving home."

Writing helps me see. After the fire, after the rains, after the hard work, sometimes even during the suffering, I spot them— those delicate blooms, breaking open. Flowers grow here.

Chapter 92

Tears in a Bottle
(fourteen months after)

Do you realize there's a scientifically proven link between our tears and wellness? Reflex tears (the tears that occur in order to cleanse our eyes of irritants) and emotional tears have a different composition. (How smart is our body? How incredible is the One who made it?) While reflex tears are simply salt water, emotional tears excrete a stress hormone. Enduring any kind of trauma takes a toll on our body. There's a build-up of hormones that flood us because of stress, and though it's normal for them to come, we need to allow our tears to "take out the trash," so to speak. Every healthy household creates waste and trash, but we don't just sit in it and let our trash bins overflow and decide to eat our meals in the midst of what has become an unconventional garbage dump. We take out the trash, we clear out space.

This is what happens when we cry. It's a much-needed release. It's not you or me (or even our kids!) being dramatic. It can feel uncomfortable for a few reasons: one, it's vulnerable, and a lot of us decided a long time ago that vulnerability is not a thing that survivors can afford. We forget that vulnerability is the lens through which we allow others to truly see us and therefore truly love us and connect with us.

A quick story involving vulnerability: Growing up, my dear, brightly-burning-light-of-a-friend had a tough relationship with her dad. She has so much grace for him, but he really wasn't (or couldn't be) the most supportive father to her in her formative years. He did some hurtful things to her whole family, especially her mom, and her parents divorced. After my friend grew up, she decided to have a real, honest talk with her dad. "I told him that I knew all of it—even all of the ugly things he'd done to my mom," she told me. "I didn't want him to think if I *really knew* what he'd done, surely, I wouldn't forgive him—I needed him to know that I saw him truly and still loved him. I told him I forgive him for every single thing. I told him that I love him and I want a better relationship with him. We were both crying at that point, and he said he loved me, too." They have a better relationship now than they ever have. I love this story for the honesty, vulnerability, forgiveness, and "I see you and still love you" parts of it. I also love this story because I dearly love my friend and am in awe of her courage and choices.

Another reason it's uncomfortable to cry in front of others is that we're the only ones doing it. Even on my first day of college—when I was either a very young adult or a very old kid, I'm not sure which—I noticed that everyone else was wearing mostly black and my bright blue L.L. BEAN book bag stood out. (And not in the artsy way I wanted). So I bought a black book bag at Aldo on my way home from my last class that first day and never used the blue book bag again. My point is, in a sea of people whose faces are not leaking salt water and stress hormones, we'd rather not be the ones whose do. But really, they should be so lucky to be taking out the trash the way we are. To be healing the way we are.

Also, I learned to cry silently while on tour and living with three wonderful roommates with whom I was not ready to share the mounting evidence of the infidelity of my husband-at-the-time. (I must say this very clearly, because I have, in the past, had too many people reach out and tell me they are so sorry to hear that me and TJ split up, etc., after reading something I wrote about me and my ex, from whom I am absolutely and happily divorced. So let it be known: TJ AND I ARE VERY MUCH TOGETHER AND I AM SO GRATEFUL FOR THIS HEADLINE IN MY LIFE. Oh, one of the more recent times I wrote about my divorce from my first husband, it was one of my older brothers' classmates from high school who reached out and was like, *Hey girl, hey*. Immediately understanding his confusion, I was like, *Hey, I'm happily married*, to which he was still like, *Hey girl hey, but do you wanna hang out?* And so I did what any decent person would do and texted my brothers and asked what in the world was up.) But I was saying that while touring, night after night, I learned that it is possible to let tears fall from your eyes and not make a sound, though I would not recommend it. I think it is far better to cry with as much sound and motion as you need—and also, to let your friends know how you really are.

Can we please remove crying from the same category as gossiping and losing our patience and forgetting to buy milk at the store—all things we should legitimately apologize for? Can we move it to the category of wonders that God has done on our behalf? The ability to cry. To heal. To remove the stress and trauma that has made its way to our precious bodies.

Every Wednesday the garbage trucks come to the end of our lane to remove all the trash we've accumulated over the past seven days. It's an amazing system, and now that I'm no longer in an apartment, I can see it and hear it, and I feel a greater measure of gratitude for the people who help us this way. Our tears do the same for us. Like the loud trash trucks that announce their presence before rumbling by, we get to hear it and see it and feel it and instead of shame or embarrassment or wondering why we are so very soft and where our self-control—our grown-up adulthood—is, what if we simply practice gratitude for this tremendous service our tears accomplish.

I cried a lot after Luca died. I still cry. Not as often as I did when his death was brand new, but when I allow my body to process that one of my babies is not physically here—when I really sit with this—I often cry. TJ, on the other hand, was so busy being my rock in those first few weeks after losing Luca, that he didn't allow himself to cry. I didn't tell him to do this, but I think our culture has done a terrible job with some of the messages it sends to men, in particular, about their emotions, and for whatever reason, he didn't cry. A few weeks into grieving Luca, I found myself sitting across from my therapist, saying, "You will never believe this, but TJ was just diag—" I am not making this up, she finished my sentence, and as cool as a cucumber (not like those very excitable and hysterical tomatoes we find in the produce aisle these days), just said, "—Let me guess, TJ was diagnosed with shingles."

I was floored. "Uh—yeah," I said, slowly, "But, how did you *know*?" She smiled compassionately and quietly told me, "Grief has a way of working its way out of the body. You can cry and process your emotions through therapy and talking with people you trust and again, letting your body really cry—or you can let the stress and trauma and grief take its toll on your body and come out in other ways. Shingles is TJ's body's way of working through grief." Here, I thought I was coming to her with some exciting—albeit awful—news and my therapist wasn't even remotely surprised. She responded to my statement as if I had told her the sky was blue.

I tell this story because tears are a healing, powerful, wonderfully accessible tool, and nobody should feel ashamed for—either their healing or their power. Also, there are consequences to not allowing our bodies to grieve in the way that is healthy. There are consequences to not allowing ourselves to cry. Now, when I see TJ holding back tears, all I need to say to him is, "You wanna shingle this, too?" and we both laugh and he also remembers that he can feel what he feels and there's no shame in sadness, grief, disappointment—any of the emotional reactions our bodies come up with when we walk through the seasons of life.

Chapter 93

We Need a Bigger Basket
(fifteen months after)

There is a story about Jesus, his disciples, a hungry crowd, and not enough food. In terms of numbers, it's nuts—like at least 5,000 people, five loaves of bread, and two fish. The crowd listens so intently to Jesus that it's suddenly dinnertime but nobody leaves. (He must be really good; no matter what I'm doing, I almost always leave at dinnertime.) When Jesus sees the crowd is hungry, he tells his disciples to feed them. This is ridiculous. The food is embarrassingly scant, and the disciples say so. Once we invited our neighbors over for dinner, and TJ had greatly overestimated the amount of broccoli we had on hand. I pulled out one small head from the fridge and alerted TJ that we didn't have nearly enough. "I won't eat any," he quickly whispered. Suffice it to say, neither of us had a vegetable that night at dinner because I would have been mortified to have let our friends leave without their fill. And this was just two extra people, let alone a crowd of 5,000. "Feed the crowd what you have," Jesus says, ignoring his disciples' logical protestations. And they do. They give away what they have, and this is when the miracle happens: it's enough. Actually, the five loaves and two fish are *more* than enough—there is even food left over.

It's 1 AM and I still haven't slept tonight. Baby Willa just settled after nursing. I'm somewhere close behind her, trying to settle, too. The stories we tell each other matter. Lately, Charlee has been asking for stories in which the heroine (usually Belle) makes bad choices. "What happens then, Mama?" she asks me at bedtime. "What happens when Belle hits someone?" I tell her the consequences, because I want her to understand that every choice is a rope we pull, bringing something new into the picture.

God knows our highest calling here on earth is to love. Maybe this story has something to do with that. At first glance, it would look as daunting as feeding a hungry crowd of 5,000 with our own meager bread and fish. Like the disciples, we'd most likely decide we can't do it. That we simply can't love that much. Sometimes being a mama feels like standing before a crowd of 5,000 and being told to feed them.

I can't.

Stay up all night?

I can't.

Nurse every hour?

I can't.

Put someone else first—like, always?

I can't.

But then you do it anyway, and just like the disciples found, that's when the miracle happens.

Birth my dead son?

I can't.

Love him and not raise him?

I can't.

Love doesn't run out. The more you give it away, the more it shows up in your basket. And you still can't, but this *can't* is different—wonderfully so. Now you can't ever run out of love to give. By giving it away, you trade the finite for the infinite. And you no longer worry if you have enough; you worry that your basket isn't big enough for what remains, what's still coming.

Chapter 94

When Happiness Eludes Us
(fifteen months after)

When I find out about my first husband's affair, a friend says, "I won't say goodnight. There's nothing good about this night for you. Instead, I'll say, 'See you soon.'"

I've been through seasons in which I was profoundly unhappy. My therapist tells me this is normal. Your husband leaves. Your baby dies. Grief and sadness ensue. In a world where social media is littered with inspirational sayings paired with selfies—which make one wonder what, exactly, someone's filtered face has to do with us "living our dreams"—there's a lot of rhetoric about happiness. About doing whatever makes you happy. And though I'm as big a fan of being happy as the next person (I love happiness and gluten and sleep—all the good things!), the more I realize that happiness is not the ultimate goal, the more I am fulfilled.

See, if I were simply trying to be happy all the time, motherhood would not be a good fit. Today Charlee wakes up at 5:30 AM, sick and angry. I have been up through the night with Willa. At one point, all three of us are crying. I call TJ because it feels so hard—managing the needs of both little girls. I'm not happy in this moment. If happiness were my end game, valuable, precious days like these would leave me feeling like a failure. I suspect there's something higher, a reason to sacrifice in the present for a greater good and happiness that will come in the future as a result of this sacrifice.

I suspect a goal more worthy than happiness alone is love. Taking care of people is exactly in line with the goal of love. Every single day, motherhood, being somebody's wife, being a sister, daughter, co-worker, fellow human—you name it—allows me to painstakingly reach for the goal of loving people well. I fail, sure; but this goal acts as a compass as I navigate my life.

A friend of mine takes leave from his job in order to care for his dying grandmother. She has dementia and is regularly nasty to him as he bathes, wipes, and feeds her. If my friend's goal is happiness, he'd walk away. But because his goal is love—both loving God and others—caring for his grandmother is in sync with what he wants for his life. "I wouldn't trade this for anything," he tells me. His voice has the sound of deep fulfillment, of being honored by the opportunity he has been given, for he is one with his goal to love well. I can't help but think of that Ram Dass quote, "We are all just walking each other home." The quote doesn't specify that we always do this happily—just that we do it. But how beautiful that my friend places love in its rightful place—higher than his own fleeting happiness—and gently walks his grandmother home.

Happiness is precarious. Deciding that life is only valuable when we're happy is devaluing a lot of important seasons. Terrible things happen, and sometimes healthy people become unhappy. We are plunged into grief, and nothing feels the same, and again, sometimes we feel unhappy as a result.

Even annoying things happen all the time. I don't particularly love making my kids lunch. For some reason, breakfast and dinner feel fine, I am emotionally prepared for the work that these meals involve. But lunch always seems to catch me off guard. Like, *I have to make these humans another meal?!* But do I not feed my kids because, at that time of day, it's not what I want to be doing? We all know the answer to this. Happiness cannot be the end goal; otherwise, we feel like failures more often than not. Otherwise, we feel like failures when we are simply walking through the seasons of life—sometimes in the shadows and sometimes in the bright light—but all of it is worthy of our time and attention. Life is still valuable, though happiness eludes us.

Jesus said, "Steep your life in God-reality, God-initiative, God-provisions. Don't worry about missing out. You'll find all your everyday human concerns will be met" (Matthew 6:33 MSG). All of that stuff boils down to love—love God and love others—and I've found that when this goal is prioritized, all of my other needs are met. I have found that deep, pervasive joy comes when I am fulfilling love's calling.

When the filter is love, the daily tasks of life become clear. When the filter is simply our happiness, the water gets muddied. Our whims, feelings, and desires change. In one moment, we might think something will make us happy, only to discover with time such things as a new car, new relationship, quitting something that is hard, etc., brings only temporary happiness. Then we are eventually right back in a place of discontent. We are right back in our own skin, dealing with feelings that didn't actually change, despite rearranging our circumstances in whatever way we can.

Now, I feel like I need to say something to the recovering people pleasers among us. Positioning love as the highest goal does not mean we walk around without boundaries. It doesn't mean we let anyone who needs something from us dictate our lives. We absolutely need to be able to say no. In a previous chapter, I referenced a verse in the Bible that speaks of leading a God-connected life and how it enables us to "marshal and direct our energies wisely" (Galatians 5:23 MSG). This means we recognize all the places our energy shouldn't go. This means we can confidently say, "No, this is not for me."

One of Luca's gifts to me is an urgency to spend my time and energy on what is mine to do, and nothing else. Writing this book falls under that category. I used to teach twelve or more fitness classes a week and train clients one-on-one in addition to that. It was awesome work, and I enjoyed it. I was up before sunrise and either out teaching others or home with my toddler. I was exhausted by evening and had no time or energy left to be creative. But I changed my schedule. I don't teach nearly as much. With some of that time I used to spend teaching and training, I now work by myself on my creative projects. I feel like I have returned to myself, and I have Luca to thank for giving me the courage to set these boundaries and the clarity to see that I need them.

I cannot love others very well if I am not also being compassionate and honest with myself. We say it all the time and it's so overused that it's kind of annoying, but the fact that one cannot pour from an empty cup still remains. In the same way, I will have a very hard time encouraging my kids and husband to be well and whole and authentically themselves if I do not lead by example. In that same letter to the Galatians, Paul, the guy who wrote about a quarter of the New Testament, writes: "For everything we know about God's Word is summed up in a single sentence: Love others as you love yourself" (Galatians 5:14 MSG). Basically, loving others well does not preclude us from loving ourselves well. To do one, you've really got to do both.

I'm relieved by this goal, because love is something I can choose to do, no matter how I feel, no matter how unhappy I am. And when my daily choices align with this major goal, everything else falls into place. It's good news that happiness— something that I am not in control of, considering I'd never have chosen for my son to die or, at the time, for my first marriage to end (I'd choose that marriage to have ended now, though—with balloons and a parade and a big old WELCOME! to the next season of my life—but I didn't know any of this then, of course). Happiness is not actually the reason I am here. If this were the case, all that grief would be wasted time—and I am sure now that it was not wasted, and is not wasted. It is actually another piece of love here on this earth. It is proof that when someone dies, our relationship with that person does not. I find it a relief that the high calling of loving others and God and being loved is ours and available all the time, no matter what I'm feeling or what my circumstances are.

Chapter 95

What Can I Do with a Broken Heart?
(sixteen months after)

Someone recently asked me: "Any advice for getting over heartbreak? It seems impossible some days."

Yes, some days it *is* impossible. And on those days, you think, *Today is not the day to get over my heartbreak. So then, what can I do with a broken heart?*

I make a list:

I can shower and brush my teeth.

I can make my bed.

I can be kind to others.

I can notice that I am not the only one hurting today.

I can move my body.

I can pray.

I can write down how I feel.

I can tell someone how I feel. (Even two strangers at a karaoke bar in New York City, right after I sing "Natural Woman." Wait—did I write 'strangers?' Because after I shared my story and they gave me the gift of listening—and buying me a drink—we were definitely no longer strangers. And after that night, I will never doubt the combined power of karaoke, transparency, a riveting story of betrayal, a couple of listening strangers, and Carol King.)

I can tie a string to a balloon called hope. Weak as I feel, I can hold onto this string, because it's just a string tied to a balloon. And both hope and balloons are really light; not nearly as heavy as this experience I'm carrying. Both hope and balloons rise. Maybe, probably, I think I will too, someday. Even with a broken heart, I can think this for five minutes. We can do just about anything for five minutes.

And just because today is not the day to get over my heartbreak, it doesn't mean tomorrow or the next is also not the day—so I keep walking forward. And someday I will realize that this is when love became more precious. This is when I started thinking "me too" when I see people who don't have enough. It's when the hope of heaven stopped being the only benefit of the gospel. Because I need a miracle right now, right here, right where doctors and medicine cannot touch: in my heart. I need the wholeness that the word *salvation* actually means. And I start to wonder: *Maybe this heartbreak is just as important as the miracle coming—for what healing comes to those who aren't first sick? What freedom comes to those who aren't first bound? And what precious, mended heart comes to one that is not first broken?*

I can listen to the rain. I love the rain. I sleep next to a window, and it is so good when rain is on the other side of it. I read somewhere that we love the sound of rain and the ocean because it sounds like our beginning. Rushing water—reminiscent of our mother's rushing blood while we're in utero—is the soundtrack of our needs being fully met. We hear it now and, like glimpsing our mother's face in a crowd of strangers, we respond: *I know this sound, I know this place.*

I cannot read about what we hear first in our mother's womb and not think about Luca. It's okay, you can relax; this is no bad thing. I'm grateful for the gift it is to think about Luca. Today while on a walk by the river with Willa, I felt deep peace. I think about Luca in these moments, too. Everyone else knows just part of the story. "She is so strong; her baby died. The one she spent the better part of a year growing inside her. How does she eat sandwiches and tell jokes and marvel at rivers and get upset about dishes piled up in the sink? How does she do all these normal things when her son is dead?"

But there is more to the story. I love the rain and the sound of the ocean and how Charlee and I chant "FREE WILLA!" every morning while I supervise Charlee un-swaddling baby Willa. I love Friday at 2 PM when TJ is home and there is nothing to do but be together, all of us, until Monday. And I also love that Luca is safe. That he is doing well, better than I am. I wish I knew him better; but there's a part of me that is convinced I do. It is the primal part; the thing in my spirit that is forever changed because I was given the gift of creation, making babies, and they were given the gift of creation, making me a mama. It is the part of me that is sure I will recognize him when I see him again someday; sure I will know him as mine, despite the time that has passed between now and the last time I held him.

Luca is safe, untouched by politics or brokenness or cruel people or even time (the thing that none of us on earth escapes). I love that when Luca died, I stopped handing Jesus a list of what I want and calling it prayer. I listen better—at least, a little. I see that Jesus, too, didn't always like being here. That it cost more than He knew He could give. But He gave it anyway, and He still found it worthwhile. When I cannot stop crying because it is too hard to be here, He says, *Yes, I know.* And then shows me it's also worth it. Not "but" it's worth it, "and" it's worth it. And I love that, since my Luca died, I truly believe it. Even with a heart that's been broken, I see it. It's worth it.

Chapter 96

Quietly Handing Each Other the Moon
(sixteen months after)

There is space between the sublime and the tragic. Tragic seasons gut-punch us until we are just skin, our insides having fled with our life, our eyes hollow and longing. Sublime seasons make us fall to our knees and thank our parents for bringing us here to experience *this*. We discover our hearts are bowls trying to capture the ocean, the love is so great. We realize our attempts to hold on are futile; we throw away the bowl, we throw up our arms in surrender, our broken heart beating in praise as we let the water take us where it will.

But the space between is ordinary. It's Monday and I'm alone with the girls, getting two little humans who have zero interest in getting ready to go to do just that. Getting them up, eating, potty-ing, diapering, changing into school-and-weather-appropriate clothes, brushing teeth, packing everything, putting one in the stroller and wearing the other—I don't think I'd call this magical. I don't forget how lucky I am to do all this—but in the midst of the mundane pressures of getting tiny children out the door on time, it doesn't feel like a mountaintop.

"We've been together thirty years today—can you believe it?" my neighbor tells me in the elevator. I love this neighbor. He brought us the most delicious blueberries I've ever had from Vermont last summer. I see him in the park from time to time, and he is not afraid to talk to me about Luca. "People ask me all the time, 'How do you two do it?'" he smiles. "How *do* you two do it?" I ask. "Some days are just okay," he says. "I don't expect the moon every day. Just commitment and love in all the spaces between."

I like this. We're busy; we keep weekends free because the weekdays go by like a stampede of wild horses. We don't often have the moon to give—but in the rushed mornings when I ask Charlee for the fourth time to please pick up her tights off the floor, I can give her love and commitment. When Willa is crying at 3 AM and I'm too tired for the moon, I can give her love and commitment. When the girls are asleep and TJ and I glimpse the life in which we first fell in love—the everything-else-dims-and-it's-just-us-forever kind of life—we quietly hand each other the moon again. But in the spaces between, when we're each tired with a thousand things to do still, we can give each other love and commitment.

Especially on the days that are just okay.

I think about how we lived immediately after Luca's death. TJ and I handling each other the way my mom handled the runt of my childhood dog's litter. Wrapped in a blanket, fed with a dropper, gently willing the pup to fight for life. We went on walks, and I told TJ how sad I was. He listened—really listened like it was new information, even though I told him this every day. I don't think we can live in open, raw grief all the time. Even divers don't build their homes on the ocean floor. They come up for air. When a body is doing what it should, a wound will eventually close up and grow some new skin again. Not to erase what happened, but to continue to be functional—to teach the world that healing often shows up as a scar.

We all need chips and TV and a couch at times (well, chips and a book and a couch is more my style). I find that I am still small minded, still so incredibly base and human, despite the moments that give me sharp clarity on life and what's worth my time and thoughts and energy and heart. I'm still annoyed at the dishes left in the sink when there's a perfectly good empty dishwasher right next to it. Still annoyed by my toddler moving at the pace of a sleeping turtle every morning while trying to get her ready for preschool. I think it's hilarious when the doctor prescribes "rest" when I'm sick. (Would the doctor also like to come over and take care of my toddler and baby so that I can follow her recommendation?) And also, I am awestruck by how many times divine gifts humble me, remind me of purpose, love, and each other—the way the evening's first star is proof that blind darkness was never God's intention.

Tonight, I see Charlee grab a paper towel and gently wipe spit up from Willa's chin and neck. For the last eleven days, we've all been sick over here. At times, I've been taking care of everyone. And isn't this why? We teach each other even when we forget we are teachers. And then your oldest is taking care of your youngest and you realize all of that taking care of everyone matters. Love, connection, and each other. It matters so sharply, so cuttingly, in tragedy; it might matter even more during the stack of days with not much to differentiate them—those "normal" days in between.

★ ★ ★

Dear TJ,

This is the message I would write in your card, but because our baby doesn't sleep by herself yet, I haven't been able to actually fill it with words. (Balance is coming.) Our wedding day is a lighthouse in my memory. But it's not the best day of my life. It's one of them, of course, but superlatives feel like limits. What about the days our babies were born, or the days we spent in Newport when it was so good between us—just closeness and our bodies and minds and spirits filling each other. What about the days after Luca came and went when we held each other's hearts the way we hold Baby Willa now (tenderly, and like this amazing being is irreplaceable and so fragile, and I will never be the one to let go). I think about those days and marvel at the juxtaposition of how much I was hurting and how close we were. It was good and awful at once, but more good than anything else. It was us; it was beautiful.

These days, I miss you so much. I'm often hungry because there never seems to be time to eat, but more than lunch, I want you. And then you finally come home and, I don't know, all of my frustration from the day and the incomplete tasks that make up my current life spill out all over the place, but I wonder if you realize that more than anything, I'm grateful to be yours and here.

If I could marry you again today, I'd do it. I'd marry you so hard that nobody would question two soulmates' journey when they pass from here to eternity. Of course we'd be together. When two are one, how could it not be so?

When Willa cries, thank you for saying: Thank God she's alive. When Charlee is wild, thank you for recognizing that it is also hilarious. Thank you for hiding smiles with me. When I cry about missing Luca, thank you for recognizing that there is room for grief and gratitude—both—in one heart. That wellness does not preclude grief. That we can move forward and not leave our tiny son behind.

I will never forget the day you asked me, "Were you always this special?" We were newly dating, and I didn't know exactly what you meant, so you clarified: "Before you were hurt so badly; before you forgave so much. Were you this special before all that?" I didn't know what to say, but I knew I was seen. And truly seeing someone is a tremendous gift to give another. I knew that redemption was no longer simply coming. It was here, and you were part of it. I knew marrying you would mean sharing everything—the bills and dishes and covers at night. I didn't anticipate sharing grief over our son, but here we are. And somehow, this grief has made our love grow. Somehow it feels like an honor to be the one who shares it with you. It feels intimate. There is nobody in the world who loves our babies like we do, all of them: our two girls and our boy. I love you so much. I like you so much, too.

Love,
Jess

Chapter 97

"It's Just the Girls Now, Huh, Mama?"
(eighteen months after)

People see Willa and ask, "Is she your first?"

"No—my third."

They ask the gender of the older two. I tell them about Charlee and I tell them about Luca.

"He died."

It's a very short story I tell about Luca. Mostly that is all I get to say, because America believes that grief and germs are best dealt with similarly—avoidance—so we don't talk about it. But this is strange. Or rather, it becomes very strange when you love someone who is not here in the way that other people can see them.

It's like going to the circus and seeing a fifteen-foot-tall elephant dancing and singing in Spanish and even making crepes that are the most delicious you've ever had. (And don't worry—this elephant auditioned and gets great wages and better healthcare than most. He even has holidays. So don't get mad about this elephant in this circus—he's doing great. Maybe be jealous about the healthcare, but not mad.) But then you leave the circus, and Aunt Millie and Uncle Bill are so blandly polite that they wonder if one should talk about such an exotic thing as a crepe-making-Spanish-speaking-dancing-and-singing-fifteen-foot elephant. Instead, they answer questions nobody is asking, least of all you. They mention the price of cotton candy and how traffic is crazy when the circus comes to town—they talk about everything, really, except what you're dying to talk about. It's a little bit like that, I guess, but not really, because we all know everyone would go on and on about that dumb and fantastic elephant and not say a word about my dead baby.

★ ★ ★

It's hard to understand why you can't talk about what has changed the shape of your heart. You can't just say, "Yes, it's cold out. Now let me tell you why I cried last night."

But there are other people out there who want to shout about what they hold buried deep in their hearts, too. You'll recognize them when you meet them. It's the dental hygienist who is telling you how wonderful your gums look (Thank you! I get that a lot!) and then you are telling her about Luca and she is telling you about her twins born at 25 weeks and the four months she spent at the hospital with them. How she was too exhausted to name them, how they were Twin A and Twin B until the NICU team forced her to name them something, and so she just let her toddler name his tiny sisters, because she was too busy surviving to be creative enough to come up with one name, let alone two.

"Also," she says quietly, "I didn't know that they'd make it. That was what really kept me from naming them," she said, while scraping my teeth. "I figured maybe it'd be less terrible, less like my own children were the ones who'd died, if I just never named them. I'm so relieved I was wrong—about all of it." Her babies made it. And thank God they did.

"How wonderful that your babies came home," you say. You both agree this is wonderful. I look at Willa and agree this is wonderful. *And God*, I think, *I miss Luca.*

* * *

I'm on the floor of my therapist's office. It's for a less dramatic reason than you probably think: Willa has a dirty diaper. After I change her, she's cooing happily on the floor, so we stay there. Want to know one of the most important lessons I've learned as the parent of a newborn? If your baby is content (unless she is about to happily fall off a cliff) DO NOT MOVE HER.

I look at Willa and that feeling comes over me. When I realize again that I'm a boat and she's an anchor and the ocean could be an entire tidal wave underneath me, but it doesn't matter because we're together always. And if the sea was joy instead of water, that might describe my insides right now.

I blurt out, "I adore this baby." And then I keep talking, "How am I supposed to wrap my heart around the fact that if Luca hadn't died, Willa wouldn't be here?" Willa changes so much. She changes what I do, where I go, what I think. A lot of my daily details are because she is here. She opens her mouth, and I smell my milk. She digs her fingernails into my skin as she nurses; *X marks the spot, you are mine, you are mine, you are mine,* these marks say.

Luca is here, because he is the same as Willa. I am a boat, and he is my anchor, and the ocean was a tidal wave underneath me that drowned me, I think. I resurfaced, and he did not—and yet, we're together always. And everything changed, sure. He was coming, and now he is gone, and that changes everything.

"You don't understand it, and that's okay," my therapist says. "You talk about the mystery, and you embrace all of it. You spend your days with your heart caring for Willa and grieving for Luca, and both are love."

Is Luca's death a terrible tragedy? Yes. Is Willa's birth an indescribable gift from God? Yes. So is this a tragedy or a blessing? Yes (depending on who you're talking about). Do I understand it this side of heaven?

No, but this dissonance is okay.

When I was little, there were many things I didn't understand, but my parents did, and that was enough. I am older, but still feel little, in a way. Certainly, grief makes me feel small. There are many things I don't understand, but maybe it's enough that I ponder it, that I try different angles again and again to peer at it from where I stand, describe it, fit it into sentences. Maybe it's okay to simply sit with something I don't quite understand—the way we all share space with people we also don't quite understand. But we get to love and honor them and ask them questions they are free to answer, and maybe we understand their choices a little more each day (or maybe we don't). And yet, we still get to love and honor them. And also— this may sound overly simple—but maybe it's enough that God understands what I simply cannot.

Charlee, my three-year-old daughter, has so much work to do at Sephora, the makeup store we both love at the mall. We are browsing the aisles of Sephora, but Charlee is unable to be contained, her feet flying across the shiny tiled floors. She runs to the fragrances and loads up on samples, spritzing and filing away. Sometimes she says, "Mama, I don't like this one," and it's tossed into the waste basket, the offending bottle put right back. She asks if she can try on lipstick.

"We don't try on lipstick that belongs to everyone, Charlee—we could get sick."

"I'm not sick."

"But someone who is sick may have just tried it."

"What about eye shadow?" she asks, switching tactics.

"Eyeshadow isn't for little kids."

"Oh. It's for six-year-olds," she sighs.

Life with Charlee is a never-ending conversation that simply pauses from about 7 PM to 7 AM every twenty-four hours. A saleslady asks if Charlee wants sparkly blush. She's not even four, but the lady is so nice, and Charlee is so happy about it that I bite my tongue. When Charlee is good and shimmery, she asks for a tissue and starts wiping it away.

"Does it smell bad?" the lady asks nervously. She presses it close to my nose, and we agree it doesn't smell bad. "Does she not like it? Is it itchy? Does she have an allergy?"

She is rapidly shooting questions at me now. I shrug. I don't know. I'm her mama, but I can't always explain her.

"I have snot," Charlee pipes up, and we all laugh.

We walk home, Willa on my chest and Charlee next to me as she says, "It's just the girls today, huh, Mama?" I squeeze her hand in mine and feel Willa's warmth against me. This is so good. This is complex. It's just the girls, and Luca isn't here, and it's good, and it is what it is.

In the Psalms, David wrote, "My cup overflows." David also lost a son. About that, he wrote, "He will never return to me, but one day I will go to him." Somehow, we can be in one place—one life—where both are absolutely true. It's just the girls, Mama. My cup overflows. He will never return, but we will go to him. My cup overflows.

Chapter 98

Sharing Luca's Story in Heels
(two+ years after)

It's two years and five months since Luca died. TJ and I are attending the Black Ties for Babies Gala in Boston—a fundraiser for a wonderful organization called The March of Dimes. This group does so much for mothers and babies in our country. Their mission is to fight for their health everywhere. They've asked me to speak at this event, to share my story about Luca. When you lose your child, you shoulder a heavy responsibility to keep them alive through your own words and actions. I've heard it said that a person dies twice. Once, when their soul departs their body, and twice, after someone on earth has remembered their name aloud for the last time. Life does not afford us many opportunities to speak about the babies we don't get to raise, so these moments when I can mean a lot.

We walk up to the stage, TJ holding my hand right next to me. I am pregnant again. I am in my third trimester with another little sibling—not only for Charlee and Luca, but for our Willa as well. I am wearing a short, long-sleeved fitted dress. I've worn it while pregnant with both Luca and Willa, too; this thought makes me smile. During the tech rehearsal a few hours earlier, those of us slated to speak were allowed to practice with the microphone as much or as little as we wanted. I walked up, grabbed the mic, and sound checked with one sentence: "My son Luca died of a cord accident at 35 weeks gestation." I told the tech I was satisfied with the levels and walked off the stage with a closed-mouth smile. He and the few other speakers in the room stared at me in silence. "Don't worry," I reassure everyone, "I'll expound a little next time I go up there."

We all laugh, and the tension and sadness in the room dissipate.

This time I'm up on stage in front of a packed and gorgeous room with a panoramic view of the entire city of Boston. Everyone is staring at me, and I start to cry. I am crying so much that I wonder if I can speak—but perhaps all my considerable practice with grief has already taught me that it is possible to cry and keep telling your story. I open my mouth to speak, and again start with a sentence that demands attention.

"Two years ago, my son Luca died from a cord accident at just short of 36 weeks gestation," I say with a shaky voice. I clear my throat and keep going, "Within hours I gave birth. Holding him was not nearly as scary as I anticipated. He was dead, but even more than that: he was my son. He *is* my son. I didn't fully realize mothering supersedes everything—even the grave— until these terribly too few hours I spent in awe of him in my arms. Too still, too quiet, too beautiful to give back." I am aware of the silence in the room as the crowd listens. I am even more aware of TJ right next to me, so cute in his tuxedo—the same one he wore when he married me. I keep speaking.

"Luca means 'bringer of light.' He continues to shine light on grief, revealing that, though heartbreaking, it is the way we love those who are no longer here. It is a part of love. He shines light on gratitude for his sisters' noisy, at times chaotic, always invaluable presence. He shines light on Heaven, showing it to be much closer with him there. And he shines light on motherhood—proving it even deeper and longer lasting than death. I'm grateful to stand with the March of Dimes, an organization that makes room for the parents and babies whose journeys are neither simple nor easy. I'm grateful to join this conversation, this cause, this fight to see all babies and mothers thrive."

I cry from the very first word I speak to the last. I walk off stage feeling connected to TJ beside me, my son inside my heart, and the grief and love that connect us always. It is not a bad feeling at all. In fact, I feel very much alive and in sync with purpose and hope. I also feel like I need to sit down as soon as possible in these three-inch stilettos. My vanity won't allow me to regret wearing them, though; a high heel does wonders for a leg, and at 30+ weeks pregnant (again!), I'll take it. TJ and I drive home through the winding Boston city streets. We hold hands and talk about how good the roasted duck was, how kind the people were, and how surprised I am that I cried so much.

"Were you embarrassed for me?" I ask him.

"I was proud. It was perfect," TJ says.

I am more surprised, however, at how much peace there is accompanying us home. I think about how, over two years ago now, we drove home from Massachusetts General Hospital. There was so much traffic outside, and so much silence inside. We had nothing to say to each other; there was no conversation that could hold the weight of our feelings. I walked through our building, my eyes downcast and swollen, my arms crossed over my suddenly too small belly—everything about me closed and telling the world to please don't ask, please stay away.

In that moment, I couldn't have imagined this peace I feel tonight.

It doesn't make the darkness from Luca's death any less terrible, but it sure makes the life we still have here so much better than I could have anticipated in those first days, weeks, months. We had to walk through the darkness to get here. You cannot cross an ocean without wading right into the deepest water. And grief can feel as endless as an ocean when you step foot into the cold water, in awe of what's in front of you. In a way, it is endless. But the thing you don't know when you first glimpse it is that the ocean is beautiful, too. Of course you don't notice. A drowning person does not think to comment on what particular shade of blue the water is. But we make it. We don't drown. And though the ocean is powerful and terrible and vast, it is full of discoveries we'd never have witnessed had we not been submerged at all, had we never walked into the wilderness and trusted that God would provide.

Perhaps the greatest discovery of all is the miracle that comes to the human heart. The shattering and unbelievable rawness where you break on the inside all over again from a simple conversation or glimpsing a newborn baby boy—but then, as great as the breaking is, there is an even more powerful healing. I am in awe of how God made our hearts to come back together in such a way that they become a deeper cup for holding compassion, love, and gratitude than they ever were before they shattered.

It's a strange kind of intersect to be like, *Here is my heart and my love and my pain and my healing, and also here is delicious duck and small talk and gosh, my feet hurt in these very high heels.* What a world and what a way the heart encompasses it all.

In a way, this kind of event—this benefit for the March of Dimes—normalizes grief, and that can be a relief for those of us who have no choice but to accept grief as normal. Also, TJ stood next to me all night long and I love him so much that his proximity must be like whatever it is between the moon and the ocean to keep its waves coming. In a storm, on a calm sunny day—just always, always being the ocean because there is the moon being the moon right next to it. I love him enough to wonder what else I can do about it besides having married him. We come home and he finds me poking around for a tiny chocolate I saw earlier in the cupboard. "I gave it to Charlee," he tells me, so I stop looking. He crawls into bed fifteen minutes later and quietly lays the chocolate next to me. "I ran to the store while taking out Luna," he says with a smile. My heart is full. I miss Luca. I'm grateful for this life I've been given.

Chapter 99

Potere: To Be Able
(two+ years after)

Recently, I was researching the word *power* for an essay I was asked to write. It comes from the Latin word *potere*, which means: "to be able." When something terrible happens to you, and you simply continue to live because, well, what else are you going to do?—the world looks on, and a lot of people use the word *strong* to describe how you're barely scraping by. They don't see the nights you cry yourself to sleep or all the social things you turn down because not only do you have zero interest in ugly Christmas sweater parties, it's actually painful to be there. It's like asking someone with a recently broken foot to run a 5K. No—it hurts. They simply cannot do it. The world doesn't see the way you wake up to grief every morning. How it is an invitation to climb a mountain when you can't even walk. How many days must I do this? you wonder, staring at this invitation that comes with the morning light across your pillow. As many days as it takes—grief takes what it takes. Nobody can tell you otherwise. Nobody can promise you that in six months you will feel better.

So you get up and climb this mountain, and nothing about what you do feels strong. But, yes—you do discover that you are able. Getting up is the very first step. And you do this over and over again, in so many ways. Laboring over Luca, delivering his still body and then holding him. Cradling him. He is dead and he is loved—he is both, and both are so incredibly powerful that you feel ended by this. We give him back. To God, to the nurse, we kiss him one last time. We are able to do this. We don't feel powerful at all—we feel incredibly, unfathomably weak—but if power is simply being able, then we discover we have it—we are powerful, after all.

Then we go home. We carve out a life without our boy—and yet with him, in ways we never could have anticipated. We are kinder and gentler to each other. We are also shorter on patience, at times; I wonder why I am easily irritated until my therapist tells me about the place where grief and all the different ways we express our anger intersect. But in a lot of ways, we are able to practice greater compassion to ourselves and each other. We are able. I am a more present mama to Charlee and Willa; I stop resenting how much they need me. I am able to get up with them through the night and hold their hands in gratitude that they are here. I am able.

I don't think that I am strong, but I think that I am able. And this is not so daunting, because nobody is asking us to be superhuman and climb our grief mountains without ropes or help or stumbling or tears. We don't have to understand it; we can be angry at the mountain before us. We can even hate it. None of this precludes being able. We are able—Luca has allowed me to see how very able our precious hearts are—to keep going, to keep loving, to keep being open and hopeful and wide-eyed at a world that is terrifying and glorious and not at all safe—all this at once. We are able to break and heal.

We are able.

We come home from an event to a messy apartment with two little girls—one sleeping and another who should be. We put her to bed. TJ takes off his suit, and I kick off my heels and pull on a tank top and the largest pair of maternity shorts I own. All of our glamor is on the floor in a pile by the bed, and it's just us now, quiet and vulnerable and needing each other in a way that keeps us close under the blanket. TJ puts his arm around me, and tonight he doesn't have to ask if I am better than I was two weeks ago, two months ago, or even two years ago.

"Is it weird that I cried so much tonight?" I ask.

"Our son died," TJ says quietly into the darkness. "How could it be weird to cry about it?"

Our son did die. And I am okay. Not okay with him being dead; rather, I am fully continuing to enter into a life that I find entirely worth living. And I am in awe of these two sentences, side by side. Just like I am in awe of the joy and grief side by side within me. And, I suppose, I am in awe of the way we all continue to be able. Still able. *Potere.* Maybe we are wrong to only ascribe power to those who are afforded mountaintop views and easier lives. Maybe what is truly powerful is the fact that we keep going, keep climbing a mountain with a terrain so difficult, we dare not stop or look around for fear we'll miss our footing. We are able, so much more able than we ever dreamed. And though happiness is so lovely and I miss it like one of my own limbs when it has flown, it does not teach me about *potere*— about continuing to be able—like grief does.

Chapter 100

On Things That Help
(two and a half years after)

Let me tell you about grief in one sentence. There is an orca whale who famously carried her dead baby for 17 days before finally letting it go. I remember hearing that story and thinking, *Yes, of course.*

Someone recently told me the date they taught their first yoga class: May 17th, 2017. *Luca's birthday*, I thought to myself but said nothing. "What a coincidence, that's when my son died," just didn't feel right.

I remember being shocked by his death. I remember being rolled over by the first wave of recognizing what this means. I remember seeing the whole ocean of waves behind that first one and realizing the commitment a mother's grief is. The forever trajectory of having a son, but not having him here. I remember being unable to reconcile the deep heart and gut and soul and everything-work of grief while answering questions about my education and insurance and listening to them decide if I could deliver him naturally or do I need a C-section. It was cognitive dissonance; it was like being told to walk on the ocean floor in just my skin, nothing to weigh me down, with all my grasping need for air driving me elsewhere. They were asking impossible things of me. Life was asking impossible things of me. And then I did it and held him and I was struck by how perfect he was (is?) and how normal it was to hold him.

There isn't a neat bow. Our son died. There is a period at the end of that sentence, but I want to write another sentence, too.

I want to keep doing this forever, concerning my relationship with my son. Luca teaches me that a person can be dead and also here. He shows me that grief brings a clarity that makes me wonder how I saw anything before.

I think about the hard passage of grief that allowed Luna Lovegood and Harry Potter to see the thestrals, and I guess I see them, too. I'd rather see Luca, but I can't, so I do my best to describe the thestrals. Also, I put on a short dress and heels the other day and asked TJ to take pictures. Whole-hearted people enter life in all sorts of ways that look like grief or tears or yoga pants or the same shirt many days in a row or a ridiculous outfit that makes no sense when you have small children begging to be held and your heels are sinking into the soft, just-rained on earth, but look at this strong body that houses this soul that grief and joy and grit and God have built.

I want to write about perceived over-sharing, and about thinking any of us have a say at all. When I had just gone through a divorce (It's weird to use past tense. The papers had been signed, but the unraveling of a marriage, a heart—surely that takes longer than ink to dry?), I sang at a women's conference. I was afraid to go. I felt safe behind a microphone, because women don't tend to interrupt mid-song to ask questions that make you cry. But there's always the bathroom and time before and after sessions that had me feeling jumpy. Sure enough, someone asked to talk. (Is there anyone who doesn't get triggered at the question, "Can we talk?" Can we retire that question entirely, and just dive in without setting off alarm bells in each other's bodies?)

We sat down, because there was nothing else I could appropriately do. She told me she was concerned. She knew I'd been in a tough season, but I was still writing dark, sad songs, and it was time to write lighter stuff. God forbid I get stuck in sadness. Shouldn't I move on? she pointed out. I thanked her and then abruptly never went to a women's conference again. (Totally kidding. I didn't thank her.)

Here is the problem with thinking we know what someone else needs when they suffer: We don't. We maybe kind of have an idea of what we need (though we learn on the fly and the learning curve is steep). Meaning, if you must sit a grieving person down and ask them to stop writing sad stuff, first look in a mirror and sit yourself down. Go wild and start by saying to yourself, "Can we talk?" and everything. See how it feels. But even if you think, *Oh this feels nice!* Then let me be the one to step in and say, it's not. It's not nice at all.

Writing helps me grieve well. The weird thing about being forced to do something is that you sort of would like to just avoid it altogether. But when you realize the only way to move at all, rather than come to a dead stop while grieving, is literally straight through it—so that your body and emotions and thoughts and even under your fingernails are covered in it—then you try to figure out how to actually do it well. Or better. Surely better than simply avoiding it. Like, embracing it in a way that allows you to eventually enter into life fully again. Writing honest words allows others to see me. When others see me, they can respond appropriately to my grief. And that helps. And I always need help.

When my brother was in a wheelchair, he couldn't use stairs. He needed a ramp. If we don't know someone is in a wheelchair, we won't know to build them a ramp. When someone gives you the gift of seeing their grief, then you have the immeasurable honor of building them a ramp. Let's pretend the building is life and everyone deserves to enter in. We cannot all enter the same way; sometimes grief needs a ramp. Needs less questions and I-Need-To-Talk-To-Yous and more ramps quietly built with a way forward.

God bless those who bravely share their grief with the world and make us realize that we are not other, not strange, not less than. We are collective. We need and build ramps, respectively. And if you need to use sad, strong, very feeling-ish words to share your grief today or in fifty years, then let me show you where there's a ramp. I know just the place.

Chapter 101

When People Think You Should Probably
Stop Grieving Now
(three years later)

A comment recently left on a social media post I had written about Luca said something to the effect of: "Losing a child is devastating. But it's been quite a while. Have you heard of therapy!" There was adrenaline in my body while reading it—a ridiculous time for adrenaline to show up since there was nothing to fight and nowhere to run, sitting alone on my couch. Also, the exclamation point. Just yelling her therapy joke on the page. It sure is something, but here is where I remind you of what I wrote earlier in this book. A long time ago, someone told me about a stillborn baby. About a funeral the parents had for this baby; how they dressed their child in tiny clothes. We agreed it seemed odd, almost macabre, and the conversation moved on.

I'm ashamed when I think about this. This is not an excuse, but I had no idea. I didn't know that babies who die before drawing breath have a death certificate, that there is a choice of a casket or an urn and what are any parents supposed to do with this other than bury their baby and pray they stay closer than you knew the dead could be.

My point is, it's possible to walk through life and know nothing about grief. It's possible to think therapy is a process in which the grieving person finally shuts up, rather than what it is: a way for the grieving person to open up, to maybe even decide to tell the world how it feels to be them. A way for the grieving person to reconcile what has happened to them with who they are, trace their foreign, scary feelings back to their own skin; to realize they don't need permission to grieve and love and make jokes and laugh and cry and still work—things that heal us, teach us it's okay to keep moving—to do all of this out loud, in the open, if you'd like.

One of my favorite scenes in the movie *Good Will Hunting* is when the therapist played by Robin Williams talks to Will about his wife who passed away. He speaks of her quirks, her imperfections, their love. It takes my breath away. It's a gift beyond words to be with our loved ones, but I cannot imagine a world where we not only lose them, but we lose the ability to talk about them, about us in relation to them.

Landmarks matter in terms of knowing where you are. So just like you'd say, *It's the house right next to the magnolia tree that is blooming all over the place right now,* the people who are side-by-side with us help us know exactly where we are. On a map, in life, forever. This is why it's important that we share the landmarks that define where and who we are. That we keep talking about our grief, our love for another human—a relationship that doesn't stop simply because one of us dies. We may even talk about all of this in the same breath, for they are different glimpses of the same relationship. And it's worth mentioning. As many times as we want or need, it's worth mentioning.

I know the joy of sharing my babies. What Charlee said today. Willa's antics. And, most recently, Noa's (our sweet fourth-born's) joy, her dimples, her pleasure to simply be. It is not fair to place the burden on a grieving mother—one who has already lost so much—to also not be able to talk about her child who the world cannot see. Talking about them allows them to still be here, don't you see? It is also not fair to come into the sacred space of another's heart and try to rearrange it. It's okay to think you would do things differently. It's okay to do things differently. But grief. Mothering our children who aren't here.

Showing the world that healing often looks like scars. These things are profoundly personal, a thumbprint of the heart. We can't tell each other exactly how to grieve; rather, we can empathize that we have to do it at all.

People ask me how to help a grieving person. *How can you possibly help when their wounds are deeper than you can see?* people wonder—the thought so daunting, that it keeps them from even trying. But you can help. You alone cannot heal it, but by being there, you can help. If you need a place to start, here are a few accessible things people did that helped me while grieving.

Send heartfelt, personal, written notes. No clichés or memes (unless they're genuinely funny, then send them to me, too, please)—just something that shows you know them, you see them, and you care.

Send food! Seriously, grieving people still need to eat. Or at least their families do. People who sent gifts of food and entire meals were incredibly helpful in terms of lifting one more burden off my shoulders. It was practical, undeniable help. I deeply appreciated it. Plus, we ate it, and it was gone. There weren't lingering signs of my dead baby in our apartment, and that also helped. Flowers are thoughtful, but they're only there briefly and then die, and personally, I found that sad.

Offer specific dates and places and times to hang out. As in: "I am going for a walk on Friday at 10 AM and would love to see you if you are up for it. No pressure." This is so much better than, "Let me know if you want to get together sometime." A grieving person (that's a mouthful, let's call this grieving person Sally, okay?) is already overwhelmed by their own insides; the last thing they need is to have to make another decision and come up with a creative plan to hang out. Even putting the onus on Sally (ah, better) to figure out something *you* can do for Sally may feel like too much. Make it simple. Take as much work for Sally out of the equation as possible. One good rule of thumb is to ask questions that can be answered definitively with a yes or no. "Do you want to walk by the river with me on Tuesday morning, Sally?" or "Do you want me to drop off dinner for you tonight, Sally?" Maybe go crazy and send both these texts at different times. Maybe keep sending them. These kinds of invitations that simplify life are a gift to Sally. Now she can text back a yes or no. Now she doesn't need to do emotional labor to facilitate you helping her. Now Sally doesn't need to come up with a plan, she can simply agree or disagree with yours.

Send texts like, "I am thinking about you, Sally." This is kind, and Sally will appreciate it. It also directly proves wrong the sneaky isolating and self-pitying thoughts ("Nobody really cares that I feel so terrible") that like to ride in undetected with the waves of grief. Sally doesn't want to think these things, but right now she is super vulnerable to them, and it's harder to fight when she is emotionally exhausted. Give Sally some clear ammunition against them, one text at a time.

Nobody hired people to clean our apartment, but let's just say I wouldn't have minded that. I think it is safe to say Sally wouldn't mind it, either. It was very helpful when people offered to watch our toddler daughter so that TJ and I could grieve together without the pressure of not wanting to be too sad around her. If you're a safe, reliable person, tell Sally you'd like to take her kid to the park for a couple of hours so she can be alone. If you're not safe or reliable, hire someone who is to babysit for Sally and stay far away from her kid.

Continue to ask how Sally is doing months, even years down the road. Let Sally know you miss their person, love their person, think about their person, too. Pray for Sally. Tell Sally you are praying for her. Then force Sally to pray for you. I am kidding about the forcing Sally to pray for you part. Please don't force anyone to pray, ever. Not Sally, not anyone. (If you've gotten nothing from this book so far, hopefully this is your takeaway.)

If you are grieving, I am so sorry. I hold hope for you; I hold hope for all of us. Your brokenness is not a curse; and once healed (for there is no brokenness that cannot be healed), that once-broken, always-beautiful place will be a wonder that both angels and those who don't know such loss will marvel at.

Until then, keep putting one foot in front of the other— and know that you are not alone. Again, *potere*, that root word where we derive the word 'power' means: to be able. And just as grieving Sally is able to text her friend back yes or no when asked if she wants to go for a walk, we are also able. We are able to help her, to carry her burden, as well. To be grace and comfort to her as we continue to reach out and, through our actions, tell her a story of how she is never alone. We are able to acknowledge she is hurting, but maybe even more than that, acknowledge she is loved. Dear grieving Sally is able; we are able. We are all more powerful than we know.

Chapter 102

Luca on a Bus
(two weeks after; two+ years after)

It's two weeks after Luca has died and the first night we are home alone—just myself, TJ, and Charlee—without any family to help distract us from our sadness. Everyone has gone back home and I didn't anticipate how hard this would be, facing immeasurable grief with nobody to pull us from the constant invitation to sit, to sink, to drown, to never resurface. Turns out our family being here with us was a band-aid that was pulled with their departure, and we finally just sit here looking at the wound. Oh, it's bigger than we thought. Oh, I'm not sure this kind of wound heals, actually. 'Sad' is not weighty enough to describe how this feels. There is no oxygen. Tonight feels unbearable; tomorrow, empty. There is no change in sight. How could there be? Luca is dead. He is dead today and tomorrow and all the days after that. Like I said: no change in sight.

At bedtime, Charlee asked me to read Nancy Tillman's sweet book, *Wherever You Are: My Love Will Find You.* It's written from the perspective of a parent to a child and goes through all the scenarios in which, no matter what, the parents' love will still be with the child. I start crying halfway through the book and can't say any more words. TJ hears me from the other room, quickly runs in and asks Charlee if she wouldn't mind if he finishes the book with her tonight. Now we're sitting on our couch, and since Charlee is asleep, there is no reason to pull ourselves up at all. Her two-year old joy and carpe diem EVERYTHING is a lifeline, but with her in the other room, that rope is out of the water.

We need help, so TJ calls his mentor, Titus. He is on speaker phone, and his voice breaks with emotion as he tells us how sorry he is. TJ starts to explain that we understand God is still God, that He has a plan. I am silent. I have no explanations to articulate; tonight, I don't understand anything at all. Titus prays for us, and this helps. He specifically prays that Charlee would have an encouraging dream to share with us in the morning. I think, *Yeah right*, because she's two and has never mentioned a dream yet. But I do feel some courage and some faith and the next breath I take is deeper. It is enough to face the night, to crawl into bed, to not be so afraid. Titus prays a very specific prayer. "God," he asks, "Please encourage TJ and Jess. Please send a dream to their daughter Charlee tonight, and may it encourage her parents in the morning." I take my pill that rocks me gently to sleep and close my eyes.

The next morning, we are back on the couch and Charlee talks to us about Luca. She is only two and a half and hasn't talked about him much. She can't understand death and never met him other than in the belly of her mama. But this morning she says, "I saw that baby Luca last night." TJ and I look at each other for a moment. "You did?" I finally say, shocked.

"Yeah. We were on a bus. He was really happy."

I start to cry, but these tears are different. Not so bitter—not really bitter at all. Every parent just wants their child to be well, to be happy. My faith tells me Luca is these things, of course, but hearing it from my daughter this morning is a revelation, an immense relief. It is a comfort beyond what I've experienced so far.

Charlee walks over and grabs some of her Peppa Pig characters. She climbs on my lap and pulls open my shirt, dropping them inside one at a time. "See mama? You don't need to be sad. Here are more babies for your belly," she says. TJ and I laugh. There are tears on my face as Charlee continues, "And Jesus is gonna give us another baby, mama." TJ and I look at each other, holding onto this oracle like the promise it is. I am not sure that I've ever seen a prayer answered so soon, so undoubtedly. For the first time since Luca died, there is a seed of hope inside. For the first time since Luca died, I can go on and I know it.

Three months later, I miscarry at five weeks pregnant. Two weeks after that, I conceive again. In the course of the first trimester, we don't tell anyone. But at around seven weeks pregnant, Charlee is lying in bed with me. She sits up, looks right at my belly, and says, "Is there a baby in there?" I don't know what to say. We weren't planning on telling her for a while, wanting to shield her from struggling to understand even more loss, should I lose this baby, too.

"Do you think there's a baby in my belly?" I finally reply.

"Yep," she says, before moving on.

★ ★ ★

I remain in awe of grief and loss, of love and the resilience of the human heart. Of the word *potere* and how it applies to each one of us; how we are both weak and powerful; and as long as we are here, we are able. Maybe more able than we ever knew until grief introduced us to ourselves anew. I never knew life was so hard and so good and so terrible and so wonderful. I didn't know about grief like this, and yet, I also didn't know about grace like this. And both change me for the better; both teach me the lesson of how to be cared for and how to care for others.

At about a week shy of nine months pregnant with Luca, I get my hair cut. Sitting next to me is another pregnant woman ,and we talk. She shares she tested positive for gestational diabetes and how upset she is about it. I tell her I'm sorry. I say it will be okay; that it's good they know so the doctors can monitor her and her baby. I say all of this not knowing my own baby has died inside of me. There is a verse in the Bible that says we see dimly—and yes. Yes, we do. I was getting my hair cut and couldn't see anything at all.

I marvel at that moment, about that girl and all she is about to face. The enormity of it. While she labors, she will be afraid to hold her baby because he's dead; but she will hold him because more than anything in the world—more, even, than him being dead—she is his mama. It is a knot that even death can't untie. She will hold him and it won't be scary; it will be strangely peaceful and holy and also terrible and giving him back will be like being told to breathe underwater. I can't; I'll die, you explain. It doesn't matter; open your mouth and do the thing that will most certainly end it all.

This girl will fall deeper in love with her husband. She will grieve differently from him and learn that part of his grief is standing up so she can lean on him. She will stop minding all the caring for her daughter in the middle of the night. She will learn that nurturing gratitude is the only thing she can do about every beautiful thing she doesn't deserve.

This girl will go on to have rainbow babies. She will wonder if these babies might die, too. (This sentence is easier to write than feel, I promise.) Her answer will come in the very best births; in two more screaming, pink babies placed on her chest, eighteen months apart. Luca's sisters. Charlee's too.

This girl will learn that when you love someone who has died, this love is present tense. The person is present tense. Heaven is closer with your son there already. Life is full. Grief is hard; grief is love.

Chapter 103

Luca's Third Birthday
(three years after)

What do you do when it's been three years exactly since you held your dead son? There is no one answer, of course. There is only the need to let your heart be the small, steady tree that it is—to let it drink from the river of emotion that runs through you. To recognize that the river is the river is the river, whether rapid and rising or placid and calm. It's all the river, as necessary as it is beautiful and treacherous. With three small people in quarantine (Oh hi. It's 2020; you might remember that there is a *pandemic*; we had nothing planned). With three small people in quarantine, we literally have nothing planned for the foreseeable future. But I did bake a cake today. Five layers of chocolate with vanilla buttercream frosting because it's Luca's birthday. And also, making something—from a song to an essay to a cake—makes me feel better. I think our calling is to discover this analogy for ourselves: Labradors are to fetching as I am to_____.

Luca helped me fill in that blank. I think words like 'destiny' and 'fate' and 'calling' sound so grandiose, that we sort of back away when we hear them, thinking it's quite a big commitment to make on a Tuesday afternoon. But however you want to say it, I know I am most myself when I am creating, when I am telling stories through whatever medium I have. Baking is how I can create with three tiny girls. Getting to artistically frost Luca's cake felt a little like the creative flow that makes me remember myself. It's a very good fit for my soul. My family will tell you they loved how the cake tasted, and I will tell you that I am not sure if I love this cake, really, but I needed to give my son something on his birthday. What I've learned is that grief is not actually the worst thing.

I have a neighbor who dives right into real talk, and after Luca died, he told me about his sister. "She lost her baby nearly full term, too, Jess," he said one night. "She never tried to have another baby, and she withdrew from a lot of relationships for good. Do what you need to do, but don't close your heart forever."

Closing your heart—I think that would be worse. The suffering of loss is terrible; those of you who know, know. It's not really worth anything, I think. Not in terms of trading your shattered heart for the lessons it brings. But, since we have no choice in the matter, we might as well marvel over how it does this incredible thing: It tells us what matters. Grief draws a hard and fast line that is inarguable and that, once you see it, makes you walk with awe and trembling at how great love is. Of course, the price for this is high; for what gift is more valuable than to love each other.

My pop planted pansies at Luca's grave and sent me a photo. What bright, hopeful velvet faces they have. I stare at their growth. I stare at how grief planted flowers, and they bloom. I thank God for how we can break and grieve and heal and love and bake cakes and narrate our stories with words and dances and lyrics and poems and, I don't know, maybe accountants even use numbers to tell their tales—but what I mean is that I am grateful to do these things as many times as I need. (Though, I will probably never tell a story through numbers. I do feel compelled to let you all know, however, that I was Captain of the Math Table in second grade. *But weren't you homeschooled, Jess?* you may be wondering, which would, of course, minimize the rank of Captain, being the only one in the class. I was not homeschooled in second grade, thank you, so you can just go ahead and maximize the rank of Captain once again.)

"Charlee," I say, blinking away tears while cutting the cake, "Today is Luca's birthday."

"*WHY?*" she says loudly. TJ and I look at each other and burst out laughing. I'm also crying. And that, I guess, is a snapshot of grieving one baby while busily raising three others. Your daughter asking why a dead baby would even have a birthday. It being so ridiculous and so refreshingly honest that you're crying and laughing at once. I love my son. I keep trying to figure out the right arrangement of words to explain how I don't know what his favorite foods are, but in the same way TJ and I found each other in New York City—two strangers coming home to each other when he held me and I realized, "Oh. I'm finally here; this is my person"—I know Luca. Ask me how well a person can know another and I will tell you his cells are in my body.

I miss him. This longing for him is as regular, as constant as my heartbeat. It is a thought in my head that has become a landmark, as permanent as the cortex and the cerebellum are in my brain. Most landmarks are visible. When I go to my childhood home, I see the big white Victorian house on the left, and I know my parents' home is the next right. That's an easy landmark to note. I spend my heart and life describing my son Luca, because, although he is not visible to the world like my other children are, he is no less a landmark that exists in close proximity to my heart.

It is a simple and lovely thing to say Luca is with God. It allows me peace and sleep and a momentum to move through life with joy—even, dare I say it, with the sweet shocking taste of happiness that still comes, even to a heart that has been claimed by grief. And it is complex because I miss him now. My language is changed. I don't say all my kids are anywhere. I say all my girls are here (I say this with gratitude). And today I say happy birthday to the boy who is three. Who is here but not here. Who is with God—which sounds dead from where we are, but I have a feeling it's way more interesting and adventurous and beautiful and alive than anything I know.

Epilogue: Marianna

It was maybe a month or so after Luca died when TJ came home from the radio station with a handwritten letter addressed to us both. "You need to read this," he said and handed it to me. I looked at the envelope, the wax seal with the letter 'M' pressed into it. *Someone cares very deeply,* I thought as I unfolded the delicate pages covered in handwriting. *Someone—a stranger—has taken a lot of time to do this,* I realized.

I proceeded to read a letter, a heartbreak, a love, a story that hasn't stopped holding me captive since.

At the time, Marianna was 24 and recently diagnosed with stage 4 ovarian cancer—stage 4 because no doctor suspected her symptoms could be indicative of something so rare for someone so young. In the letter, she told me how much it meant to her to read about my grief over Luca. She told me she grieved him, too—and that she even had any spare feelings of grief to spend on someone else at all bowled me over.

TJ and I asked if we could meet her and before too long, we drove down to CT to have breakfast with her and her dear sister Kelly. I'm not sure Marianna has ever met a stranger, and I'm pretty sure she could draw a scintillating conversation out of one of those British Tower guards who aren't even supposed to do so much as smile. Needless to say, it's not hard to love her instantly. I was still warm from the bed of grief, only hanging around people who didn't mind if I stayed nestled deep in it— who could enter a room without me getting up, so to speak—but it was different with Marianna. I got up, I drove to CT, I ate a pancake across from her, and I felt better for having done all of it. At one point I stifled a yawn and caught her eye. "Sorry," I said sheepishly, "I had a rough night last night. I was pretty low." She didn't try to talk me out of it or tell me to take a nap or that I'll feel better soon. She simply said, "me too," and I believed her. I took another bite of my pancake and marveled at how I could be eating the comfort food of my childhood—a kind of cake we were miraculously allowed to eat for breakfast—while faced with the realization that life is impossibly hard sometimes. I looked down at my lap and saw the impossibility of it all, and I looked across the table at this beautiful, vibrant, curious, hilarious, very thin girl and saw it, too.

But then we talked about God.

And I think what is so hard is that we are looking for an oven manual and expecting life to be an oven, when the reality is that life is the ocean—deeper and wider and more mysterious and impossible to see all of it from here or there or anywhere. And God is the Maker, the Lover, the Giver, the Good and Beautiful One. But like C.S. Lewis says of Aslan, though He is a *good* Lion, He is not a *tame* Lion. God is the Storyteller and at times we close our eyes and say, *I cannot bear to watch this story any longer!* and yet, the story continues and the ground crumbles underneath us and we shake our fists and are crushed all over again at the way this does absolutely nothing but eventually tire us out.

(But the story continues, it always does.)

This past Friday TJ and I got to spend time with Marianna. She was very sick, her body a flickering flame, her eyes large and bright and closing more than I'd ever seen them close before. "I think often about what you told me about Charlee and the elevator," she said, and I knew exactly what she meant. When we lived in a big building in Cambridge, Charlee would run in just a few steps ahead of us. She'd round the corner before us, and for a few moments, she was out of my sight. We'd always catch up at the elevator and I never worried because she was only out of my sight for a bit.

When Luca died, it comforted me that he is only out of my sight for a little bit. That we'll all catch up at the elevator.

"We'll catch up to you," me and TJ told Marianna on Friday. Her wonderful, doting dad was right next to us, breaking my heart. "I can't wait for you to show me around Heaven, sweetie," he said.

We sang, we prayed, we cried, we laughed. We lived, really lived in these frail fragile moments that land on us like snowflakes, melting away before we're ready, trading time in over and over again, exchanging it for something unrecognizable; introducing a new rhythm and a new dance before we'd mastered the last one.

"What does your name mean?" I asked Marianna on Friday. She didn't know, so we looked it up. "Grace," TJ said. "Unmerited favor from God," I said. *Yes*, we all agreed. That is Marianna—her razor-sharp humor and incandescent personality are only a gift from God. Her resilience and grace as she lived and died—these are the things God does in and through and for us.

Marianna died this morning. She wasn't afraid, she died in peace. Her dad had a beautiful dream last night that isn't mine to share, but it's the kind of evidence of God's grace I will tuck deep into my heart. It's bread for hungry times.

What is wild to me is how death continues to teach me about life. How her faith walked her into a rebirth that I don't fully understand but my heart remains buoyed by. And how she's only out of sight for a few moments, and we'll all catch up at the elevator.

About the Author
Jessica Latshaw

Jessica Latshaw grew up reading Cinderella every time she was sad. That happily ever after kept her coming back. Eventually, she looked around for books with less cartoon mice (now, however, she is mature enough to once again appreciate cartoon mice), and she couldn't stop reading stories (shout out to homeschooling and  all the time to read). Then she learned to dance and sing and act and told stories on stages across North America and Asia with different Broadway shows. And all the while, she wrote down her life on her blog. She has a BFA in dance performance from the University of the Arts and has written and performed music on a lot of beautiful stages (and equally beautiful living rooms). Her home in Pennsylvania is always spotless, lol just kidding; but it is filled with three beautiful daughters, her husband TJ, a few dogs, a piano, a fireplace, and a lot of good books.

Subscribe to Jessica's newsletter at JessicaLatshaw.com.